# 2000ˢ

**All-American Ads**

# Imprint

Want to see more? Visit *taschen.com* to view our current publications, browse our latest magazine, and subscribe to our newsletter.

**EACH AND EVERY TASCHEN BOOK PLANTS A SEED!**
TASCHEN is a carbon neutral publisher. Each year, we offset our annual carbon emissions with carbon credits at the Instituto Terra, a reforestation program in Minas Gerais, Brazil, founded by Lélia and Sebastião Salgado. To find out more about this ecological partnership, please check: www.taschen.com/zerocarbon
**Inspiration: unlimited.**
**Carbon footprint: zero.**

© 2025 TASCHEN GmbH
Hohenzollernring 53, D–50672 Köln
**www.taschen.com**

Introduction © 2025 Steven Heller
German translation: Anke Caroline Burger, Berlin
French translation: Alice Pétillot, Bordeaux

Printed in Slovakia
ISBN 978–3–8365–6802–9

page 1: *Target, 2000*
above: *Kellogg's, 2003*
right: *42BELOW, 2010*
page 10–11: *Hard Rock, 2004*
page 16–17: *Five Star, 2000*
page 22–23: *Shell, 2007*

# 2000s

## All-American Ads

**Edited by Jim Heimann**
**with an introduction by Steven Heller**

Steven Heller:

ALL-AM

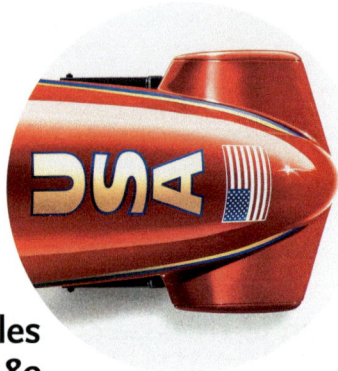

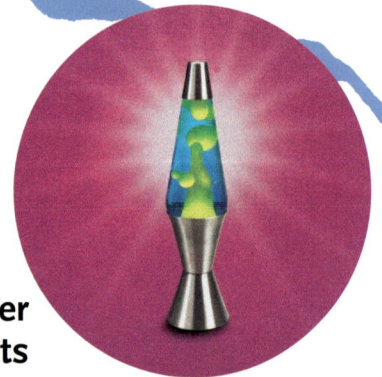

RICAN

# The 2000s

## The Beginning of the End

by Steven Heller

Advertising did not change when the Times Square ball fell at the stroke of midnight on January 1, 2000, but the industry began its creative decline in the early 2000s. Here are several indicators to support this claim: For one, the traditional print outlets for advertisements, notably magazines and newspapers, sharply declined in numbers (some turning to digital-only) during the late 1990s and early 2000s. Major advertisers were cutting print budgets and earmarking creative talent for television work. TV had already plucked away many of the most imaginative ad-people during the preceding decades, and print slipped lower down on the hierarchical ladder. Furthermore, some of the best campaigns produced and published during the early 2000s were originally conceived (and became iconic) during the preceding decade.

Yet every doomsayer pronouncement is riddled with exceptions—and mine is no exception: One of the best known and memorable, forward-facing campaigns of the millennial decade was the ubiquitous 2001 campaign for the iPod, featuring startling posters, print ads, and television commercials showing black silhouettes of dancers and musicians in frozen motion, wearing white earbuds and set against fluorescent, flat-color backgrounds. This work left almost all other advertising of the era, regardless of the product, in the dust. It also sold lots of iPods, which became a household fixture.

Although it is premature to pass wholesale judgement on the advertising industry during the first decade of the 21st century, it is an incontrovertible fact that what was produced, much of it fine, nevertheless fell far short of igniting a brand-new Creative Revolution, or resuscitating the old one. Other than TWBA\Chiat\Day's Apple ads, there were no Doyle Dane Bernbach-style Big Ideas that stand up to intense scrutiny (well, my own scrutiny, at least). Despite the creative consistency of work coming from certain key agencies—notably including Weiden and Kennedy—there were inexorable reasons for a creative devolution.

The aughts were a roller coaster fraught with social, political, and cultural disruptions. 9/11 certainly unhinged the American sense of exceptionalism and security. The boom and bust economy (recalling the tech bubble bursting in 2000), triggered by a flux in the technology, communication, and transportation industries, as well as the failure of many start-ups to actually start-up and succeed, had grave consequences on advertising. These, coupled with shifts in food and fuel consumption and energy sustainability, impacted environmental factors, causing marketplace volatility. A slew of demographic shifts further altered consumer loyalties and contributed to the ad-verse results during this period, which reduced the incentive of advertisers to take chances on untried ideas.

One might argue that the first decade of the 2000s was a last gasp before traditional advertising across all media transformed into something "other." It was just prior to what would become the first juggernaut of social media and artificial intelligence, which has forever changed advertising's form, content, distribution, and reception (influencers, anyone?).

Some of America's most popular legacy products succumbed to the pressures of fickle tastes and habits. Producers and corporations were forced to refocus on unexplored new markets to survive among new and distinctive competitive brands.

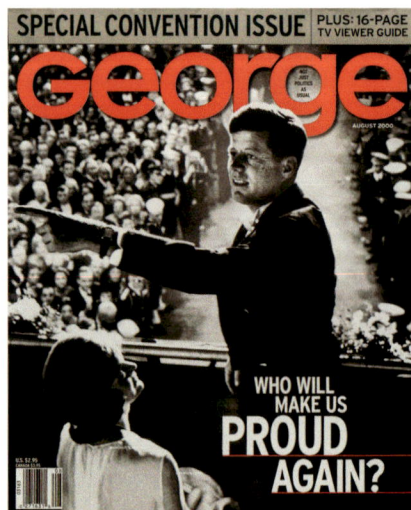

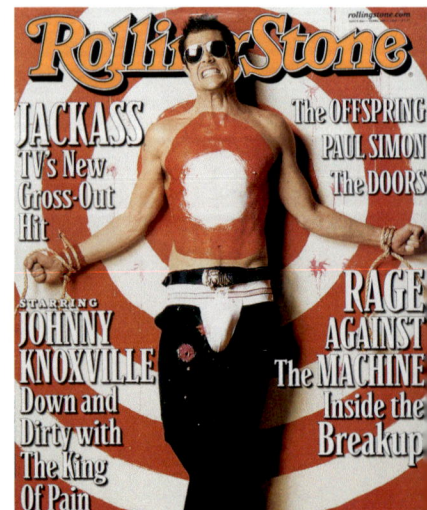

In the process, the American advertising paradigm was threatened by (mostly) young upstarts that developed clever tactics for spreading "brand awareness" throughout the culture, and overtly and covertly into the hearts and minds of brand conscious

**"One of the best known and memorable, forward-facing campaigns of the millennial decade was the ubiquitous 2001 campaign for the iPod, featuring startling posters, print ads, and television commercials…"**

consumers (which was similar to the existential reevaluations advertising had to reconcile and reinvent to cope with the age of TV in the 1950s).

In the Digital Age, terminology began to change: "Strategic branding," "brand story"—in short, branding this and that enveloped the distinct yet symbiotic fields of corporate identity and product-focused campaigns. Graphic design was becoming a larger factor in what the "agency of the

future" promised the client. The work of 1960s and 1970s "mad men" smothered conventional establishment agencies at Art Directors Club award competitions, spawning the innovative Big Idea creative dynamic where exceptional art directors and copywriters made witty, ironic, and suggestive slogans and visuals. But, by the early 2000s, these teams started to cede their dominance with, among the other social factors, the death of many national print magazines and the failure of television networks to retain large audiences in the face of cable. This also happened thanks to the precipitous upward rise of the internet's role in commerce and consumption.

The early part of the new millennium was not, however, a total washout for advertising. This book is evidence that brand recognition and the embrace of new products flourished if the fundamental brand was seared into the consumer's brain. Also, a bevy of futurist products and high-tech gadgets—from smart phones, pads, and pods to music and video streaming services, and other lifestyle accessories—were among the mass-ticket items. Moreover, high-end status merch was ripe for "fresh creative"

advertising, the most memorable being Apple products that sent droves of consumer lemmings to purchase these compact big-bang wonders. There were many other digital product ads but none that found the secret to capture consciousness: Sony, Panasonic, Palm, Blackberry, Razr, Samsung, and others tried to rise above mediocrity but they only really showed a product—not an idea—and sometimes a requisite celebrity holding or using it. With such innovative merchandise to sell, creatives should have been churning out "fresh creative" as fast as technology was advancing. How come they did not?

Maybe the public wasn't emotionally ready or intellectually open to visualize the future. In 1995, Microsoft's Bill Gates was mocked when he tried to explain "the big new thing," the internet, to a skeptical David Letterman before millions of TV viewers. Gates held his ground but maybe he should have presented a demo. Without seeing the product in action, the skeptic had the upper hand. Skepticism is anathema to good advertising. But skepticism can be overcome with witty and/or alluring copy and imagery. There are plenty of examples of both in

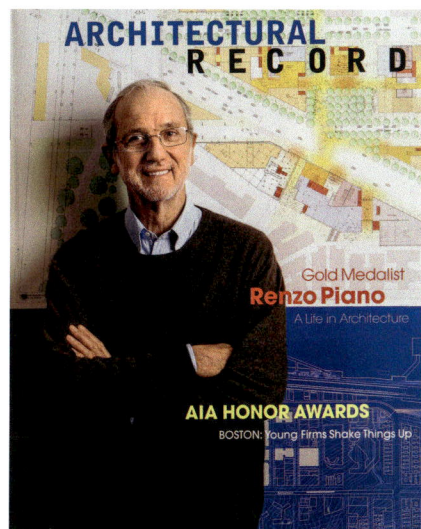

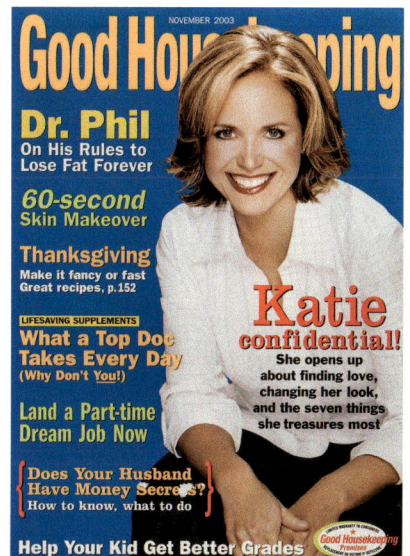

this book, yet on the whole, they don't rise above the bar set by the previous Big Idea generation.

Fashion is one of the all-star advertising genres where photography reigns supreme, whether as celebrity model poses and portraits (Tommy Hilfiger), still life products, or fantasy tableau *vivant* (Dolce & Gabbana). Indulging in fantasy is what makes these ads (Cesare Paciotti) perennial favorites. Moreover, there is apparently more chance to push artistic boundaries with fashion (Havaianas). These are the "this can be you" variety of persuasion. Otherwise, a menu of tabletop and food photos for most other packaged products use familiar fashionista conventions in attempts to whet the viewer's appetite, with various degrees of success. Often maintaining convention is part of the strategy (for Armani, following formula with nuanced deviations is essential for the brand identity).

Fashion is nonetheless routinely vibrant, and elegant photography is the grand standard since the 1970s, if not before. The best ads of the early 2000s were ostensibly studio shots, and Calvin Klein's brand of advertising has been constant throughout

the years: black and white, sexually charged, nude and seminude photos of men in underwear and women with nothing on. Reebok Classic is a good example of making the audience interested. Instead of products, these ads leverage fame (Ice Cube posing in denim and classic sneakers) and eccentricity (a naked Steve Dodos holding a Komodo dragon, while wearing Reebok sneakers). For me, the most effective approach to fashion from this era is an ad for Khaki Jeans from Macy's that implements

## "... brand recognition and the embrace of new products flourished if the fundamental brand was seared into the consumer's brain."

a novel use of various words in multiple styles of type formatted in the shape of a human torso wearing a pair of jeans. Without any of the above-mentioned tropes, it is a Big Idea and fresh concept in a genre that gets a lot of wear and tear.

Health and beauty are also mash-ups of conventions, each one playing with how to express fragrance or wellness, showcasing

celebrities and other props that represent aspiration. For men, the ads usually are head-on portraits of celebs, like Michael Jordan and David Beckman, promoting their own signature brands—while they look like real-life heroes, the ads are conceptually mundane. Yet some such ads are sexually playful, if also degrading, in a pre-Me-Too way: take the ad for Candies where a half-naked man is playfully pulling down the shirt of a buxom woman, while spraying a spritz of fragrance, with the questionable tagline "Anywhere You Dare."

Food is a complicated area for visual innovation. Food styling leans pretty much toward accepted conventions of product shots, however, occasionally there is an ad that makes the audiences' collective mouths water. Dove Bar accomplished that with an extreme close-up of a cropped version of delicious chocolate slowly engulfing ice cream on a stick. The stick is the hook on which the word mark for Dove Bar is prominent. Humor is tricky when applied to food, but a silly ad for Campbell's soup pulled it off, showing a little girl in a window sucking on a long noodle that emerges from a billboard that says "Only Campbell's is Made With

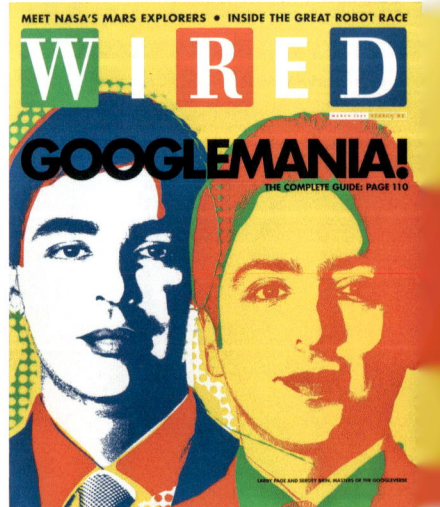

Fresh Egg Noodles. 32 Feet in Every Can." It's a silly concept but a laudable attempt at using wit with dull product photography.

In addition to tech and fashion, alcoholic beverages and some beer advertising have the most to gain and little to lose with dramatic photography, in which the product is the message. The 1980 Absolut campaign that ran for 25 years—and grandfathered into the 2000s—represents the quintessential marriage of object and word (*sachplakat*, German for "object poster"). It never seems to get old, either, because each special label is the name of the age. The art, culture, and celebrity recipe for making an Absolut advertisement has succeeded beyond expectation to engage an audience whether they are drinkers or not. It is possible the campaign could have gone on forever without becoming stale. Now that's a brand story without compare.

The less said about tobacco the better. Camel, infamous for its seductive, universally criticized for luring in kids, Joe Camel character barrage, continued its "Pleasure to Burn" ad in the early 2000s with codes directed at young adults. Winston applied playful female dominance in an ad showing a frolicking man and woman wrestling on the beach with the nonsensical tagline "Hostile Takeover" for a line of cigarettes claiming to have "no additives."

As long as America is a consumer's paradise, as long as competition is what drives the economy, and as long as the buying public is attracted to the best promoted brands there will always be advertising. It goes beyond selling—it is American vernacular. How this will be forever more ingrained in our consciousness is up to how advertisements are best received and acted upon. The nascent years of the new century was the beginning of the end, but as Winston Churchill might have said, the start of the 2000s was the end of the beginning ... of advertising.

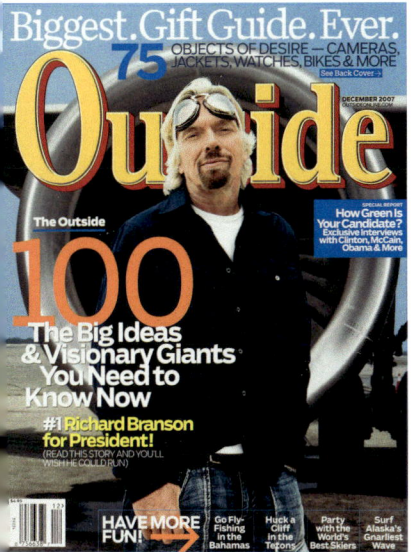

# Die 2000er

## Der Anfang vom Ende

von Steven Heller

Die Werbeindustrie veränderte sich nicht auf einen Schlag am 1. Januar 2000. Aber in den ersten Jahren des neuen Jahrtausends setzte der kreative Niedergang sehr deutlich ein. Diese Behauptung stützt sich auf mehrere Indikatoren: Zum einen ging die Zahl der Zeitungen und Zeitschriften, in denen Anzeigen bis dahin erschienen, in den späten 1990ern und frühen 2000ern dramatisch zurück (manche gab es nur noch digital). Die großen Werbekunden kürzten ihre Budgets für die Drucksparte und konzentrierten ihre talentierten Kreativen in der Fernseharbeit. Auch während der vorausgehenden Dekaden hatte sich das Fernsehen schon die kreativsten Köpfe im Marketing gekrallt, aber nun rutschten die Printprodukte in der Hierarchie noch weiter nach unten. Etliche der besten Kampagnen, die in den frühen 2000ern produziert und veröffentlicht wurden, waren ursprünglich im vorhergehenden Jahrzehnt konzipiert worden (und genossen zum Teil bereits Kultcharakter).

Doch bei jeder Schwarzseherei gibt es Ausnahmen – so auch bei mir: Eine der bekanntesten und unvergesslichsten Kampagnen nach 2000 war die progressive, allgegenwärtige Kampagne für den iPod aus dem Jahr 2001. Sie zeigte auffällige Plakate, Anzeigen und Fernsehspots von Tanzenden und Musikern in schwarzer Silhouette, mitten in der Bewegung eingefroren vor einem flachen, einfarbig bunten Hintergrund, weiße Kopfhörer in den Ohren. Diese Idee ließ quasi die gesamte restliche Werbung des Jahrzehnts, unabhängig vom Produkt, weit hinter sich. Außerdem wurden eine Menge iPods damit verkauft, die sich plötzlich praktisch in jedem Haushalt fanden.

Es mag noch zu früh sein, um ein Pauschalurteil über die Werbeindustrie im ersten Jahrzehnt des 21. Jahrhunderts zu fällen. Aber es ist eine unwiderlegbare Tatsache, dass viel von dem, was produziert wurde, zwar hübsch, aber weit davon entfernt war, eine brandneue kreative Revolution zu entfachen oder die alte Kreativität zumindest wiederzubeleben. Abgesehen von der TWBA\Chiat\Day-Kampagne für Apple gab es keine großen, neuen „Big Ideas" im Stil von Doyle Dane Bernbach, die einer eingehenden Prüfung standhalten könnten (zumindest nicht meiner ganz persönlichen Prüfung). Trotz der beständigen Kreativität der großen Agenturen – vor allem der Agentur Wieden+Kennedy –, war der un-aufhaltsame kreative Niedergang der Werbeindustrie in vollem Gang.

In den Nullerjahren herrschte soziale, politische und kulturelle Instabilität. Die Terroranschläge vom 11. September 2001 versetzten dem amerikanischen Gefühl der Sicherheit und Einzigartigkeit einen schweren Dämpfer. Der Boom-Bust-Zyklus der Wirtschaft (der an das Platzen der Tech-Blase im Jahr 2000 gemahnte), ausgelöst durch große Umwälzungen in der Technologie-, Kommunikations- und Transportbranche und das vorschnelle Ende vieler Start-ups, hatte tiefgreifende Auswirkungen auf die Werbung. Dazu kam ein Wandel des Konsumverhaltens und bei der Treibstoff- und Energienachhaltigkeit, was Auswirkungen auf Umweltfaktoren hatte und zur Instabilität der Märkte beitrug. Veränderungen in der Bevölkerungszusammensetzung führten zum Wandel in der Markentreue bei den Verbrauchern und erzeugten Negativergebnisse in der Werbebranche, sodass die Werbekunden noch weniger Lust verspürten, mit Unerprobtem Risiken einzugehen.

Man könnte sagen, dass die Nullerjahre ein letztes Röcheln darstellten, bevor sich die Werbung quer durch alle Medien hin-

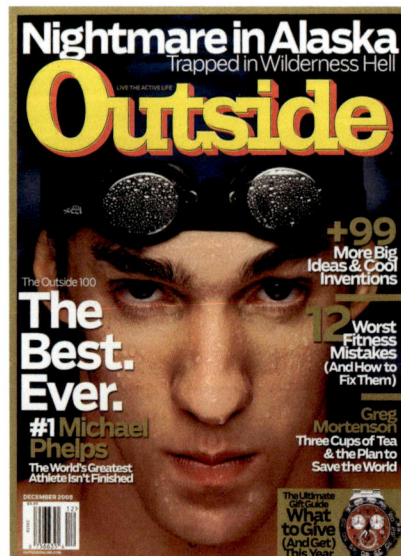

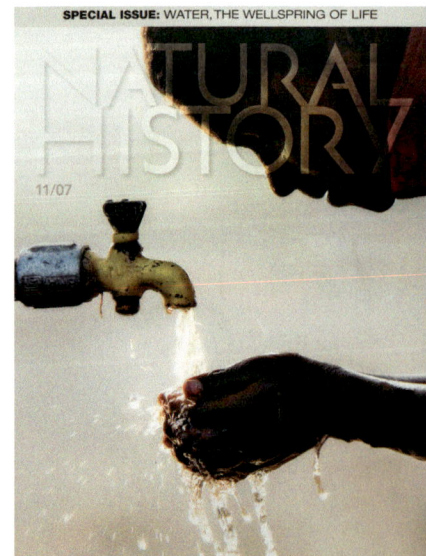

weg in etwas „Anderes" verwandelte. Der erste große Ansturm der sozialen Medien und der künstlichen Intelligenz, der Form, Inhalt, Verbreitung und Wahrnehmung von Werbeinhalten für immer verändern sollte (man denke nur an die Influencer!), stand kurz bevor.

Einige der populärsten amerikanischen Traditionsmarken erlagen dem Druck der flatterhaften Geschmäcker und Gewohnheiten. Etablierte Produzenten und Firmen waren gezwungen, sich auf unerprobte, neue Märkte zu fokussieren, um zwischen neuen und besonders markanten Mitbewerbern zu überleben. Gleichzeitig wurde das bislang herrschende amerikanische Werbeparadigma von zumeist jungen Emporkömmlingen bedroht, die clevere Strategien für die Verbreitung von „Brand Awareness" quer durch die ganze Gesellschaft entwickelten und sich offen und versteckt in die Köpfe und Herzen von markenbewussten Konsumenten stahlen (diese Phase des Umbruchs ähnelt der tiefgreifenden Neubewertung der Werbeindustrie im aufkommenden Zeitalter des Fernsehens in den 1950er-Jahren).

Mit dem digitalen Zeitalter kam auch eine neue Terminologie auf: „Strategic Branding", „Brand Story" – plötzlich ging es immer ums Branding, das die voneinander getrennten, aber symbiotischen Felder Corporate Identity und produktfokussierte Kampagnen umfasste. Grafikdesign wurde zum wichtigen Faktor bei dem, was die „Agentur der Zukunft" den Kunden versprach. In den 1960ern und 1970ern stellte das Werk der „Mad Men" die Arbeit der herkömmlichen Werbeagenturen bei den Preisverleihungen des Art Directors Club immer wieder in den Schatten; von diesen „Mad Men" stammte die innovative Dynamik der „Big Idea". Das bedeutete, dass außergewöhnliche Art-Direktoren und Werbetexter eine zusammenhängende Erzählung mit witzigen und doppeldeutigen Slogans und Visuals erschufen. Mit dem neuen Jahrtausend büßten diese Kreativteams jedoch ihre Vorherrschaft ein, weil viele amerikanische Zeitschriften eingingen, andere soziale Faktoren dazukamen und das Fernsehpublikum zu den Kabelkanälen abwanderte. Auch die sprunghaft zunehmende Bedeutung des Internets für Handel und Verbraucherverhalten spielte dabei eine große Rolle.

Die Nullerjahre stellten aber auch keine totale Pleite für die Werbung dar. Dieses Buch ist Beweis, dass Markenwiedererkennung und Akzeptanz neuer Produkte florierten, wenn sich die Marke erst einmal ins Gehirn der Konsumenten eingebrannt hatte. Futuristische Produkte und Hightechgeräte – von Smartphones, Pads und Pods bis hin zu Streaminganbietern von Musik und Filmen und anderen Lifestyle-Accessoires – verkauften sich in großen Mengen. Hinzu kam, dass teures „Status Merch" geradezu nach „frischer, kreativer" Werbung schrie; besonders die Apple-Produkte stachen heraus, und Horden von Konsumenten standen wie die Lemminge vor den Apple-Läden Schlange, um diese neuen kleinen Wundergeräte zu kaufen. Es gab viele, viele andere Anzeigen für Digitalprodukte, aber außer Apple schaffte es niemand, den Zeitgeist und das neue Bewusstsein einzufangen: Sony, Panasonic, Palm, Blackberry, Razr, Samsung und andere versuchten, Besseres als reines Mittelmaß zu bringen, zeigten im Grunde aber nur ein Produkt – keine große Idee – und manchmal vielleicht noch den obligatorischen Promi, der das Gerät benutzte. Wenn es derart innovative Produkte zu verkaufen galt, hätte die Werbeindustrie Frisches, Kreatives mit derselben Hochge-

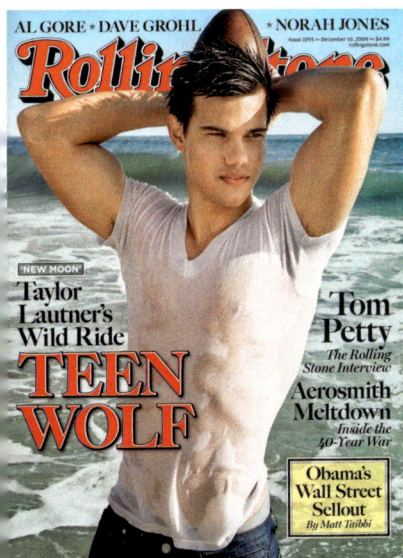

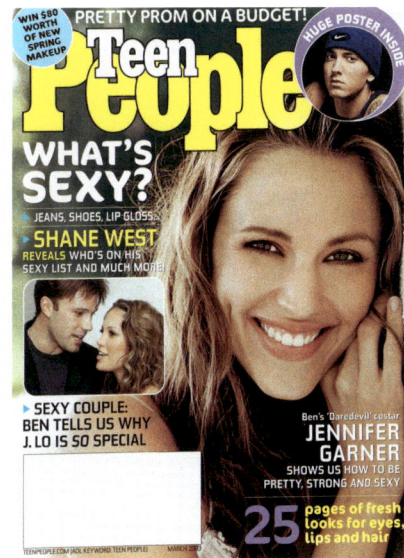

schwindigkeit produzieren müssen, in der sich auch die Technologie weiterentwickelte. Warum passierte das nicht?

Vielleicht war die Öffentlichkeit ja innerlich noch nicht bereit oder intellektuell offen genug, um sich die Zukunft vorzustellen. 1995 wurde Microsoft-Chef Bill Gates verspottet, als er dem skeptischen David Letterman und Millionen von Fernsehzuschauern „das große neue Ding" Internet erklären wollte. Gates ließ sich nicht einschüchtern, hätte aber vielleicht besser demonstrieren sollen, was das Internet war. Weil man das Ganze nicht in Action sah, behielten die Skeptiker die Oberhand. Und Skepsis ist ein Gräuel für jede gute Werbestrategie, lässt sich aber durch witzige Texte und/oder verführerische Bildgestaltung überwinden. In diesem Buch sind eine Menge Beispiele für beides zu finden, aber im Großen und Ganzen wachsen sie nicht über das hinaus, was von der vorigen „Big Idea"-Generation erreicht worden war.

Die Mode ist eine der All-Star-Werbesparten, in der die Fotografie die Alleinherrschaft ausübt, seien es nun Porträts von Supermodels (Tommy Hilfiger), Produktstillleben oder raffiniert inszenierte, laszive lebende Bilder (Dolce & Gabbana). In diesen Tableaus werden Fantasien aller Art ausgelebt, sie machen die Werbung (Cesare Paciotti) unwiderstehlich. Auch scheint es in der Mode mehr Gelegenheiten zu geben, die künstlerischen Möglichkeiten voll auszureizen (Havaianas). Dazu gehört auch die betörende Spielart: „Das könntest du sein." Ansonsten werden die meisten abgepackten Waren als Stillleben oder wie Nahrungsmittel fotografiert, damit der Kundschaft beim Betrachten das Wasser im Mund zusammenläuft. Oft gehört es auch zur Strategie mit dazu, nicht gegen Konventionen zu verstoßen (für Armani zum Beispiel ist es essenzieller Bestandteil der Markenpositionierung, dieselbe Formel mit kleinen Nuancierungen beizubehalten).

Andererseits ist Fashion natürlich immer strahlend schön, und elegante Modefotografie ist seit mindestens den 1970er-Jahren, wenn nicht sogar schon vorher Standard. Die besten Kampagnen der frühen Nullerjahre waren offensichtliche Studioaufnahmen; der provokante Stil der Calvin-Klein-Werbung ist im Lauf der Jahre unverändert geblieben: Schwarz-Weiß-Fotos von hypererotisierten, nackten und halbnackten Männern in Unter- hosen und gänzlich unbekleideten Frauen. Reebok Classic ist ein gutes Beispiel dafür, wie man das Interesse der Käufer weckt. In der Kampagne stehen nicht die Produkte im Mittelpunkt, sondern Stars (Ice Cube zeigt sich in Denim und Classic Sneakers) und exzentrisch aus dem Rahmen Fallendes (der nackte, nur mit Reebok Sneakers bekleidete Steve Dodos hält einen Komodowaran in der Hand). Für mich persönlich ist der effektivste Ansatz in der Modewerbung eine innovative Macy's-Anzeige für Khaki Jeans, bei der verschiedene Worte in mehreren Schrifttypen die Form einer menschlichen Silhouette mit einer Jeans am Leib bilden. Es ist eine „Big Idea" und ein frisches Konzept in einem Genre, das manchmal etwas abgenutzt wirken kann, und verwendet keines der oben genannten Motive.

Im Bereich Gesundheit und Kosmetik herrscht ebenfalls ein Mischmasch der Konventionen, jede Werbung sucht nach dem besten Ausdruck für Duft oder Wellness und präsentiert zu diesem Zweck Promis und Accessoires, die für Verlangen stehen. Für Männer sind das frontale Porträts berühmter Sportler wie Michael Jordan und David Beckham, die ihre eigenen Kosmetika bewer-

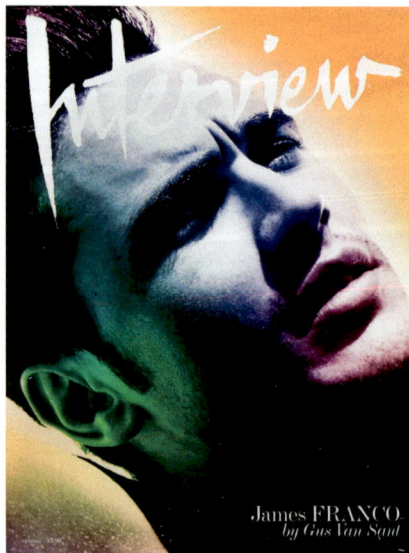

James FRANCO.
by Gus Van Sant

Find your
New Look
What to wear now

„Man könnte sagen, dass die Nullerjahre ein letztes Röcheln darstellten, bevor sich die Werbung quer durch alle Medien hinweg… verwandelte."

ben – sie mögen wie ganz große Männerhelden aussehen, aber konzeptionell sind die Anzeigen eher Durchschnitt. Einige der Werbungen sind in ihren sexuellen Anspielungen frauenfeindlich auf eine Art, die seit #MeToo so nicht mehr möglich ist: zum Beispiel die Candies-Werbung, in der ein halbnackter Mann einer drallen Frau spielerisch von hinten das Hemd herunterzieht und ihr Parfüm in den Ausschnitt spritzt, begleitet von dem fragwürdigen Slogan „Anywhere You Dare" („Überall, wohin Sie sich trauen").

Im Bereich Nahrungsmittel ist visuelle Innovation schwierig. Das Foodstyling orientiert sich meist an den akzeptierten Konventionen der Produktfotografie, aber hin und wieder gibt es mal eine Anzeige, bei der jedem das Wasser im Mund zusammenläuft. Der Dove-Schokoladenriegel schafft das durch die extreme Nahaufnahme köstlich flüssiger Schokolade, die langsam ein Eis am Stiel umfließt. Der Eisstiel ist der Aufhänger, für den die Wortmarke Dove Bar berühmt ist. Wenn es ums Essen geht, ist Humor immer tricky, aber eine alberne Werbung für Campbell's Dosensuppe schafft es: Sie zeigt ein Fenster mit einem kleinen Mädchen darin, das an einer langen Nudel saugt,

die aus einer Plakatwand mit der Aufschrift „Nur Campbell's wird mit Frischeinudeln hergestellt. 11 Meter in jeder Dose" kommt. Es ist eine alberne Aussage, aber ein löblicher Versuch, langweilige Produktfotografie mit etwas Witz aufzupeppen.

Neben technischen Geräten und Mode haben Alkoholika und Bier, bei denen das Produkt die Werbebotschaft ist, durch dramatische Fotografie wenig zu verlieren und am meisten zu gewinnen. Die aus dem Jahr 1980 stammende Absolut-Werbekampagne lief 25 Jahre lang – bis ins neue Jahrtausend hinein – und repräsentiert die vollkommenste Vereinigung von Objekt und Wort. Die Absolut-Werbung wird nie langweilig, weil der Schriftzug immer spezifisch für die jeweilige Ära ist. Der Cocktail aus Kunst, Kultur und VIPs, aus dem eine Absolut-Anzeige zusammengemixt wurde, hat das Publikum nie kaltgelassen, ob es nun Wodka trinkt oder nicht – eine Brand Story mit beispiellosem Erfolg.

Je weniger wir über Tabakprodukte sprechen, desto besser. Camel, berüchtigt und von allen Seiten kritisiert für die Verführung Minderjähriger zum Rauchen durch seine allgegenwärtige Comicfigur Joe Camel,

führte seine eindeutig an junge Erwachsene gerichtete „Pleasure to Burn"-Anzeigenserie bis in die frühen 2000er fort. Winston bediente sich spielerisch weiblicher Dominanz in einer Werbung, die einen Mann und eine Frau zeigte, die sich am Strand miteinander balgten, der sinnfreie Slogan dazu lautete „Hostel Takeover", geworben wurde für Zigaretten „ohne Zusatzstoffe".

In Amerika wird es immer Werbung geben, solange die USA ein Verbraucherparadies bleiben und der Wettbewerb die Wirtschaft am Laufen hält und solange sich die kaufende Öffentlichkeit am stärksten zu den am besten beworbenen Marken hingezogen fühlt. Aber es geht nicht nur um das Verkaufen – Werbung ist ein uramerikanisches Metier. Wie diese uramerikanische Sprache für immer in unserem Bewusstsein verankert bleibt, beeinflusst, wie Werbung wahrgenommen wird und welches Kaufverhalten sich daraus ableitet. Die ersten Jahre des neuen Jahrtausends waren der Anfang vom Ende, aber wie sagte Winston Churchill doch gleich? „Dies ist nicht das Ende. Es ist nicht einmal der Anfang vom Ende. Aber es ist, vielleicht, das Ende vom Anfang" … der amerikanischen Werbung.

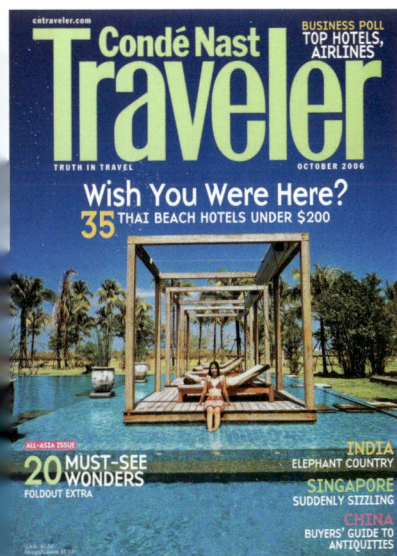

# Les Années 2000

## Le commencement de la fin

de Steven Heller

La publicité n'a pas changé à l'instant où la boule de Times Square est tombée, au premier coup de minuit le 1er janvier 2000, mais elle a bien entamé son déclin créatif au tout début du nouveau millénaire. Plusieurs indicateurs en attestent : d'abord, ses supports de diffusion imprimés traditionnels, notamment les magazines et journaux, ont fortement diminué en nombre entre la fin des années 1990 et le début des années 2000, certains se convertissant au tout numérique. En effet, ces annonceurs majeurs ont réduit leurs budgets dédiés aux publications papier et réservé leur talent créatif à la télévision. Le petit écran avait déjà capté la crème des publicistes au cours des décennies précédentes et la presse écrite dégringola un peu plus dans l'échelle hiérarchique. Enfin, certaines des meilleures campagnes produites et publiées au début des années 2000, devenues culte, ont été conçues au cours de la décennie précédente.

Toute affirmation catastrophiste possédant sa cohorte d'exceptions, la mienne n'en est pas exempte. Une des campagnes avant-gardistes les plus fameuses et mémorables de cette première décennie du millénaire a été celle pour l'iPod, omniprésente en 2001 à grand renfort d'affiches, d'annonces dans la presse et de spots télévisés montrant les silhouettes noires de danseurs et de musiciens figés dans leur mouvement, écouteurs blancs dans les oreilles, sur un fond monochrome fluo. Ce travail a laissé presque toutes les autres campagnes de l'époque sur le carreau, quel que soit le produit. Il a aussi fait vendre beaucoup d'iPods, devenus des accessoires domestiques standard.

Il serait prématuré de tirer des conclusions définitives sur l'industrie publicitaire au cours de la première décennie du XXIe siècle, mais il est indéniable que ce qui a été produit entre 2000 et 2010, souvent de très bonne facture, n'a pas su déclencher une nouvelle Révolution créative, ni ressusciter l'ancienne. Hormis les campagnes Apple de TWBA\Chiat\Day, aucune Grande Idée à la Doyle Dane Bernbach n'en ressort qui résiste à un examen minutieux (au mien, tout au moins). Malgré la cohérence créative du travail fourni par certaines agences – parmi lesquelles Weiden et Kennedy – la décentralisation créative était inexorable, pour plusieurs raisons.

Ces années ont été une période marquée par des vagues de perturbations sociales, politiques et culturelles. Les attentats du 11 septembre ont bien sûr ébranlé le sentiment d'exception et de sécurité des Américains. Les hauts et les bas d'une économie fébrile (qui rappellent l'explosion de la bulle Internet en 2000) provoqués par l'activité fluctuante des industries de la technologie, de la communication et des transports, ainsi que par l'incapacité de nombreuses start-up à croître au-delà du statut de jeune pousse, ont eu de graves conséquences sur la publicité. Cette conjoncture, associée à l'instabilité des marchés de l'alimentation, du pétrole et de l'énergie, mis face à leurs responsabilités environnementales, a généré une grande volatilité. Une flopée de changements démographiques ont fini d'altérer la loyauté des consommateurs et ont contribué aux résultats négatifs enregistrés sur la période, si bien que les publicitaires échaudés sont devenus frileux et peu enclins à tenter des idées nouvelles.

On pourrait dire que la première décennie du XXIe siècle fut le dernier soupir de la publicité traditionnelle avant que, tous médias confondus, elle se mue en « autre chose ». C'était juste avant le raz-de-marée des réseaux sociaux dopés à l'intelligence

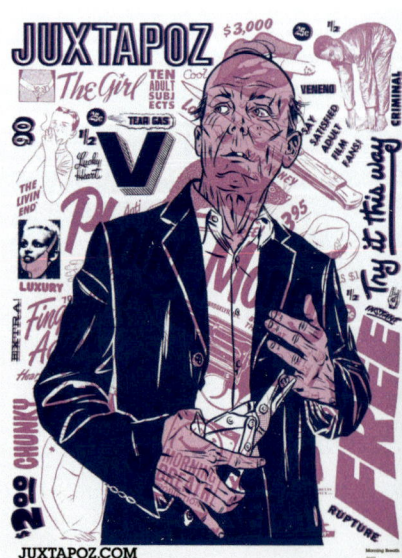

artificielle, qui ont changé à jamais la face de la publicité – sa forme, son contenu, sa diffusion et sa réception (des influenceurs, dans le coin ?).

Certains produits emblématiques du consumérisme américain ont succombé

« Une des campagnes avant-gardistes les plus fameuses et mémorables de cette première décennie du millénaire a été celle pour l'iPod, omniprésente en 2001 à grand renfort d'affiches, d'annonces dans la presse et de spots télévisés… »

à la pression capricieuse des goûts et des tendances. Producteurs et entreprises ont été contraints de se recentrer sur des marchés jusqu'alors inexplorés pour survivre à une concurrence effrénée. Le paradigme publicitaire américain s'est trouvé menacé, principalement par de nouveaux acteurs qui ont développé des tactiques astucieuses pour diffuser leur « notoriété de marque » dans la culture populaire et s'immiscer, ouvertement ou sournoisement, dans le

cœur et l'esprit des consommateurs amateurs de marques à l'identité forte (une réévaluation et une réinvention similaires à celles que l'industrie publicitaire a dû mener à l'arrivée de la télévision, dans les années 1950).

À l'ère numérique, la terminologie s'est mise à changer : « stratégie de marque », « histoire de la marque » – en bref, le *branding* a pris le dessus sur les champs distincts mais symbiotiques de l'identité d'entreprise et des campagnes axées sur le produit. La création graphique a pris une part plus importante dans ce que ces « agences du futur » promettaient au client. Le travail des *Mad Men* des années 1960 et 1970 avait escamoté les agences conventionnelles les plus établies au palmarès des clubs de directeurs artistiques, engendrant la dynamique créative novatrice de la *Big Idea*, dans l'élan de laquelle des directeurs artistiques et des rédacteurs exceptionnels ont conçu des slogans et des visuels spirituels, ironiques et suggestifs. Au début des années 2000, ces équipes ont commencé à perdre leur ascendant avec, entre autres facteurs, la mort de nombreux magazines papier nationaux, l'échec des chaînes de

télévision traditionnelles à conserver un large public face à la concurrence du câble, et le rôle prépondérant qu'Internet a si vite joué dans le commerce et la consommation.

Pour autant, la publicité n'a pas vécu un fiasco total aux premières heures du nouveau millénaire. Ce livre montre que la reconnaissance de marque et l'adoption de nouveaux produits ont perduré lorsqu'une marque était bien ancrée dans le cerveau des consommateurs. La multitude de produits futuristes et de gadgets de haute technologie qui fleurit alors – smartphones, tablettes et *pods*, services de streaming pour la musique et les vidéos et autres accessoires du quotidien – est une manne. En outre, le marché haut de gamme appelle une publicité créative « fraîche », les campagnes les plus mémorables étant celles d'Apple, qui poussent à l'achat des nuées de consommateurs avides de nouveauté. Beaucoup d'autres publicités pour des produits numériques n'ont pas su se faire une place dans nos consciences : Sony, Panasonic, Palm, Blackberry, Razr, Samsung et d'autres ont tenté de se hisser au-dessus de la médiocrité ambiante, mais n'ont réussi qu'à montrer un produit – et non une idée –

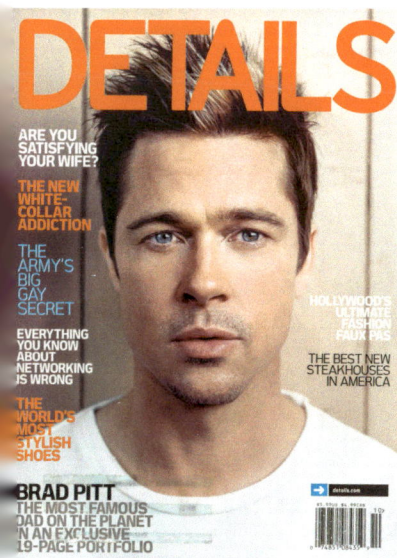

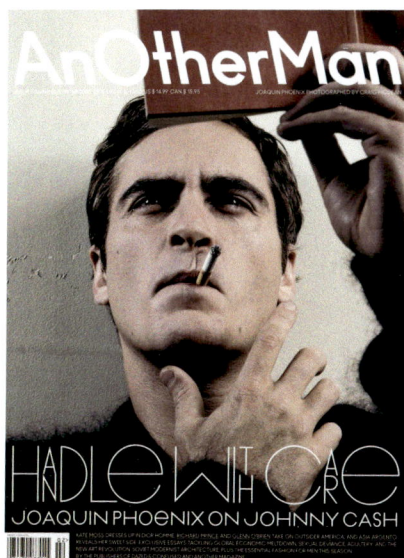

parfois assortie d'une célébrité en guise de VRP. Chargés de vendre une marchandise si novatrice, les créatifs auraient dû produire de la « fraîcheur » à tour de bras, au même rythme trépidant que le progrès technologique. Pourquoi ne l'ont-ils pas fait ?

Peut-être le public n'était-il pas prêt, émotionnellement ou intellectuellement, à imaginer l'avenir. En 1995, le créateur de Microsoft, Bill Gates, a fait l'objet de moqueries quand il a tenté d'expliquer ce « nouveau truc énorme » qu'était l'Internet à un David Letterman sceptique devant des millions de téléspectateurs. Gates ne s'est pas démonté, mais peut-être aurait-il dû en faire une démonstration. En l'absence du produit en action, le sceptique a pris le dessus. Et le scepticisme jette l'anathème sur la bonne publicité. Une narration et une imagerie intelligentes et/ou séduisantes peuvent toutefois circonvenir ce scepticisme. Les exemples ne manquent pas dans ce livre, même si, dans l'ensemble, ils n'égalent pas les campagnes emblématiques de la *Big Idea* de la génération précédente.

La mode est un des domaines publicitaires de choix où la photo règne en maître, qu'il s'agisse de poses et de portraits de stars ou de mannequins célèbres (Tommy Hilfiger), de natures mortes ou de tableaux vivants fantasmatiques (Dolce & Gabbana). C'est l'expression du fantasme qui fait de ces publicités (Cesare Paciotti) d'éternelles favorites. La mode se prête au dépassement des limites artistiques (Havaianas). C'est la stratégie de persuasion du « ça pourrait être vous ». Pour aiguiser l'appétit des consommateurs, les agences recourent aux codes et conventions connus des fashionistas, comme les photos de plats et de tables bien garnies, pour vendre la plupart des autres produits industriels, avec plus ou moins de succès. Préserver les conventions fait souvent partie de leur stratégie – chez Armani, par exemple, suivre la formule éprouvée en n'y apportant que des variations nuancées est essentiel pour l'identité de la marque.

Familière, la mode n'en demeure pas moins vivante et la photo élégante en est un standard, au moins depuis les années 1970. Les meilleures publicités du début des années 2000 ont été ostensiblement réalisées en studio, comme les campagnes Calvin Klein, toujours cohérentes dans leur style : noir et blanc, à forte charge sexuelle, images d'hommes nus ou en sous-vêtements et de femmes dénudées. Dans un autre genre, Reebok Classic a su capter l'attention du public. Au lieu de se centrer sur le produit, ses publicités jouent avec la célébrité (Ice Cube posant en jean, les célèbres baskets aux pieds) et l'excentricité (Steve Dodos nu et chaussé de Reebok, tenant un dragon de Komodo). De mon point de vue, l'approche la plus efficace de la mode s'incarne dans une campagne pour les Khaki Jeans de Macy's, où l'argumentaire de vente est décliné en différentes polices pour former le torse de « vrais hommes ». Sans recourir à aucun des tropes susmentionnés,

« ... la reconnaissance de marque et l'adoption de nouveaux produits ont perduré lorsqu'une marque était bien ancrée dans le cerveau des consommateurs. »

elle incarne une *Big Idea* et un concept « frais » dans un genre prompt à l'usure.

La santé et la beauté aussi se vendent en respectant un mélange de conventions :

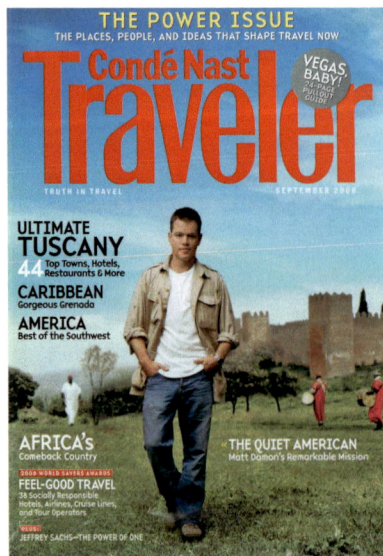

« ... la première décennie du
XXI<sup>e</sup> siècle fut le dernier
soupir de la publicité
traditionnelle avant que,
tous médias confondus,
elle se mue en "autre chose". »

il s'agit toujours d'exprimer un parfum, ou un bien-être, grâce à des vedettes ou des accessoires symboles d'aspirations sociales ou intimes. Pour les hommes, les publicités se limitent en général à des portraits de célébrités, comme Michael Jordan et David Beckman, qui promeuvent les marques dont ils sont les égéries. Mais si elles évoquent des héros du quotidien, elles ne présentent aucun intérêt conceptuel. Certaines jouent avec la sexualité, quitte à tomber dans un sexisme décomplexé pré-MeToo, comme cette pub pour Candies où un homme torse nu tire sur le décolleté d'une planétureuse jeune femme pour y vaporiser du parfum, avec le fâcheux slogan « partout où tu oses ».

L'alimentation est un domaine où l'innovation visuelle est complexe. La mise en scène de la nourriture s'en tient encore beaucoup aux conventions du genre en la montrant dans l'assiette, mais parfois une pub réussit à faire saliver le public autrement. C'est le cas de Dove Bar qui montre en très gros plan un eskimo lentement nappé de délicieux chocolat et grave son nom sur le bâton autant que dans les esprits. Il n'est pas facile de manier l'humour sur ce marché, mais une pub pour la soupe Campbell's a su le faire avec cette petite fille qui aspire une très longue nouille émergeant d'une affiche où est écrit : « Seule la soupe Campbell's est faite avec des nouilles fraîches aux œufs. Dix mètres dans chaque boîte. » Le concept est tout bête, mais c'est une tentative louable d'associer un trait d'esprit à une insipide photo du produit.

Comme pour la technologie et la mode, les promoteurs d'alcools forts et de certaines bières ont tout intérêt à opter pour des visuels spectaculaires où le produit est le message. La campagne de 1980 pour Absolut, qui tourna pendant 25 ans et survécut à l'an 2000, représente l'union essentielle entre l'objet et le mot (incarnée par le *Sachplakat* du siècle précédent, l'affiche-objet). Elle donne l'impression de ne pas vieillir, notamment parce qu'elle a connu plus de 1500 déclinaisons pour coller à l'esprit du temps. Associer art, culture et célébrité s'est révélé un pari gagnant puisque la campagne a aussi marqué ceux qui ne buvaient pas d'alcool. Cette campagne aurait pu perdurer à l'infini sans jamais se tarir. Voilà une histoire de marque qui sort du lot.

Moins on parle du tabac, mieux c'est. Camel, très critiqué pour avoir créé le personnage débonnaire de Joe Camel, populaire auprès des enfants, continue sur sa lancée pyromane au début des années 2000 avec sa campagne « Pleasure to Burn », qui cible cette fois les jeunes adultes. Winston exploite les codes d'une domination féminine joyeuse dans une publicité pour des cigarettes soi-disant « sans additifs », où un homme et une femme batifolent sur la plage, avec ce slogan incompréhensible : « Hostel Takeover » (« reprise de l'auberge ») !

Tant que l'Amérique sera un paradis consumériste, que la concurrence sera le moteur de l'économie et que le public acheteur sera séduit par les marques les mieux promues, la publicité existera. Cela dépasse la notion de vente – c'est une langue vernaculaire américaine. Elle sera d'autant plus imprimée dans nos consciences que nous saurons recevoir la publicité et la faire perdurer par l'action. Les premières années du nouveau siècle ont marqué le commencement de la fin, mais aussi, comme l'aurait dit Winston Churchill, la fin du commencement ... de la publicité.

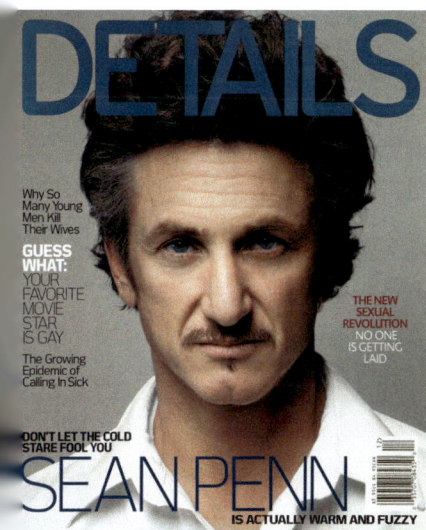

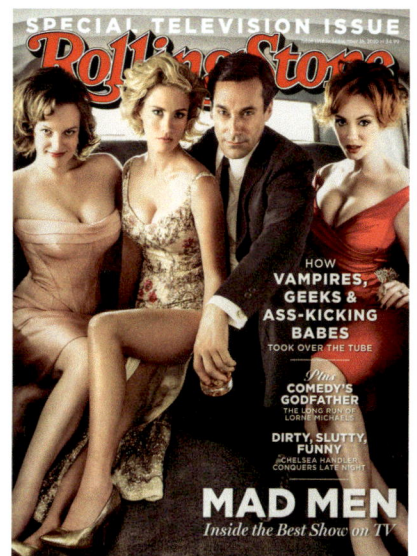

SURGEON GENERAL'S WARNING: Smoking By Pregnant Women May Result in Fetal Injury, Premature Birth, And Low Birth Weight.

*Marlboro, 2000*

regulars

**100% additive-free natural tobacco**

For a sample CARTON call:
1-800-872-6460 ext. 13001

SURGEON GENERAL'S WARNING: Smoking By Pregnant Women May Result in Fetal Injury, Premature Birth, And Low Birth Weight.

No additives in our tobacco does **NOT** mean a safer cigarette.

SURGEON GENERAL'S WARNING: Cigarette Smoke Contains Carbon Monoxide.

*Kahlúa, 2001* ◄ *American Spirit, 2003*

*Camel, 2006*

*Marlboro, 2000*

KAHLÚA SKREW

Pour 1 part Kahlúa, 1 part vodka and 4 parts orange juice over ice. Drink with a circle of friends.

ANYTHING GOES™

Grand Marnier, 2002

JERRY LEWIS
**ABSOLUT VEGAS**

One in a series of 20 portraits celebrating ABSOLUT VODKA's 20th anniversary.

*Absolut, 2000*

# ABSOLUT KRAVITZ.

download the full experience at absolutkravitz.com

# ABSOLUT BOWIE.

Miller Lite, 2003

Cabana Cachaça, 2008

Alizé, 2004 ◄ Michelob Ultra, 2004

LUXURY REBORN

www.belvedere-vodka.com

Terry Richardson

*Belvedere Vodka, 2007*

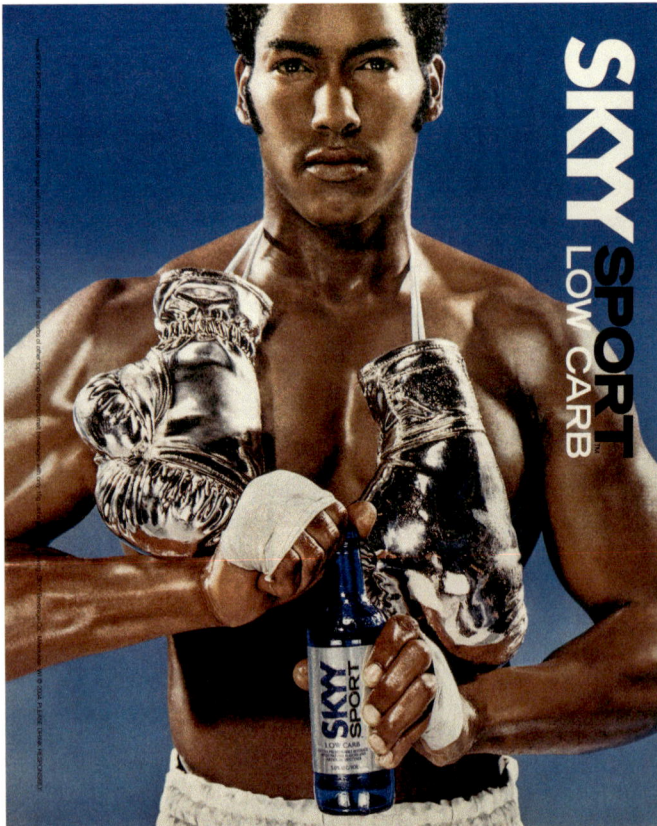

SKYY **SPORT** LOW CARB

*SKYY Vodka, 2004*

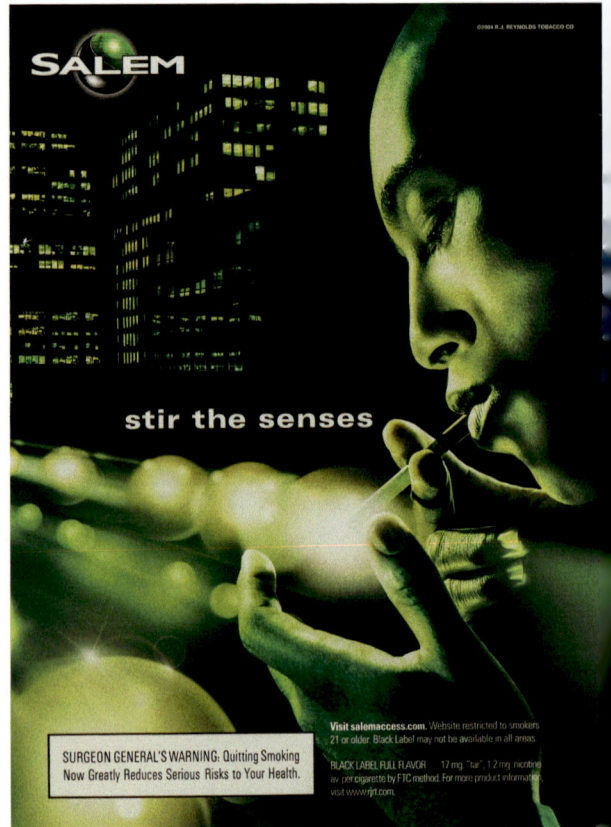

SALEM

stir the senses

**SURGEON GENERAL'S WARNING:** Quitting Smoking Now Greatly Reduces Serious Risks to Your Health.

*Salem, 2004*

*Camel, 2005*

Redwood Creek, 2009

Little did he know, his "ex" would be on the scene.

Bombay Spirits, 2005

Bushmills, 2008

Fernet-Branca, 2005

▶ Martini & Rossi, 2008

GRAND
CANAL
VENICE

*andy Warhol*

MARTINI & ROSSI® recognized Andy Warhol's unique talent and commissioned him to develop an advertising campaign, which ran in the U.S. from 1956 to 1963. It was during this time that Warhol began to develop his famed "blotted line" technique, which he used to create a series of four advertisements promoting vermouth cocktail usage in the United States.

DISTINCTIVE SINCE 1953

DISTINCTIVE SINCE 1830

Tanqueray
IMPORTED

LONDON DRY GIN

Hef says drink responsibly

IMPORTED LONDON DRY GIN 47.3% ALC./VOL., 100% GRAIN NEUTRAL SPIRITS, SCHIEFFELIN & SOMERSET CO., NEW YORK, N.Y. © 2002 GUINNESS UNITED DISTILLERS & VINTNERS AMSTERDAM B.V.

*Tanqueray, 2002*

*1800, 2004*

*Winston, 2004*

*Moët & Chandon, 2007*

*SKYY Vodka, 2002*

*Evan Williams, 2003*

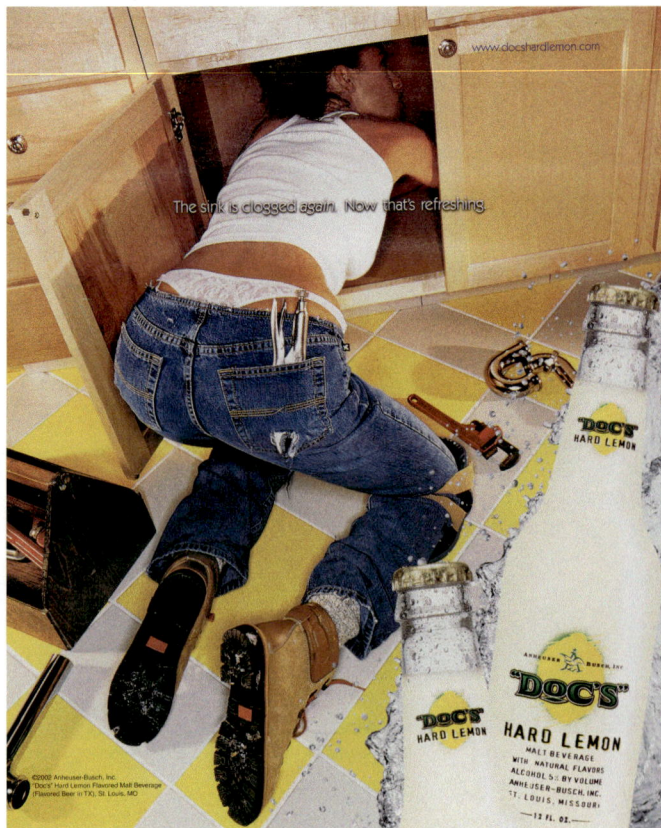

*"Doc's" Hard Lemon, 2002*

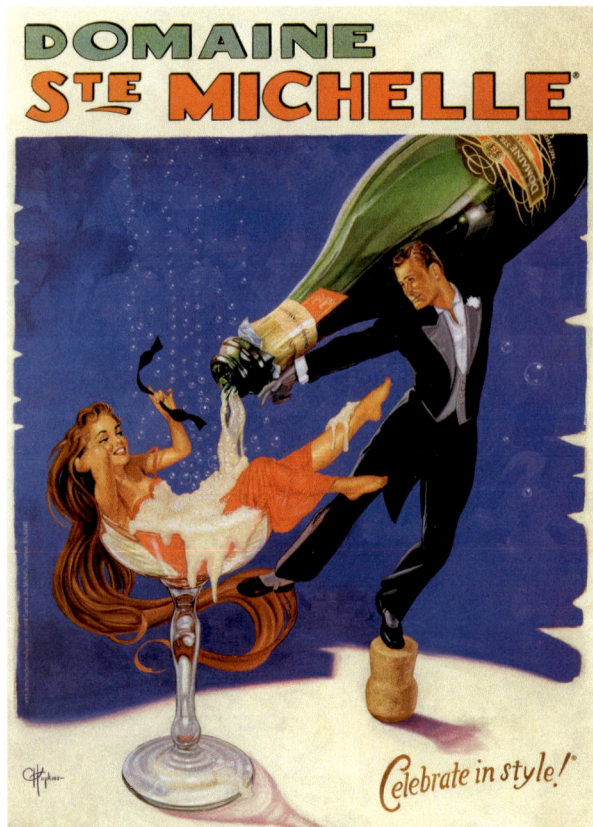

*Domaine Ste. Michelle, 2004*

*Crown Royal, 2001*

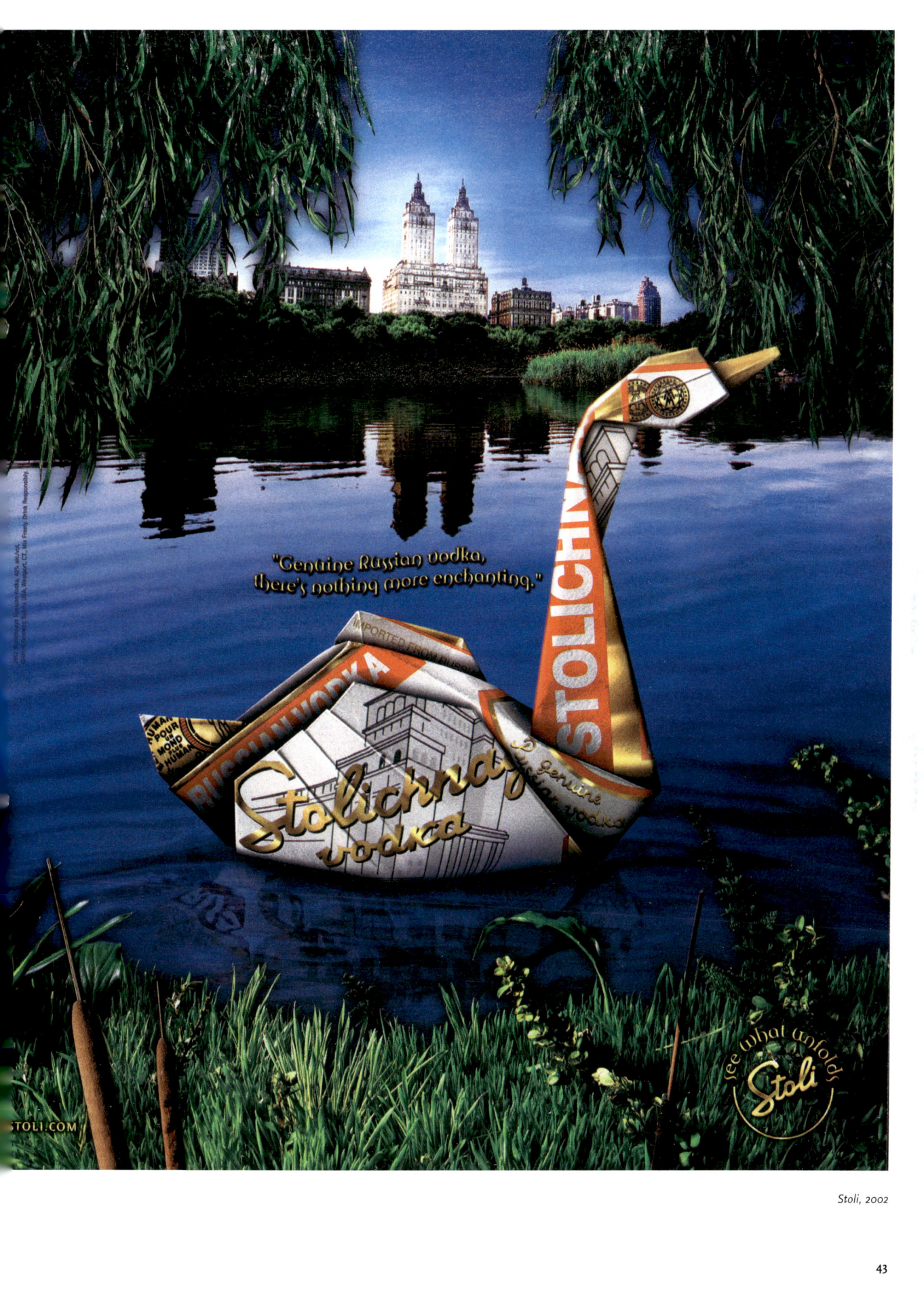

"Genuine Russian vodka, there's nothing more enchanting."

see what unfolds

*Stoli, 2002*

43

*Seagram's, 2006*

*Seagram's, 2005*

*SVEDKA, 2007*

*Chopin, 2005*

*Chopin, 2005*

*Coors, 2005*

YOUR DAD HAD GROUPIES

He soloed. People paid to see him. He drank cocktails. But not in martini glasses. They wer whisky cocktails. Made with Canadian Club. Served in a rocks glass. They tasted good. DAMN RIGHT YOUR DAD DRANK I

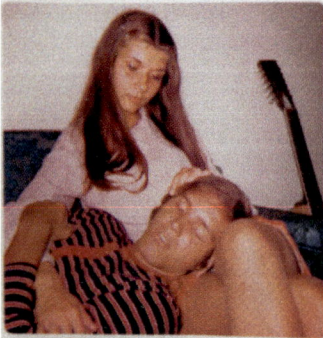

Canadian Club® Blended Canadian Whisky, 40% Alc./Vol. ©2007 Canadian Club Import Company, Deerfield, IL.

Canadian Club.

Canadian Club, 2008

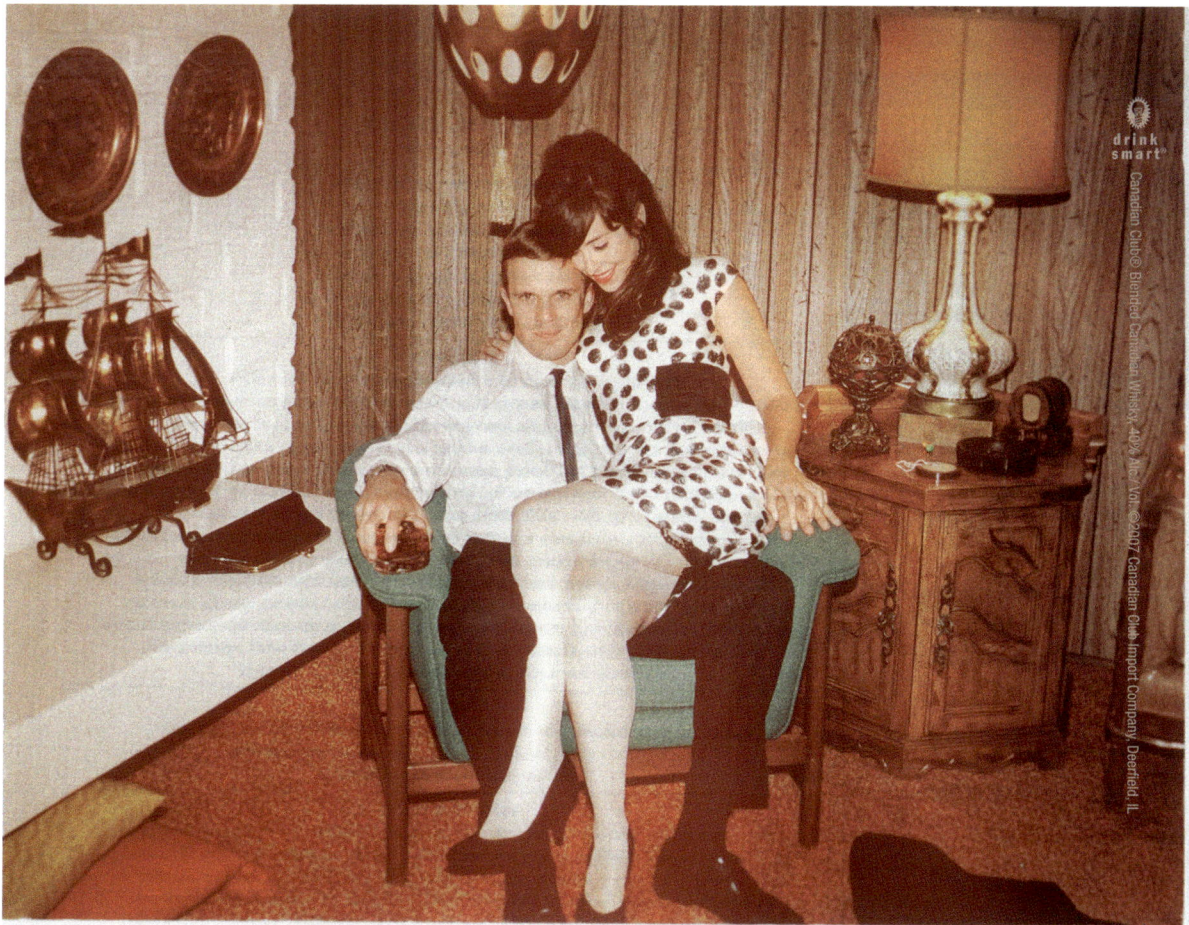

YOUR MOM WASN'T YOUR DAD'S FIRST

He went out. He got two numbers in the same night. He drank cocktails. But they were whisky cocktails. Made with Canadian Club. Served in a rocks glass. They tasted good. They were effortless. DAMN RIGHT YOUR DAD DRANK IT

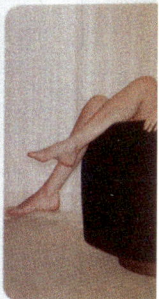

*Canadian Club*

*Canadian Club, ca. 2008*

YOUR DAD DIDN'T PUT ON HIS OWN LOTION

He chose the beach. Picked his spot. And decided when it was time for some drinks.
C.C. and Gingers. Smooth. Refreshing. **DAMN RIGHT YOUR DAD DRANK IT™**
And brought to him in his beach chair.

*Canadian Club.*

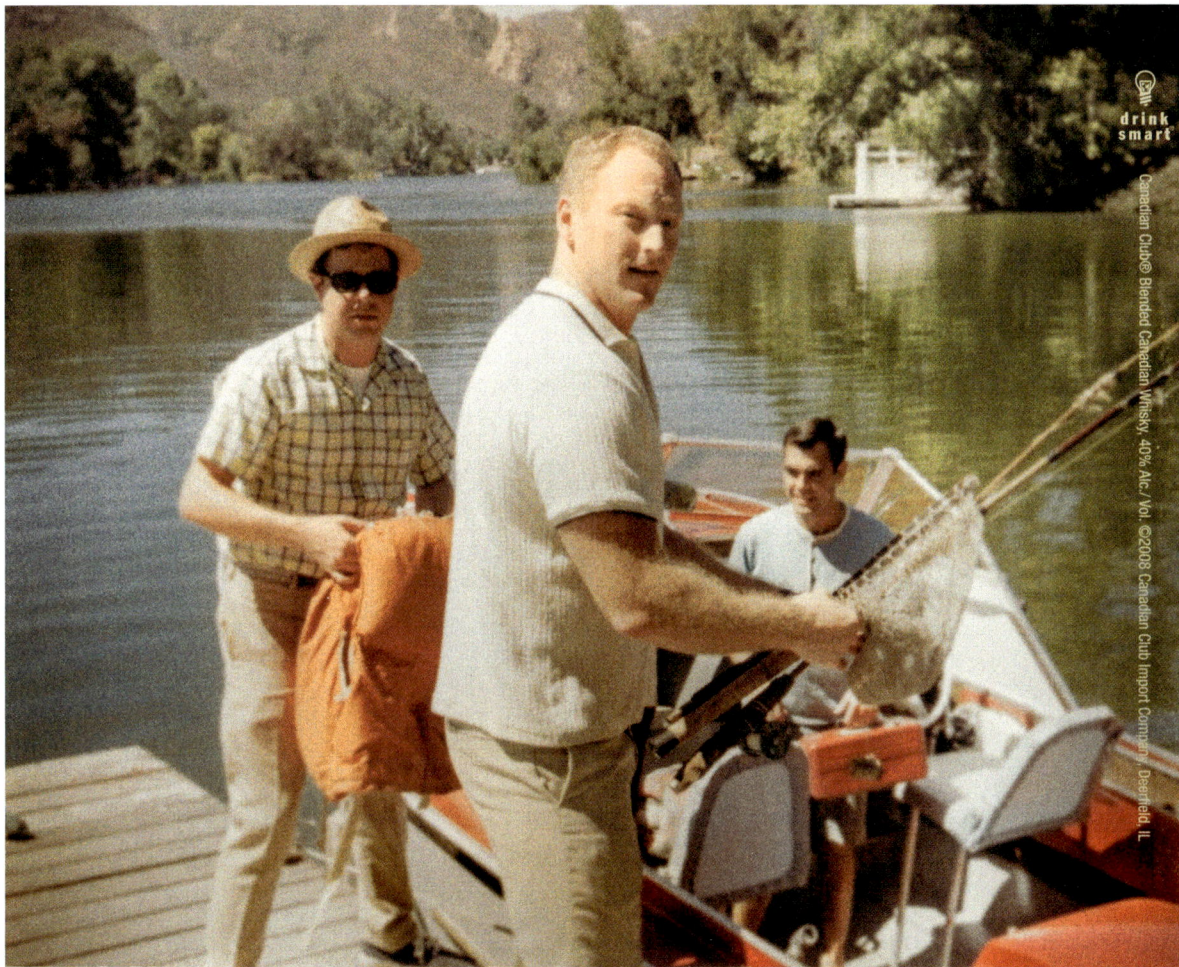

YOUR DAD WAS NOT A METROSEXUAL

He didn't do pilates. Moisturize. Or drink pink cocktails. Your Dad drank whisky cocktails. Made with Canadian Club®. Served in a rocks glass. They tasted good. They were effortless.

DAMN RIGHT YOUR DAD DRANK IT

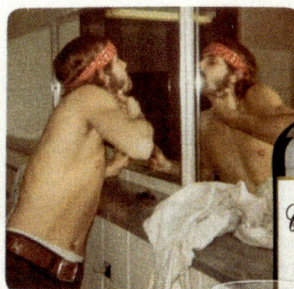

Canadian Club.

*Canadian Club, 2008*

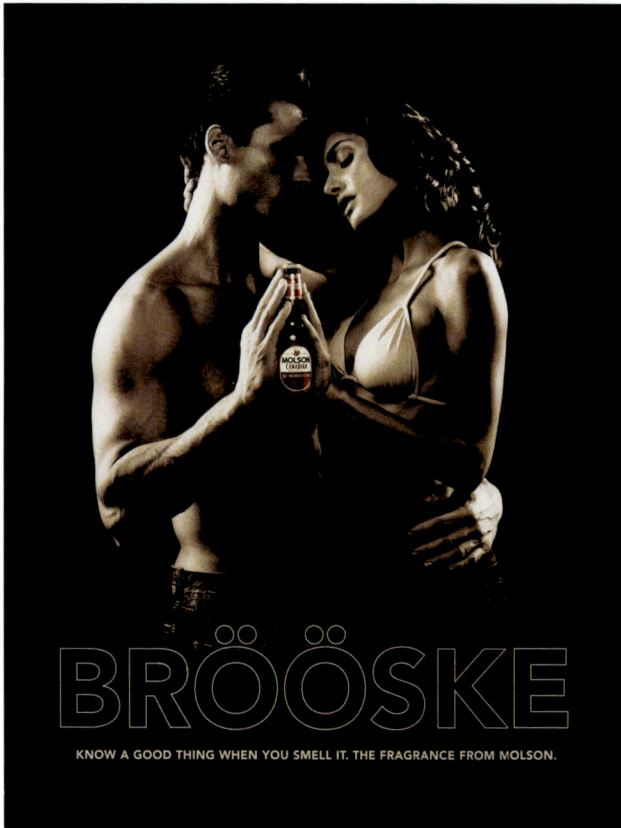
Molson, 2005

Hennessy, 2006

Punch, 2004

Jack Daniel's, 2006

► Amstel, 2006

*Stoli, 2008*

*Budweiser, 2006*

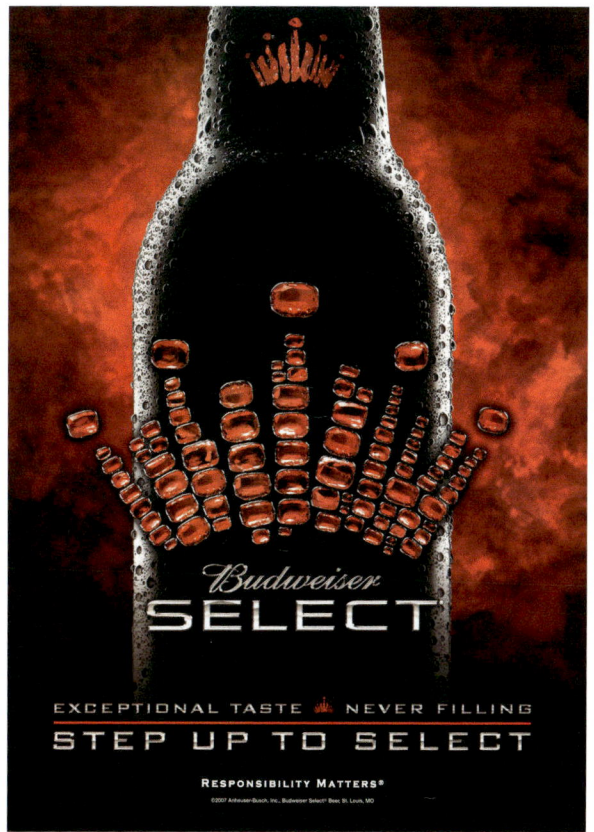

*Budweiser, 2007*

*Yellow Tail, 2006*

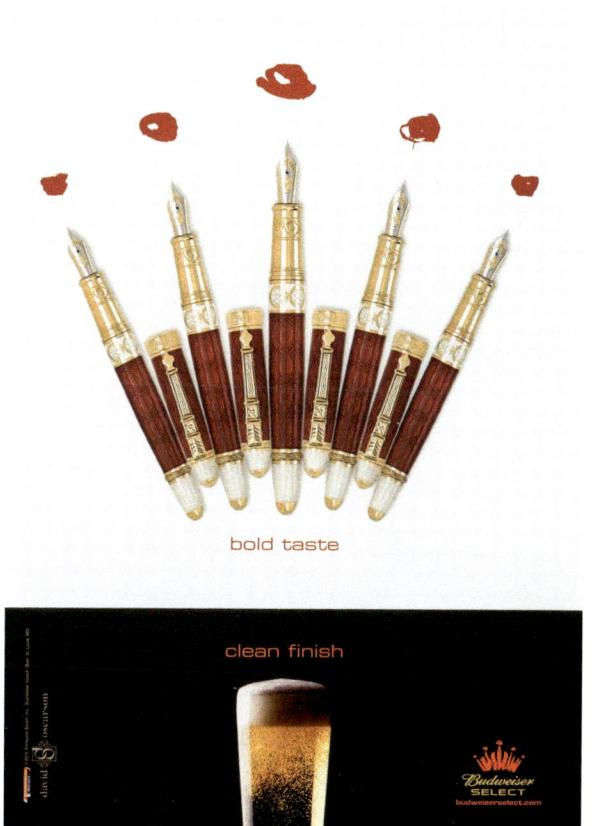

*Budweiser, 2006*

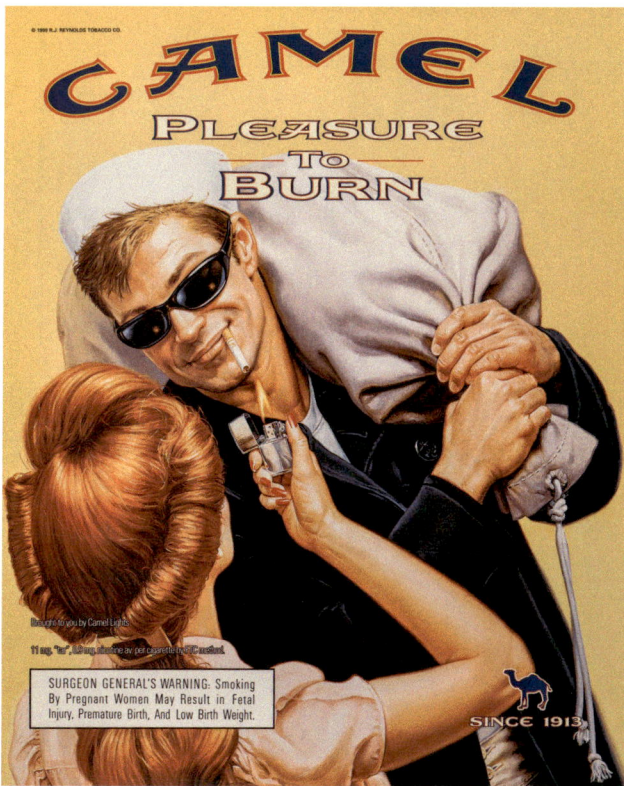

*Camel, 2000*

*SKYY Vodka, 2001*

*Moët & Chandon, 2002*

*Beefeater, 2002*

Chivas Regal, 2002

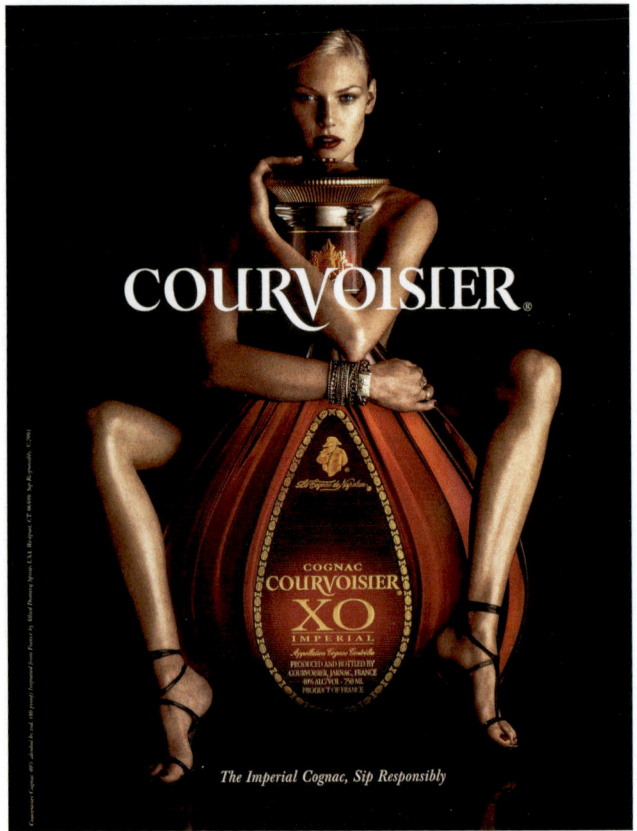

Courvoisier, 2004

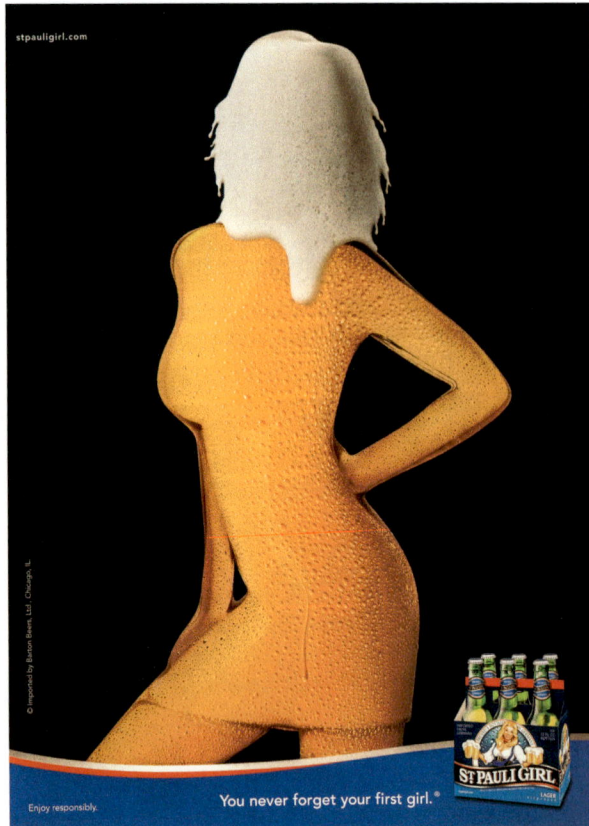

St. Pauli Girl, 2006

Jose Cuervo, 2006

34

*Kool, 2006*

FULL FLAVOR

# PARLIAMENT

OUT OF THE CLEAR BLUE

DISTINCTLY SMOOTH

For more information about PM USA and its products, visit www.philipmorrisusa.com or call 1-877-PM USA WEB.

Lights: 10 mg "tar," 0.7 mg nicotine – Full Flavor: 15 mg "tar," 1.0 mg nicotine av. per cigarette by FTC method.

Full Flavor available in limited areas. © Philip Morris Inc. 2000

*Parliament, 2000*

Knob Creek, 2001

Bulleit Bourbon, 2007

Peroni, 2007

Peroni, 2007

*C'est ma folie.*

Why create beers as imaginative as they are delicious? Ask New Belgium's brewmaster Peter Bouckaert and you'll get an earful about Surrealist art, untranslatable Flemish sayings, and why he painted his house blue. Which is to say, the answer is best tasted.

*newbelgium.com*

Hey, get your own New Belgium beer glass! Available at your favorite beer store.

NEW BELGIUM BREWING

FAT TIRE AMBER ALE

*Follow your folly. Ours is beer.*

*New Belgium Brewing, 2008*

Nada Zilch Zip

Rien

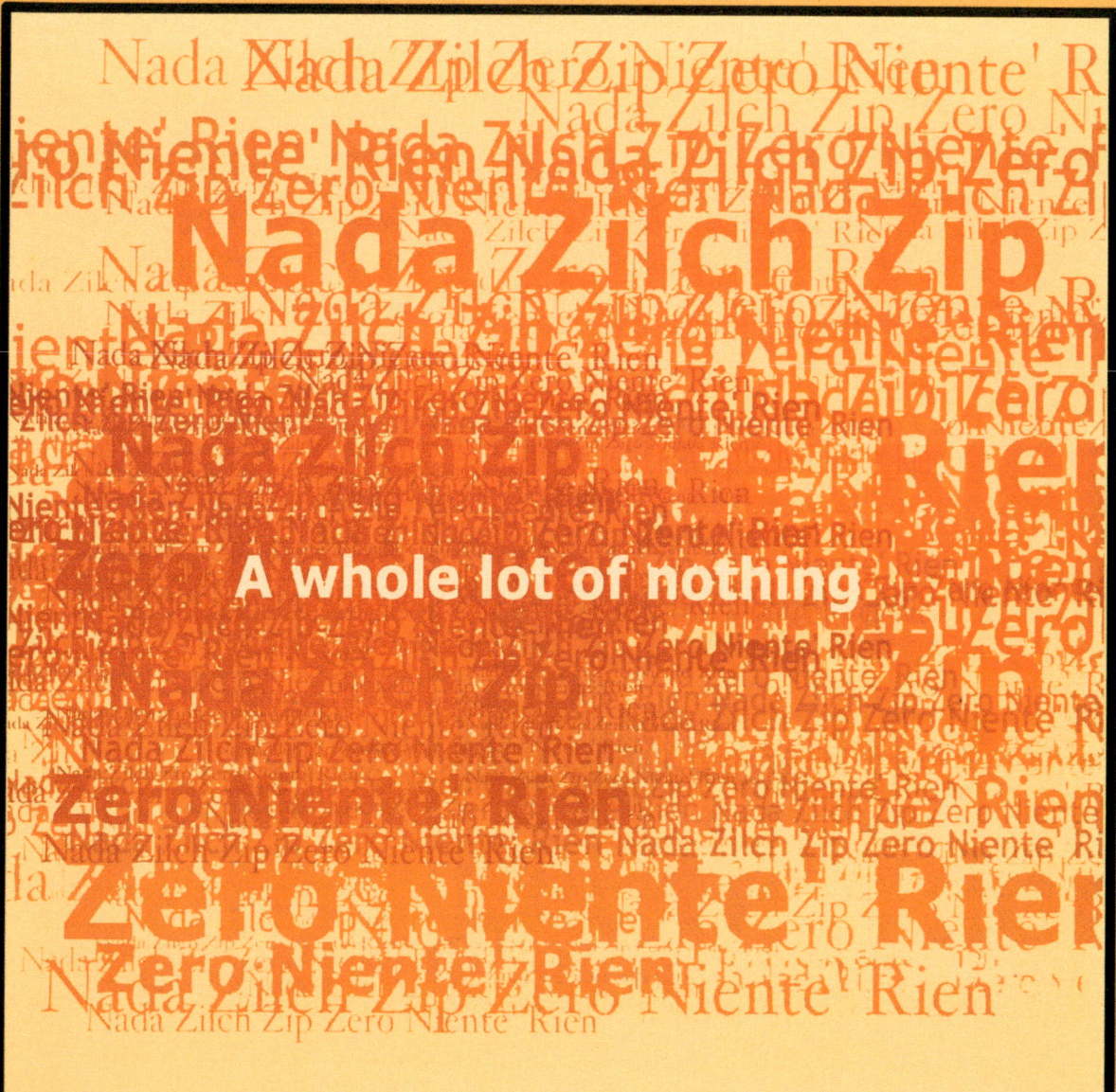

A whole lot of nothing.

Zero Niente Rien

Zero Niente Rien

Zero Niente Rien

When you're counting carbs, Smirnoff vodka, Crown Royal, Johnnie Walker and Tanqueray gin have none.

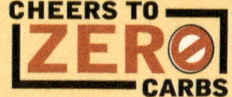

SMIRNOFF

Crown Royal

JOHNNIE WALKER

Tanqueray
DISTINCTIVE SINCE 1830

CHEERS TO
ZERO
CARBS

Please drink responsibly • Check out zerocarbparties.com

*Zero Carbs, 2004*

# HOW 42 BELOW

## MET THE MARTINI

Actually, our friend Paul tried it. And he was all like, "This is so good I would bathe in it." So being the marketing guys at 42BELOW, we let him. Is that so wrong?

**IT'S VODKA. FROM NEW ZEALAND.**

42BELOW.COM

SKYY BLUE

THE MOTHER OF ALL VODKAS FROM THE MOTHERLAND OF VODKA

GENUINE RUSSIAN VODKA
STOLICHNAYA
КЛАССИЧЕСКАЯ Р...

STOLICHNAYA
IMPORTED RUSSIAN VODKA
Stolichnaya vodka
RUSSIAN VODKA

CHOOSE AUTHENTICITY

STOLICHNAYA RUSSIAN VODKA

DRINK RESPONSIBLY
© STOLICHNAYA® Russian Vodka. 40% Alc./Vol. 100% Grain Neutral Spirits. ©2007 Imported by Pernod Ricard USA, Purchase, NY.

*Stoli, 2007*

Paint the town Pucker™

FIVE TECHNICOLOR FLAVORS OF SWEET AND SOUR SCHNAPPS.

*Pucker, 2000*

▶ Abso

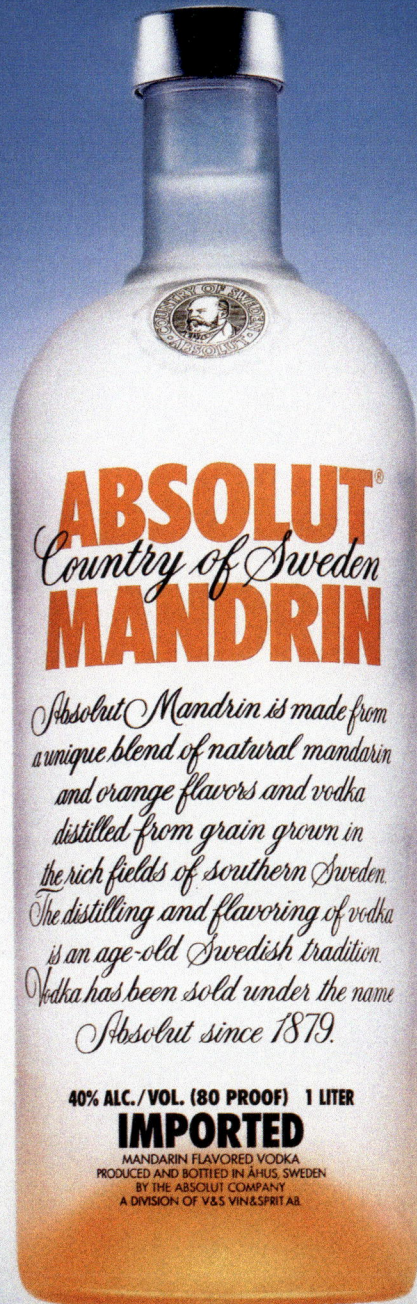

**ABSOLUT OBSESSION.**

ABSOLUT® VODKA. PRODUCT OF SWEDEN. 40 AND 50% ALC/VOL (80 AND 100 PROOF). 100% GRAIN NEUTRAL SPIRITS. ABSOLUT COUNTRY OF SWEDEN VODKA & LOGO, ABSOLUT, ABSOLUT BOTTLE DESIGN, ABSOLUT CALLIGRAPHY AND ABSOLUT.COM ARE TRADEMARKS OWNED BY V&S VIN & SPRIT AB. ©2001 V&S VIN & SPRIT AB. IMPORTED BY ABSOLUT SPIRITS CO., NEW YORK, NY. PHOTOGRAPH BY SERGE PAULET. ENJOY OUR QUALITY RESPONSIBLY. absolut.com

*Absolut, 2002*

*Sagatiba, 2007*

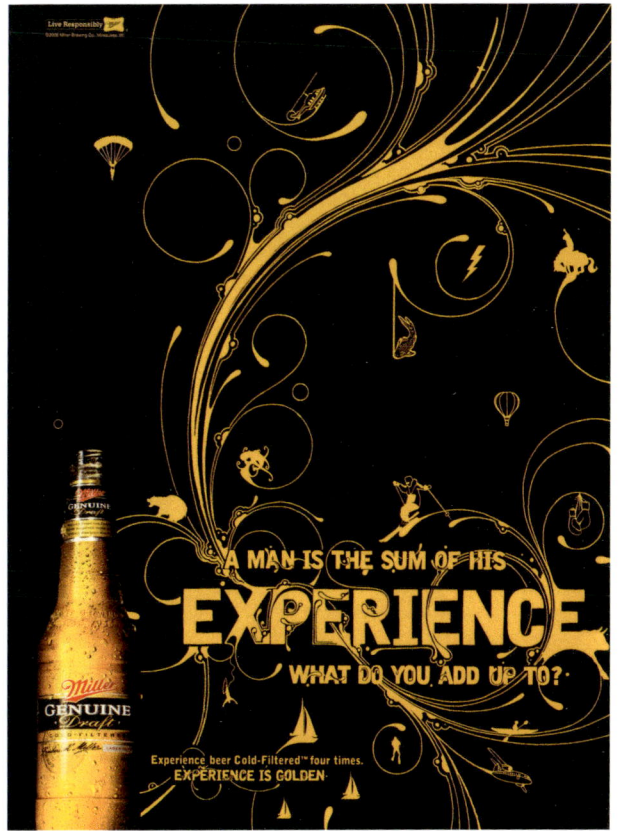

*Miller, 2006*

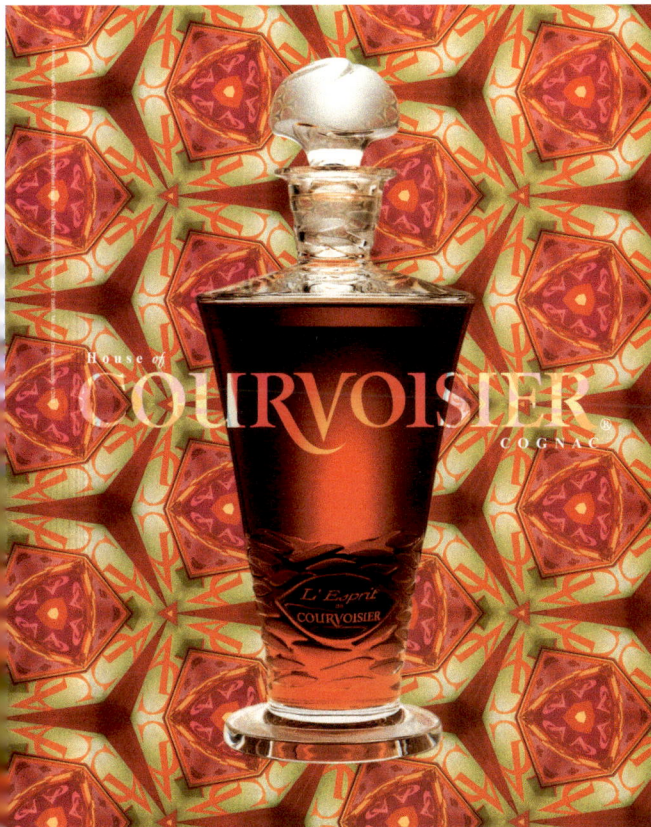

*Courvoisier, 2002*

*Jose Cuervo, 2007*

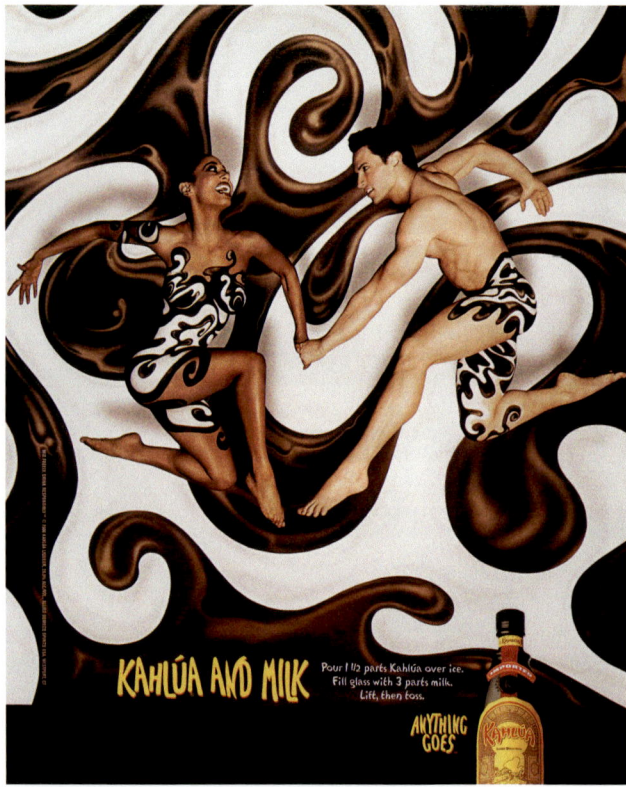
Kahlúa, 2001

Kahlúa, 2000

Hpnotiq, 2005

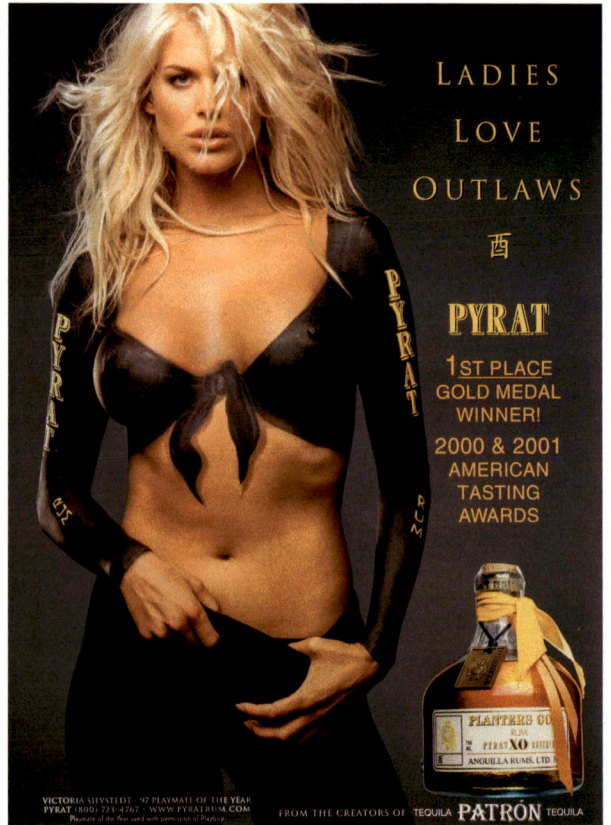
Patrón, 2002

*Cutty Sark, 2001*

*Tanqueray, 2009*

*Tanqueray, 2000*

*Absolut, 2007*

*Johnnie Walker, 2007*

NA ZDROWIE, MOM & DAD.

I **have** more friends than foes.
I **have** a signed copy of "Kind of Blue."
I **have** a conscience.
I **have** many stories to tell.
I **have** no regrets.

ARE YOU PRIVILEGED?

Hennessy
*Privilège*
V.S.O.P
COGNAC

buenas noches

Corona Extra

LA CERVEZA MAS FINA

BEER    12 FL OZ

Brewed and bottled by
CERVECERIA MODELO, S.A. DE C.V
MEXICO, D.F.

relax
responsibly
Imported by Crown Imports LLC, Chicago, IL 60603

# And the winner is...

## Cut It Out

Just when you thought it was safe to drink beer without a dose of sex, here comes this tits-and-ass gem that harkens back to the days when dad stashed a secret pinup behind closed garage doors. Times change, but beer makers seem to know that sex always sells. Women beware: this beverage is "BREWED for a MAN'S TASTE."

## Perfekt gebaut

Gerade dachte Mann noch, er könne mal in Frieden ein Bier trinken, ohne ständig an Sex denken zu müssen, da kommt diese scharfe Schnitte mit ihrer Kreissäge daher. Sie scheint direkt aus den Zeiten zu stammen, in denen Papa heimlich ein Pin-up hinter der geschlossenen Garagentür hängen hatte. Die Zeiten haben sich verändert, nur die Bierbrauerei scheint es noch zu wissen: *Sex always sells*. Aber Achtung, dieses Dosenbier ist nichts für Frauen: „BREWED for a MAN'S TASTE."

## Taillée sur mesure

Alors que l'on pensait pouvoir déguster sereinement une bière sans évoquer le sexe, voilà que ce petit bijou sexy nous renvoie à l'époque où papa planquait des photos de pin-up dans le garage. Les temps changent, mais les brasseurs savent que le sexe fait toujours vendre. Mesdames, gare à vous! Cette boisson est « BRASSÉE pour PLAIRE À L'HOMME ».

▶ *Milwaukee's Be*

FASTEN YOUR SEAT BELT AND

# TIE DOWN THE DOG.

MINI COOPER S

**THE ALL-NEW MINI CONVERTIBLE. ALWAYS OPEN.**

# It's an environmental movement all by itself.

How many cars does it take to change the world? Just one, perhaps. Introducing the Honda Insight. It's America's first gasoline-electric hybrid automobile.

Nothing short of an engineering breakthrough, the new Insight achieves an astounding 70 miles per gallon on the highway, 61 miles per gallon in the city, and a phenomenal 700-mile range on one tank of fuel. How? Simply by combining an efficient three-cylinder gasoline engine with an electric motor that's powered by nickel-metal hydride batteries which never need to be plugged in. Then add a lightweight body, and a world-class aerodynamic design, and you have the ultra-low-emission Insight. It's the result of years of research and development into lighter, more fuel-efficient, cleaner cars. In other words, technology with a conscience. Then again, what else would you expect from a car powered by Honda?

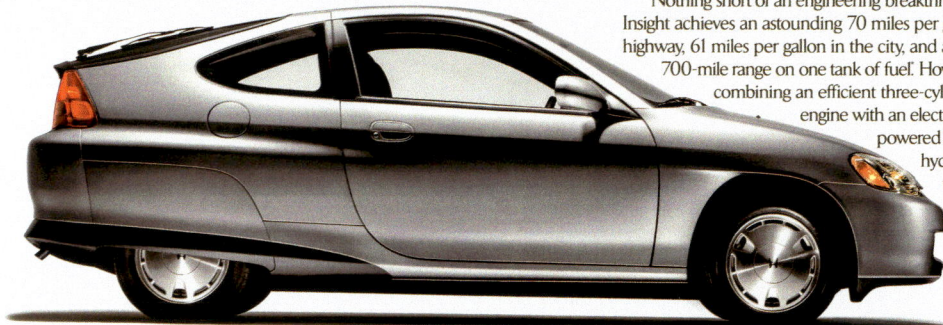

**HONDA**
Thinking.™

*Toyota, 2002* ◄◄   *Honda, 2000*

---

THAT WAS **THEN.**   THIS IS **WOW.**

IN 1935, THERE WAS NOTHING ELSE QUITE LIKE THE CHEVY™ SUBURBAN. NOW, NEARLY 65 YEARS LATER, IT'S STILL AN ORIGINAL.   THE ALL-NEW 2000 CHEVY SUBURBAN HAS A MORE COMFORTABLE INTERIOR, SMOOTHER RIDE,

MORE POWERFUL VORTEC™ V8 ENGINES, AND IMPROVED TOWING AND HAULING CAPABILITIES. **THE BEST SUBURBAN**   **YET** ISN'T MERELY AN EXTENSION OF ITS HERITAGE. IT'S THE BEGINNING OF A NEW ERA.

**SUBURBAN**
**LIKE A ROCK**

*Mini, 2009* ◄   *Chevrolet, 2000*

0·60?

Yes.

Drivers wanted. VW

*VW, 2000*

Are we the cutting edge of avant-garde? ................................................................. Well, no.

The New I·S. Starting At $30,995.*
It's Sufficiently Radical.

Race-inspired cockpit, Formula One-style shifting, drilled-aluminum foot pedals, 17" performance alloy wheels.† 215 horsepower. Radical. Without being ridiculous. lexus.com. THE RELENTLESS PURSUIT OF PERFECTION. LEXUS

*Lexus, 2000*

Boldly go.

**2001 PT CRUISER**   Enough of the lifeless commute. The new Chrysler PT Cruiser will recharge your ride. Aggressive stance. Pronounced grille. Chrome accents. Clearly, this is no vehicle for the mild-mannered. Peeling back its rebel skin reveals a Boy Scout resourcefulness. 26 seating configurations,* a foldout tailgate table, handy power outlets* and an amazing price. From $16,000 to $19,995.** So, don't just simply go. Boldly go. 1.800.CHRYSLER or www.chrysler.com.

*Optional. **Base MSRPs include destination, exclude tax. Model with options shown/described: $19,995.

**CHRYSLER**

*Chrysler, 2000*

**How we look at every Five Star dealer.**

Now there's a process that puts dealers and their dealerships under the microscope so you don't have to. It's called Five Star — an innovative certification process that totally redefines the way cars and trucks are sold and serviced. • This 21-point process scrutinizes every aspect of the car-buying experience. It looks at what each person in the dealership does, how they do it and, most important, how they can do it better. • Take a closer look at a Five Star certified Chrysler, Plymouth, Jeep, or Dodge dealer. You'll really like what you see — but only where you see the Five Star sign. **Five Star. It's Better. We'll Prove It.**

For more information, call us at 1-800-677-5-STAR or visit www.fivestar.com. Jeep is a registered trademark of DaimlerChrysler.

**Dodge**   **CHRYSLER Plymouth Jeep**

*e Star, 2000*

www.toyota.com • 1-800-GO-TOYOTA ©2000 Toyota Motor Sales, U.S.A., Inc. Buckle Up! Do it for those who love you.

4-pist in caliper front disc brakes for exceptional stopping power.

Double-wishbone front suspension enhances ride comfort.

Single-piece frame rails with nine cross members increase rigidity.

Load-sensing proportioning valve for stable braking with heavy cargo.

Trust me, fellas. Your view is better than mine.

**Sometimes the best way to judge a truck is to look under one.**
The Toyota Tundra. It has an i-FORCE V8 that's the only 32-valve dual overhead cam engine in a full-size pickup. Plus, enough technology underneath to make your friends look silly.

**TOYOTA TUNDRA**
Better from the ground up.

*Toyota, 2001*

85

"Hey, there's a black one."

Drivers wanted.

© 2000 Volkswagen. 1-800 DRIVE VW or VW.COM

*VW, 2001*

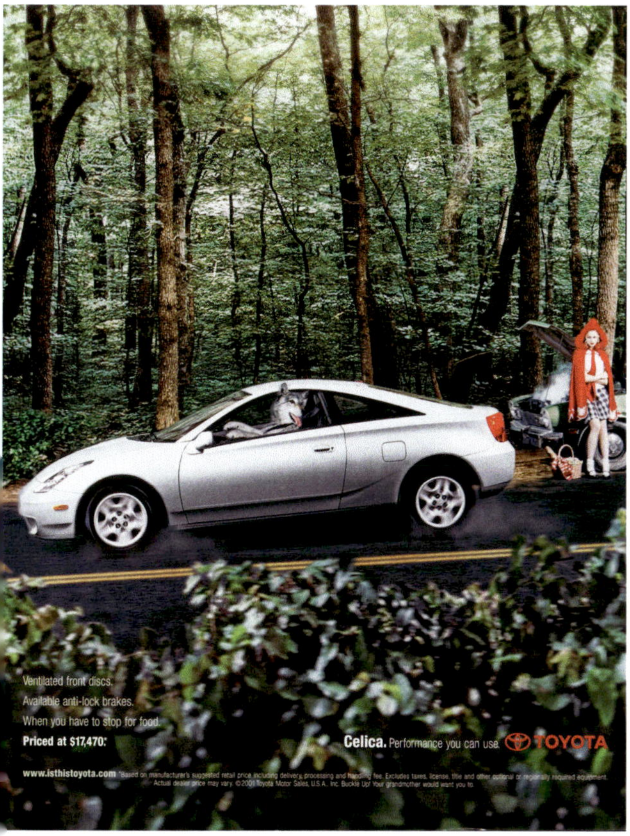


*Toyota, 2001*

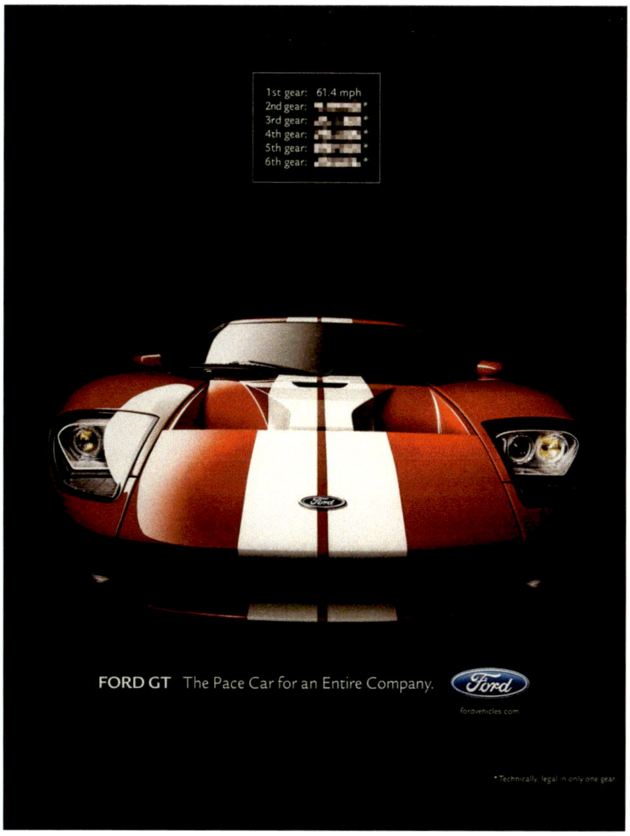


*Ford, 2004*

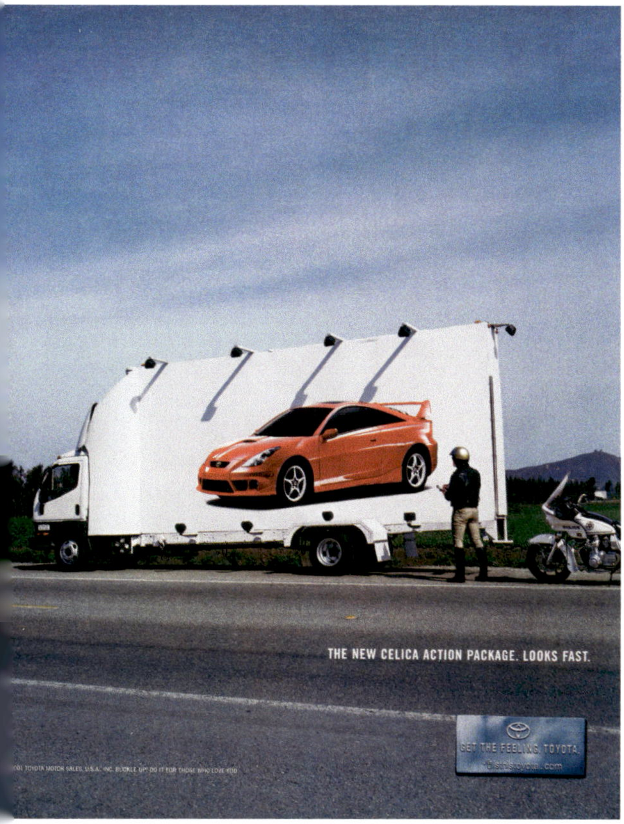


*yota, 2002*

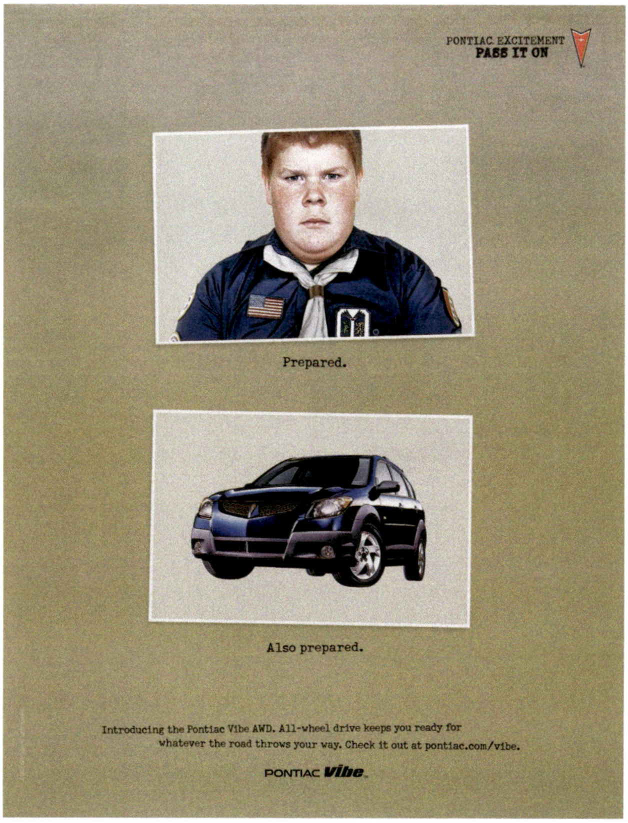


*Pontiac, 2002*

"Hey, there's a blue one."

Drivers wanted.

*VW, 2001*

**Scion By Rico, Installation Artist**

xB pricing starts at $14,165* well equipped, including A/C, Pioneer AM/FM/CD system, power windows, door locks, mirrors, chrome exhaust tip, anti-lock brakes, vehicle stability control and choice of 3 wheel cover options. Over 30 accessories are available to customize your car. *MSRP includes delivery, processing and handling fee. Excludes taxes, title, license and optional equipment. Actual dealer price may vary.

© 2003. Scion and the Scion logos are trademarks of Toyota Motor Corporation and Toyota is a registered trademark of Toyota Motor Corporation. For more information, call 866-70-SCION (866-707-2466) or visit scion.com.

"Original ideas are worth preserving" ... Rico.

**Scion xB**

**Scion xA**

Personalization begins here.

what moves you
scion.com

*Scion, 2003*

IT ONLY LOOKS LIKE THIS BECAUSE IT'S BADASS.

THE NEW H2. **HUMMER**® LIKE NOTHING ELSE.™

**Scion By State of Grace, Tattoo Artist**

xB pricing starts at $14,165* well equipped, including A/C, Pioneer AM/FM/CD system, power windows, door locks, mirrors, chrome exhaust tip, anti-lock brakes, vehicle stability control, and choice of 3 wheel cover options. Over 30 accessories are available to customize your car. *MSRP includes delivery, processing and handling fee. Excludes taxes, title, license and optional equipment. Actual dealer price may vary.

"When you make your mark, make sure it means something" ... State of Grace.

Cadillac, 2007

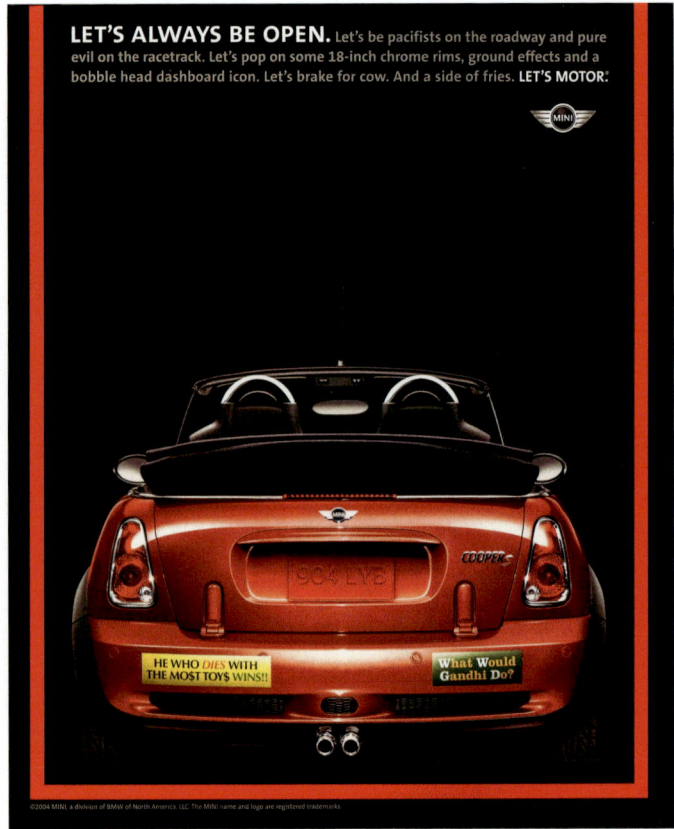

Mini, 2005

Audi, 2005

IT HAS A POLARIZING EFFECT ON EVERYONE.
EVERYONE BUT CRITICS.

THE AWARD-WINNING PT CRUISER

It's united the critics for one very good reason. Quality. In fact, PT Cruiser won Strategic Vision's Total Quality Award™ for compact cars in '01, '02 and '03 (tie)* And while it may never be a vehicle for everyone, it's already a vehicle for everything—with over 120 cubic feet of interior space, 160 possible interior configurations and enough room for five. PT Turbo starts at $21,865! This 220-horse-power, turbocharged GT monster runs $25,995! PT Cruiser. **CUSTOMIZE YOUR LIFE**

**CHRYSLER**
**PT CRUISER**

*Chrysler, 2003*

HHR UNBLEND.

**HHR** DEPART FROM THE ORDINARY FAST WITH THE HHR™ ECOTEC® ENGINE, TOURING SUSPENSION,' AND AVAILABLE 17-INCH POLISHED-ALUMINUM WHEELS.' WHAT ARE YOU WAITING FOR? GO TO CHEVY.COM AND CHECK OUT THE NEW HHR.

*Chevrolet, 2005*

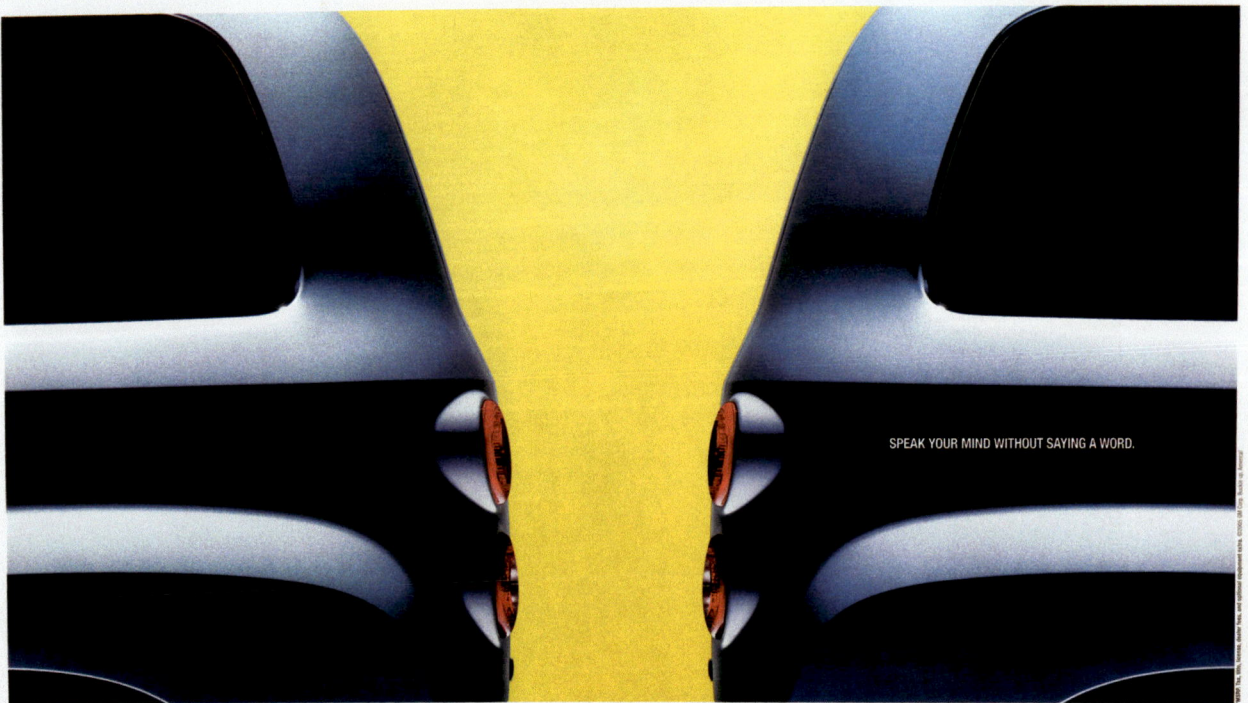

SPEAK YOUR MIND WITHOUT SAYING A WORD.

**HHR** THE HHR™ IS ROLLING PROOF THAT COOL CAN BE USEFUL AND USEFUL CAN BE COOL. GET INTO THE LATEST FORM OF SELF-EXPRESSION FOR JUST $15,990.' AS SHOWN $18,790.' THE NEW CHEVY™ HHR.

*Chevrolet, 2005*

It's got punch.

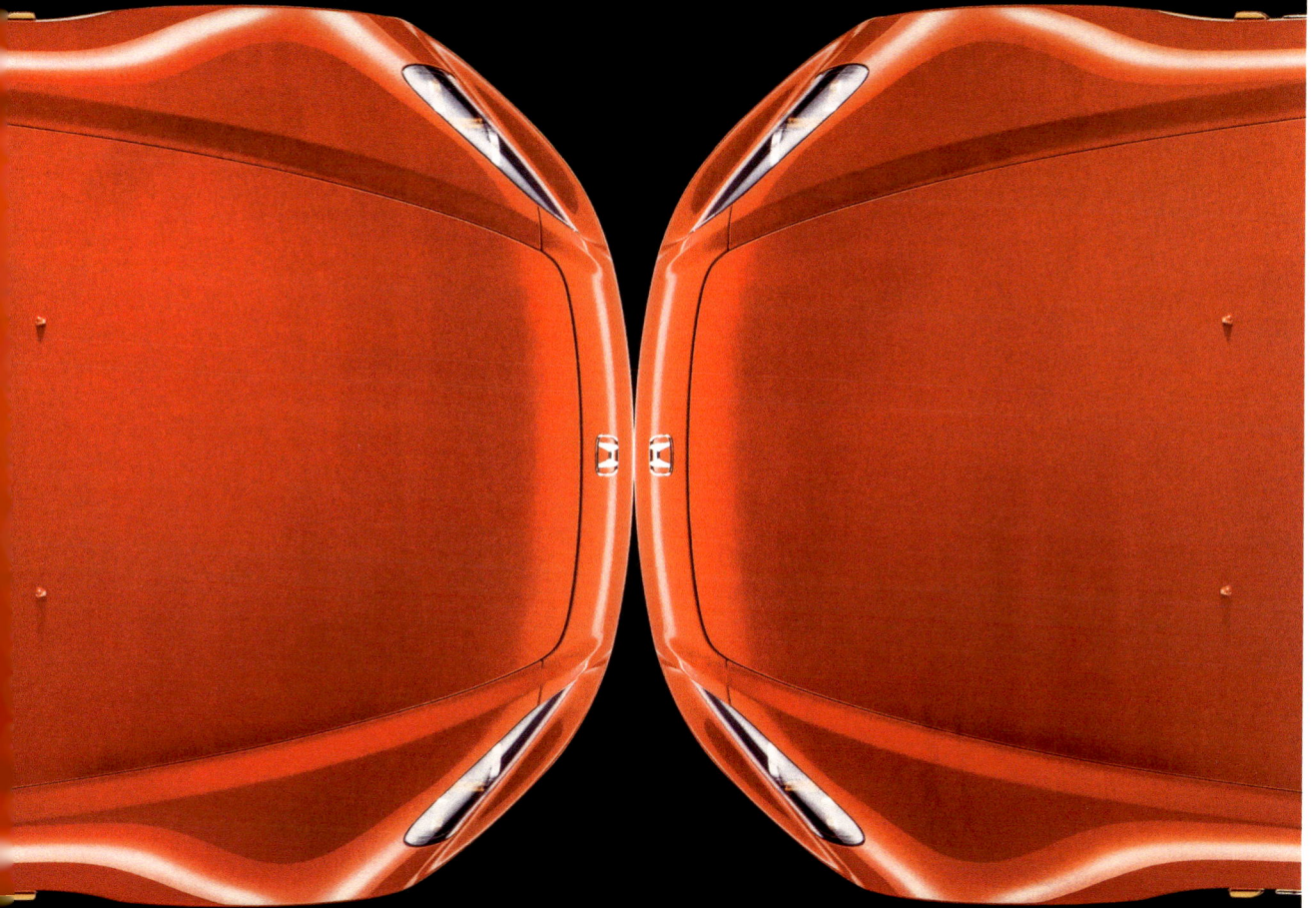

When it's time to go toe-to-toe, the S2000's 237-hp engine and 8000-rpm redline will definitely give you the upper hand.

honda.com 1-800-33-Honda ©2005 American Honda Motor Co., Inc.

S2000 HONDA

*Honda, 2006*

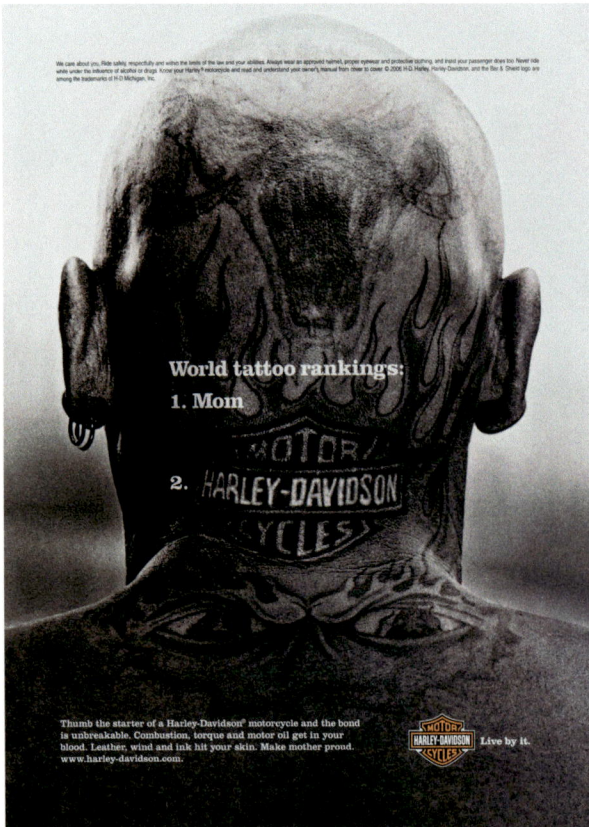

Harley-Davidson, 2007

Cadillac, 2006

Cadillac, 2006

Toyota, 2005

Toyota, 2009

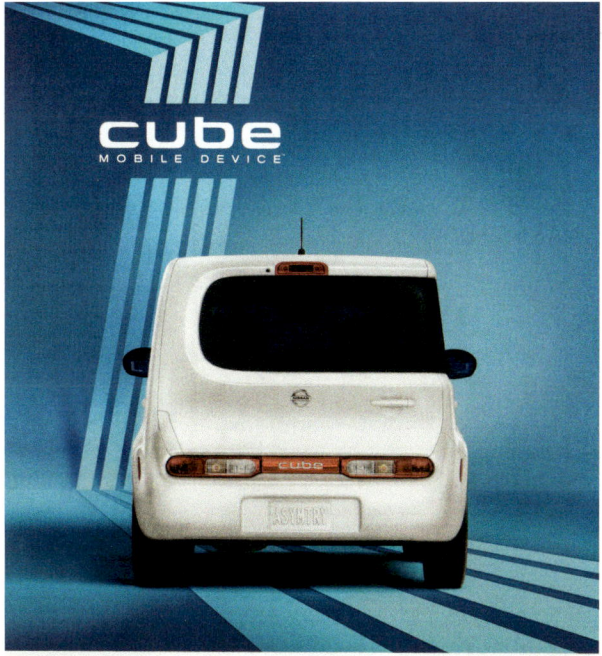

Nissan, 2009

▶ Scion, 2006

# PERSONALIZATION

**2006 Scion xB**
**Starting at $14,395***

## Standard features include

Six-speaker Pioneer CD stereo • iPod® and MP3 player capable • Satellite radio ready • 30 city/34 hwy. MPG† as estimated by EPA • Choice of three wheel-cover designs • Power windows, door locks and mirrors • Chrome exhaust tip • Anti-lock brakes • 5-year, 60,000-mile Powertrain warranty‡

## Customization accessories include

Fog light kit • Rear spoiler • Clear-lens rear tail lights • Sport pedal covers • Color steering wheel • Quickshifter • Interior light kit • Sport muffler • Struts/shocks kit • Performance clutch • Lowering springs kit • Tube subwoofer • Yakima roof rack • Billet oil-filler cap

**Wheel-cover Designs**

**60/40 Split Rear Seat**

**iPod-ready Pioneer CD Stereo**

**Sport Pedal Covers**

**SCION**
what moves you
scion.com

# 1.5 Liters of
# Micro Muscle Fury!

True technology.

The all-new Nissan Altima Coupe

NISSAN

SHIFT_

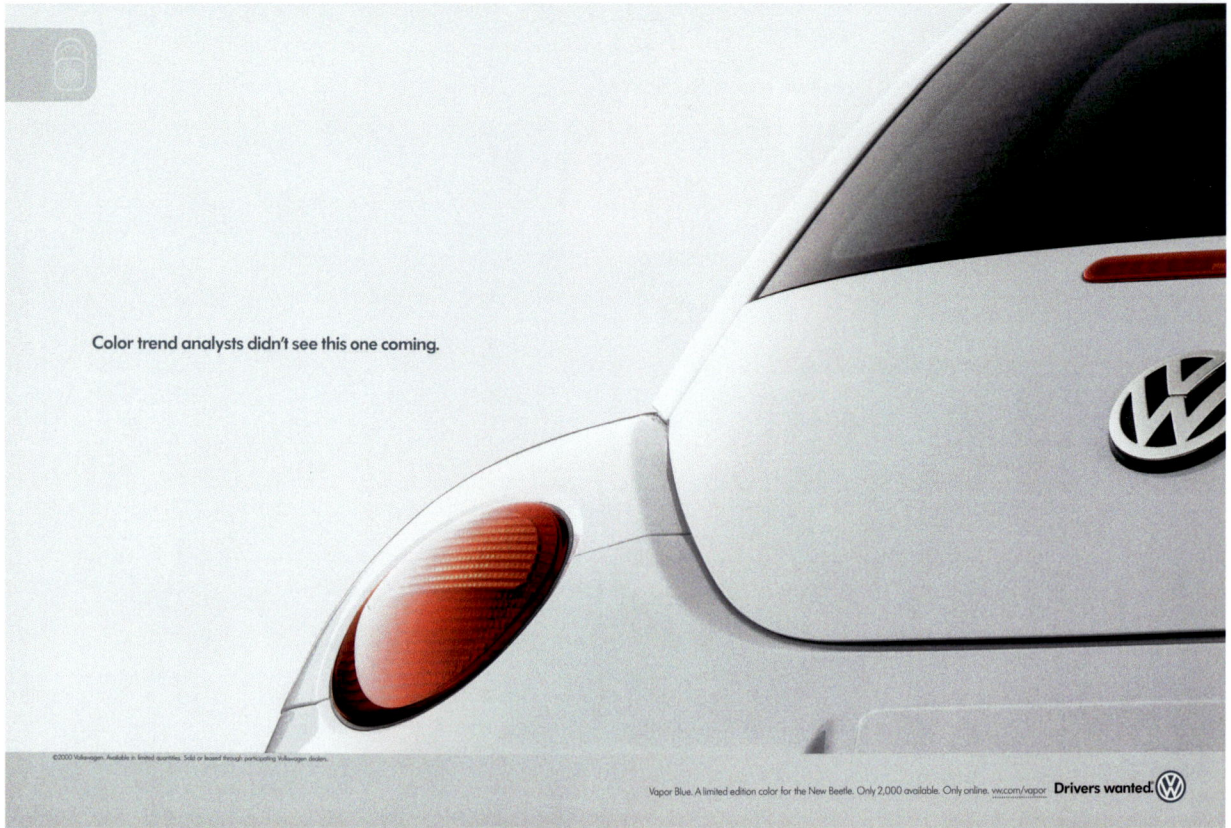

Color trend analysts didn't see this one coming.

©2000 Volkswagen. Available in limited quantities. Sold or leased through participating Volkswagen dealers.

Vapor Blue. A limited edition color for the New Beetle. Only 2,000 available. Only online. vw.com/vapor **Drivers wanted.**

*VW, 2000*

Eliminates the need to know the guy working the door.

Ford *Thunderbird*
fordvehicles.com

*Ford, 2001*

Maybe we're taking this sponsorship thing a bit too far.

CHEVY
WE'LL BE THERE

*Chevrolet, 2001*

**Hydrogen. It's gonna be huge.** Which is why GM is proud of our partnership with *The Weekly Reader* to provide teachers and students with lesson plans and classroom activities that focus on hydrogen and fuel cell technology. Because we believe that someone should be committed to preparing the children of today for the possibilities of tomorrow.

Only **GM**

onlyGM.com

*GM, 2006*

*Toyota, 2007*

**WHO SAYS MEN ARE AFRAID OF COMMITMENT?**

*Indian, 2000*

Harley-Davidson, 2007

Yamaha, 2005

Yamaha, 2005

► Honda, 2004

REALITY EXCEEDS THE FANTASY.

Ford, 2002

Toyota, 2005

Pontiac, 2007

▶ Jeep, 2006

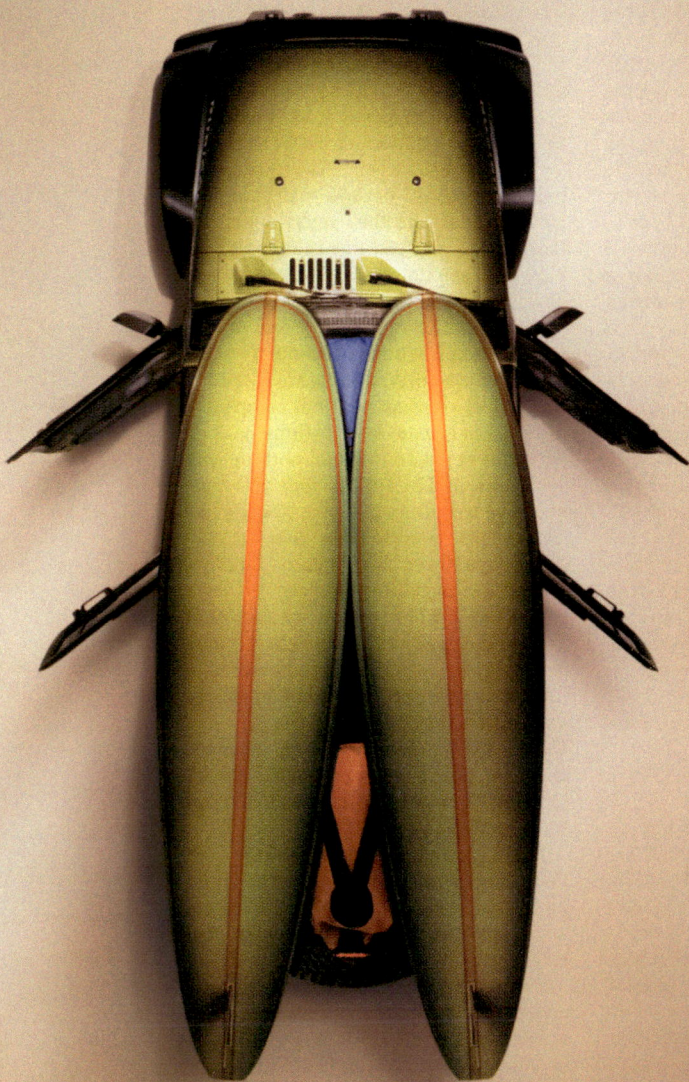

2007 WRANGLER UNLIMITED
*Four-dooricus Rockcrawlerus*

A new species from Jeep.

It's time to fight back.

When it comes to reducing our dependency on oil, Michelin® *HydroEdge*® tires certainly do their part. They're the longest-lasting, most fuel efficient tires in their category,* and just one of many things we're doing to reduce our impact on the environment. To learn about our efforts, like reforestation and tire recycling, and how you can help, visit michelinman.com/green.

**MICHELIN**
*A better way forward*

*Michelin, 2007*

**The Soul.** A new way to roll.

🎵 MP3 Input  ⓑ Bluetooth  ⚙ 50+ Accessories  ⛽ 31 MPG/HWY  💲 Starting under $14k  💻 kiasoul.com

**KIA MOTORS**
*The Power to Surprise*

*Kia, 2009*

113

**INTRODUCING JEEP® COMPASS. THE URBAN RECREATIONAL VEHICLE.**

It's time to start having fun with the city. The all new 2007 Jeep Compass comes with an advanced 172 hp 2.4L engine that gets up to 30 miles per gallon*, an available four-wheel-drive system, Electronic Stability Program (ESP) with Brake Assist, as well as a Five-Star side-impact safety rating† All for a starting price of $15,985†

‡Limited model 4X4 as shown, $22,235. MSRPs exclude tax.
*2.4L engine EPA estimate of 26 city/30 highway for 5-speed manual-equipped 4x2 models.
†Based on NHTSA crash testing.
**Jeep is a registered trademark of DaimlerChrysler Corporation.**

**Jeep**

**INTRODUCING JEEP COMPASS. THE URBAN RECREATIONAL VEHICLE.**

It's time to start having fun with the city. The all new 2007 Jeep Compass comes with an advanced 172 hp 2.4L engine that gets up to 30 miles per gallon,* a Five-Star side-impact safety rating,† MP3 compatibility, an available 9-speaker Boston Acoustics® Premium Sound Group with flip-down liftgate speakers. Starting at $15,985.‡

‡MSRP excludes tax.
*2.4L engine EPA estimate of 26 city/30 highway for 5-speed manual-equipped 4X2 models.
†Based on NHTSA crash testing.
Boston Acoustics is a registered trademark of Boston Acoustics, Inc.
**Jeep is a registered trademark of DaimlerChrysler Corporation.**

**Jeep**

The Cabrio. Drivers wanted. Ⓥ

# And the winner is...

### 360 Degrees of Nothing

What's going on here? Is this any way to sell an automobile? Are potential Lexus owners expected to turn their heads upside down to read the tiny copy and decipher what the obscure images mean? Too many questions and too few answers. This ad agency gets a F–. They did not passionately pursue perfection.

### 360 Grad nichts

Was soll diese Anzeige? Verkauft man so etwa Autos? Sollen die zukünftigen Lexus-Besitzer sich den Kopf um 180 Grad verdrehen, damit sie den winzigen Text lesen und herausfinden können, was es mit den obskuren Bildern auf sich hat? Zu viele Fragen, zu wenige Antworten. Diese Werbeagentur kriegt von uns eine Sechs. Von wegen „Passionate Pursuit of Perfection"!

### 360 degrés de rien

Il se passe quoi, là ? C'est comme ça qu'on vend une voiture ? L'acheteur potentiel d'une Lexus est censé se tordre le cou pour déchiffrer le lettrage minuscule et comprendre le sens des images ? Trop de questions, pas assez de réponses. Cette agence de pub mérite un zéro pointé. Loin d'elle la quête passionnée de la perfection.

ALL-AMERICAN

▶ Le

180°

180°

CAKES
ALL NATURAL
FAT FREE

The new, more powerful 2001 GS 430. Featuring a larger 4.3-liter engine, responsive handling and the power to reach 60 mph in 5.8 seconds.* Visit lexus.com for a closer look.

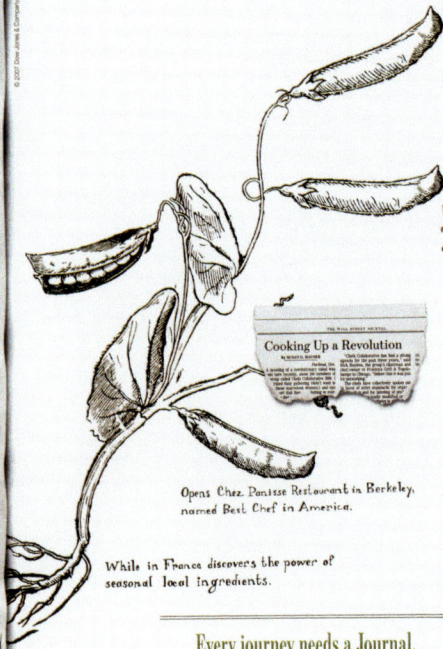

Champions edible education
for every child in America.

journey.wsj.com/alicewaters

Launches Edible Schoolyard,
connecting food, health,
and the planet.

Cooking Up a Revolution

Opens Chez Panisse Restaurant in Berkeley,
named Best Chef in America.

While in France discovers the power of
seasonal local ingredients.

**Every journey needs a Journal.**

The Wall Street Journal, 2007

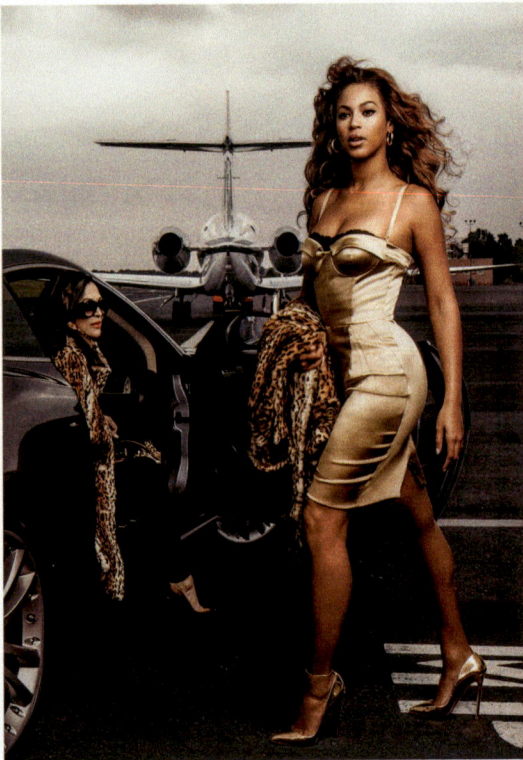

Cardmember ___Beyoncé Knowles___

Member Since ___2001___

Occupation ___Singer / Actress___

Proudest accomplishment ___Winning my 1st Grammy___

Perfect day ___Lounging in the sun, on a boat, in the middle of nowhere, with the people I love___

Most unusual gift ___Rhinestone Studded Pedicure Toe spacers___

Recent impulse buy ___Lorraine Schwartz Diamond Monkeys (See no Evil, Hear no evil, speak no evil)___

Retail therapy ___Shopping with my mom at Designer and Boutique Stores___

Can't shop without ___My American Express Card. Because I know I'll be taken care of.___

My card ___Is there for me, wherever I go, for whatever I buy.___

*Visa, 2007* ◄ *American Express, 2007*

Here's to every single one of you

Here's to the first users, the forefathers of our community
Here's to the early adopters and the trendsetters,
Who knew we would not go by the way of the pet rock
And here's to the ones who just joined the party
To you, we say make yourself comfortable, and welcome
There's room for everyone here

**Things to know
when you do it eBay**

*Buy It Now* Don't want to bid on an item? If the thing you want has the "Buy it Now" icon next to it, you can buy it right away without waiting.

*New* Thousands of brand new items are being bought and sold here everyday. With eBay, you have a choice of new, used and collectible items.

Every eBay user has a feedback rating. This rating is based on past transactions. It helps ensure we all know who we're dealing with.

*Live Help* Live Help is eBay's support line for new users that's available via live computer chat to answer any questions you may have.

Do it eBaY

AOL keyword: eBay

*eBay, 2002*

search ebay.com/fuse boxes
/scissors
/pots and pans
/toasters
/garbage cans
/nose studs
/no-parking signs

/wedding bands
/tripods
/pocket watches
/mp3 players
/golf putters
/karaoke microphones
/baby strollers

/DVD recorders
/radio-controlled cars
/reading glasses
/tool sets
/motorcycles
/fountain pens
/belt buckles

you can get it on ebaY

*eBay, 2006*

Now, my life is complete.

What would it take to make you happy? Whatever it is, try boxLot.com, or call 1-877-4boxLot. There's no better find in online auction and commerce.

boxLot.com

Finders. Keepers.

*BoxLot.com, 2000*

▶ *Amazon, 20*

# Over one bazillion gazillion plus infinity children's titles to choose from.

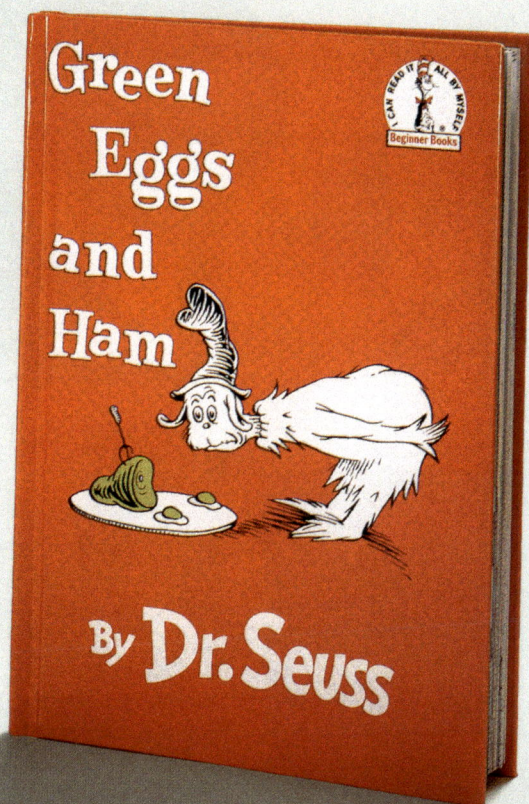

*Green Eggs and Ham* is one of more than 300,000 children's titles available at Amazon.com

Smarter business for a Smarter Planet:

# Is it possible to build a supply chain that delivers intelligence?

The opportunities of an interconnected world come with a host of challenges for today's supply chains: rapid wage inflation, spikes in commodity prices, unpredictable currency rates. Transportation costs alone can fluctuate by as much as 250% per year. IBM helps companies manage cost volatility by building flexibility into supply chains—interconnecting everything from customers to suppliers to IT systems. Allowing businesses to shift workloads around the globe, adjust inventory based on changing demand and respond to currency fluctuations by realigning global partnerships. This kind of flexibility is helping companies in industries as diverse as healthcare, retail and electronics adapt to market changes and cut costs. In fact, last year, IBM helped build flexibility into 17 of the world's top 25 supply chains.[1]

A smarter business needs smarter thinking.
Let's build a smarter planet. ibm.com/managecosts

IBM, 2009

a) oil

b) natural gas

c) wind

d) solar

e) biofuels

✓ f) all of the above

bp

beyond petroleum®

bp.com/us

*BP, 2008*

127

AT&T, 2006

FreeAgent.com, 2000

Visa, 2008 ◄ FreeAgent.com, 2000

Visa, 2007

Last year, computer hackers cost businesses 45 billion dollars.
**THIS IS JUST A WARM-UP.**

Introducing beTRUSTed
With advanced levels of security and verification, people all across the European Union are sending and securing everything from multi-million dollar transactions to single e-mails. Now you can too. The doors of global e-commerce are finally wide open.

get the full story at
www.beTRUSTed.com

PRICEWATERHOUSECOOPERS
Join us. Together we can change the world.

*PricewaterhouseCoopers, 2000*

SUITS AREN'T NECESSARILY BAD.
WHEN THEY'RE WORKING FOR YOU.

Your portfolio is growing. So's the list of things you want to do with your life. How do you keep maximum control of your investments? Work with someone who knows even more about managing money than you do: a Financial Consultant at Salomon Smith Barney. For your free copy of "NetImpact: 10 Stocks For The Future Economy Revealed" call 1-800-EARNS-IT, extension 1802. salomonsmithbarney.com

SALOMON SMITH BARNEY
SEE HOW WE EARN IT™

A member of citigroup®

*Salomon Smith Barney, 2000*

Is running your business getting in the way of running your business?
Get QuickBooks and spend less time on your paperwork and more time on your business. It's the easiest way to:
CREATE INVOICES • PAY BILLS • TRACK SALES
Get back to business.

QuickBooks
Pro 2008

You can buy QuickBooks at:

*QuickBooks, 2008*

Chili's big mouth burgers
for you and your date: $15

(finding a nice way to tell her she has ketchup on her face: priceless)

The best place to hook up with friends is at Chili's. With burgers, babyback ribs, fajitas, molten chocolate cake – Chili's has everything you crave. So bring your date. Bring your friends. Bring your MasterCard.® there are some things money can't buy. for everything else there's MasterCard.™

MasterCard

*MasterCard, 2005*

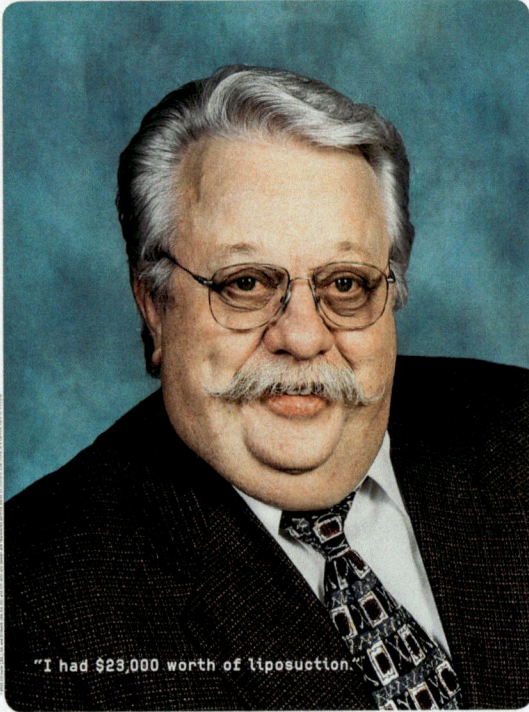

*Citi, 2003*

*Sun Microsystems, 2005*

**It didn't seem right to us, either.**

With Fraud Early Warning, when we see uncharacteristic or suspicious
spending, we'll alert you and stop it. It's part of Citi® Identity Theft Solutions.
That's using your card wisely. Call 1-888-CITICARD or visit citicards.com.

citi
**Live richly.**

5424 1801 2345 6789

*Citi, 2004*

Speed. Control. Omnipotence. Verizon Broadband gives online gamers the upper hand in any competition. Visit richerdeeperbroader.com and tell us what game you're playing.

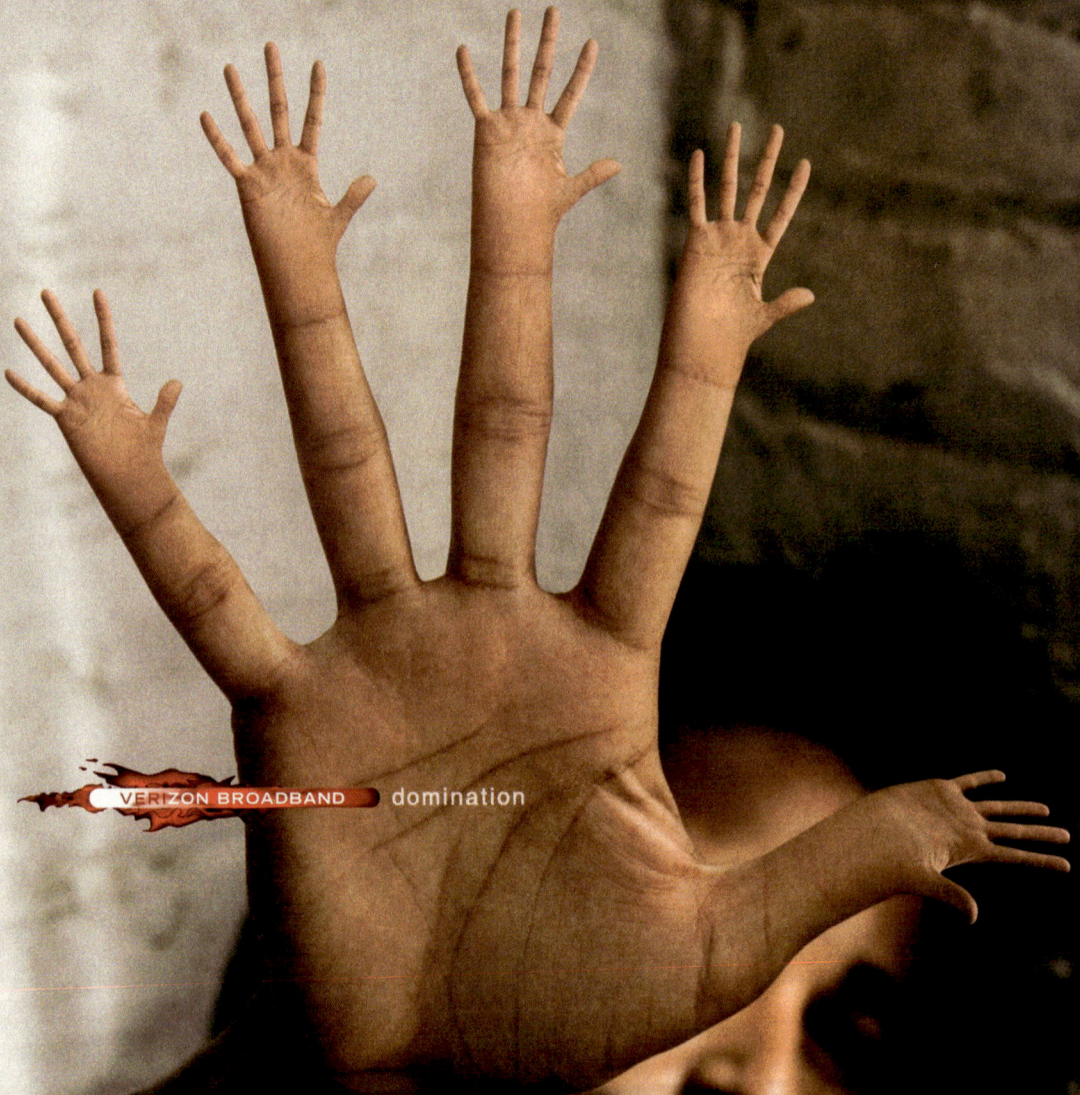

VERIZON BROADBAND domination

RICHER.DEEPER.BROADER

verizon

*We never stop working for you.*

© 2005 Verizon. All Rights Reserved.

Verizon, 2005

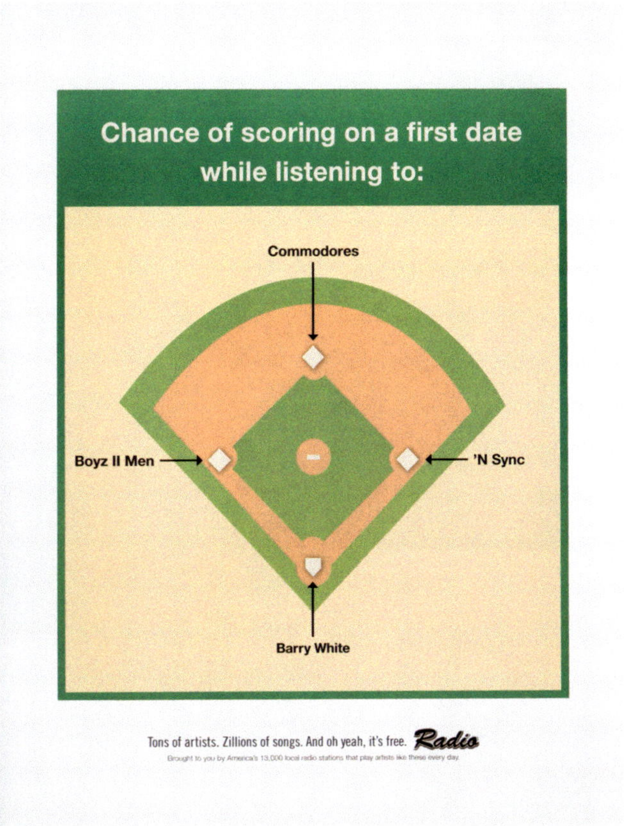


Radio, 2005

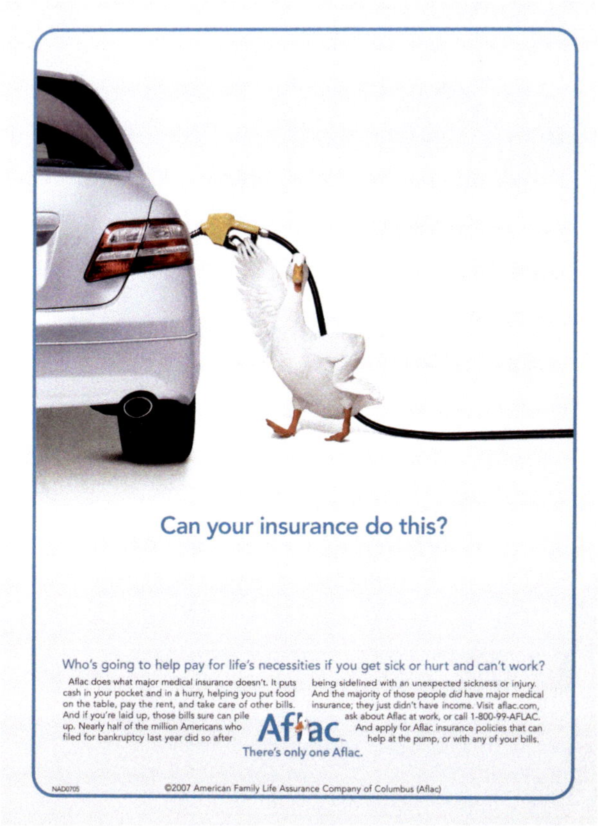


Aflac, 2007

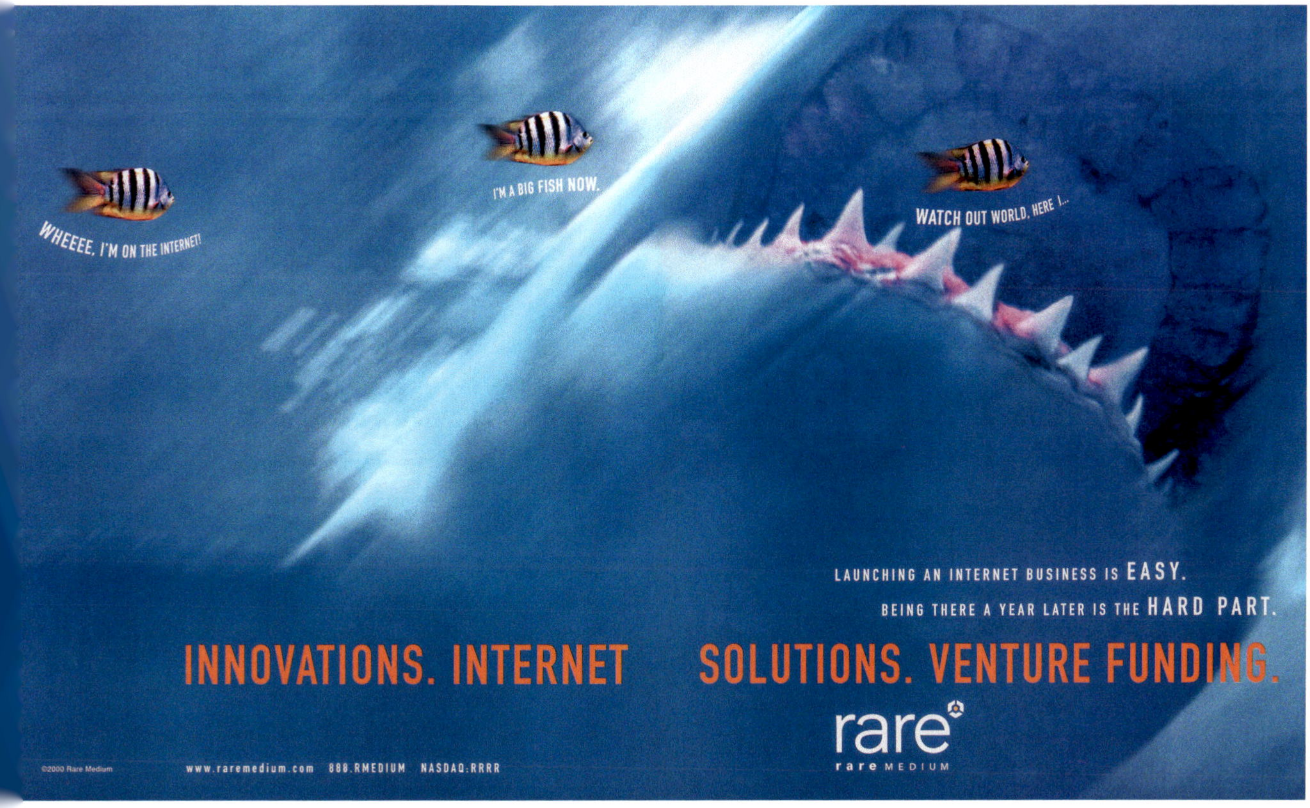


are Medium, 2000

*FedEx, 2001*

*Gilbert, 2004*

*Sallie Mae, 2010*

*Geico, 2005*

$654

: priceless

: priceless

: priceless

: priceless

: priceless

: priceless

: priceless

MasterCard
priceless.com

MasterCard, 2008

EARTH DAY 2009

WWW.EARTHDAY.NET

Buy this poster or t-shirt at earthday.net/estore and support Earth Day Network's non-profit work to stop climate change, provide environmental education, build green schools for our children and create healthier communities.

*Earth Day Network, 2009*

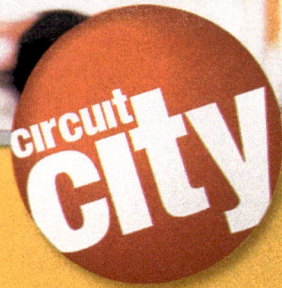

*Circuit City, 2002*

# Not Cool.

Temperatures are rising thanks to **global warming**. That means we can expect more frequent heat waves along with increased air pollution, smog and infectious diseases. The number of deaths from global warming are projected to double over the next 15 years.

**It's time to do something. Now.**

Global warming isn't cool. Stopping it is. Visit **www.ClimateStar.org**

ORLANDO BLOOM,
CLIMATE STAR

PHOTOGRAPHER: ALEX KESHISHIAN • DESIGN: MOONLIGHT DESIGN, VENICE, CA

©2003 ECO

Union of Concerned Scientists

Produced in partnership with the Steven & Michele Kirsch Foundation

EARTH COMMUNICATIONS OFFICE

ClimateStar.org, 2005

*Shell, 2008*

*Shell, 2007*

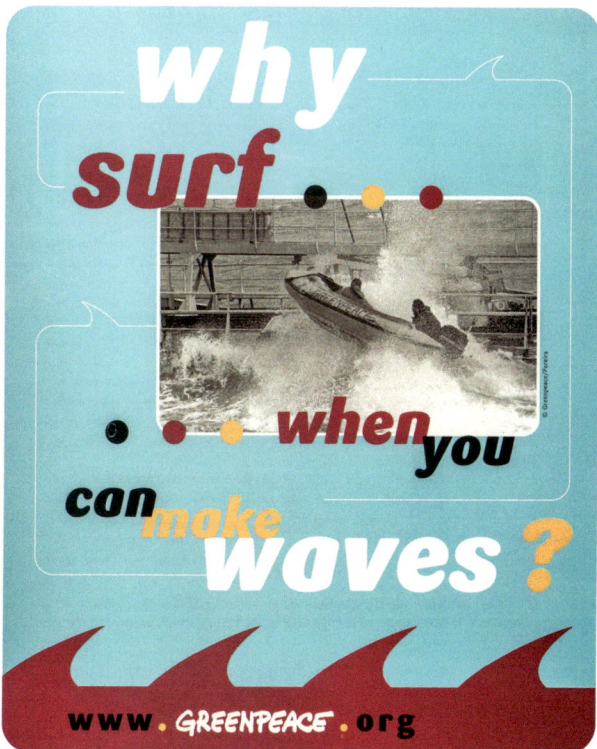

*Greenpeace, 2000*

*International Advertising Association, 2009*

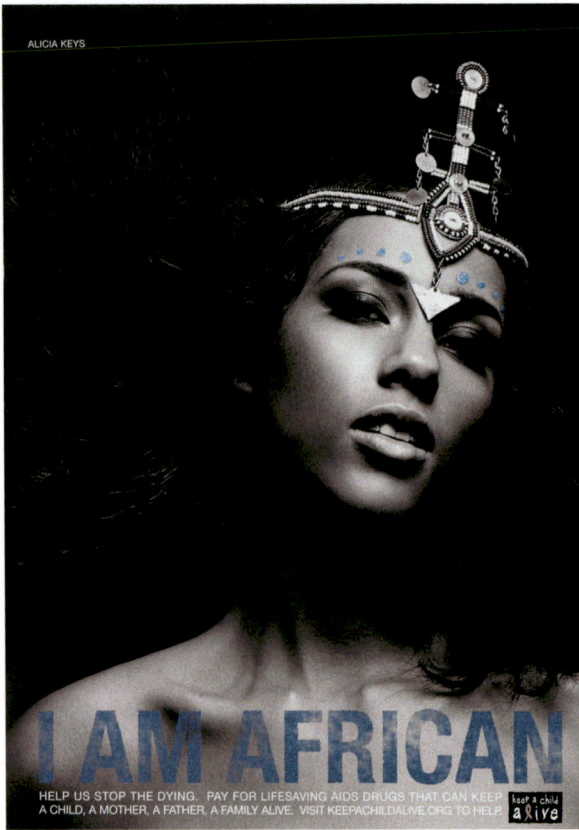

*Keep a Child Alive, 2007*

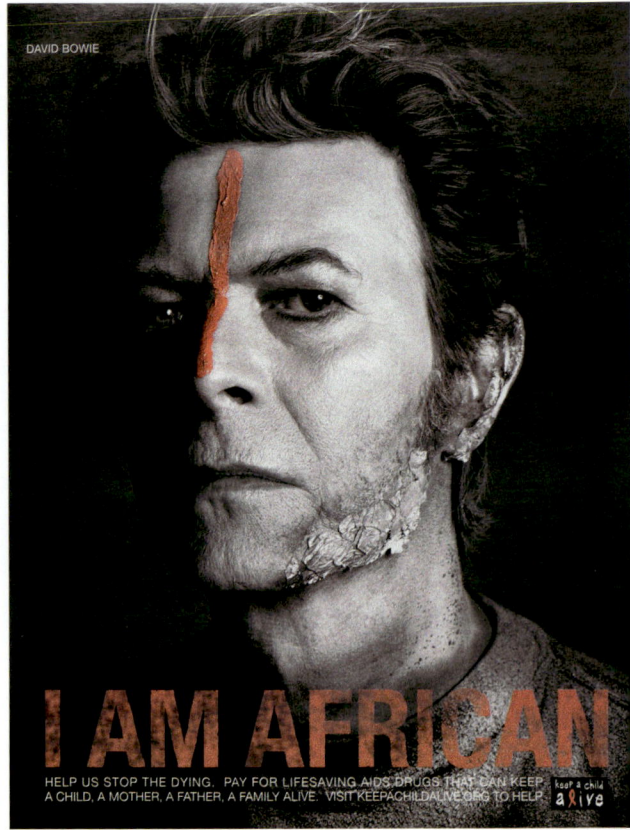

*Keep a Child Alive, 2007*

*Until There's A Cure, 2006*

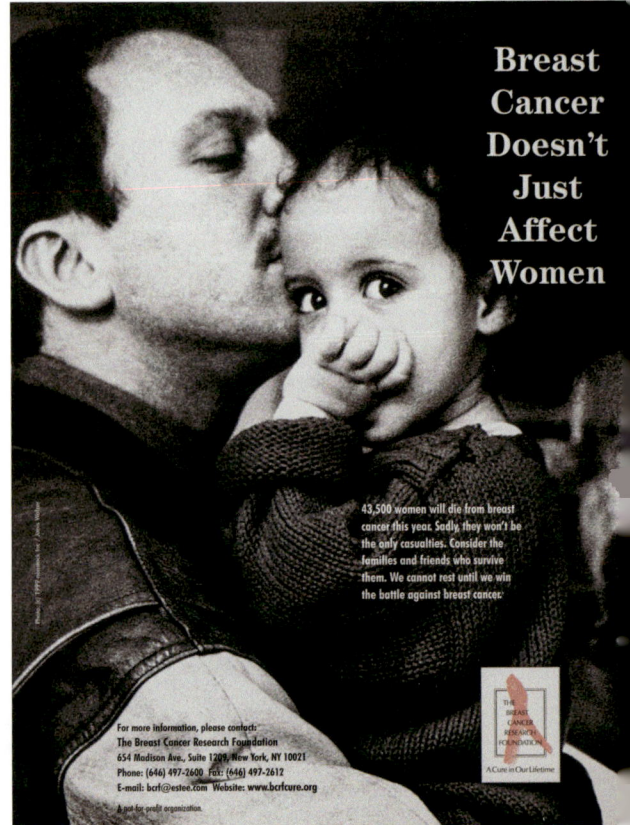

*The Breast Cancer Research Foundation, 2000*

THE BEAUTY OF
BREAST CANCER **RESEARCH**
IS THAT IT WILL **CHANGE**
THE **FUTURE.**

At The Breast Cancer Research Foundation,
more than 85 cents of every dollar donated goes to
breast cancer research and awareness programs.

Our targeted funding has led to breakthrough
advances in detection, prevention and treatment.

BCRF is the most highly rated breast cancer
organization in the U.S., consistently receiving
the highest rating – 4 stars – since 2002 from
Charity Navigator and outperforming over
5,000 other charities.

RESEARCH TODAY SAVES LIVES TOMORROW.

The
**Breast
Cancer**
Research
Foundation.

THE BREAST CANCER RESEARCH FOUNDATION.  •  FOUNDED IN 1993 BY EVELYN H. LAUDER  •  WWW.BCRFCURE.ORG  1.866.FIND.A.CURE

*The Breast Cancer Research Foundation, 2009*

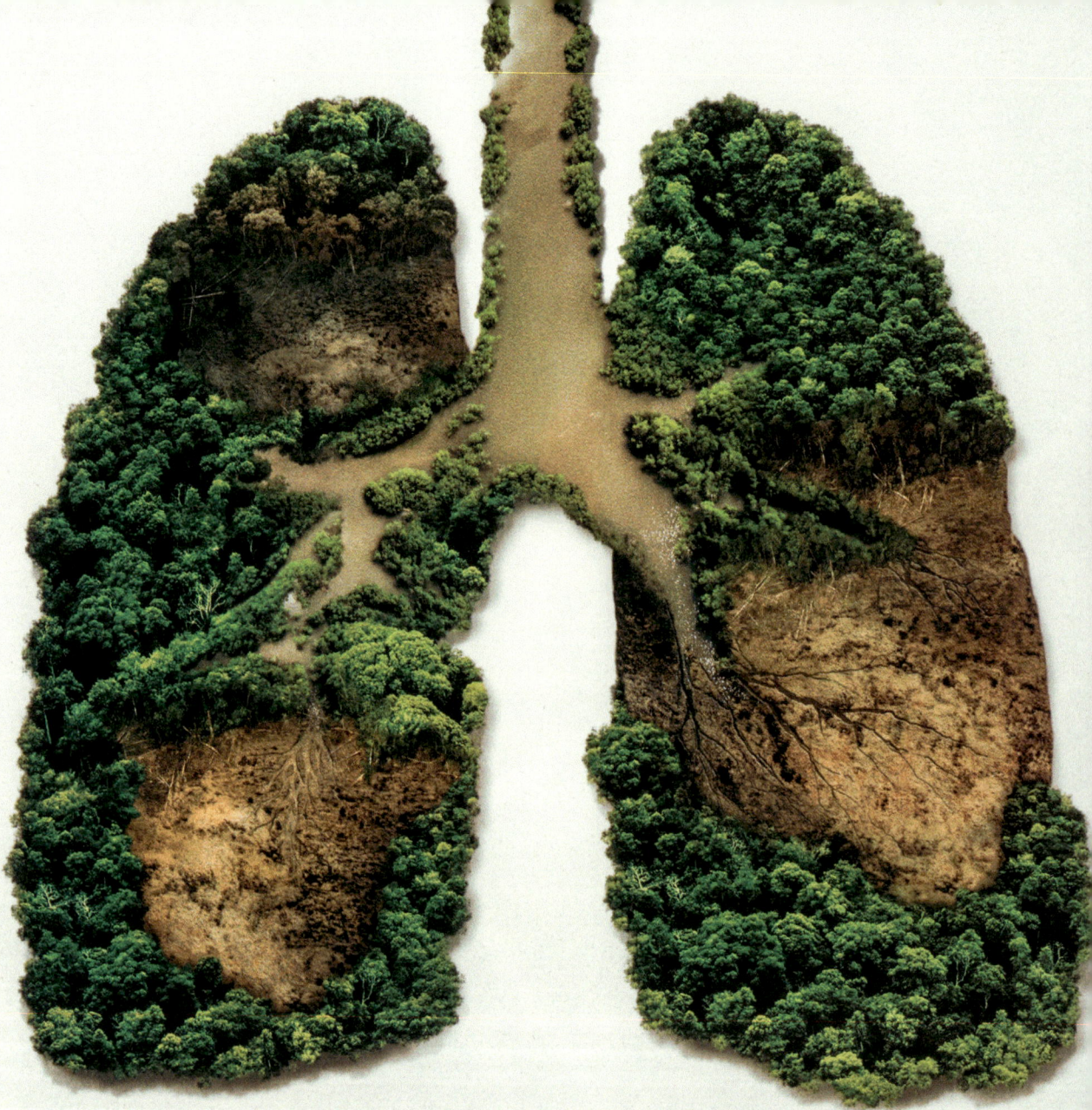

# LOST THERE, FELT HERE.

When rainforests are slashed and burned, it affects every one of us.
It releases carbon into the air that we breathe. It changes our climate.
Deforestation accounts for 20% of all carbon emissions, which is more than the
amount that all the cars, trucks and planes in the world emit, combined.
Join Team Earth on **conservation.org** and help stop climate change, even if
it's just one acre at a time. Or we'll all feel it.

CONSERVATION
INTERNATIONAL

AN AMAZING
PLACE...

DON'T LET IT
VANISH WITHOUT
A TRACE.

1.800.CALL.WWF
www.worldwildlife.org/act

*Get your free World Wildlife Fund Action Kit and help leave our children a living planet.*

WWF

# BOOT CAMP STARTED LONG BEFORE RECRUIT TRAINING WITH US.

Thanks to you, your son is well-behaved, respectful and courteous. You taught him to stand up straight, know right from wrong and to always respect his elders. And that nothing in life worth having ever comes easy. In short, you've given him the qualities we look for in a U.S. Marine. Now, give him a chance to serve his country with honor — where he'll develop character traits like self-discipline, leadership skills and the ability to keep his cool under pressure. All thanks to you. And you thought you were just being a good parent.

For more information, visit us online at MARINES.COM, or call 1-800-MARINES.

**MARINES**
THE FEW. THE PROUD.

*Marines, 2006*

The Wounds of War are not always Easy to See.

www.giveanhour.org

Give an Hour
Give help | Give hope
www.giveanhour.org

*YouthAIDS, 2005*

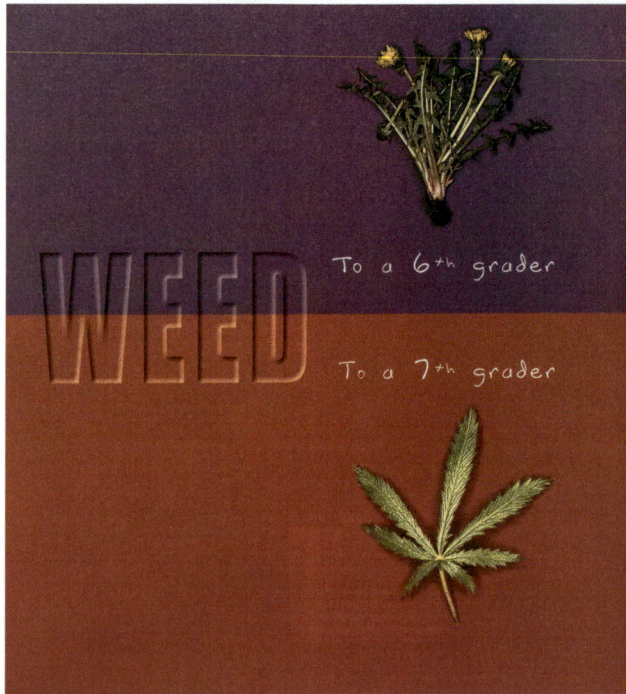

*Partnership for a Drug-Free America, 2000*

*Slow Food Nation, 2008*

*Don't Serve Teens, 2009*

PRESCRIPTION DRUGS CAN GET YOUR TEENS JUST AS HIGH.

Office of National Drug Control Policy / Partnership for a Drug-Free America®

Rx Prescription Medication

Safeguard all prescription drugs in your home.

Learn more at theantidrug.com.

PARENTS.
THE ANTI-DRUG.

*Partnership for a Drug-Free America, 2009*

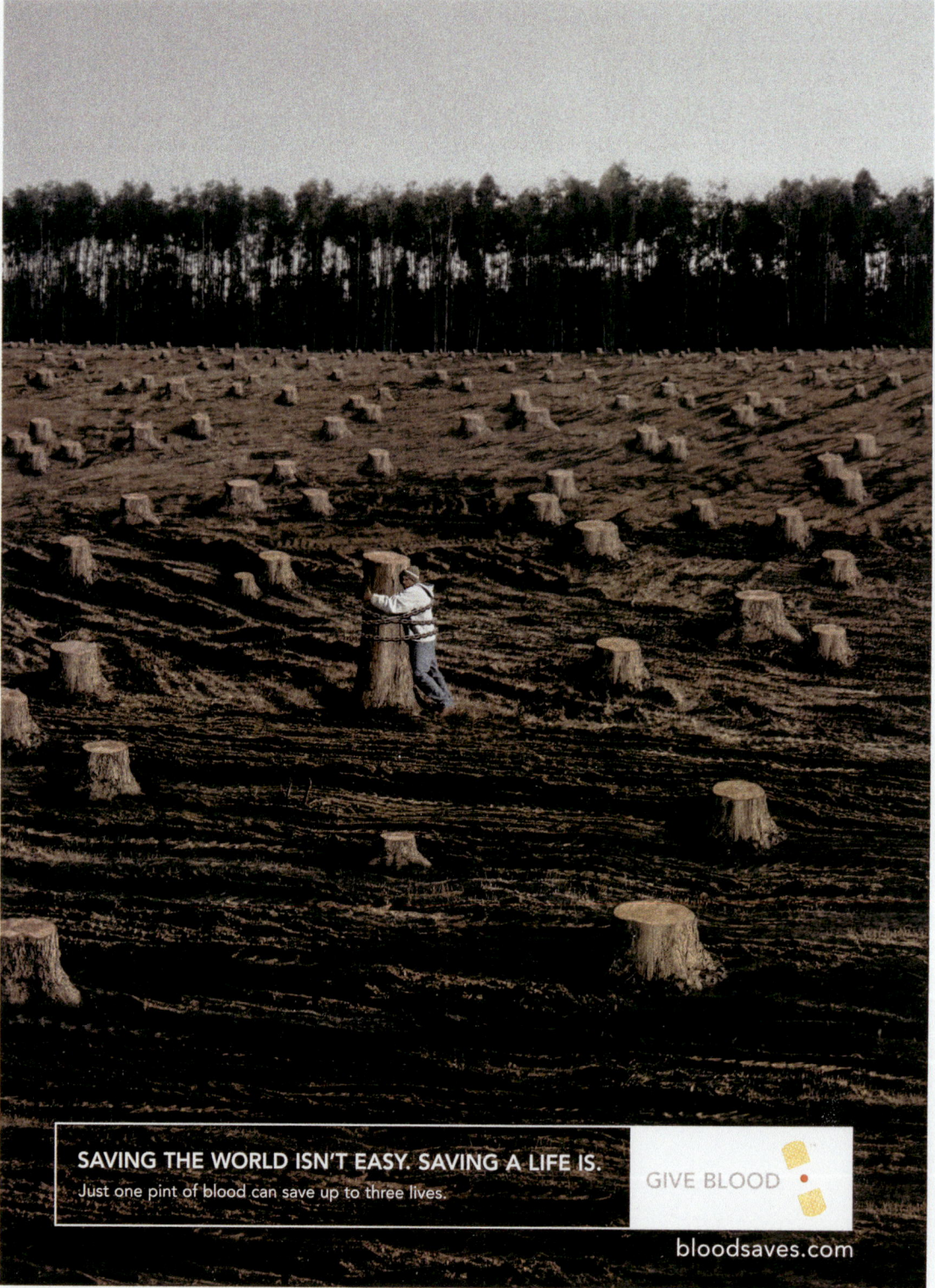

SAVING THE WORLD ISN'T EASY. SAVING A LIFE IS.
Just one pint of blood can save up to three lives.

GIVE BLOOD

bloodsaves.com

Ad Council

"This **flag** has the **power** to grant a **wish**."

Jimmie & Chandra Johnson

The NASCAR Foundation® and the Make-A-Wish Foundation® make magical days together. And it's more than tickets, autographs and pictures. We always make sure to do something that the kids will never forget. Little Simon was handed a mike and he uttered one of the most famous lines in sports. The crowd went nuts. What a cool wish! Chandra and I love the opportunity to bring a smile to any child with a life-threatening medical condition. It makes your heart race.

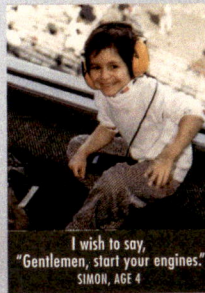

I wish to say,
"Gentlemen, start your engines."
SIMON, AGE 4

We all have the power to grant a wish. Start your journey with Destination Joy® at Wish.org

**MAKE·A·WISH.**

SHARE THE POWER OF A WISH®

© 2008 Make-A-Wish Foundation of America

The name and likeness of Jimmie Johnson, and other trademarks and copyrights, are used with the permission of Jimmie Johnson Racing II, Inc.

*Make-A-Wish Foundation, 2008*

151

**GET OFF** (Okay, it may seem like I hate my parents, but I'm really demonstrating what a therapist would call "asserting my identity," so I can grow up to be a well-adjusted individual. Sure, I say I want freedom, but without parental supervision, I'm much more likely to smoke pot and stuff. I hope my parents don't try to act like my friends. What I really need is parents.) **MY BACK.**

Office of National Drug Control Policy/Partnership for a Drug-Free America

**TALK. KNOW. ASK. PARENTS. THE ANTI-DRUG.**

For information contact us at 1-800-788-2800 or www.theantidrug.com

*Partnership for a Drug-Free America, 2003*

▶ *Partnership for a Drug-Free America, 2000*

☐ **Jewelry Box?**      ☐ **Hiding Place?**

Looks innocent enough. But this is just one of over a dozen spots listed on our site that kids use to hide drugs and drug paraphernalia. Visit drugfree.org to learn more from professionals and other parents about drug prevention and raising healthy teens. Because kids who learn about the risks of drugs from their parents are up to 50% less likely to use them. **Do you know enough to have the conversation?**

**drugfree.org**

The Partnership ⦿ for a Drug-Free America®

# And the winner is...

### Bare Bottom Blues

I don't care what you are selling—no one wants to see an aging man's hairy back and sagging gluteus maximus splashed full-page in a magazine. Of the endless images the stock photo agency had to offer, this was the one they felt would help them sell rights to millions of photos?

### Der Blues vom nackten Hintern

Mir egal, was ihr zu verkaufen habt – kein Mensch will den haarigen Rücken und das schlaffe Gesäß eines nicht mehr ganz jungen Mannes seitenfüllend in einer Zeitschrift sehen. War von den endlos vielen Fotos, die es bei der Agentur zu kaufen gab, das hier wirklich das Bild, mit dem sich die Rechte an Millionen von Bildern besser verkaufen lassen?

### Blues de la déculottée

Peu importe ce que vous vendez – personne n'a envie de voir ce dos plissé poilu et ces vieilles fesses molles s'étaler en pleine page d'un magazine. Parmi la multitude de photos que l'agence avait en stock, ils se sont vraiment dit que c'était celle-là qui les aiderait à vendre les droits de millions de photos ?

► C

corbis®
start here

corbis.com                    800.260.0444

CIRCLE 1 ON CONNECTIONS CARD

Philips Somba.™ Finally a 13" TV you can love.

The **PHILIPS SOMBA** combines futuristic design with fun. A backlit analog alarm clock that can wake you to the sound of a xylophone, a harp, even a rooster crowing. Translucent feet that glow for a cool night-light effect. And a stereo sound system you can program to suit your individual taste. Even when it's turned off, the Somba is on. **I've got to admit it's getting better. www.philipsusa.com/men**

© 2000 Philips Electronics North America Corporation

**PHILIPS**

*Let's make things better.*

*Target, 2001*

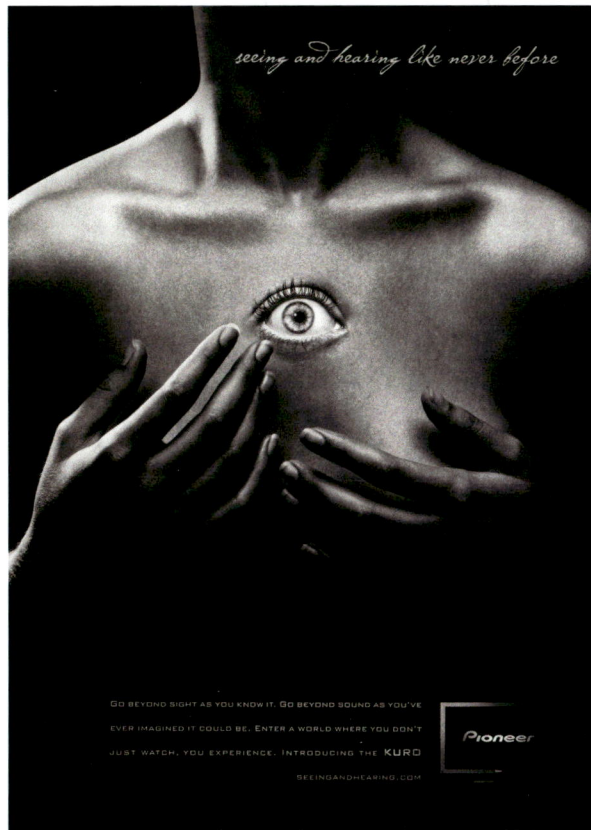

seeing and hearing like never before

GO BEYOND SIGHT AS YOU KNOW IT. GO BEYOND SOUND AS YOU'VE
EVER IMAGINED IT COULD BE. ENTER A WORLD WHERE YOU DON'T
JUST WATCH, YOU EXPERIENCE. INTRODUCING THE KURO
SEEINGANDHEARING.COM

*Pioneer, 2007*

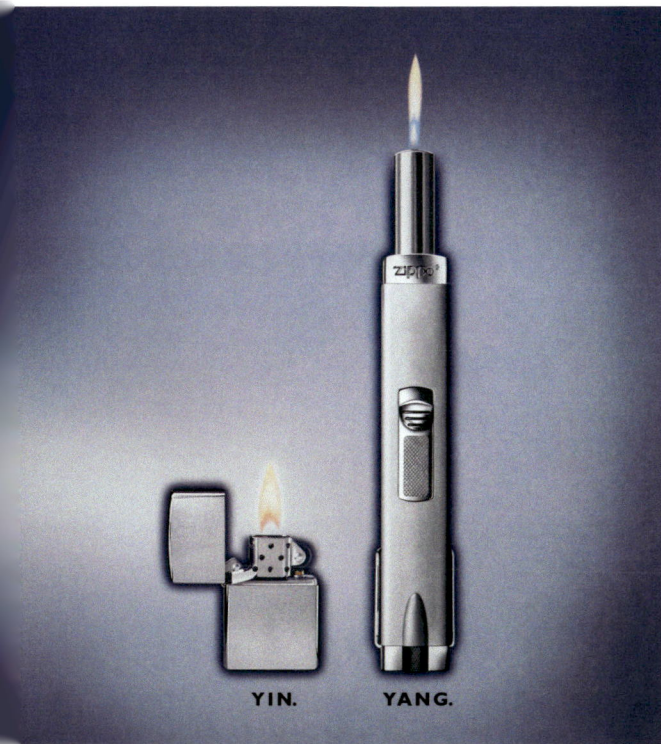

YIN.    YANG.

Introducing the Zippo Multi-Purpose Lighter. Like its soul mate, it's tough, dependable, easy to refill and guaranteed for life. It also has an adjustable
flame, a fuel indicator and is perfect for lighting fireplaces, grills, candles and more. The new Zippo MPL comes in silver or black. Get one today
by visiting any **Things Remembered** store, going to thingsremembered.com or calling 800-274-7367. It will bring zen-like balance to your life.

*Zippo, It works or we fix it free.™ • zippo.com*

**Zippo**
F O R   R E A L

*00, 2002*

IT'S WHO WE ARE.
Every Zippo lighter tells a story. ZippoStories.com

*Zippo, 2007*

*Kodak, 2008*

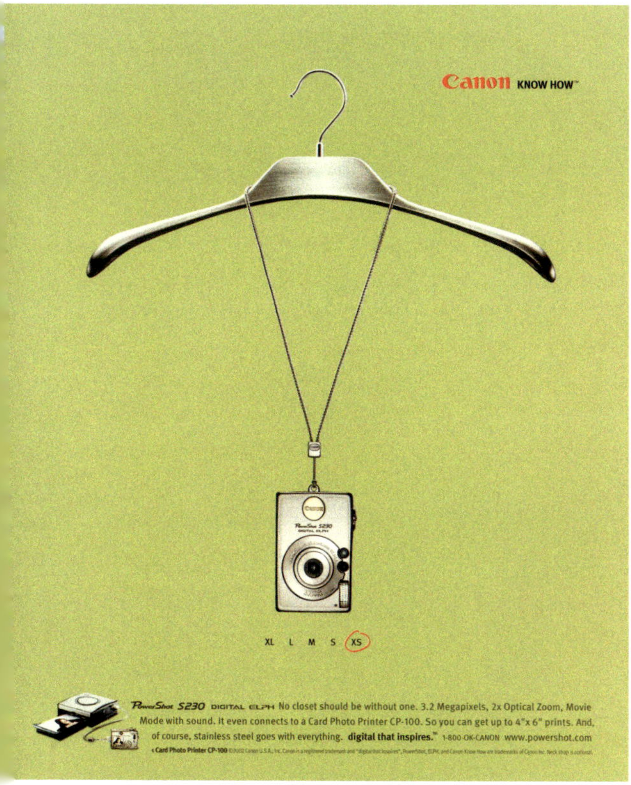


anon, 2002

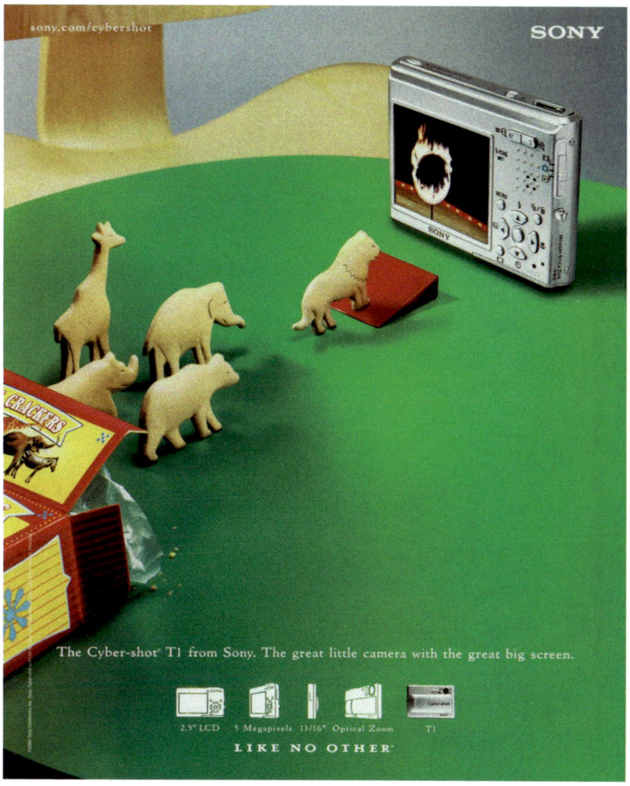


Sony, 2004

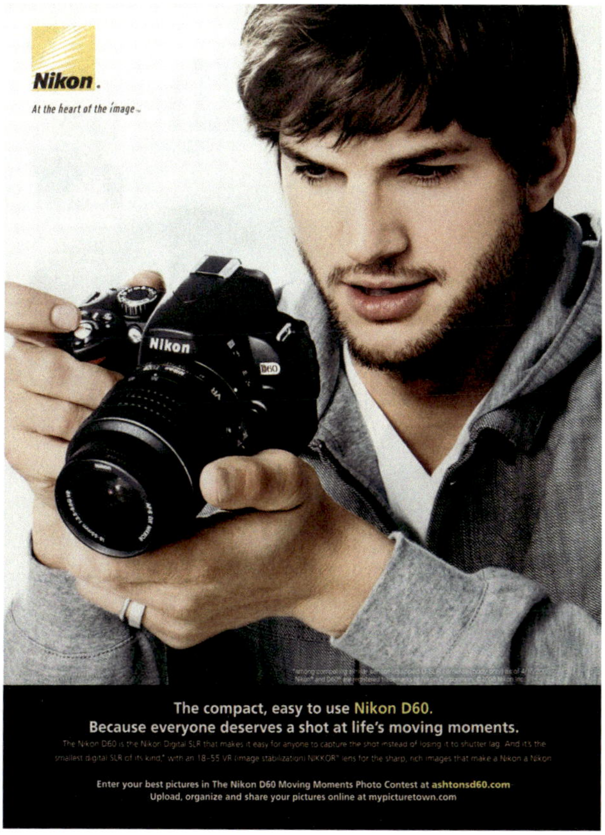


Nikon, 2008

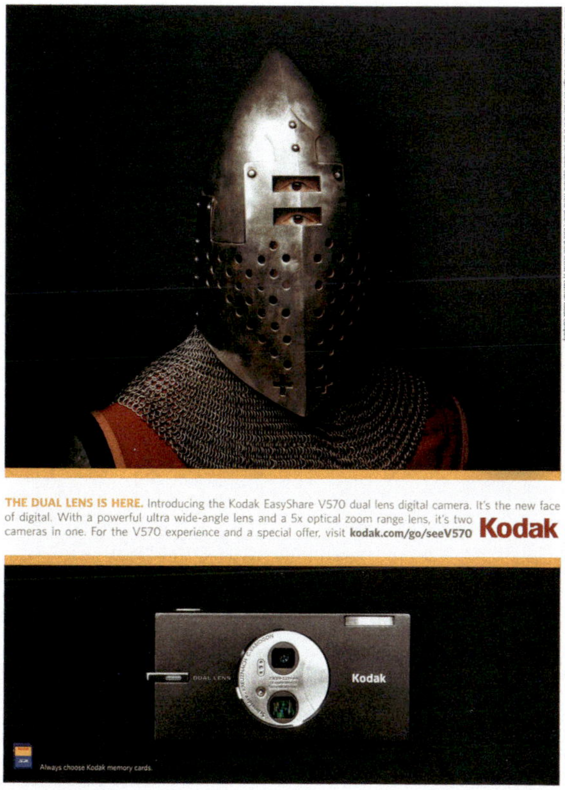


Kodak, 2006

**because**
a great workout deserves a standing ovation.

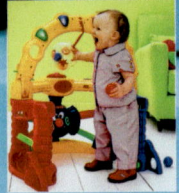

**crawl & cruise playground™**

twinkling lights, fun music, engaging activities. our playground actually encourages each exciting milestone. from crawling, to pulling up and cruising, all the way to standing tall. and with you as her coach, how could she not reach her goal.

discover what's possible™...www.fisher-price.com

**Fisher-Price**
*Oh, the possibilities!*

*Fisher-Price, 2002*

**because**
your first set of wheels should be a convertible.

**stride-to-ride walker™**

dancing lights and engaging music encourage baby's first steps. then converts to a ride-on where the lights and sounds keep her confidence growing. ball toss play makes for fun rest stops along the way.

discover what's possible™...www.fisher-price.com

**Fisher-Price**
*Oh, the possibilities!*

*Fisher-Price, 2002*

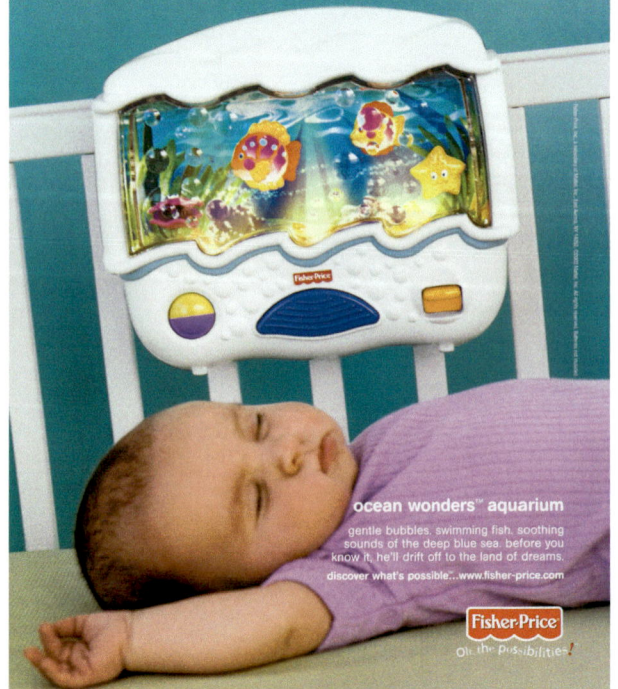

**because**
there's nothing like an oceanfront view.

**ocean wonders™ aquarium**

gentle bubbles, swimming fish, soothing sounds of the deep blue sea. before you know it, he'll drift off to the land of dreams.

discover what's possible™...www.fisher-price.com

**Fisher-Price**
*Oh, the possibilities!*

*Fisher-Price, 2002*

BEST BUY
Thousands of Possibilities | GET YOURS

BestBuy.com

© 2004 Best Buy

*Best Buy, 2004*

*Target, 2000*

NOW MAKE ROOM FOR BOTH BIG AND SMALL.

Room for one more? Sometimes it's easier said than done. Especially when it comes to plugging those bulky, oversized power adapters into a surge protector. There's never enough space. Unless you go to RadioShack and pick up an 11-outlet surge protector. It has four reserve outlets designed specifically to house those plus-sized plugs right alongside normal-sized plugs. Plus, it protects your computer, phone and USB with a $50,000 properly connected equipment guarantee. The RadioShack 11-outlet surge protector. Just one of many innovative, quality accessories you can find now, at your neighborhood RadioShack store.

11 outlets give your plugs more space.

**R** RadioShack®
You've got questions. We've got answers.®

165

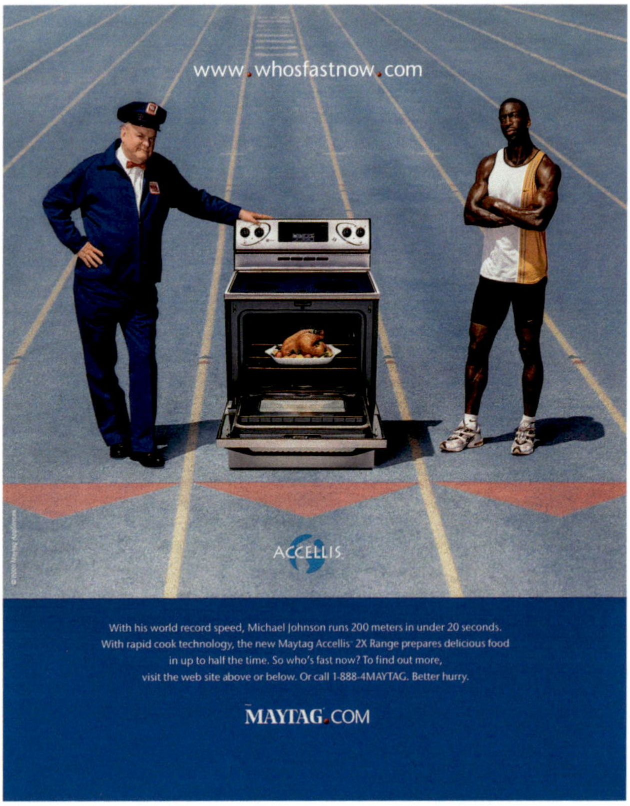


*Maytag, 2000*

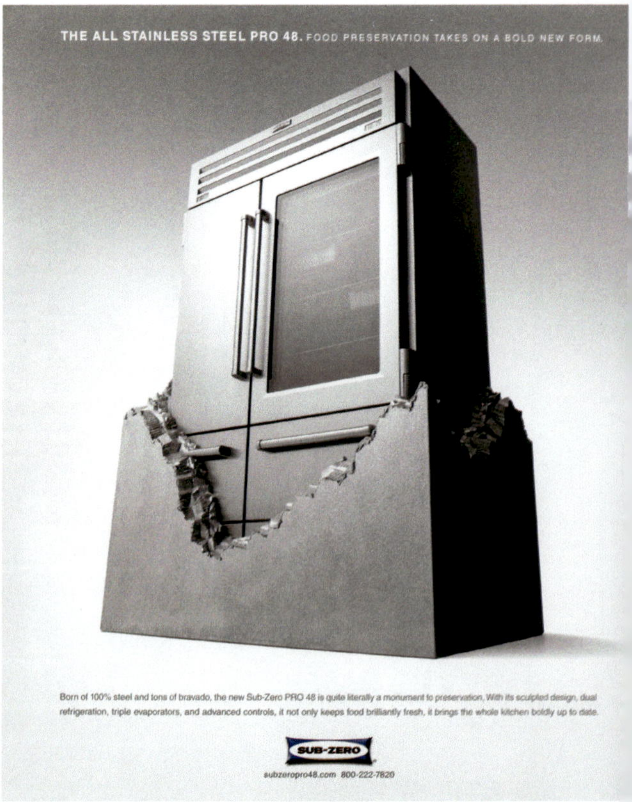


*Sub-Zero, 2006*

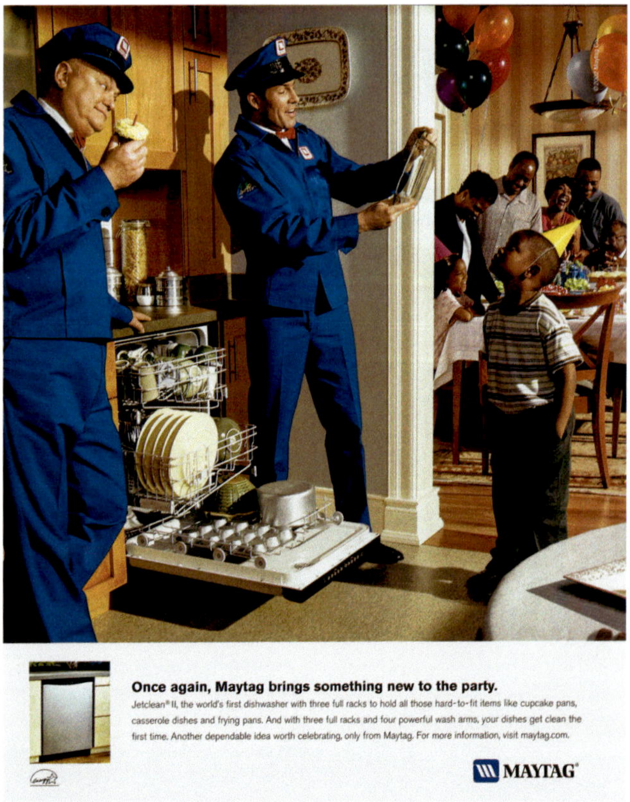


*Maytag, 2002*

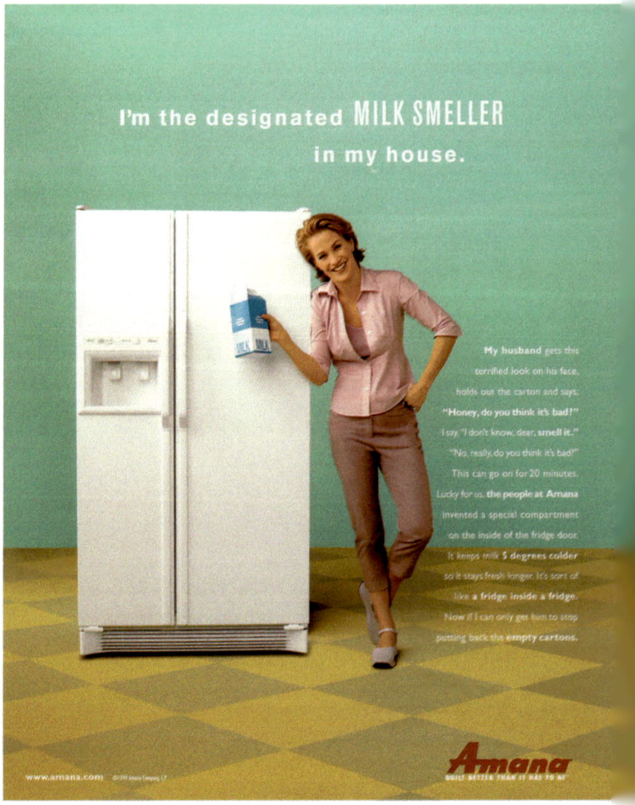


*Amana, 2000*

KitchenAid, 2008

Sears, 2005

Braun, 2003

Target, 2000

*Ziploc, 2000*

*Kleenex, 2000*

*Glad, 2000*

The ultimate grilling accessory.

Eat out every night.™ **weber**

www.weber.com
Shown: Summit® 450 gas grill. ©2000 Weber-Stephen Products Co.

The only bag with a revolutionary new diamond texture that stretches to prevent rips and tears.

GLAD
FORCEFLEX
STRETCHABLE STRENGTH

*Cottonelle, 2002*

*Scott, 2006*

*ad, 2005* ◄ *Clorox, 2006*

*CyberRebate, 2000*

HEROES
*always get*
THEIR MAN.

Wanna capture your man? Then capture his heart with the FTD® Sweet Surprise® Bouquet. Visit your local FTD Florist or online at FTD.COM.

© 2000 FTD. ®, "M", "M&M's," and the "M&M's" Characters are trademarks of Mars, Incorporated. © Mars, Incorporated. Manufactured and distributed under license by FTD.

FTD

BE A HERO

Hungry for clogs.

*Liquid-Plumr, 2009*

Earlier today

# YOUR HUSBAND WASN'T QUITE AS ACCURATE

as he likes to think he is.

Don't just clean. Clean and Disinfect.
www.clorox.com

*Clorox, 2005*

Moments ago the

# BLOODY JUICE FROM A RAW CHICKEN

collected in a sticky pool on this counter.

Don't just clean. Clean and Disinfect.

*Clorox, 2005*

**MAID FOR YOUR SHOWER.**

Just press the button once a day. Your shower is sprayed 360° with a powerful formula that cleans soap scum, mold & mildew stains without scrubbing.
AutomaticShowerCleaner.com

*rubbing Bubbles, 2006*

FRESH SCENT OF LAVENDER. SAME POWERFUL CLEAN.

*Pine-Sol, 2005*

PAM HELPS YOU PULL IT OFF™

The bleach you can pour directly on your whites.

# THE UNEXPECTED BLEACH

clorox.com

# UPPERDECKSTORE.COM

## A CONVENIENT PLACE TO PICK UP ALL THOSE HARD TO PRONOUNCE GAMES YOUR KIDS JUST HAVE TO HAVE.

SHONEN JUMP'S

**Yu-Gi-Oh!™**

**TRADING CARD GAME**

Available November 29
Base set of Yu-Gi-Oh!
Collectible Trading Pins $9.99
($2.99 for expansion packs)

Choose from six
Yu-Gi-Oh! TCG Collectible Tins
$24.99

Yu-Gi-Oh! TCG Box of
24 Magician's Force Booster Packs
$94.99

The Yu-Gi-Oh! TRADING CARD GAME is on every kid's wish list this holiday season.

Call 800-551-8220 or log onto upperdeckstore.com and check out our exciting holiday line up of Collectible Tins, Pins and Magician's Force Booster Packs. Your kids will love them and more importantly you won't have to visit every toy store in town. Unless you like that sort of thing.

WWW.UPPERDECKSTORE.COM

*Konami, 2003*

*Lowe's, 2009*

*Hawthorne Village, 2009*

*Swatch, 2008*

*Swatch, 2009*

{EVERY TIME YOU TURN IT ON A HIPPIE GETS ITS WINGS}

# Crate&BarrelHoliday

Hive Modern, 2008

bludot.com

BLU DOT

Group therapy doesn't have to be so depressing.

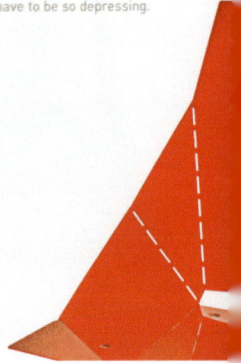

Blu Dot, 2008

Kartell

LOUIS GHOST
Designed in six colors by Philippe Starck
for your chateau.

866 854 8823 • info@kartellus.com • kartellus.com
Atlanta • Boston • Los Angeles • Miami • New York • San Francisco

Kartell, 2003

*Tommy Hilfiger, 2000*

183

As I See It, #1 in a series by David LaChapelle.

The San Raphael™ Power Lite Toilet with an exceptionally quiet .2-hp. pump. Strong, silent and remarkably clean. No, you can't marry it.

1-800-4-KOHLER, ext. LA5
kohler.com/sanraphael

THE BOLD LOOK
OF **KOHLER**

©2003 Kohler Co.

*Kohler, 2003*

► Ko

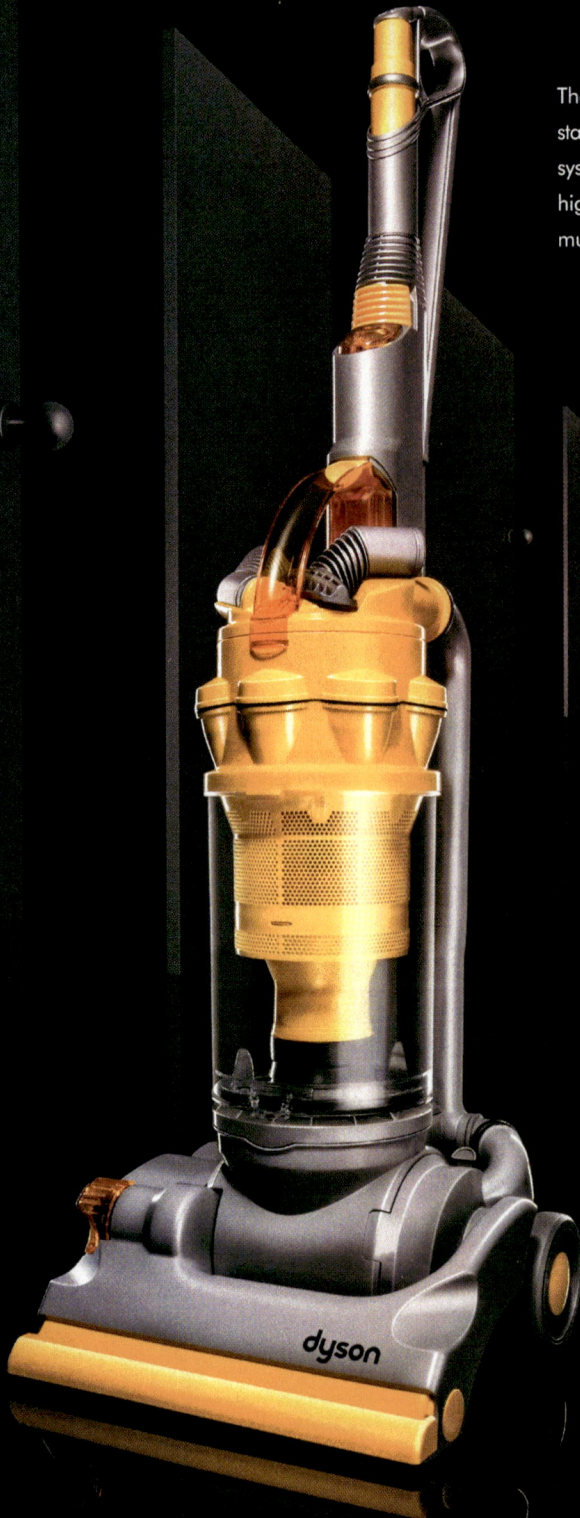

**A**rt marries technology.

If you're partial to art, you'll find it here. From dramatic curves and contoured surfaces to the sleek expanses of stainless steel. After all, when it comes to appliances, art does matter.

If you're partial to technology, you'll find it here. From sensor-controlled cleaning to true European convection cooking. After all, when it comes to appliances, technology does matter.

GEAppliances.com

GE *Profile*™

, 2003

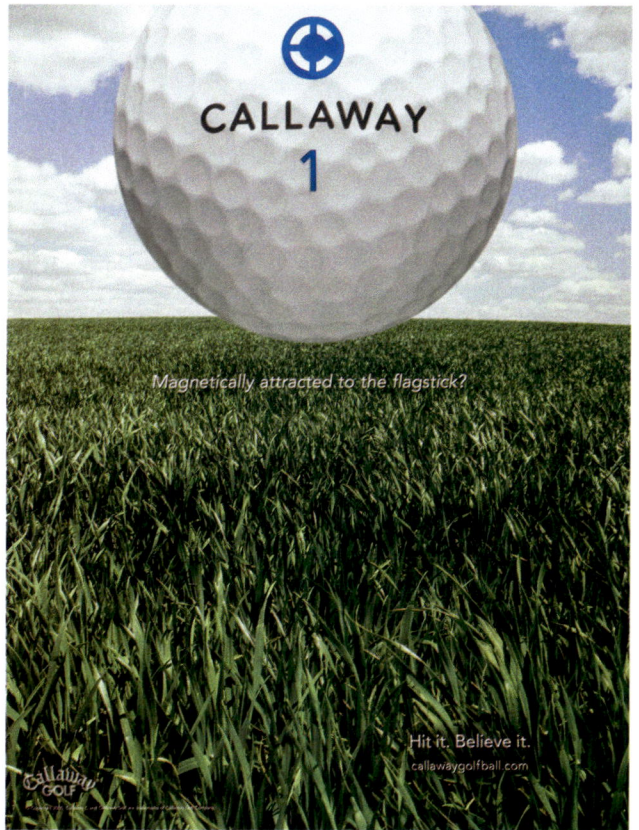

CALLAWAY
1

*Magnetically attracted to the flagstick?*

Hit it. Believe it.
callawaygolfball.com

Callaway GOLF

Callaway Golf, 2000

It gives you a buzz
before you take a sip.

Miele

Transform your kitchen with a jolt of European design sophistication, blended with a taste of café elegance. Miele's unique integrated coffee system lets you brew coffee just the way you like it with the simple push of a button, cup by perfect cup. You can also create delicious latte, cappuccino, hot chocolate or tea using the frothing wand and hot water dispenser. The Miele built-in coffee system generates a buzz before you savor one perfect drop. For the Miele dealer nearest you, call toll free 1-888-346-4353 or log on at miele.com.

**Miele**
anything else is a compromise

n, 2005 ◀ Miele, 2003

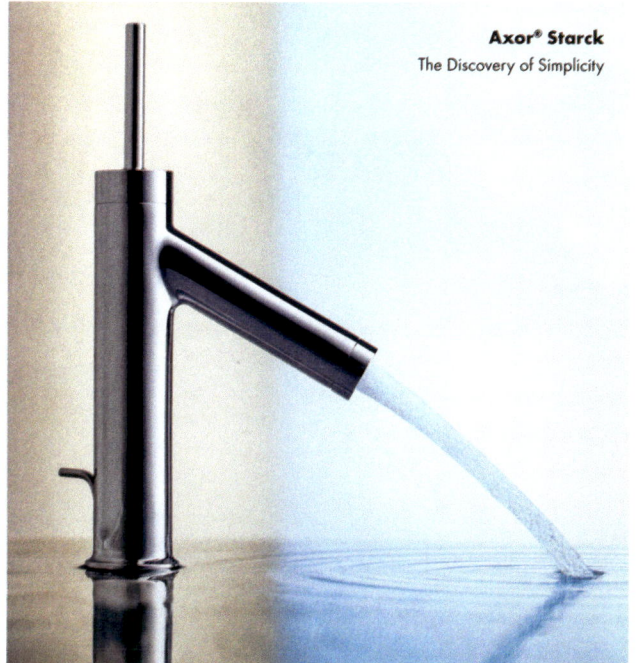

**Axor® Starck**
The Discovery of Simplicity

With Philippe Starck's unique bathroom vision, beauty doesn't need embellishment to be striking and timeless. The Axor Starck collection perfects minimalism and allows us to relax without distractions. The collection features a wide selection of products to create your perfect bath environment—from the two-handle design and stylish showers to wall-mounted faucets and universally appealing accessories. See the entire Axor Starck collection at www.hansgrohe-usa.com, or call 800-334-0455 to add the serenity and purity of Axor Starck to your home.

**AXOR®**
hansgrohe

Axor, 2008

Corinna's Salmon Wontons with Ginger Soy Sauce left the entire family breathless.

Even her sister-in-law stopped talking.

Sometimes the most gratifying praise is silence. And the Oster® Food Processor, with its versatility and reliability, ensured that Corinna's efforts were amply rewarded. That the awe-inspiring recipes at oster.com left everyone speechless goes without saying.

**Oster**

*Inspire*

The Oster® Inspire™ line
Visit Oster.com for a retailer near you.

Oster, 2004

We've been there.

From defending the fruits of our labor to maintaining that perfectly green lawn. It's why our tools and local advice are right for whatever you take on next.

**True Value**
START RIGHT. START HERE.

truevalue.com • 800-642-7392

*True Value, 2006*

# And the winner is...

## Wipeout

Trying to connect the family pet and the use of toilet paper is a stretch to say the least. Whose bottom is getting wiped? Fido does look content, but with the sensitive nature of this product wouldn't it have been better to feature something, or someone, other than the family pet?

## Abgang

Die geistige Verbindung zwischen Haustier und Toilettenpapier herzustellen, ist, gelinde gesagt, zumindest schwierig. Wessen Po soll hier gewischt werden? Fido sieht natürlich zufrieden aus, aber wäre es nicht besser gewesen, bei einem so delikaten Produkt etwas oder jemand anderen abzubilden als den Haushund?

## Bérézina

D'accord, faire le lien entre le toutou de la famille et le papier toilette n'était pas chose facile. Quel postérieur s'agit-il d'essuyer? Toutou a l'air très content, mais étant donné la nature sensible de ce produit, n'aurait-il pas mieux valu montrer autre chose (quelqu'un, peut-être?) que le chien?

▶ Cotto

Simply Color

Simply Palm

*Game Boy, 2001* ◂ *Palm, 2000*

## "One Wedding and an iMac"

**Apple introduces Desktop Movies.** How do you make love endure? Turn those special life moments into pro-quality movie classics:

*Plug your digital camcorder into iMac's FireWire port and presto. You're in show business.*

Complete with dissolves, sound tracks and scrolling titles. Just plug your digital camcorder into iMac's FireWire port, launch the remarkable iMovie software and start directing. Then

*Transfer your movie to video-cassette so everyone can share all your magic moments.*

you can share your movies with family and friends or post them on your website for the world to

*Add titles, sound effects and music. Just like Hollywood pros.*

see. It's as simple as saying "I do." Visit www.apple.com or call us at 1-800-MY-APPLE. 🍎 **Think different.**

*Apple, 2000*

Farewell, mousepad. The optical mouse. Now standard on every Mac. 🍎 Think different.

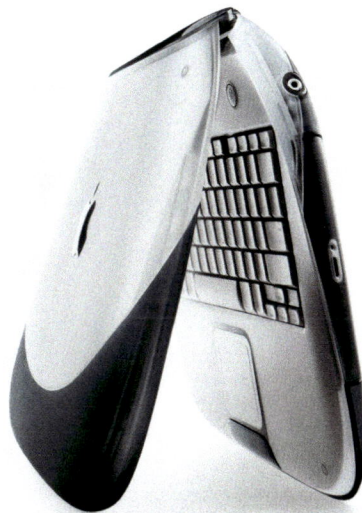

# Black tie optional.

🍎

### Think different.

*e, 2000*

*Apple, 2000*

Say hello to iPod.

*iPod's main menu lets you access your music the way you want to – by playlist, artist or song.*

*Your iTunes playlists are automatically downloaded into iPod, so select your favorite mix with just a click.*

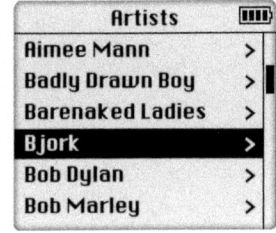

*Or choose the artists you're in the mood for, then select their best album or songs.*

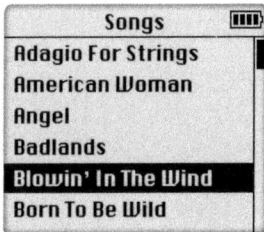

*Or zip through an alphabetical list of titles to find the song you're looking for in no time.*

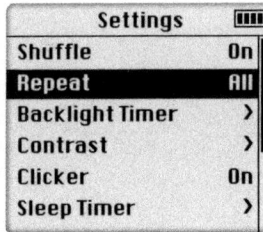

*Then set iPod to play your favorite songs again and again, or shuffle through your entire library.*

*Finally, adjust the volume and fully enjoy iPod's breathtakingly pure and dynamic digital sound.*

The new iPod.
$399*§§

Think different.

*Don't steal music.*

*Apple, 2001*

## Rip.

The new iMac with iTunes lets you take all your favorite songs,

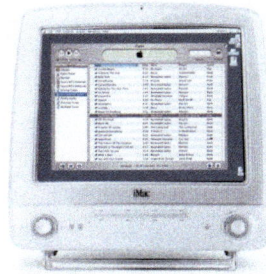

## Mix.

organize them into an MP3 library, put them in any order you want

## Burn.

and then create your own custom CDs. After all, it's your music.

# Think different.

"I can't believe she has on the same phone as me."

**Introducing the camcorder phone from LG.**

Capture and send video* with the new VX7000 camcorder phone. With digital zoom, a rotating lens, an embedded camera with flash and a sleek, sophisticated design, it will get just as much attention as anything else you're wearing.

WWW.LGUSA.COM

Life's Good

Samsung u740

imagine a phone that will transform the way you text

The new Samsung u740 pivots from a phone to a keyboard faster than you can say QWERTY. And it does so with a surprisingly slim profile. So now you can switch from talking to texting on a dedicated keyboard with one pivot. With the Samsung u740, it's not that hard to imagine. Visit www.samsungmobileusa.com/u740.

SAMSUNG

verizon wireless

Motorola, 2006

Motorola, 2006

Compaq, 2000

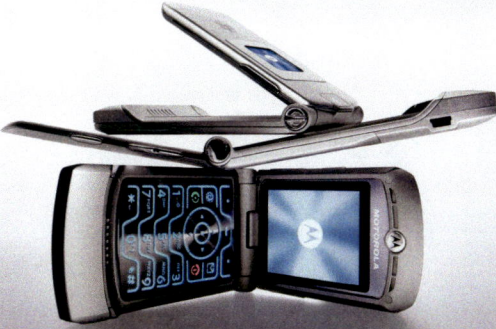

THE NEW MOTO RAZR V3

2.2" hi-res screen

digital camera

video playback

picture caller ID

color external display

class 1 bluetooth® wireless technology

# MOTORAZR

laser-etched keypad

mp3 ringtones

J2ME™ applications

speakerphone

quad-band

all in a 13.9 mm thin

anodized aluminum case

available only at X cingular WIRELESS

hellomoto.com

*Motorola, 2004*

SONY

DREAM ON▸▸▸▸

FILES YOUR NEW AGE TUNES. FILES YOUR METAL TUNES.

## THIS, FRIENDS, IS AN ORGANIZER.

The great thing about an electronic organizer is that it helps keep all your stuff, well, organized. Your appointments. Your phone numbers. And, if it's a Sony CLIÉ™ Handheld, your music. Is the CLIÉ a powerful business tool? The CLIÉ's Palm OS® operating system answers that question. But the CLIÉ also comes with cool entertainment features. Like? Like an MP3 audio player. Not to mention a high resolution color display. Memory Stick® media expansion slot. 16MB total memory.* Jog Dial™ navigator. Even a built-in image viewer and software to view and listen to color video clips. CLIÉ. Reggae, meet rap. Rap, meet reggae. Visit your local retailer or www.sony.com/clie today.

■ Memory Stick® media stores and transfers all your data – pictures, music, video, and files.

©2001 Sony Electronics, Inc. All rights reserved. Reproduction in whole or in part without written permission is prohibited. Sony, the Sony logo, CLIÉ, the CLIÉ logo, and Dream On are trademarks of Sony. Palm OS and the Palm Powered logo are registered trademarks of Palm Computing Inc. Screen image is simulated. *16MB internal memory plus 8MB Memory Stick media

CLIÉ™

*Sony, 2001*

# WEB W/O WIRES

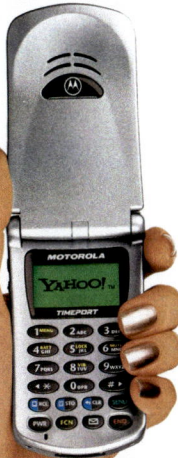

TIMEPORT WEBPHONE MINI-BROWSING CAPABILITIES, E-MESSAGING, INFORMATION AND BANKING SERVICES.
GET THE WEB W/O WIRES IN YOUR HANDS AT MOTOROLA.COM OR 1.800.331.6456.

Subscription and service provider dependent. (M) Motorola and Timeport are trademarks of Motorola, Inc. © 1999 Motorola, Inc. "Yahoo" is a trademark of Yahoo, Inc.

(M) MOTOROLA

*Motorola, 2000*

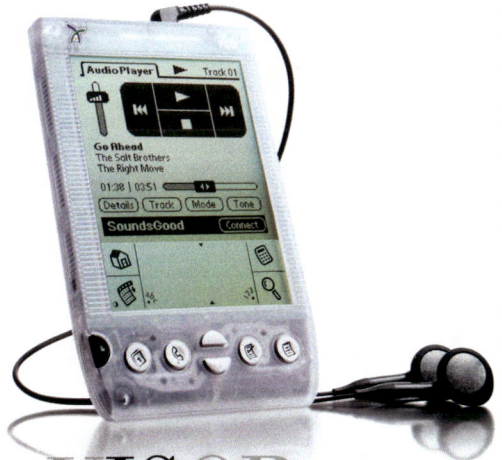

# VISOR

clearly into music.

More than just an electronic organizer, Visor has

an optional MP3 player and countless other things

that will rock your world. Visit us online for availability.

handspring

www.handspring.com

*Handspring, 2000*

# PLAN A

# PLAN B

## CALL IT OCEAN. DON'T CALL IT A PHONE.

Ocean is the world's first dual-slider with both a numeric keypad and a separate full QWERTY keyboard. Designed to make the perfect call, crank out an email or just send your friend a quick instant message. Ocean is without equal. Take its new HTML browser for a test drive on an advanced nationwide 3G network and you'll see that Ocean delivers a superior web experience paired with smart technology that delivers all of your Yahoo!® AOL,® Windows Live,™ Gmail™ accounts and more into a single inbox. You can even sync your Microsoft® Office Outlook® email, contacts and calendar right there on your Helio. Just one more way that Ocean makes you look like a mastermind.

www.helio.com

*Helio, 2007*

# STARLET

## CALL IT THE NEW HELIO HEAT.™
## DON'T CALL IT A PHONE.™

The new Helio Heat isn't just the hottest thing on the red carpet. It's also the most talented. Available in Onyx and exclusive, new Gold, the Heat stylishly delivers on-demand music and streaming video over our advanced nationwide 3G network. There has simply never been a device so small, yet so powerful. The Heat is even equipped with GPS-enabled Google Maps,™ which means it won't just get you into the party. It will actually help you find it.

www.helio.com

*Helio, 2007*

YOUR HAND CONFIRMS WHAT YOUR EYES PREDICTED
THE SATISFYING WEIGHT, THE QUALITY OF THE MATERIALS
THE PRECISION OF THE COMPONENTS, THE SENSE OF CRAFTSMANSHIP

THIS IS YOUR PHONE

THE NEW ASCENT | Ti

Forged from solid titanium. Finished
in sapphire crystal and ceramic.
Vertu Fortress technology for secure
data backup. Twenty-four hour
concierge service.

# VERTU

+ 1 914 368 0432
VERTU.COM

*Vertu, 2007*

**verizon**wireless

# RAZR2

EXTERNAL MUSIC CONTROLS. EXPANDABLE MEMORY. STEREO BLUETOOTH. SHARPER THAN EVER.

IT AIN'T WHERE YOU FROM

WHERE YOU AT

Includes Nationwide Boost™ Walkie-Talkie
Boost Mobile™ Pay-As-You-Go.

Check out **boostmobile.com** for all the latest information.

**boost** mobile®

*"Where you At?"*

# GET MORE BLACKBERRY®
# OUT OF YOUR BLACKBERRY.

**BlackBerry Tour**

## The new BlackBerry Tour™ runs better on America's Largest and Most Reliable 3G Network.

With an ultra fast processor, a brilliant screen, global voice and data coverage, and the Network, you can do more with your BlackBerry than ever before.

### ONLY $199⁹⁹

$299.99 2-yr price less $100 mail-in rebate debit card. New 2-yr activation on voice plan with email feature, or email plan req'd.

**1.800.2 JOIN IN**    verizonwireless.com/tour

*Verizon, 2009*

100% Jesse.

Custom gas tank art skin,
vintage mullet photos,
Gmail to send project updates,
Chaproid™ helicopter game,
mobile banking app.

Introducing the first phone that becomes 100% you.
The new T-Mobile® myTouch™ 3G with Google.

T-Mobile and the magenta color are registered trademarks of Deutsche Telekom AG. myTouch, myTouch 3G, the myTouch design and 100% you are trademarks, and stick together is a registered trademark, of T-Mobile USA, Inc. Google, Gmail and the Google logo are trademarks of Google, Inc. © 2009 T-Mobile USA, Inc.

*T-Mobile, 2009*

**Now with 3G.**

The revolutionary new iPhone is now available at Apple stores and resellers in selected countries.

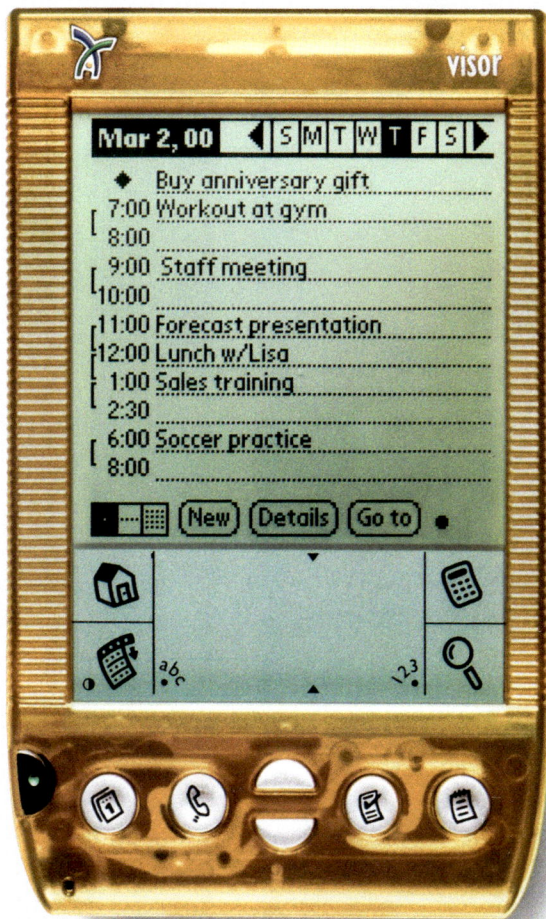

VISOR

having a nice day.

More than just an electronic organizer,

Visor is technology that relieves stress instead of causing it.

handspring™

www.handspring.com

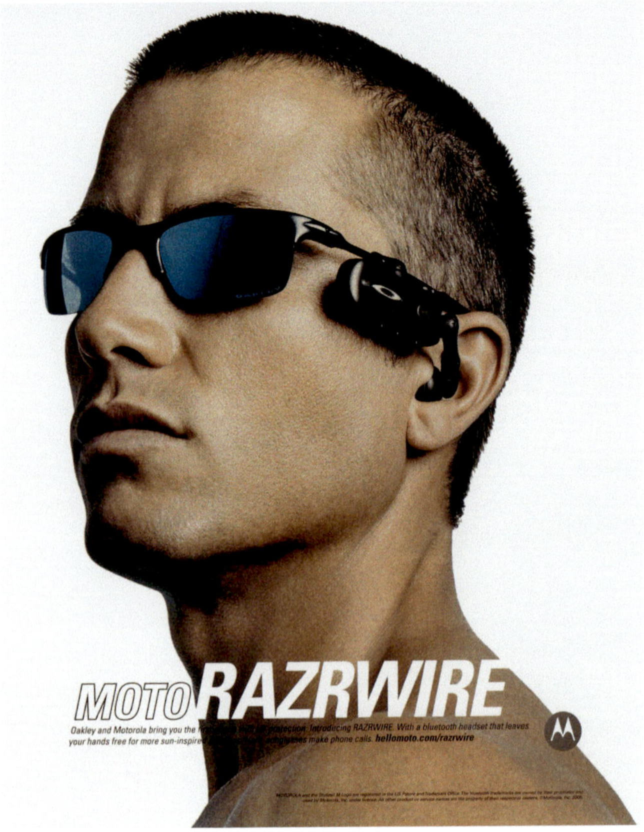


Motorola, 2005

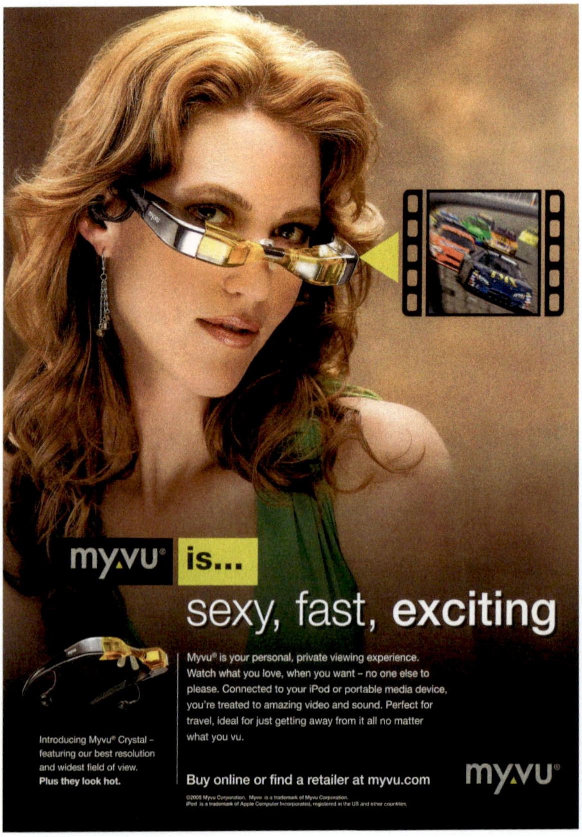


Myvu, 2008

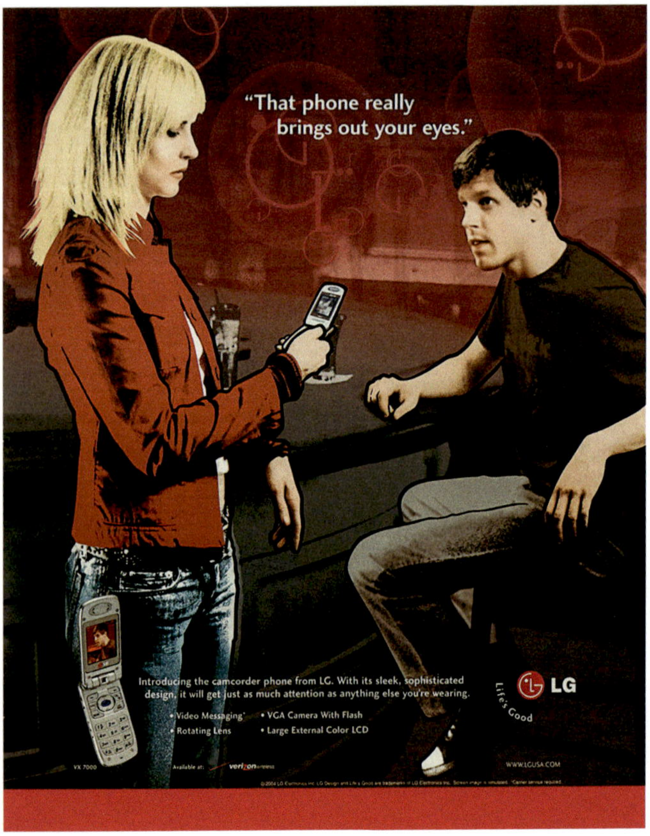


LG, 2004

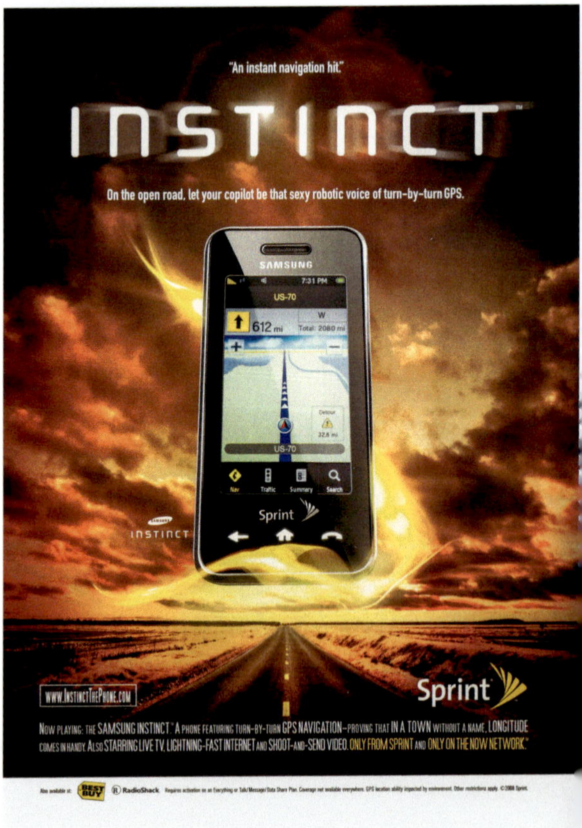


Samsung, 2008

T-Mobile, 2009

Palm, 2005

Sanyo, 2006

Nokia, 2005

The new Palm® Centro™ In it you'll find **email**, **text**, **IM**, **voice**, **web**, and a killer DJ.

It's designed for a more social life. To learn more, visit palmcentro.com

Socializing

It's a Palm thing.

palm

Samsung, 2007

BlackBerry, 2008

Palm, 2008 ◄   AT&T, 2018

Motorola, 2009

*Nikon, 2008*

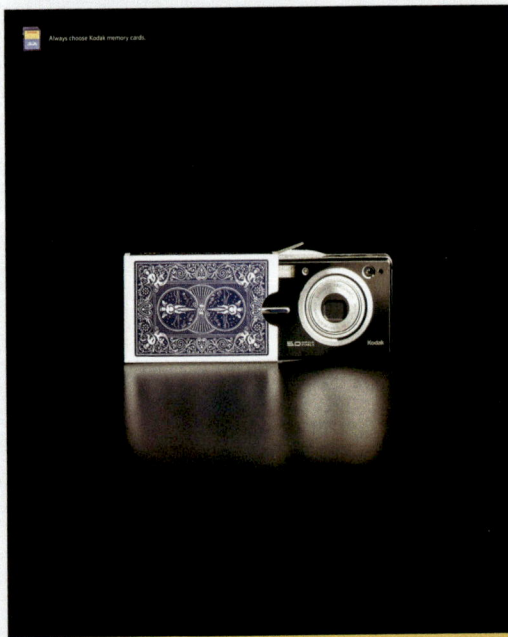

*Kodak, 2005*

*Panasonic, 2000*

satisfy your creative sweet tooth.

www.imation.com

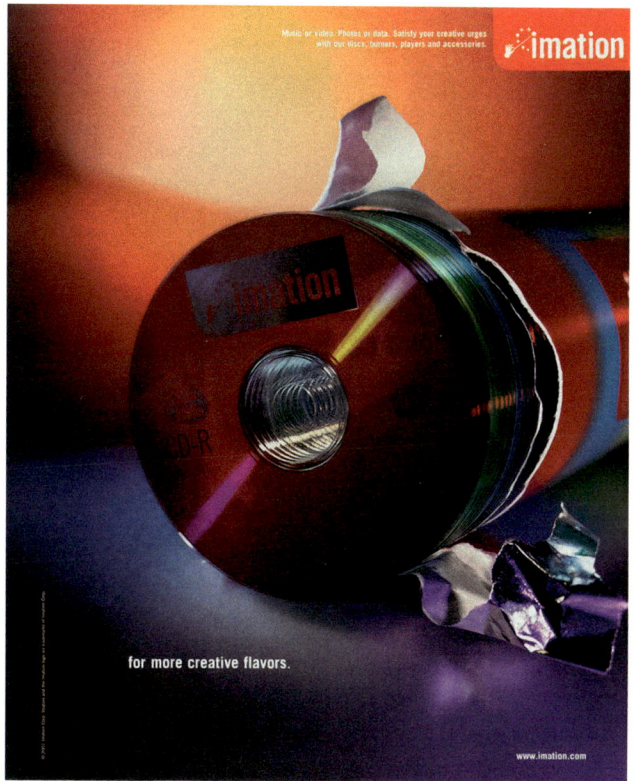

Imation, 2001

for more creative flavors.

www.imation.com

Imation, 2001

Digital Cameras

Now you can take pictures for your desk top as well as your desktop.

**FinePix 4700zoom** Why relegate your digital pictures to a screensaver? The Fujifilm FinePix 4700zoom digital camera, equipped with revolutionary new Super CCD technology, gives you brilliant color and remarkable clarity and sharpness, all with the convenience of a digital camera. Create 4.3 million pixel files. Record up to 80 seconds of video with sound. And use the color LCD monitor and speaker to instantly review what you've just shot. Then start shopping for a worthy picture frame. For more information on the FinePix 4700zoom and other Fujifilm digital cameras, call 1-800-800-FUJI, or visit www.fujifilm.com.

FUJIFILM digital
Get the picture

Film, 2000

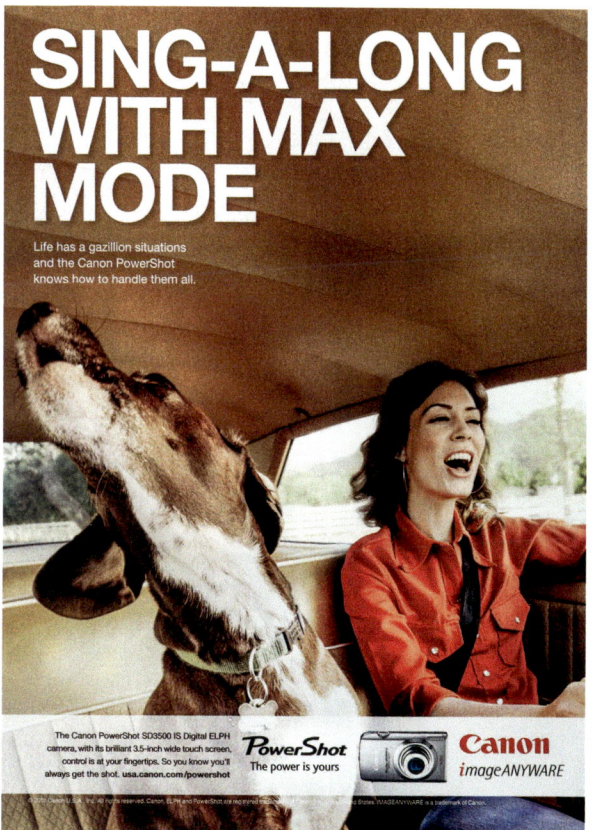

# SING-A-LONG WITH MAX MODE

Life has a gazillion situations and the Canon PowerShot knows how to handle them all.

The Canon PowerShot SD3500 IS Digital ELPH camera, with its brilliant 3.5-inch wide touch screen, control is at your fingertips. So you know you'll always get the shot. usa.canon.com/powershot

**PowerShot** The power is yours

**Canon** imageANYWARE

Canon, 2010

Apple, 2003

Apple, 2005

XM SATELLiTE RADiO

**LISTEN LARGE™**
America's Largest Playlist

**The Perfect Holiday Gift**

*XM Satellite Radio, 2005*

Sony, 2002

## 1,000 songs in your Mac.

Apple's award-winning iTunes™ software makes it easy to put your entire music collection right on your Mac.™ You can rip MP3s, create playlists and burn custom CDs™ all from one refreshingly simple interface. And now iTunes 2 offers even more features — like MP3 CD burning, crossfading and an equalizer. iTunes makes it simple and fun to build your very own digital music library on your Mac. Now, imagine having all of that incredible music with you wherever you go — even when you're away from your Mac.

## 1,000 songs in your pocket.

Presenting iPod.™ The first MP3 player to pack a mind-blowing 1,000 songs™™ and an 8-hour battery™ into a stunning 6.5-ounce package you can literally take everywhere. But iPod™ isn't just a revolution in portability, it's also a revolution in simplicity. Just plug it into your Mac and all of your iTunes songs and playlists are automatically downloaded into iPod at blazing FireWire® speed. With iPod, it's that easy to take your entire music collection with you wherever you go, in the pocket of your choice.

Apple, 2001

All the music you want
10 bucks a month

Rhapsody

GET THE APP FOR IPHONE®, IPOD TOUCH® AND ANDROID™

Listen to anything and everything in the catalog for one low monthly price. A Rhapsody subscription gives you millions of songs to choose from. Listen online, through home audio systems, and now with mobile apps for iPhone, iPod touch and Android.

www.rhapsody.com

*apsody, 2010*

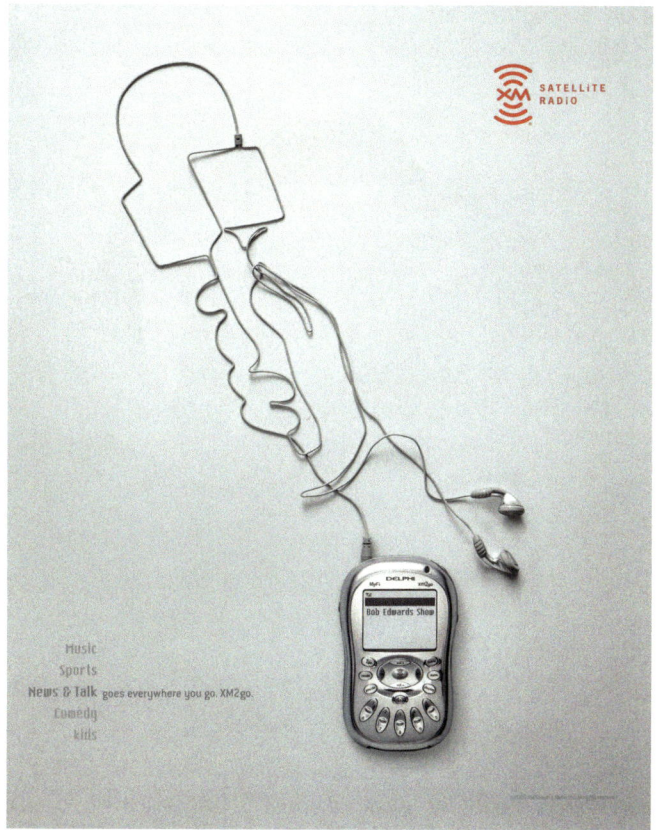

Music
Sports
News & Talk goes everywhere you go. XM2go.
Comedy
Kids

*XM Satellite Radio, 2005*

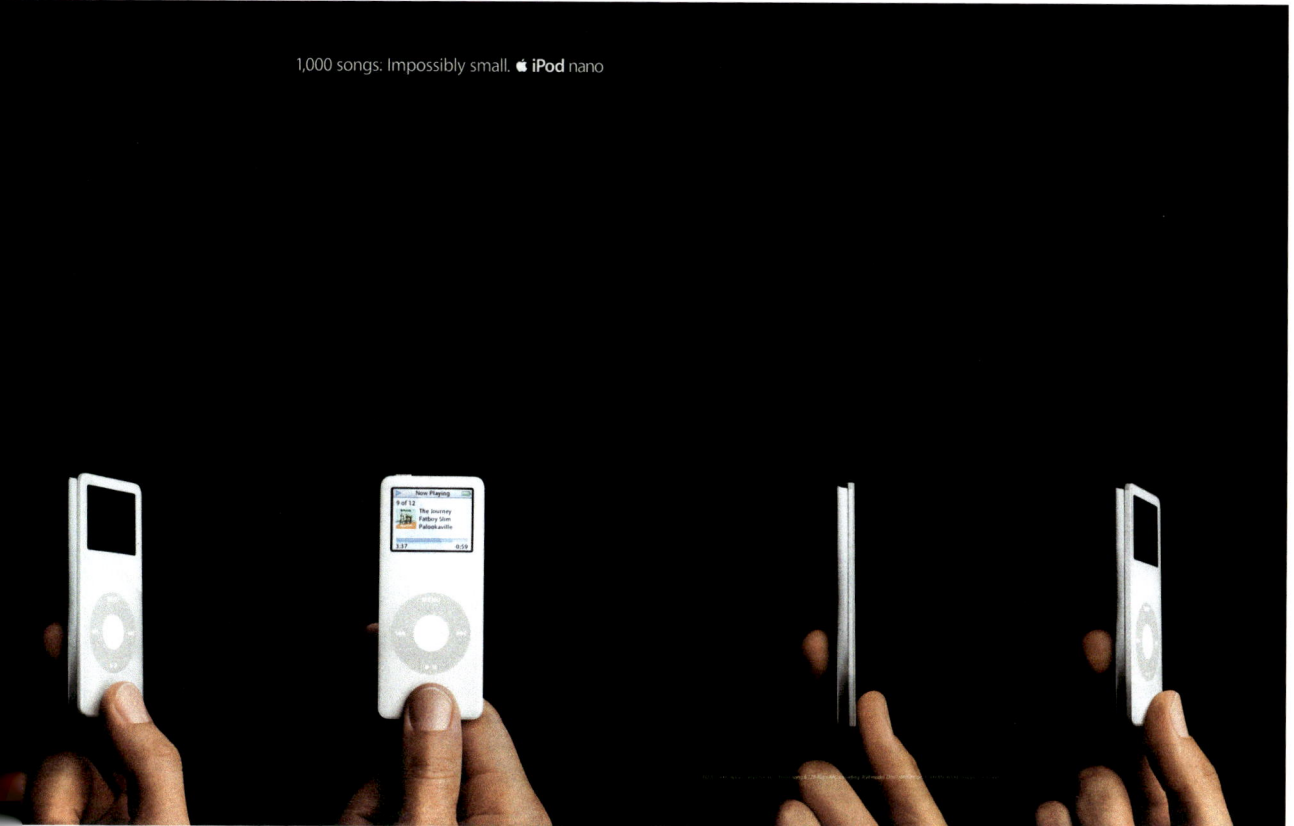

1,000 songs. Impossibly small. ᴓ iPod nano

*e, 2005*

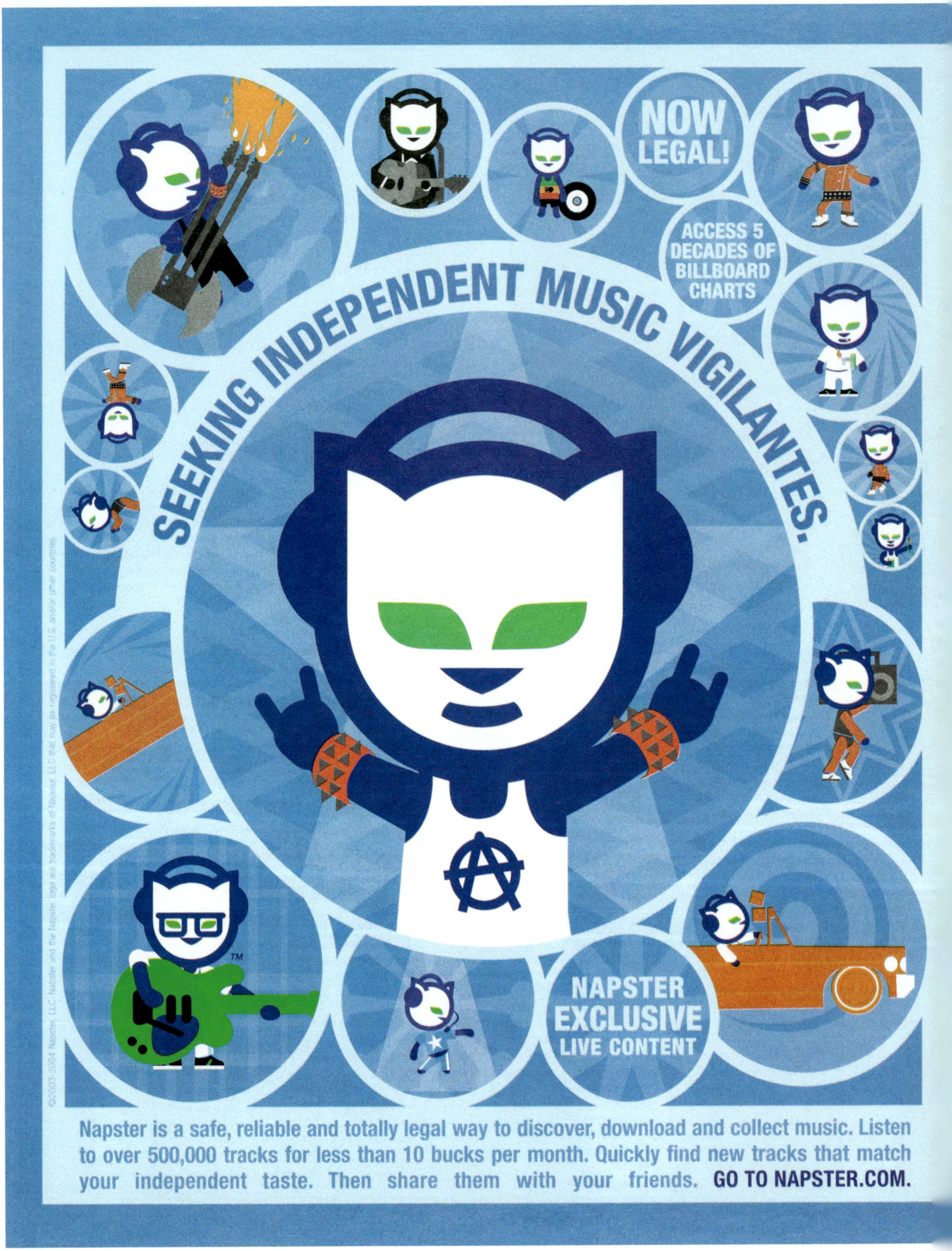


*Napster, 2004*

THERE'S NO MILLION ITEMS OR LESS LANE.

With one click you can enjoy all your favorites and discover new music quickly, safely and legally. A Napster subscription gives you unlimited access to our massive catalog of music. Get it all for just $9.95 a month and you'll never buy a CD with only one good track again.

Try it for free at Napster.com

napster™

*Napster, 2004*

1,000 songs* in your pocket.  iPod+iTunes

you make it you

**A little video for everyone.** Now the world's most popular music player also plays your favorite TV shows, movies and videos. 4GB and 8GB. From $149. iPod nano

*Apple, 2007*

iPod mini. It's the world's smallest 1,000-song player, comes in 5 colors, weighs a mere 3.6 ounces and works with your PC or Mac. Just $249.

iPod mini

*Apple, 2004*

# I'M LISTENING.™

Rio
riohome.com

Sony, 2001

Sony, 2001

ROCK, POP, JAZZ, HIP-HOP, COUNTRY, R&B, DANCE.

DID WE LEAVE ANYTHING OUT?

YEAH, THE COMMERCIALS.

RIDE WITH THE BIG DOG,
SIRIUS SATELLITE RADIO.

When you Ride with the Big Dog, SIRIUS Satellite Radio, you get everything you want to hear without all the stuff you don't. You want over 120 channels, including 65 with commercial-free music? With SIRIUS you get that, plus news, talk and the best sports programming around. For those who never want to miss an NFL game, SIRIUS comes with its exclusive NFL Sunday Drive. It's live play-by-play action of the entire NFL. With SIRIUS, you get everything for just $12.95* a month. See, when you get all the stuff you really want, that's radio your way. That's SIRIUS Satellite Radio. RIDE WITH THE BIG DOG.

GREAT GIFT FOR THEM.
GREAT DEAL FOR YOU.
NOW GET $30 BACK
WHEN YOU GET SIRIUS
FOR SOMEONE THIS HOLIDAY.

With a SIRIUS Plug & Play receiver, you can listen to your music in the car, move it in the house or take it wherever you go.**

**SIRIUS**
SATELLITE RADIO

sirius.com

*Sirius Satellite Radio, 2004*

start
something
Sonic Start discovering new music. Collecting the old stuff.
Start recording your own. Mixing and mashing. Taking it on the road.
Start creating your personal soundtrack.

With a world of software and devices that run on Windows® XP, the choice is yours.
Go to windows.com and start anything you like.

Windows·xp

*Microsoft, 2005*

Sony, 2005

"I speak four languages. ¿Y tú?"

Match.com member: HablaWithMe Online Now!

You could meet HablaWithMe or any of the 20,000 new people who join Match.com every day. We guarantee you'll find someone special in 6 months or we'll give you **6 months FREE!*** Get started today.

find someone special in 6 months **guaranteed!**

match.com®
IT'S OKAY TO LOOK®

*See site for details.
Subscription required. ©2009 Match.com, LLC

*Match, 2009*

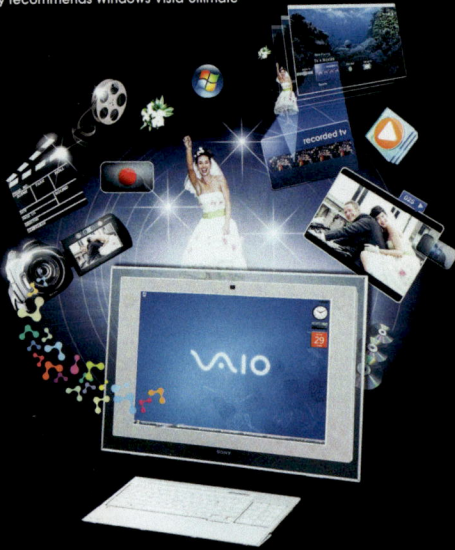

Sony, 2008

Sony, 2007

Sony, 2008

Panasonic, 2007 · ▶ Hewlett-Packard, 2008

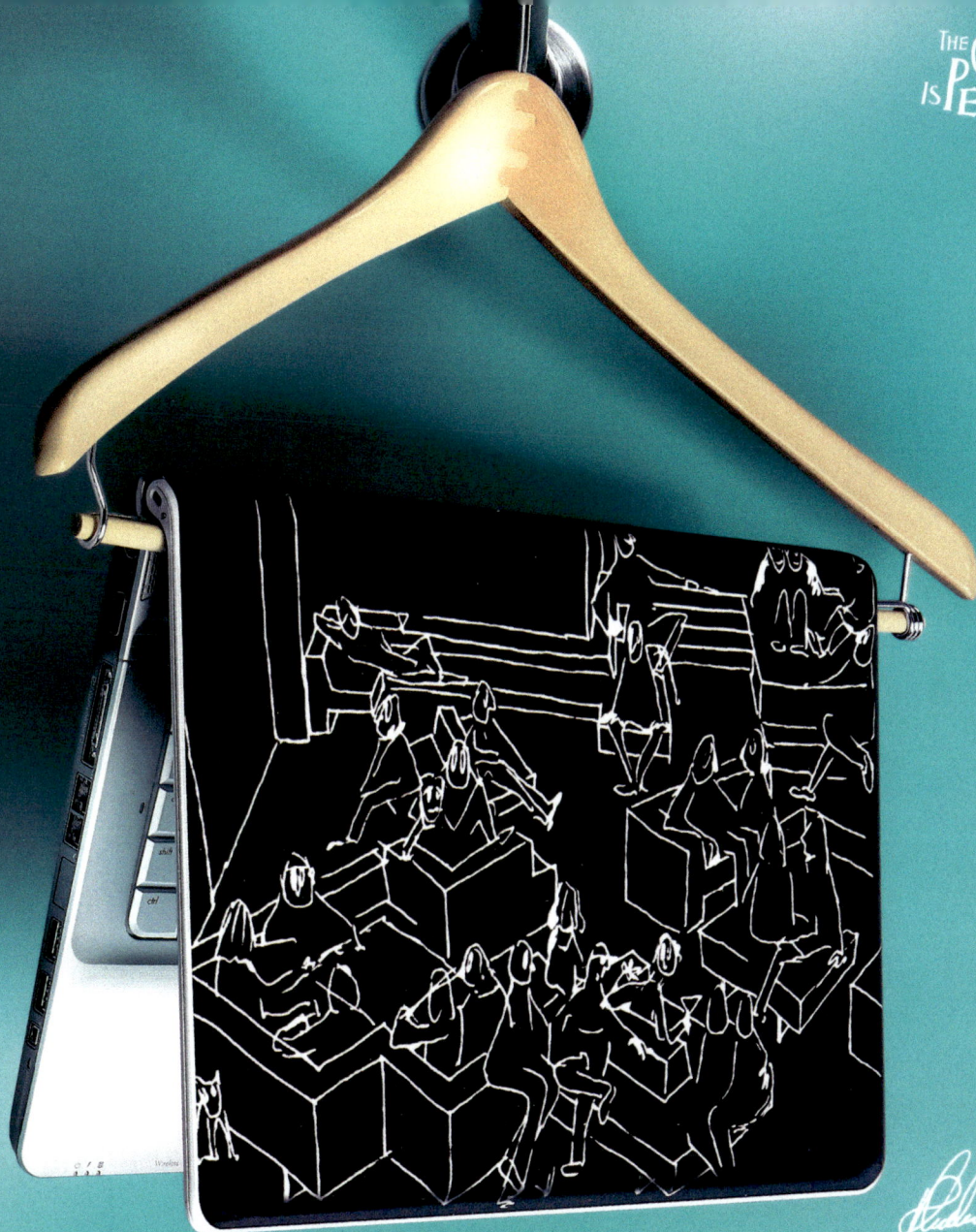

THE COMPUTER IS PERSONAL AGAIN.

The Standard by designer Vladimir Kagan

It knows it's haute. Add an elegant accent to an already chic HP entertainment notebook. Three design icons have created three fashionable skins exclusively for HP. Only 500 of each design are available. All proceeds go to DIFFA: Design Industries Foundation Fighting AIDS. Personalize your notebook today at hp.skinit.com.

**Introducing the Diane von Furstenberg Limited Edition Sidekick 3 from T-Mobile.**
Now you can stay connected in style with e-mail, Web browsing and IM. You can only find this exclusive Sidekick 3 online at **www.sidekick.com/LE** and at select T-Mobile retailers.

**T··Mobile· stick together**

# EVEN
# OUR STYLE
# HAS SUBSTANCE.

Introducing the New Dell™ XPS™ M1330 Notebook.

This wedge shape isn't just for good looks. In fact, it allows us to make the XPS M1330 notebook less than one inch thick, making it the thinnest 13.3" notebook on the market. Designed for Performance. Yours is here.

**XPS**

New Dell™ XPS™ M1330
Starting at
**$1449**

GET YOURS AT WWW.DELL.COM / MAXIMMAG | 1-800-822-3781

**DELL**
YOURS IS HERE

*Dell, 2007*

## Introducing the MacBooks, the world's newest power couple.

Meet the MacBooks, the two newest members of the Mac™ family. Both feature Intel Core Duo processors right out of the box, and the award-winning iLife® '06 suite of software that lets you easily create

for blazing performance, 13-inch glossy widescreen displays, built-in iSight™ cameras for video-chatting blogs, podcasts, photo albums, movies and more. The MacBook™ starts at just $1,099.* 🍎 **Mac**

*Apple, 2006*

Your life in sync.

Logitech® Cordless Desktop® MX™5000 Laser

ep all your Bluetooth devices in sync. A multimedia keyboard with LCD screen shows your email
essages and music tracks. And a laser mouse provides pixel precise tracking on almost any surface.

etooth    www.logitech.com

Logitech

Designed to move you™

*Logitech, 2005*

# Thinnovation.

The world's thinnest notebook. 13.3-inch widescreen display. Full-size keyboard.   MacBook

Toshiba recommends Windows Vista™ Business.

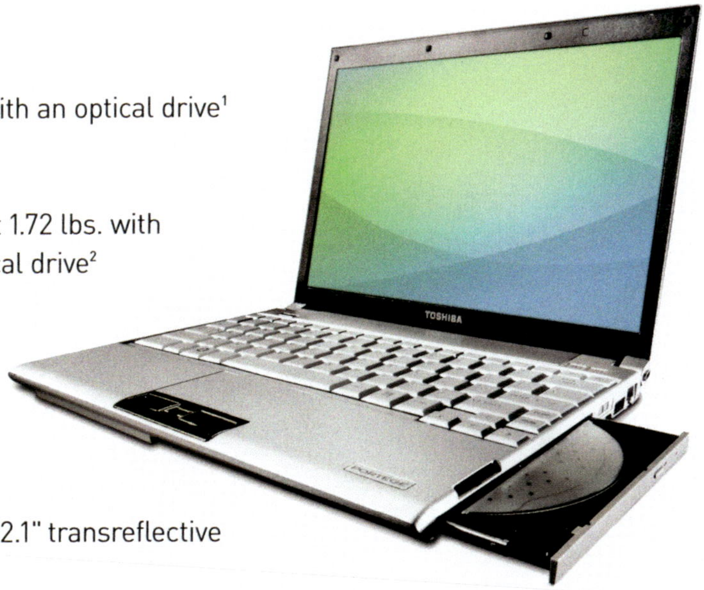

**World's thinnest**
widescreen 12.1" notebook with an optical drive[1]

**World's lightest**
widescreen 12.1" notebook at 1.72 lbs. with solid state drive and no optical drive[2]

**World's longest**
battery life in a widescreen 12.1" notebook[3]

**World's first**
indoor/outdoor widescreen 12.1" transreflective LED backlit display

# Introducing the Portégé® R500 Notebook PC Series.

**The world's thinnest** widescreen 12.1" notebook with an optical drive[1] or **the world's lightest** widescreen 12.1" notebook with 64GB[4] solid state drive[2] featuring Intel® Centrino® Duo processor technology and the Windows Vista™ Business operating system — and everything you need to be more productive no matter where business takes you. **Learn more at toshiba.com/R500.**

**TOSHIBA**
**Leading Innovation »»**

1. Copy protection technology may prevent or limit recording or viewing of certain optical media (e.g., CD or DVD). 2. Lightest model configuration of 1.72 lbs is based on a 64GB solid state drive (SSD), a 3-cell battery and no optical disk drive. The Portégé R500 with the solid state drive will not be available until the end of July 2007. 3. Battery life may vary considerably from specifications depending on product model, configuration, applications, power management settings and features utilized, as well as the natural performance variations produced by the design of individual components. 4. Hard drive capacity may vary. 1 Gigabyte (GB) means $10^9$ = 1,000,000,000 bytes using powers of 10. See Hard Disk Drive Capacity Legal Footnote at www.info.toshiba.com. Portégé is a registered trademark of Toshiba America Information Systems, Inc. and/or Toshiba Corporation. Intel and Centrino are trademarks or registered trademarks of Intel Corporation or its subsidiaries in the United States and other countries. Windows Vista is either a registered trademark or trademark of Microsoft Corporation in the United States and/or other countries. All other trademarks are the property of their respective owners. While Toshiba has made every effort at the time of publication to ensure the accuracy of the information provided herein, product specifications, configurations, prices, system/component/options availability are all subject to change without notice. For the most up-to-date product information about your computer, or to stay current with the various computer software or hardware options, visit Toshiba's website at pcsupport.toshiba.com. "World's" claims are based on data as of June 5, 2007. © 2007 Toshiba America Information Systems, Inc. All rights reserved.

*Apple, 2008* ◄

*Toshiba, 2007*

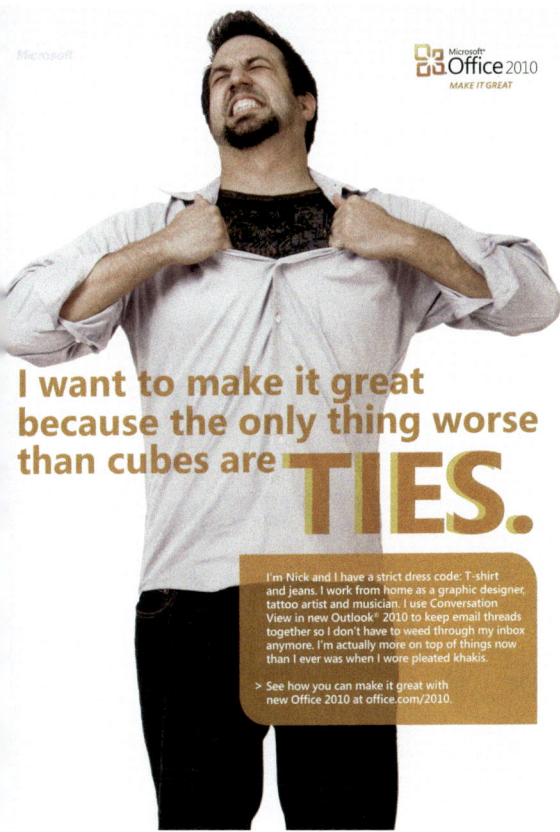

I want to make it great because the only thing worse than cubes are TIES.

I'm Nick and I have a strict dress code: T-shirt and jeans. I work from home as a graphic designer, tattoo artist and musician. I use Conversation View in new Outlook® 2010 to keep email threads together so I don't have to weed through my inbox anymore. I'm actually more on top of things now than I ever was when I wore pleated khakis.

> See how you can make it great with new Office 2010 at office.com/2010.

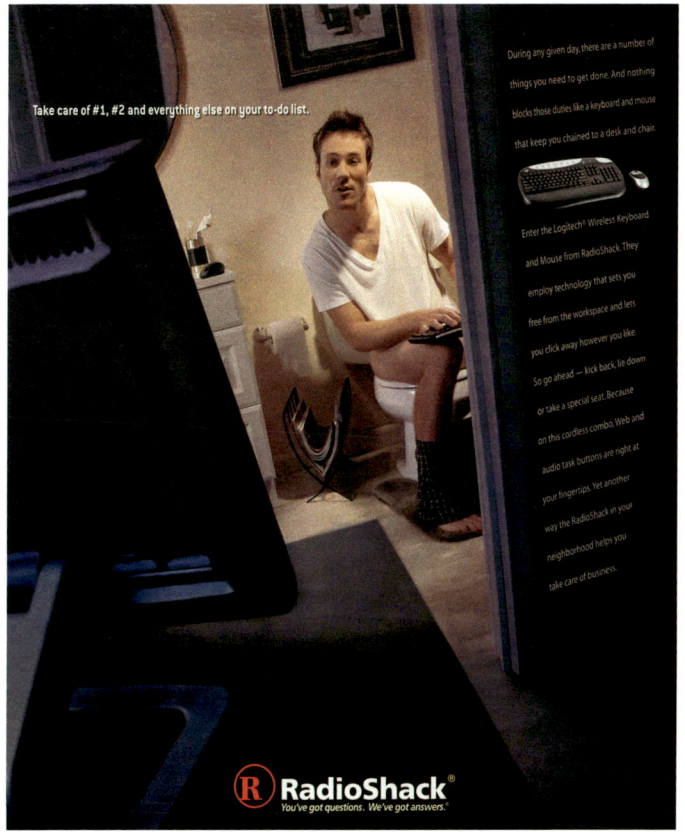

Take care of #1, #2 and everything else on your to-do list.

During any given day, there are a number of things you need to get done. And nothing blocks those duties like a keyboard and mouse that keep you chained to a desk and chair.

Enter the Logitech® Wireless Keyboard and Mouse from RadioShack. They employ technology that sets you free from the workspace and lets you click away however you like. So go ahead — kick back, lie down or take a special seat. Because on this cordless combo, Web and audio task buttons are right at your fingertips. Yet another way the RadioShack in your neighborhood helps you take care of business.

RadioShack®
You've got questions. We've got answers.®

*Microsoft, 2010*                                   *RadioShack, 2004*

SONY

Sony recommends Windows Vista® Home Premium

It could be the world's best-dressed music collection.

For special offers and to learn more about the beautiful Sony® VAIO® notebook with Windows Vista® go to sonystyle.com/vaiovista.

like.no.other

Windows Vista
Home Premium

*Intel, 2006* ◄ *Sony, 2008*                          ► *Toshiba, 2008*

Windows.® Life without walls.™

Imagine your life without walls. Where everything's connected. Where it's easy to manage both your photos and your finances. Working against walls is what Windows Vista® is all about. Because life is better without walls.

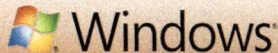

**Windows**®

# In 1985, Toshiba brought you the laptop. 6,927 patents later, we're bringing you its future.

**SET YOURSELF FREE WITH SATELLITE® SERIES LAPTOPS PREINSTALLED WITH GENUINE WINDOWS VISTA® HOME PREMIUM.**

At Toshiba, we're building a future where laptops set you free— free from technology that dictates how you work. That's why we're pioneering simple, intuitive and human-based innovations to help you achieve more. Features like USB Sleep-and-Charge, which keeps your electronic devices charging even when your laptop is asleep or turned off, and technologies we're working on will charge a battery to 90% capacity in about 10 minutes. See what else Toshiba, the Laptop Expert, has in mind for the future at **laptops.toshiba.com.**

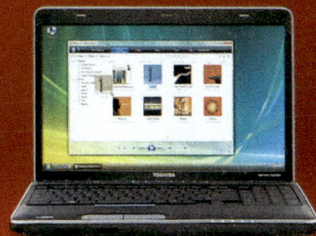

## TOSHIBA
### Leading Innovation >>>

# Amazon's #1 Bestselling Product

Free 3G wireless. No monthly bill. No contract. Think of a book and start reading it in 60 seconds.

Long battery life. Read for up to 2 weeks without recharging.

New York Times Best Sellers and top new releases.

Over 420,000 of the most popular books, newspapers, magazines, and blogs.

Paper-like display is easy to read, even in bright sunlight.

**amazonkindle**

**Madelyn's Kindle**                3G            amazon.com

**Browse:**
Books
Newspapers
Magazines
Blogs

**New York Times Best Sellers**

**Kindle Top Sellers** - *The Apothecary's Daughter*

**New & Noteworthy Books** - *The First Rule*

**Kindle Daily Post** Wed, February 10, 2010 3:04 PM PST
In *Buried Alive*, contractor Roy Hallums recounts the harrowing ten months he was held captive by Iraqi insurgents, the heroic rescue by American troops and the...

**Recommended for You**

See All

*Begin typing to search*          Q search store

PREV PAGE

NEXT PAGE

HOME

NEXT PAGE

MENU

BACK

Kindle carries your library for you and holds up to 1,500 books. Just over 1/3 of an inch thin, Kindle is as thin as most magazines. At 10.2 ounces, Kindle is lighter than a typical paperback.

**amazonkindle**

*amazon.com/kindle*

# The All-New Kindle
## Smaller, Lighter, Faster, with 50% Better Contrast

Kindle
$139

Kindle 3G
$189

**Think of a book and start reading it in 60 seconds.**

Carry your library—up to 3,500 books.

Easy to read even in bright sunlight.

8.7 ounces—lighter than a paperback.

Long battery life—up to one month.

Free 3G wireless on Kindle 3G. No monthly bills, no annual contract.

**amazon**kindle

*Learn more at **amazon.com/kindle***

Macs and PCs have never been so compatible.

Microsoft® Office v. X makes Macs and PCs more friendly. It lets Mac users effortlessly open, share, edit, and save any Office file, to make working with PCs a breeze. Complete with easy-to-use, exclusive Mac tools that simplify complex tasks. And it's built specifically for Mac OS X, so it's the most reliable, stable, easygoing Office yet. Go www.officeformac.com to download a free 30-day trial of Office v. X today.

Office:mac

*Microsoft, 2003*

Have you seen these personal trainers you can get for your TV? They're awesome. I got one and NOW MY TV Is a Lean, Mean Entertainment Machine. Seriously, this little high-tech trainer has really whipped my television into shape. Now it only shows me programs about stuff I like, plus it plays music through my entertainment system and lets me look at digital photos huge onscreen. I mean, my TV was thin and all before, but now it's buff, too.

TiVo

You've got a life. TiVo gets it.™

*TiVo, 2004*

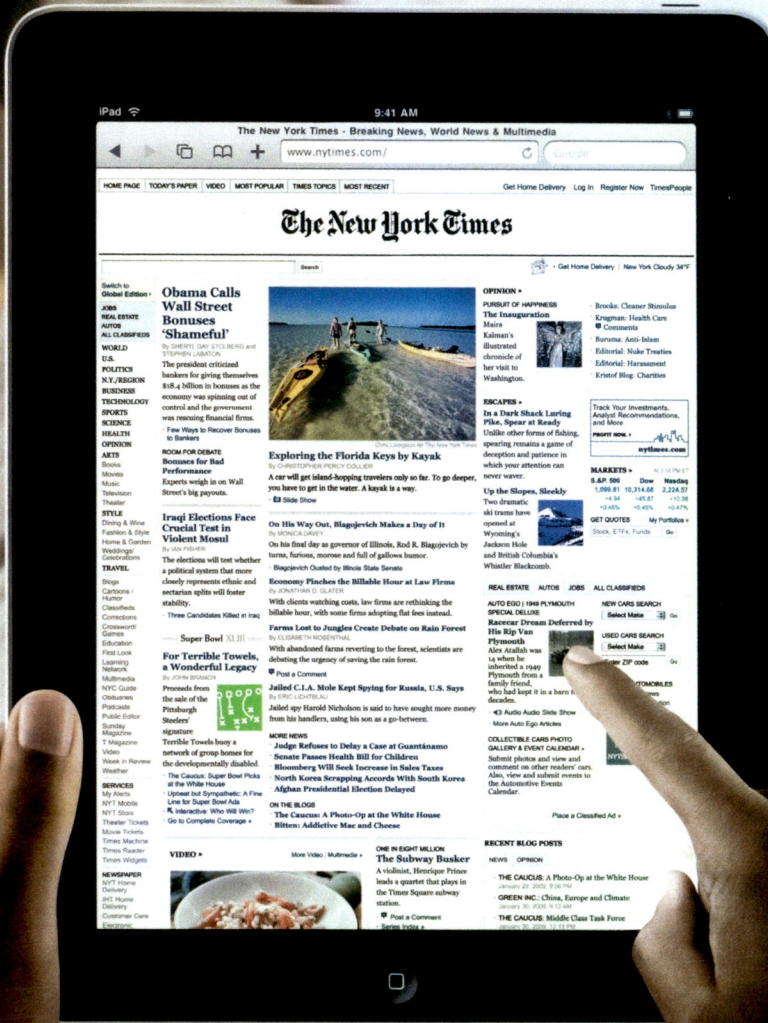

*Apple, 2010*

Look !

SOCCER_M0M47

**USED CAR**

PTA member since '98

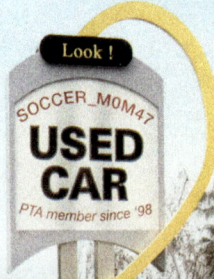

*Meet the car dealer next door.* eBay Motors is simply a better way to buy a car. Search national or local listings, and research prices. Get eBay Vehicle Purchase Protection up to $20,000.* And review sellers' feedback so you feel good about who you're buying from. And even better about the car you drive home.

You can get it on

**eBay Motors**

*eBay, 2007*

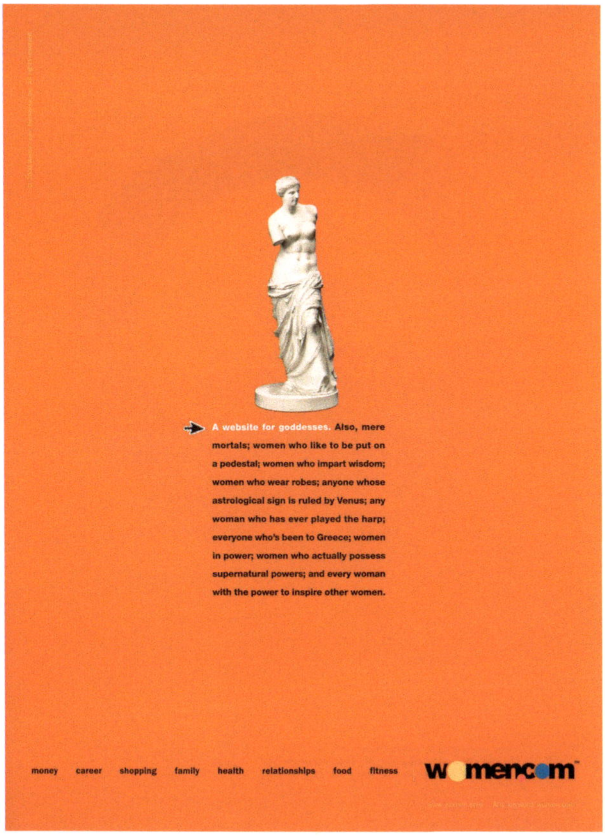


*Women.com, 2000*

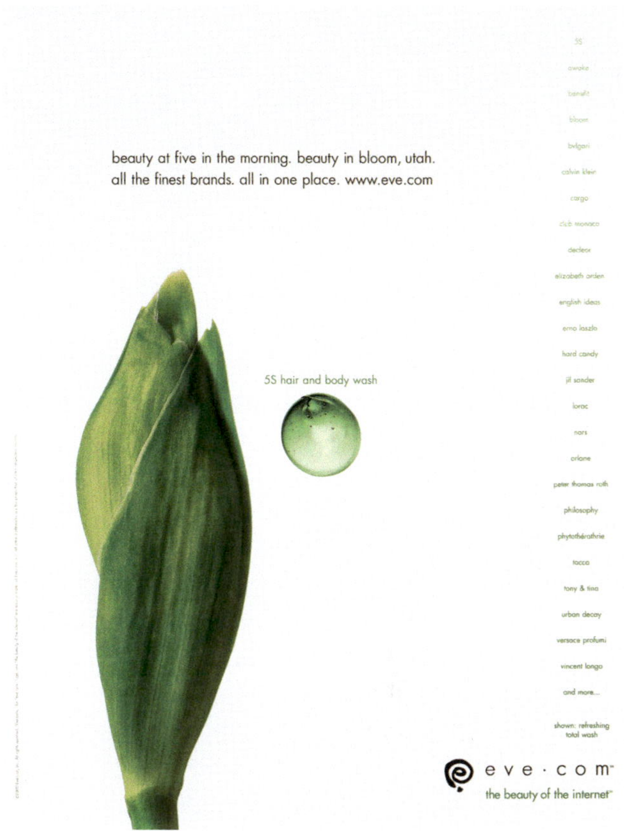


*Eve.com, 2000*

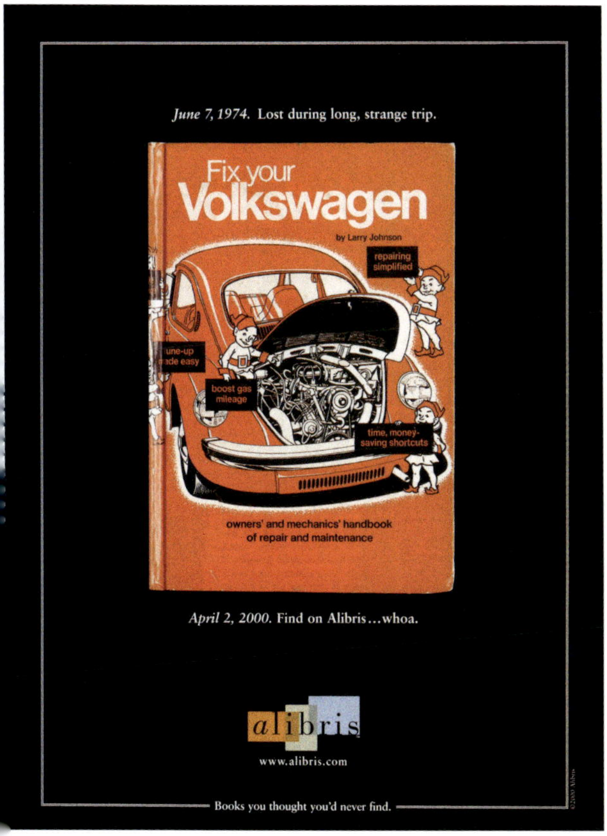


*Alibris, 2000*

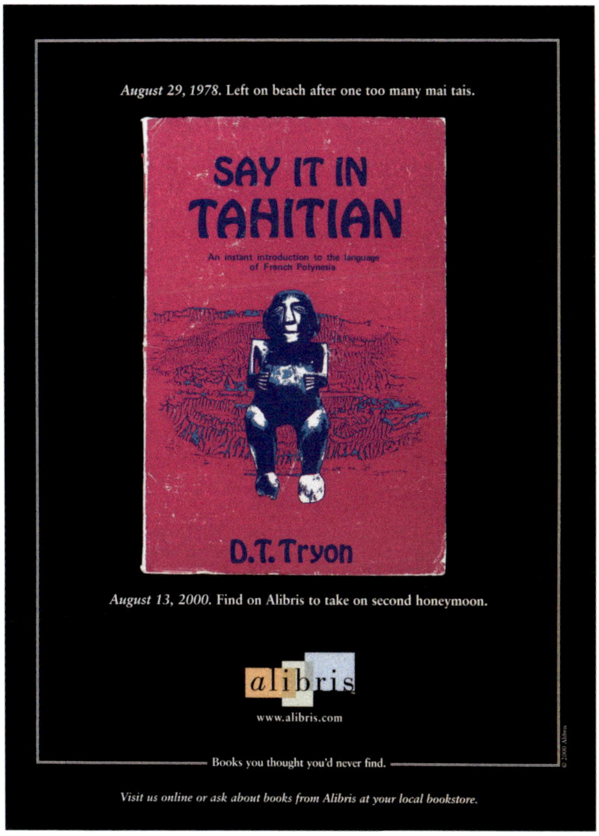


*Alibris, 2000*

**MEAT TENDERIZER**

**You need it. We've got it.** Nothing can turn the joy of cooking into a tedious chore faster than using the wrong equipment. So, whether you're looking for a new recipe, or the best tools from brands like Calphalon, KitchenAid or Wüsthof, Cooking.com is the premier resource for all your cooking needs. Order now and get free shipping.*

**Cooking.com**
Cookware. Recipes. Advice.

Visit us at www.cooking.com or AOL keyword: cooking.com.*Coupon code: C11194. Expires 4/15/00.

*Cooking.com, 2000*

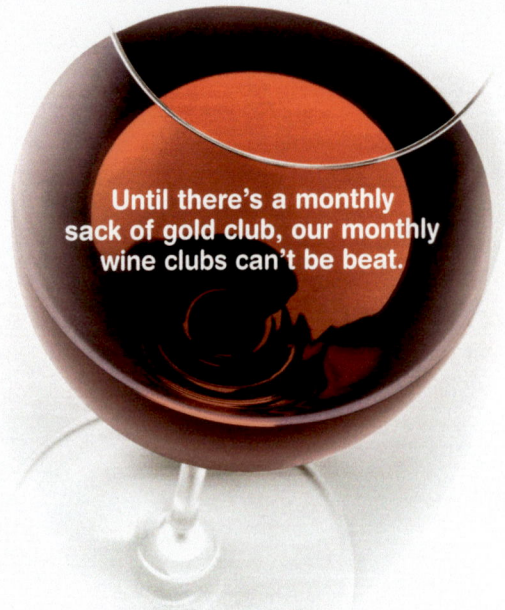

Until there's a monthly sack of gold club, our monthly wine clubs can't be beat.

Whether you want to learn about new wine every month or fill your cellar with the exceptional, we've got a wine club for you. No secret knock required.

**wine.com**
*The best of wine*

*Wine.com, 2000*

Is running your business getting in the way of running your business?

Then get QuickBooks and spend less time on your paperwork and more time on your business. It's the easiest way to:

CREATE INVOICES
PAY BILLS
TRACK SALES

www.QuickBooks.com

**Intuit QuickBooks**
Pro 2008

Get back to business.

*QuickBooks, 2008*

Needle, thread and a mother's love managed to do
what all the king's horses and all the king's men couldn't.

I'm quite simple, really — made in a time when just
being me was enough to bring a smile.

I've played house, kept secrets and dried tears for generations.

And when there was no one left to pass me down,
a man named Jack saw something special in me.
Now others see it, too — in room 15 at The Inn at Occidental,
Sonoma Valley, California.

There's no room like it on Earth,
but there are plenty like it everywhere.

23,000 UNIQUE PROPERTIES | GIFT CERTIFICATES | INN TRAVELER NEWSLETTER | ONLINE BOOKING   BedandBreakfast.com

*BedandBreakfast.com, 2000*

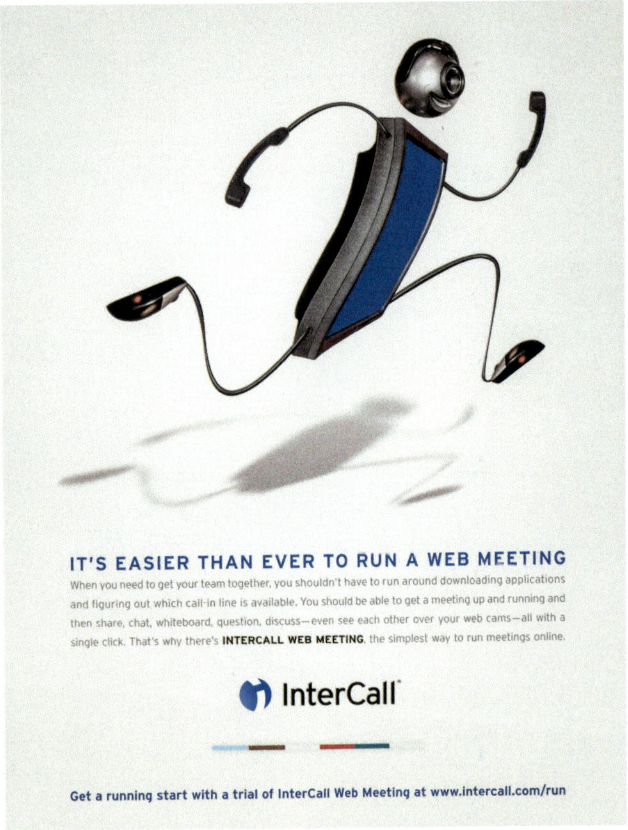


*InterCall, 2008*

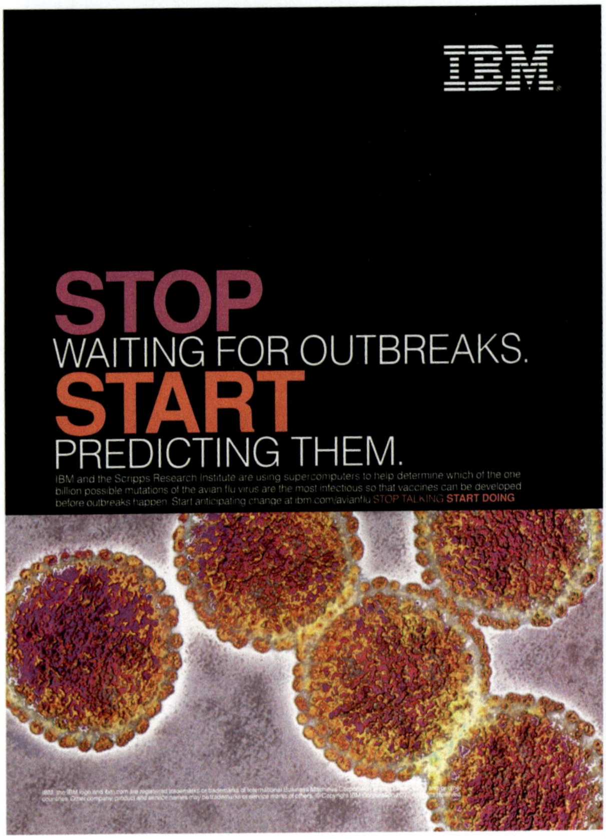


*IBM, 2008*

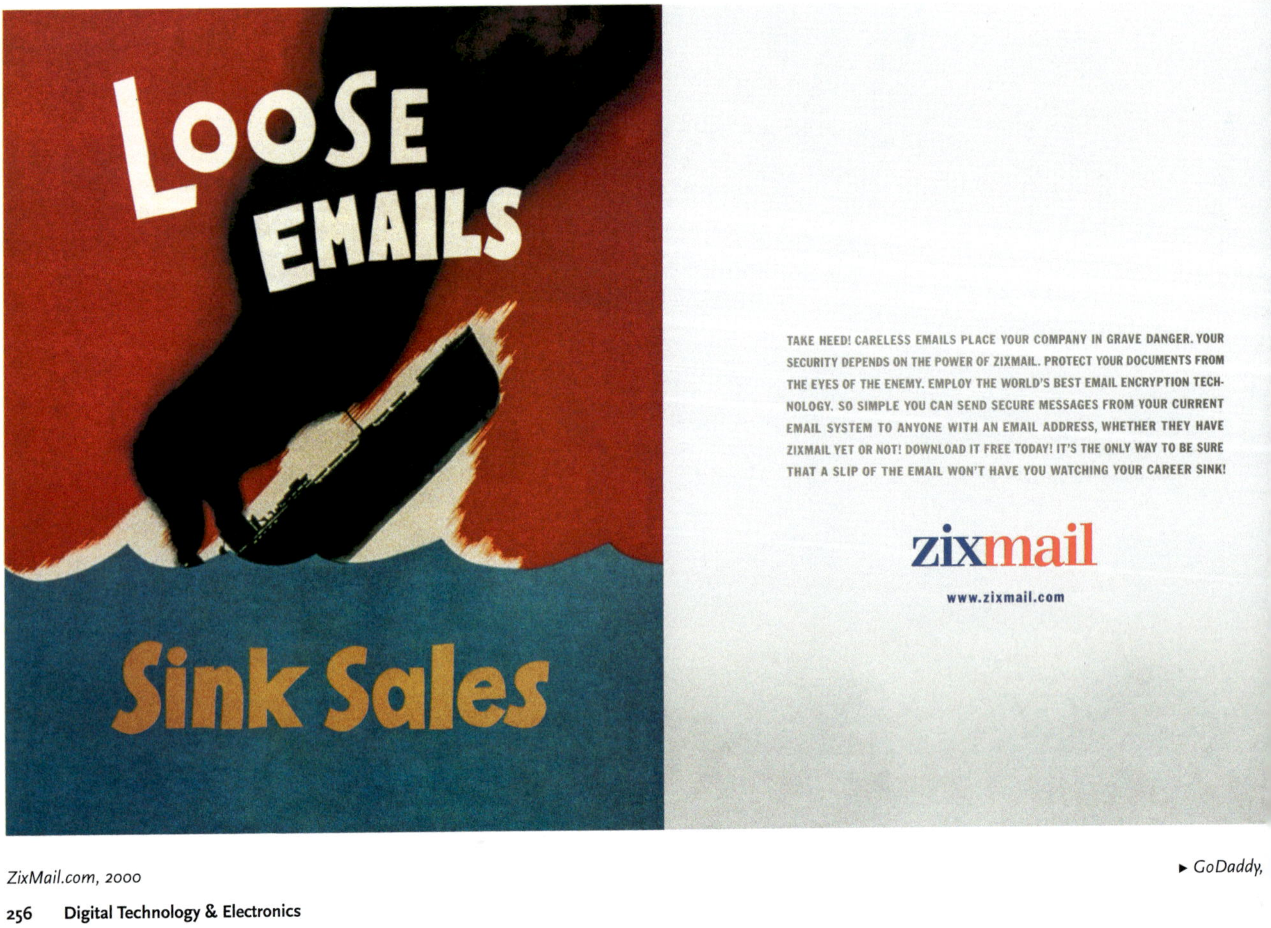


*ZixMail.com, 2000*

▸ *GoDaddy,*

THINK YOU'VE SEEN IT ALL?

go•daddy•esque (adj.)

1. Edgy
2. Innovative
3. Slightly Inappropriate

*Zero Knowledge, 2000*

*Gay.com, 2008*

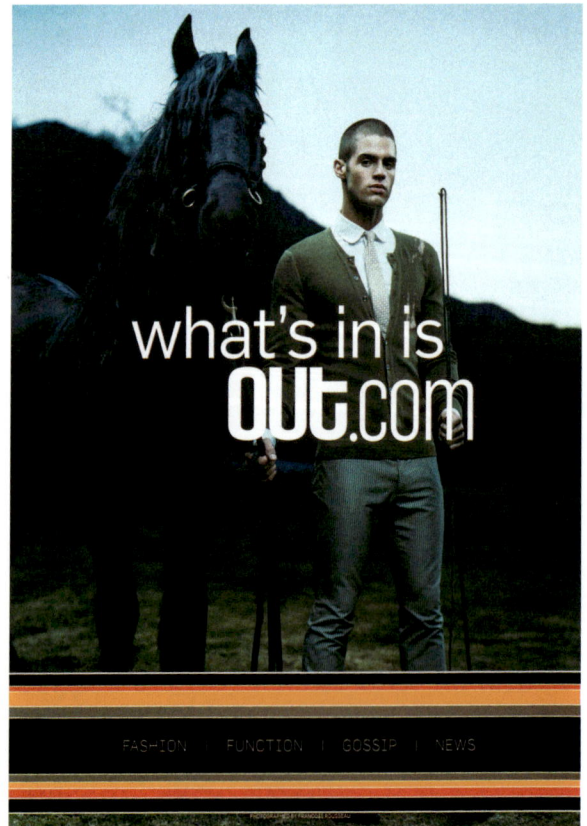

*Out.com, 2008*

ove is complicated.
match.com is simple.

match.com®

# epicurious

## get closer to your food

Visit epicurious.com for over 25,000 tested recipes, menus for any occasion, guides to cooking in and dining out, essential technique videos, and all the great food writing you can eat.

**www.epicurious.com**

*Epicurious, 2008*

# Now what's hard to find isn't.

Introducing EthnicGrocer.com. Thousands of the world's most sought-after ingredients, recipes and ideas.
So all you have to do is point and click, and we'll deliver to your door. Now how hard is that?

## EthnicGrocer.com™
877-604-3846 (toll-free)

*EthnicGrocer.com, 2000*

TiVo, 2004

IBM, 2000

Microsoft, 2004

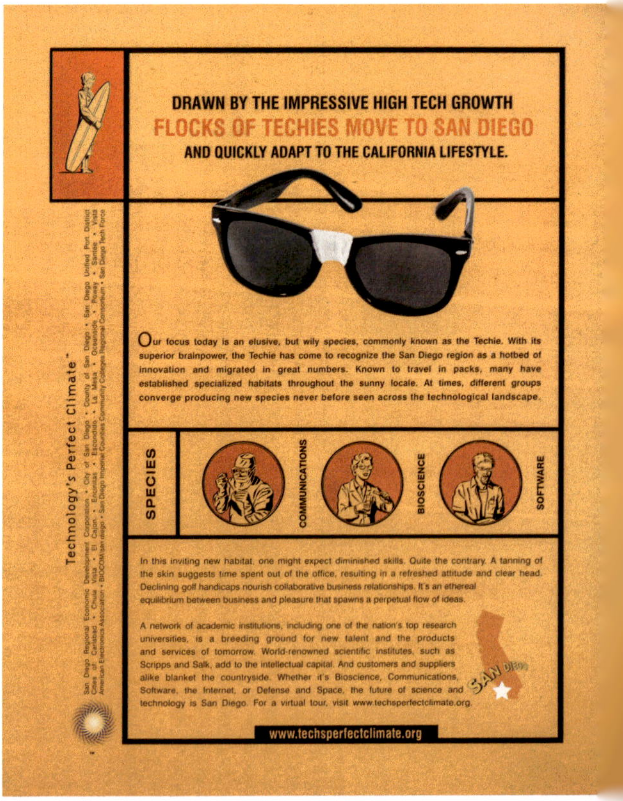

Technology's Perfect Climate, 2000

Feed Me!

**Watch it.** This thing is ravenous. Music, videos, photos—he devours it all. With up to 20 hrs battery life and an expanding microSD™-card-slot stomach, he's like a tweaked-out trucker at a Vegas buffet. Get ready for some serious feeding, 'cause this MP3 player is one hungry Lil' Monsta.

Lil'Monsta.com

Sansa™
e200

*SanDisk, 2006*

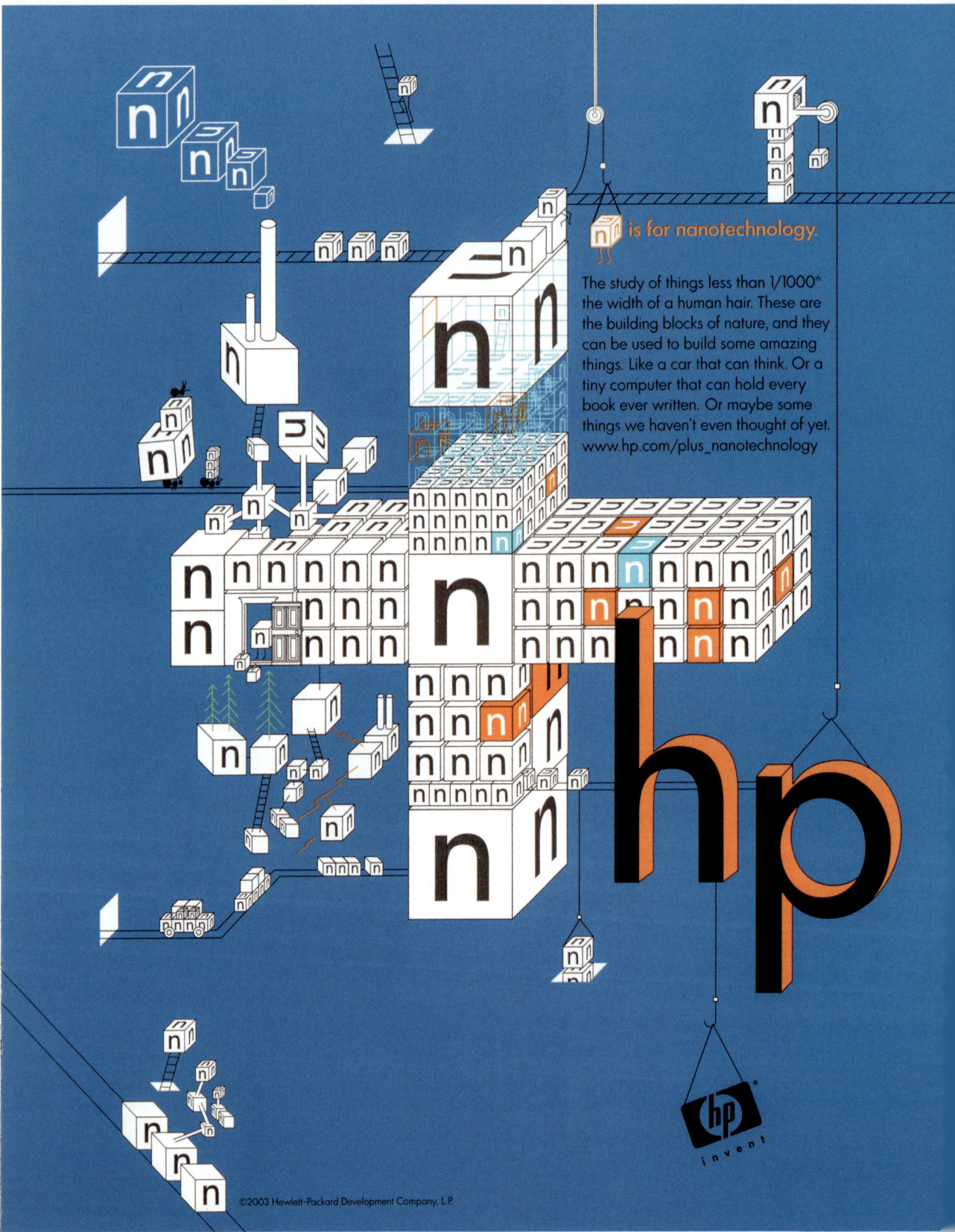

**n** is for nanotechnology.

The study of things less than 1/1000$^{th}$ the width of a human hair. These are the building blocks of nature, and they can be used to build some amazing things. Like a car that can think. Or a tiny computer that can hold every book ever written. Or maybe some things we haven't even thought of yet. www.hp.com/plus_nanotechnology

hp invent

*Hewlett-Packard, 2004*

It's a small universe after all.

Walt Disney Imagineers had a dream: create an attraction that allowed visitors to experience the thrill of space flight. The technological expertise of HP engineers and Walt Disney Imagineers made it possible. Relying on HP IT architecture, workstations and servers, the teams collaborated to create Mission: SPACE, a space flight simulator so real, even astronauts say it's accurate. www.hp.com/plus_disney

disney + hp

= *everything is possible*

invent

*Hewlett-Packard, 2004*

**6:23 PM AyumIAMi: get out of your cubicle already! you'll less. Now come meet me at the playground. I'm on the swing thing.**

**IM** E-MAIL TEXT
ON THE MOVE. **SEND WORD.**

unlimited usage as low as $17.99 per month.* no annual contract quick start-up
Ogo currently $99.99 (suggested retail price $129.99, mail-in rebate $30). get one now

www.attwireless.com/ogo
800.844.1217

**ogo**™

AT&T Wire

Access any existing AOL®, MSN®, or Yahoo!® account.

AMERICA Online    **msn**    YAHOO!

*Unlimited service only applies to e-mail, compatible IM, and domestic text messaging services on your device from the Ogo Service Area. International and premium text messaging charges, various taxes, surcharges, fees and other asse
(e.g. Universal Connectivity Charge) apply. You must either add Ogo service to an existing, qualified AT&T Wireless GSM account or activate using an approved credit card. Credit approval applies for add-a-line; deposit may be required. Og
and $19.99 activation fee required. Not available for purchase or use in all areas. Availability, timeliness and reliability of service are subject to transmission limitations. You will not be able to place or receive any calls. Documents cannot be
or viewed. Limited time offer. Other restrictions apply. Subject to Service Agreement and printed materials. *Mail-In Rebate:* Must be active for 30 days and when rebate is processed. Allow 8-10 weeks for the rebate check. See rebate for
details. Mail-in rebates not available in CT. ©2004 AT&T Wireless. All Rights Reserved.

*AT&T, 2004*

start something
DEDICATED
START TRACKING YOUR TEAMS.
IMPROVING YOUR SWING.
ANALYZING THE STATS. COACHING LIKE A PRO.
TRAINING FOR NEXT YEAR.
START ELEVATING YOUR GAME.

With a world of software and devices
that run on Windows® XP, the choice is yours.

Go to windows.com and start anything you like.

Windows xp

*Microsoft, 2005*

Do you believe anything is possible?

We do. We believe in a High Speed world without viruses, spyware or online identity theft. A place where your information can be safe from scammers and online intruders. We believe the Internet can be something wonderful again. We've got the tools to make that dream come true. With a little imagination and a lot of hard work we're making unbelievable things happen every day. Call 1-866-EARTHLINK and start believing today.

High Speed offers starting at $19.95 a month for the first 6 months.

www.earthlink.net

**EarthLink**
*We revolve around you.*

*EarthLink, 2005*

WE PROMISE TO USE OUR
**FREAKY KNOWLEDGE**
OF COMPUTERS FOR GOOD

Geek Squad
24 HOUR COMPUTER SUPPORT TASK FORCE

1 800 GEEK SQUAD

Agent 1571

I SWEAR THAT "VIGILANT" IS MY MIDDLE NAME.
ACTUALLY, IT'S CHARLES, BUT "VIGILANT" WOULD BE COOL.

REPAIR • UPGRADES • WIRELESS NETWORKING • SECURITY

© 2006 GEEK SQUAD 29344-2    HIGHLY SENSITIVE INTEL CONTAINED HEREIN

*Geek Squad, 2006*

*Zappos.com, 2008*

*Game Boy, 2001*

*Sirius Satellite Radio, 2004*

izon, 2007

Adobe, 2005

rola, 2009

Why.com, 2000

eYada.com, 2000

Sports Illustrated, 2010

Virgin Mobile, 2004

PC Tools Software, 2008

▶ AllAutograph.com, 2010

The compact Sony Cyber-shot® P1 Camera has 3.3 mega pixels for optimal resolution. And with 3X optical zoom and an LCD screen, it's high style and high tech.  www.sony.com/di

*Sony, 2000*

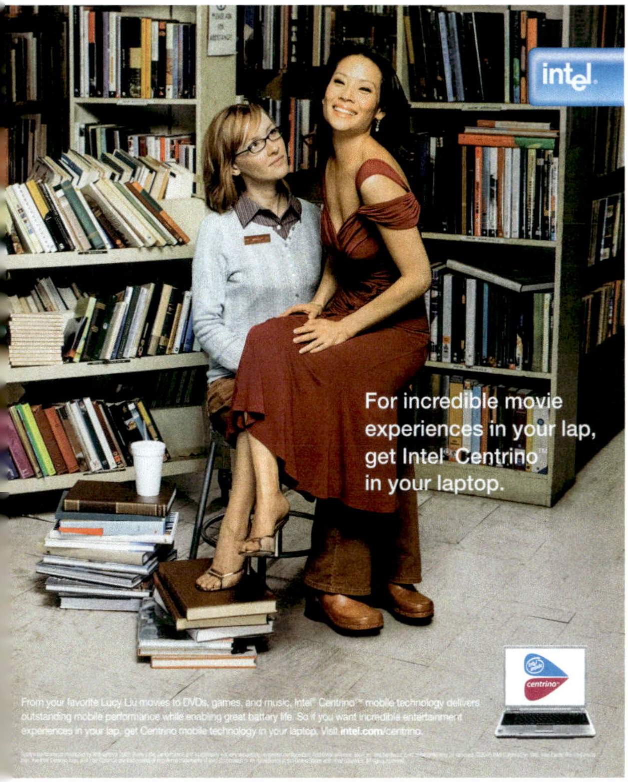


ntel, 2005

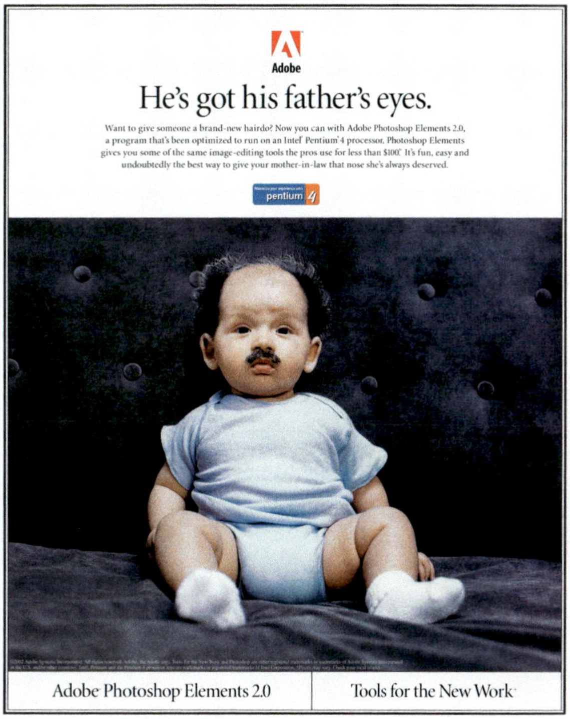


Adobe, 2003

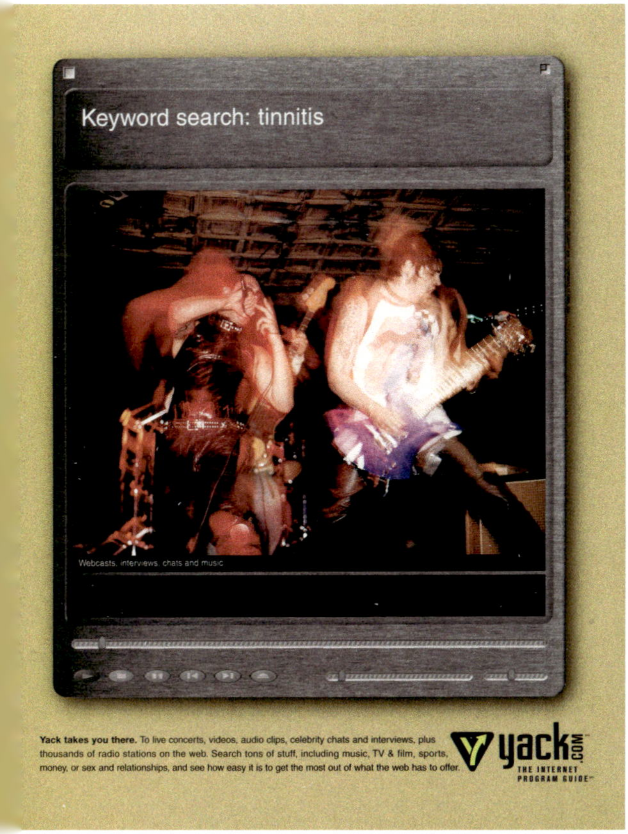


ck.com, 2000

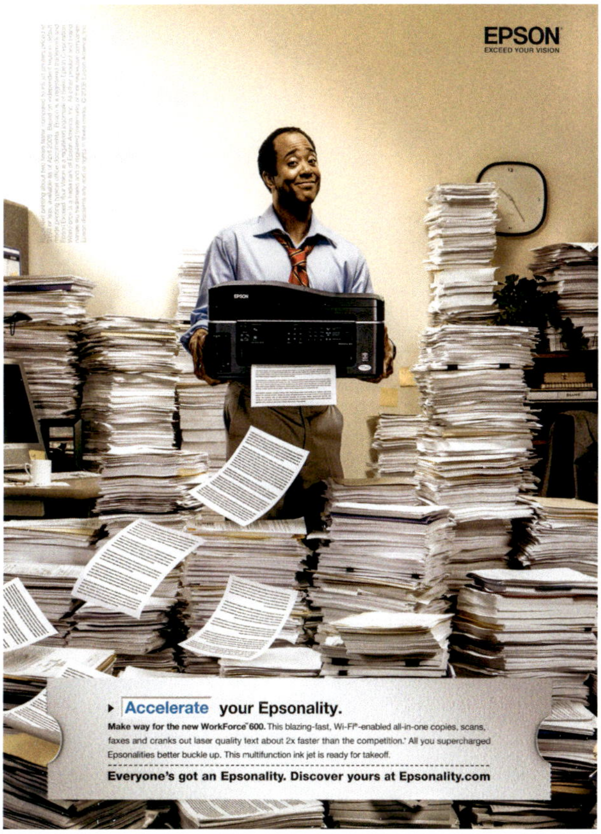


Epson, 2008

*Nike, 2005*

*Nike, 2005*

*"You don't just charge people fees and not tell them. That's Sunday School 101."*

Pay As You Go by *Virgin* mobile *Live without a plan.*

virginmobileusa.com

*Virgin Mobile, 2004*

▶ *Sun Microsystems, 20*

Introducing the world's first eco-responsible server.
The Sun Fire™ T1000 with CoolThreads™ technology. Visit sun.com.

Sun microsystems

*Magazine.org, 2005*

*MySimon.com, 2000*

*Yahoo, 2004*

*Yahoo, 2000*

278 Digital Technology & Electronics

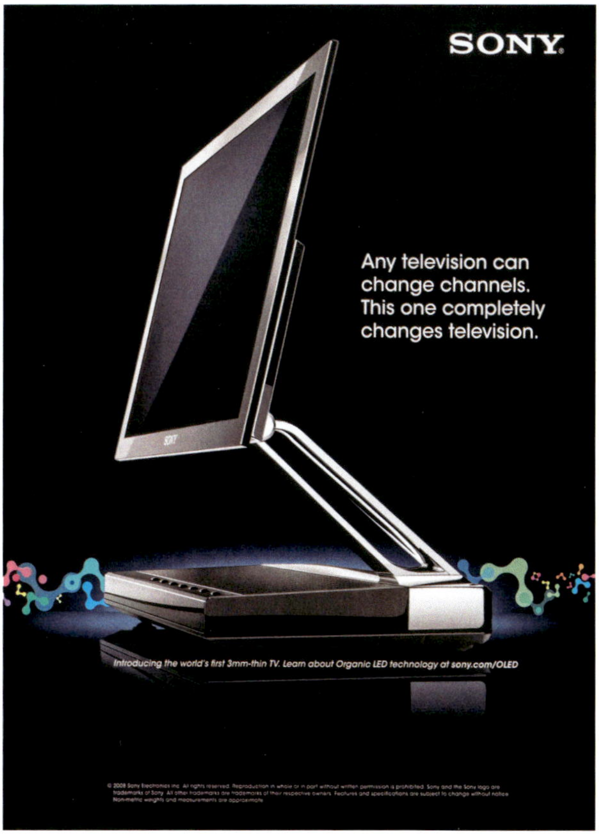


*Sony, 2008*

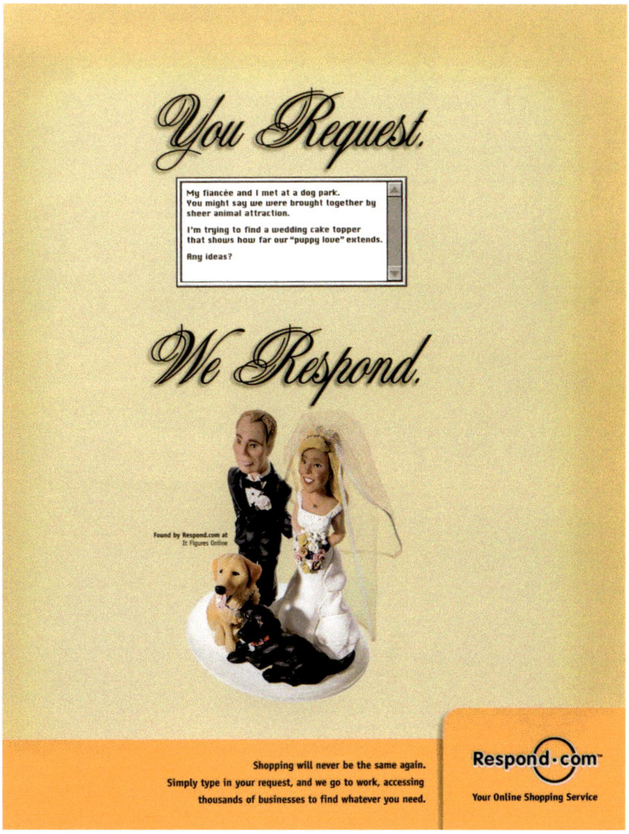


*Respond.com, 2000*

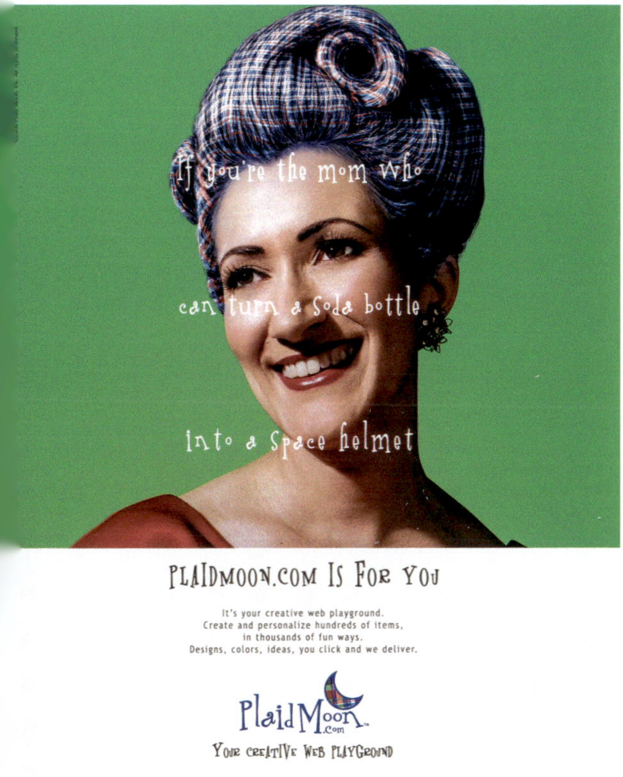


*dMoon.com, 2000*

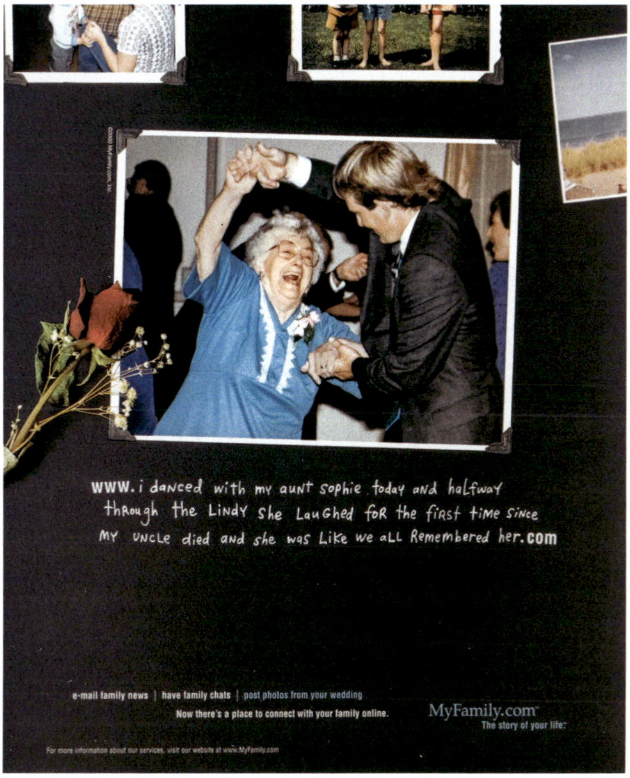


*MyFamily.com, 2000*

*MailStation, 2000*

*Garmin, 2004*

*Intel, 2001*

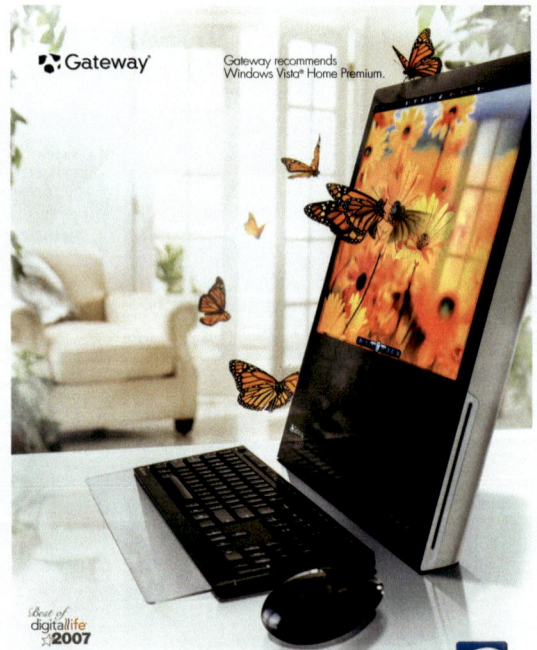
*Gateway, 2008*

# If you get one of these,    you'll need one of these.

Digital cameras have arrived. And the new iMac is designed to make the most of them. Just plug your camera in and your pictures will appear on the screen in seconds. Then easily save, organize and share them in some pretty amazing ways.

*Apple, 2002*

What's the point of capturing life's special moments on videos you can only play on your camcorder? Now, with the new Power Mac G4 and Apple's revolutionary iDVD software, you can organize and preserve your favorite memories on DVDs you can watch again and again on almost any standard DVD player. iDVD's simple drag-and-drop interface makes it easy to create professional-looking DVD menus in minutes.

You can even include slide shows of your favorite photos right alongside your movies.

Then you can use the new G4's aptly named SuperDrive to burn your own custom DVDs. No more dusty videotapes and crumpled photos. Just ultra-crisp digital video and CD-quality sound ready to be shared with friends and family anywhere. To see how you can make your memories last forever, visit www.apple.com or call 1-800-MY-APPLE.   Think different.

*e, 2001*

# And the winner is...

### I Can't Get No Satisfaction

Here we go again. Drag out the old sex theme to sell a product. Fabulous fashion? Was the sex so boring that the woman immediately had to go online to shop for satisfaction? And what's up with that giant phallic cactus? Men, kids, and home be damned—women only shop to get satisfaction.

### I Can't Get No Satisfaction

Schon wieder das alte Thema Sex, um ein Produkt zu verkaufen. Fabelhafte Mode? War das Liebesspiel so gähnend langweilig, dass die Frau sich umgehend ins Internet einloggen und shoppen muss, um ein bisschen Befriedigung zu verspüren? Und was macht eigentlich der phallische Riesenkaktus da? Vergesst Männer, Kinder und Haushalt – Frauen shoppen nur, um mal richtig abzugehen.

### I Can't Get No Satisfaction

Et c'est reparti. On ressort la bonne vieille thématique sexuelle pour vendre. Merveilleuse mode? Cette femme s'est-elle ennuyée au lit au point de se rabattre sur le shopping en ligne pour se satisfaire? Et puis c'est quoi, ce cactus phallique géant? Que les hommes, les gosses et le ménage aillent au diable... les femmes n'achètent que pour le plaisir.

▶ *BlueFly*

satisfaction guaranteed.

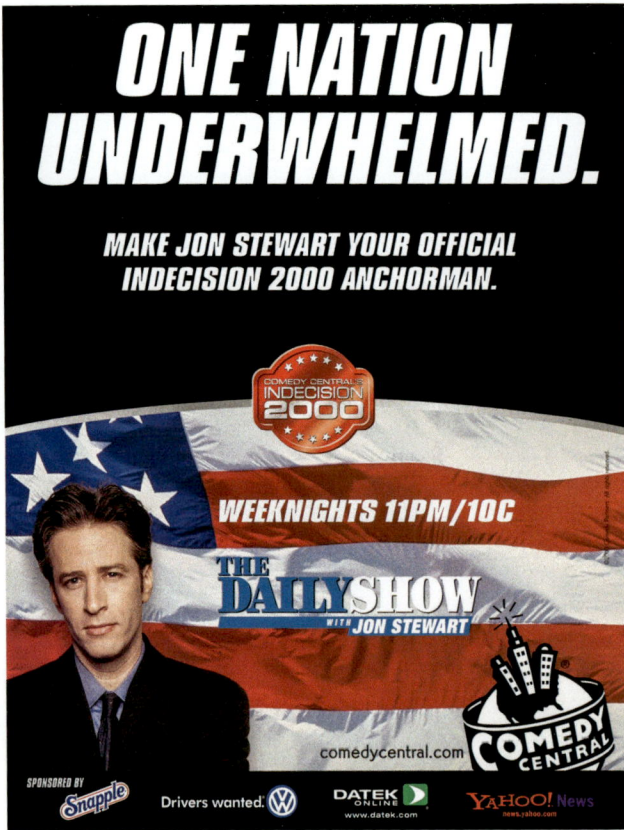

The Daily Show, *2000*

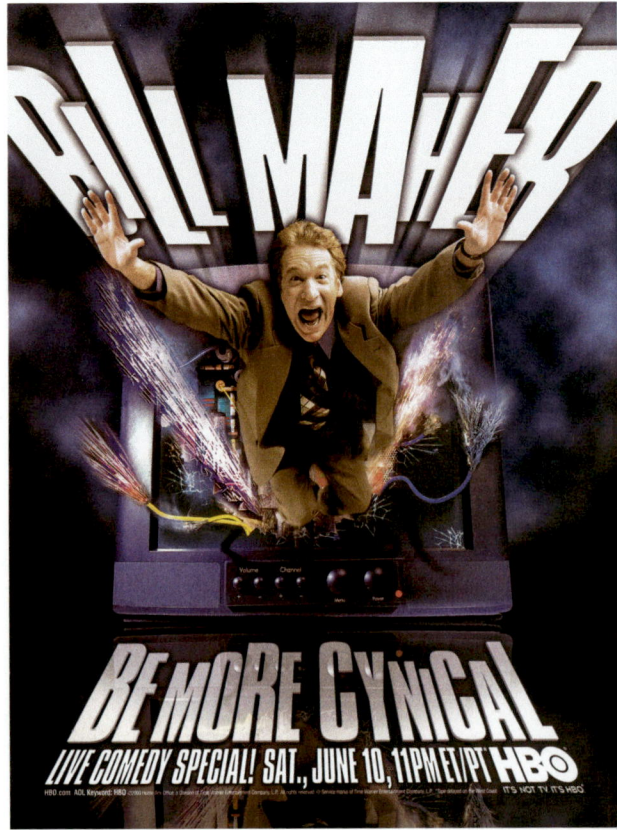

Bill Maher: Be More Cynical, *2000*

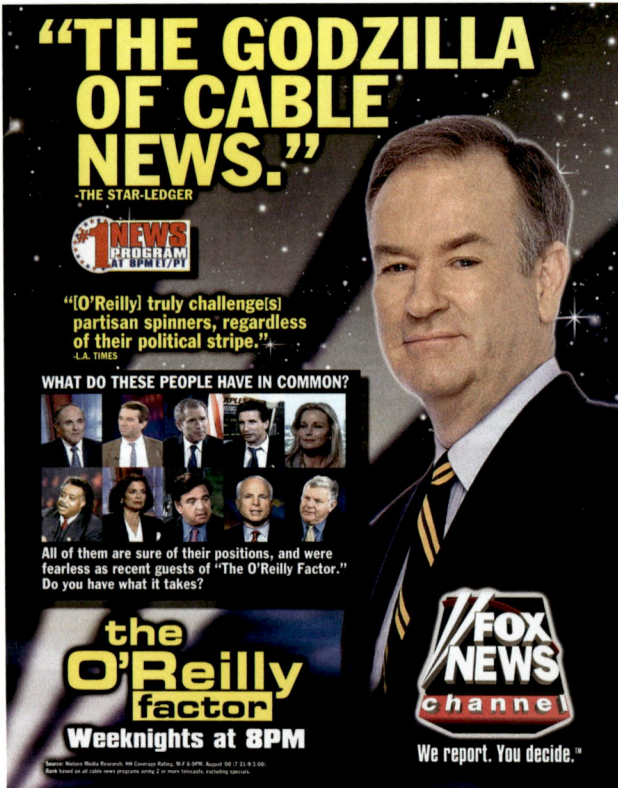

Sesame Street, *2000* ◄   The O'Reilly Factor, *2000*

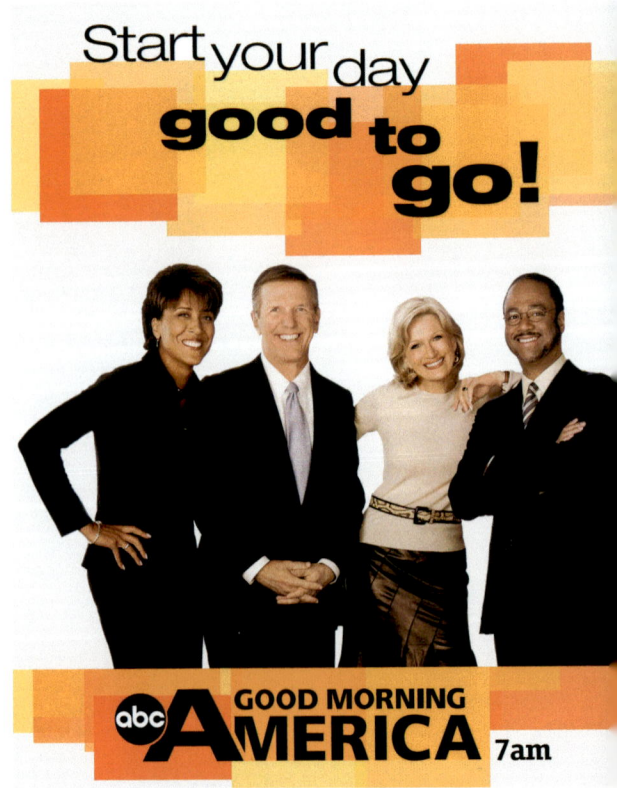

Good Morning America, *2000*

# LIGHTS. CAMERA. PRESSURE.

# WIN OR GO HOME.

## NBA PLAYOFFS START APRIL 22

*NBA Playoffs, 2000*

South Park, *2000*

Get Ready.

new episodes
**south park**
WED NOV 6 10PM|9c

COMEDY CENTRAL®
comedycentral●com

jackass

The name speaks for itself.

Hosted & co-produced by **Johnny Knoxville**

Featuring **pranks, jackass antics, stupidity and plenty of poo.**

premiering **SUNDAY OCTOBER 1** at **9pm**

**only on mtv.**

Jackass, *2000*

Queer As Folk, *2000*

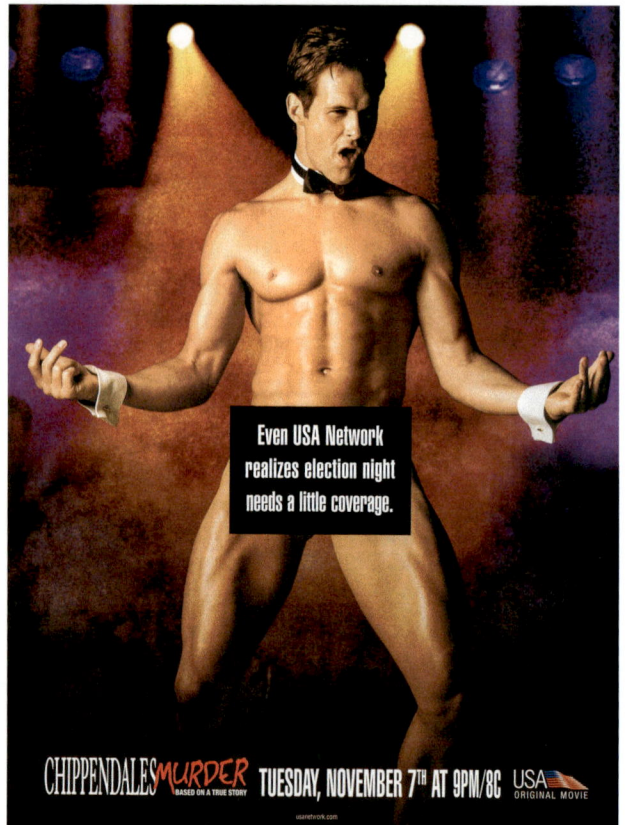

Even USA Network realizes election night needs a little coverage.

Chippendales Murder, *2000*

THE NAKED CHEF

**food** NETWORK

premiering saturday,
november 4th 9:30pm et/pt

To see more on the Naked Chef visit *foodtv.com*

If you do not receive Food Network, call your local cable operator or satellite dealer for details.
©2000 Television Food Network, G.P. All Rights Reserved.

The Naked Chef, *2000*

Ellen DeGeneres: The Beginning, 2000

From Martha's Kitchen, 2000

Wolfgang Puck, 2001

Boston Legal, 2005

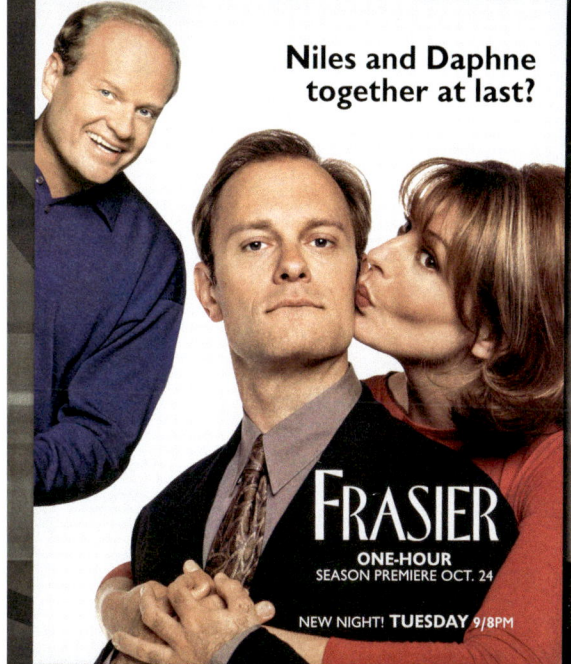
Frasier, 2000

▶ Sex and the City, 2000

Ready

FROM EXECUTIVE PRODUCER DARREN STAR

EVERY SUNDAY AT 9PM/8C

ENCORE PLAYS TUESDAY 11PM/10C

THE COMPLETE FIRST SEASON ON VIDEOCASSETTE AND DVD, AVAILABLE WHEREVER VIDEOS ARE SOL

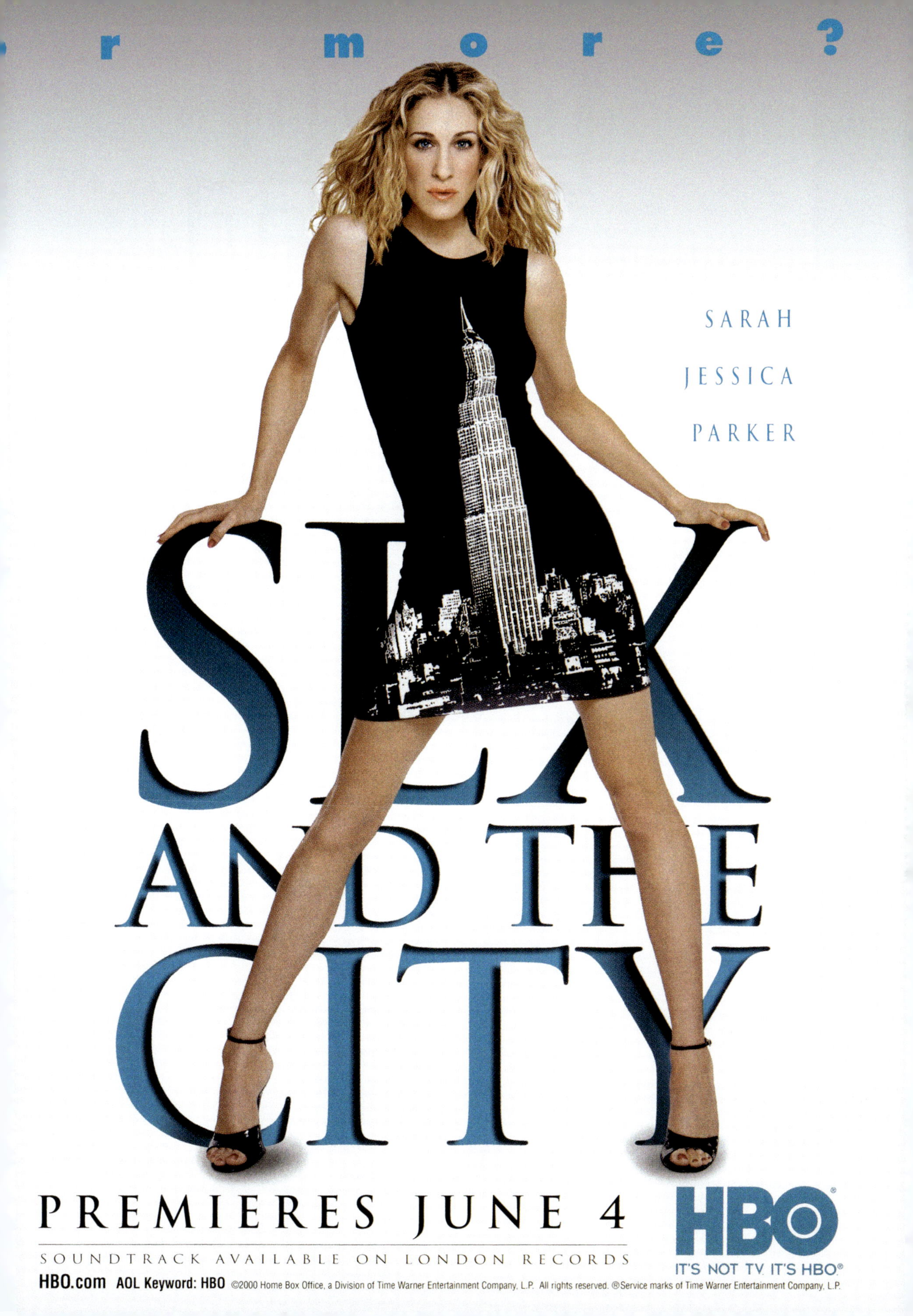
r more?
SARAH JESSICA PARKER
SEX AND THE CITY
PREMIERES JUNE 4
SOUNDTRACK AVAILABLE ON LONDON RECORDS
HBO
IT'S NOT TV. IT'S HBO®
HBO.com AOL Keyword: HBO
©2000 Home Box Office, a Division of Time Warner Entertainment Company, L.P. All rights reserved. ®Service marks of Time Warner Entertainment Company, L.P.

...nd Theft Auto: Vice City, 2002 ◄

*Ultimate Fighting Championship, 2001* ► The Sopranos, *2004*

Hell hath no fury like the family.

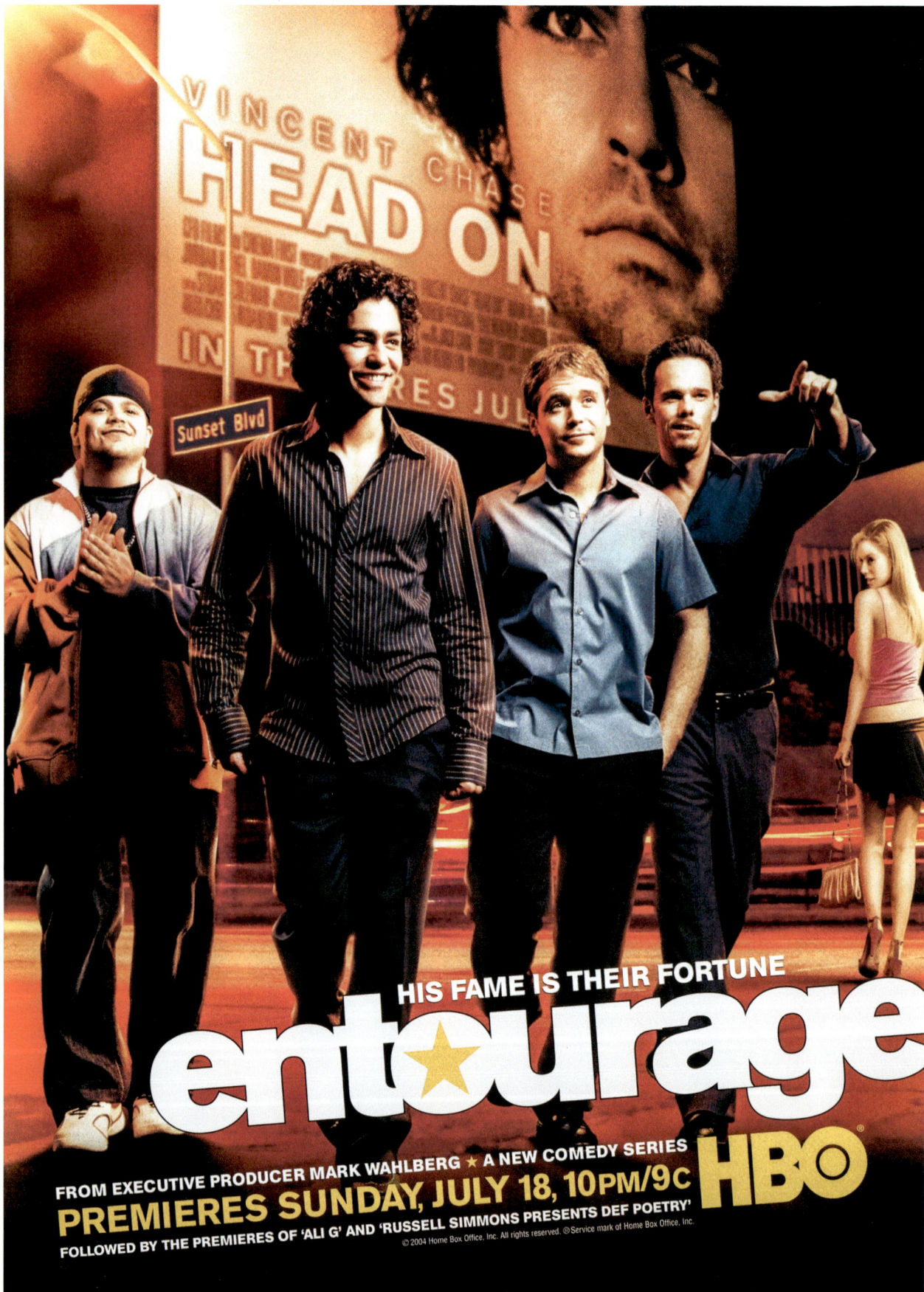

*Entourage, 2004*

**TV with Teeth**

Put the bite on your Sunday night. Go dangerously close to five ferocious shows about wild animals, and even wilder people who love looking danger in the face.

8:00 Great African Wildlife Rescues

8:30 Vets in the Wild

9:00 **THE CROCODILE HUNTER**

10:00 O'Shea's Big Adventure

10:30 Aquanauts

**SUNDAYS 8-11pm** ET/PT

**Animal Planet**

Check out Animal Planet at discovery.com

Call your local cable or satellite company and growl for ANIMAL PLANET

©2000 DCI

*Animal Planet, 2000*

X Games, *2001*

Six Feet Under, *2001*

The Osbournes, 2002

Oz, 2003

Skin, 2003

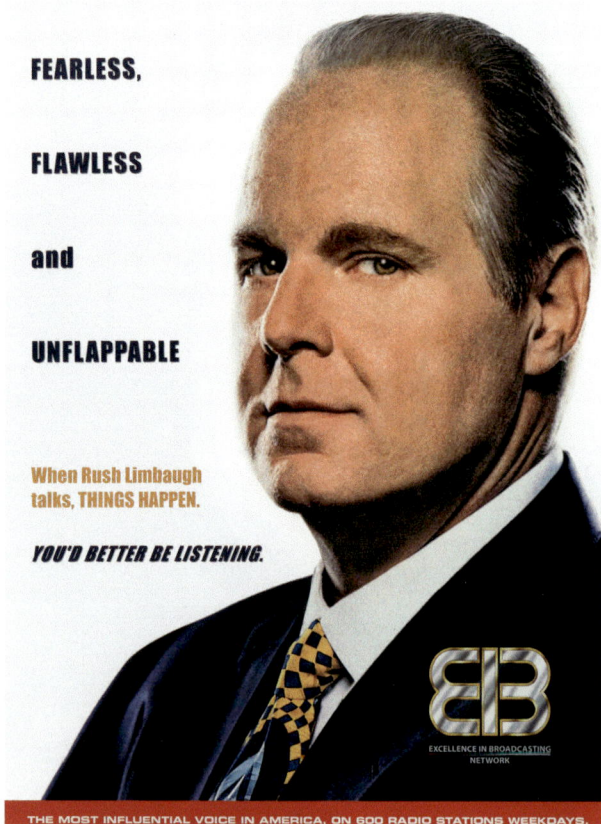

The Rush Limbaugh Show, *2003*

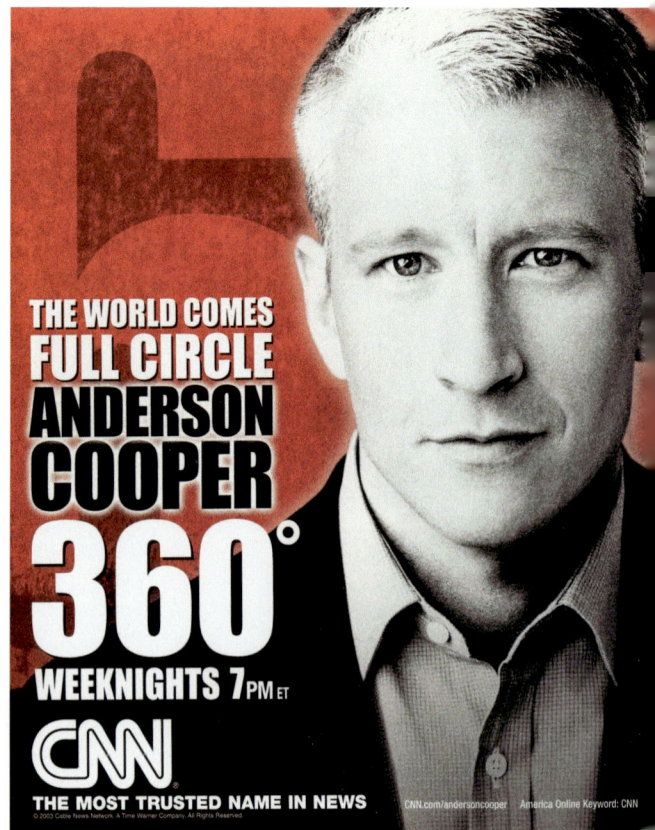

Anderson Cooper 360°, *2003*

Jimmy Kimmel Live, *2003*

# Aha!

## The Power of a Moment.

The **Oprah Winfrey** Show

LIVE YOUR BEST LIFE

WWW.OPRAH.COM

The Oprah Winfrey Show, *2002*

*NBC News, 2000*

*dingTree, 2003*

*Dr. Phil, 2003*

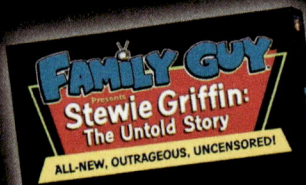

Family Guy, 2005

ANIMATION DOMINATION

Surrender your Sundays!

MATT GROENING

KING OF THE HILL   Malcolm in the Middle   THE SIMPSONS   FAMILY GUY   AMERICAN DAD!

THE NEW FOX SUNDAY BEGINS MAY 1ST
FOX

*Ultimate Fighting Championship, 2001*

*Ripley's Believe It or Not, 2001*

*The Man Show, 2005*

*QVC, 2005*

The Rebel Billionaire: Branson's Quest for the Best, *2004*

...mes, 2004

Lost, 2006

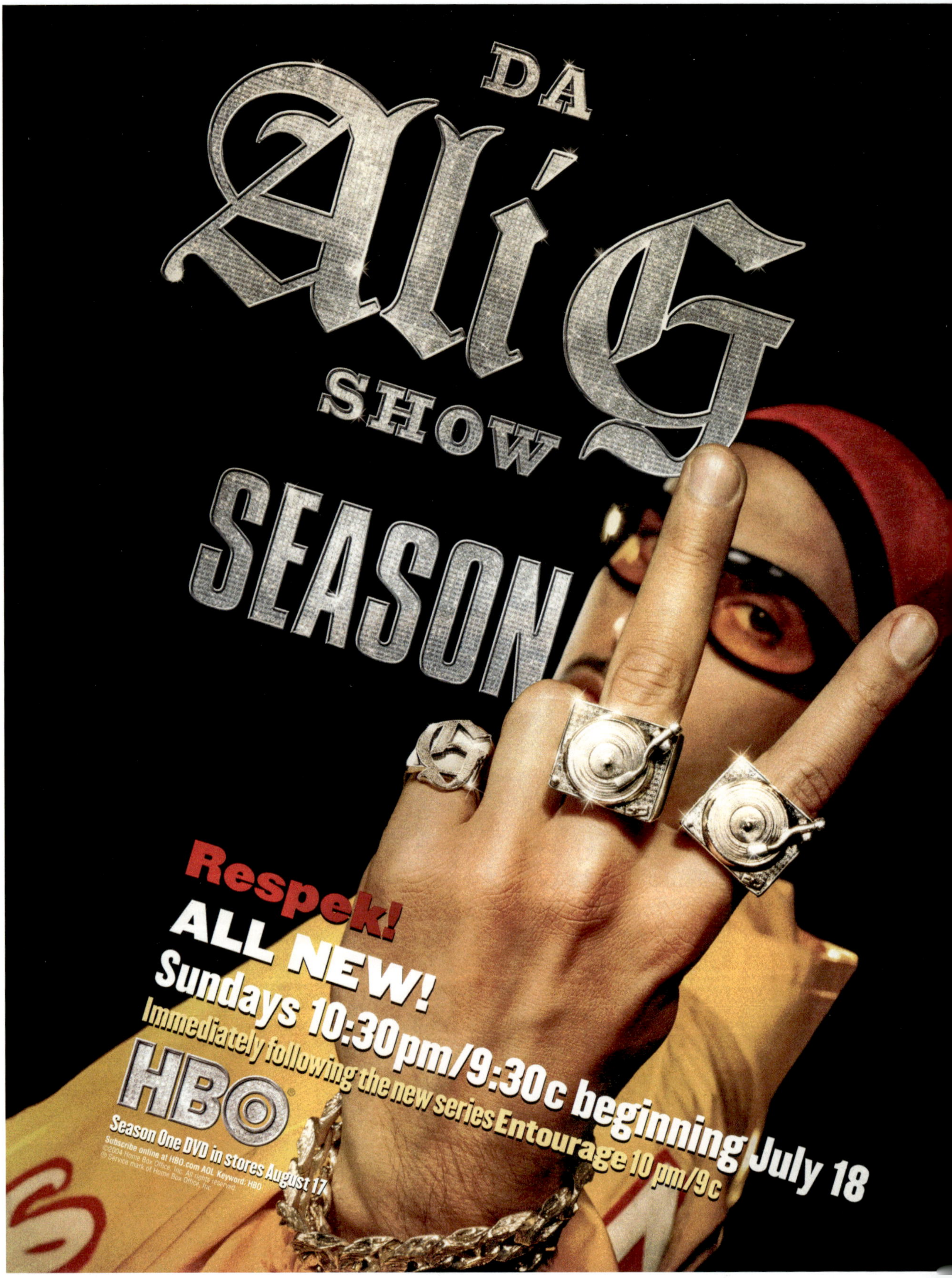


Da Ali G Show, *2004*

Chris Rock: Never Scared, *2004*

Wanda Does It, 2004

Dave Chapelle: Killin' Them Softly, 2009

Strictly Sex With Dr. Drew, 2005

Grammy Awards, 2004

SEE SNOOP AT THE
*Projekt Revolution*
TOUR

ACCESS
TO THE
SHOW
SWEEPSTAKES

GRAND PRIZE-
HANG WITH SNOOP

Snoop Dogg

BROUGHT TO YOU BY
MLB AUTHENTIC COLLECTION
AND FINISH LINE
THE ONLY PLACE
TO GET EXCLUSIVE
ARGYLE JERSEYS

1st   prize (1) attend all
      '04 World Series® games

2nd   prize (1) flat screen tv, dvd dream system,
      computer & mp3 player

3rd   prize (25) MLB™ memorabilia
      signed by the bands

4th   prize (100) $50 Finish Line gift cards

ENTER AT ANY ONE OF OUR
550+ FINISH LINE STORES

finish line

www.finishline.com

*See store for details. No purchase necessary.
MLB trademarks and copyrights are used with permission of
Major League Properties Inc. Visit the official website at MLB.com

MLB Authentic
COLLECTION
ACCESS TO THE SHOW™

*Projekt Revolution, 2004*

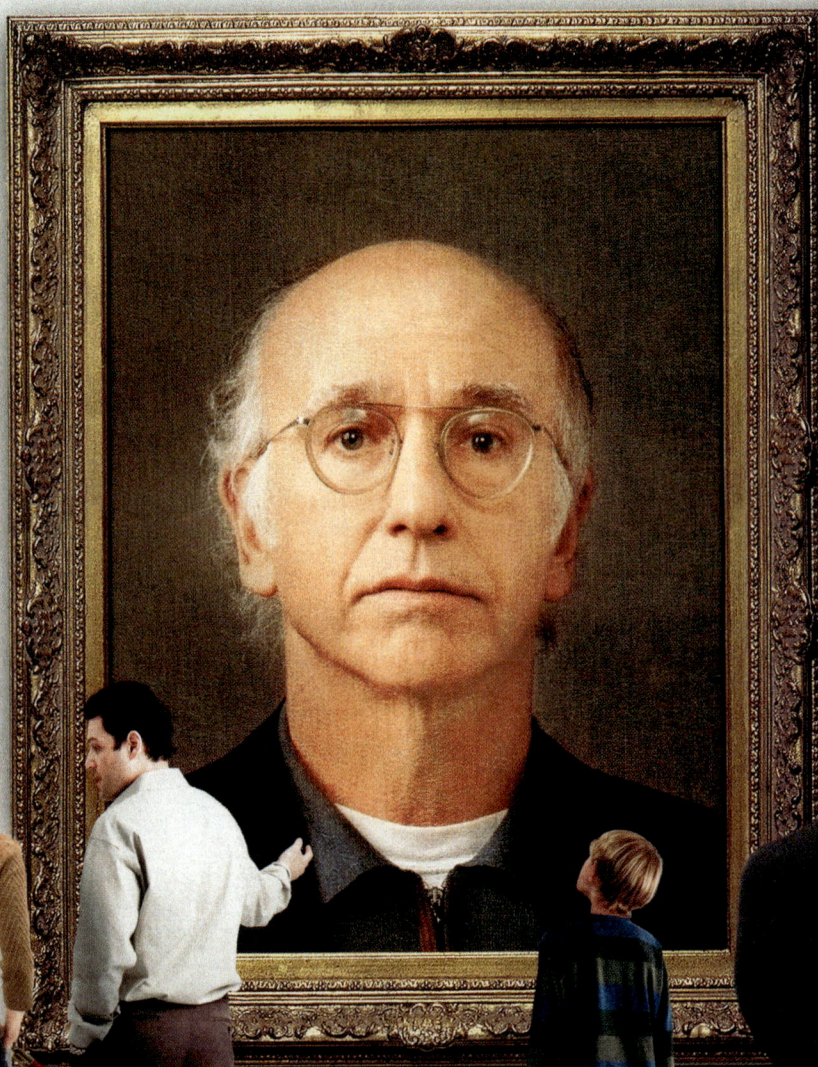

Curb Your Enthusiasm, *2007*

The New Adventures of Old Christine, *2006*

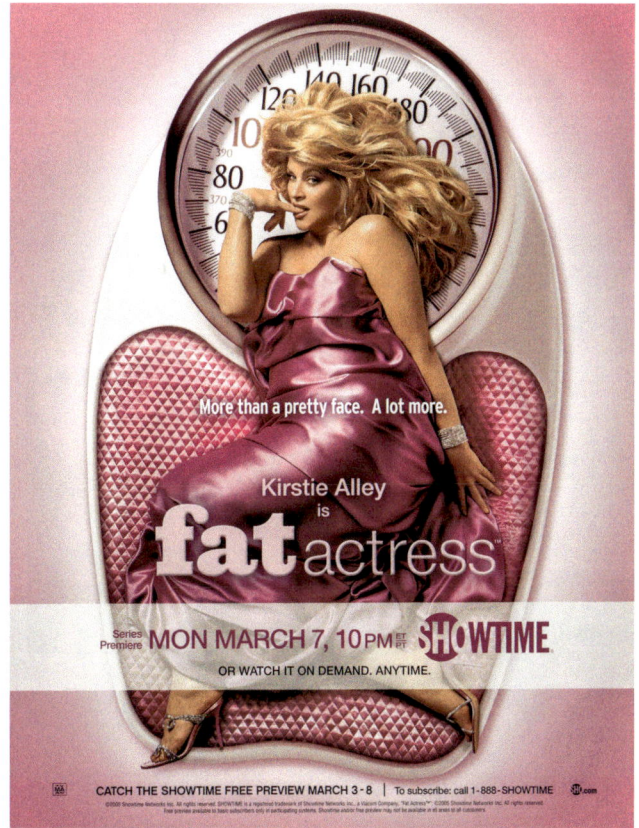
Fat Actress, *2005*

Two and A Half Men, *2005*

American Chopper, *2007*

THE NEW SEASON
# CSI:
CRIME SCENE INVESTIGATION

THURSDAYS 9/8c ◉CBS

©2005 CBS Broadcasting Inc.

cbs.com

CSI: Crime Scene Investigation, *2005*

Desperate Housewives, 2005

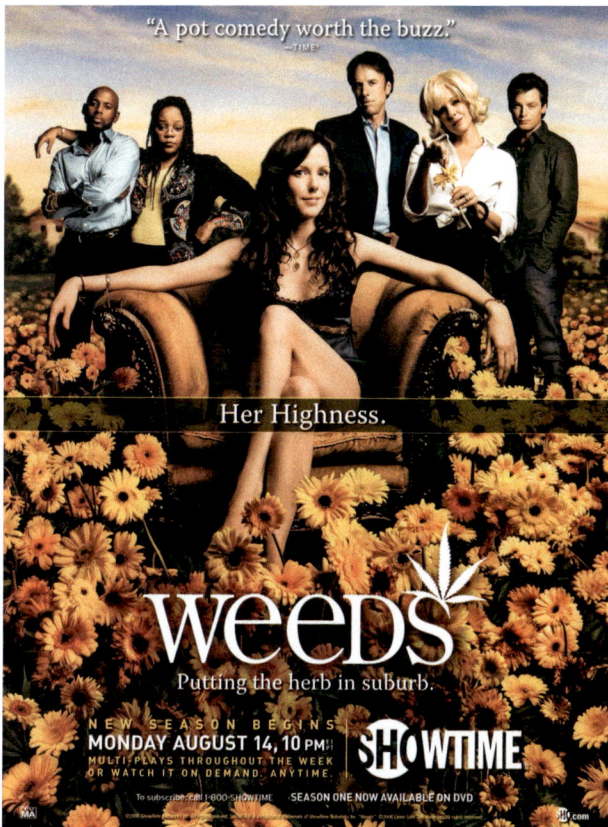

Weeds, 2006

LA Ink, 2007

30 Rock, 2006

The Wire, 2006

Rome, *2005*

Spartacus, *2010*

Deadwood, 2005

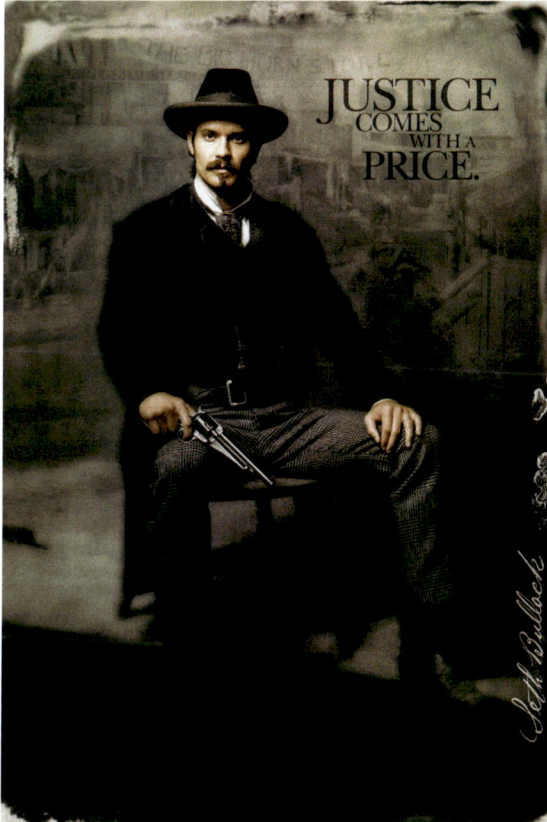

Deadwood, 2005

*NBA All-Star Weekend, 2010*

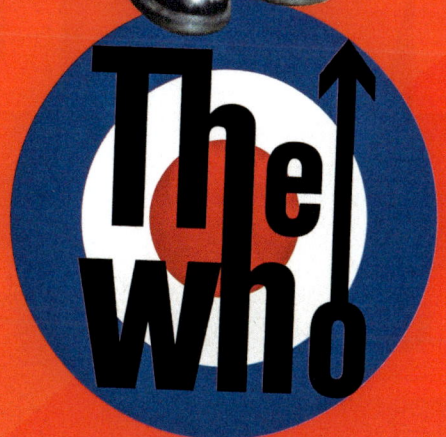

Bridgestone Super Bowl XLIV Halftime Show, *2010*

"TV'S BEST SHOW"
- ROLLING STONE

MAD MEN

EMMY® AND GOLDEN GLOBE® WINNER FOR BEST TV DRAMA

Presented by
BMW
The Ultimate
Driving Machine®

Premieres August 16
Sundays 10p/9c

aMC
amctv.com

© 2009 American Movie Classics Company, LLC.

SONS OF ANARCHY

SEASON 2

SEPT 8
TUES 10
FX
THERE IS NO BOX™

Available on FX HD FXnetworks.com

*Sons of Anarchy, 2009*

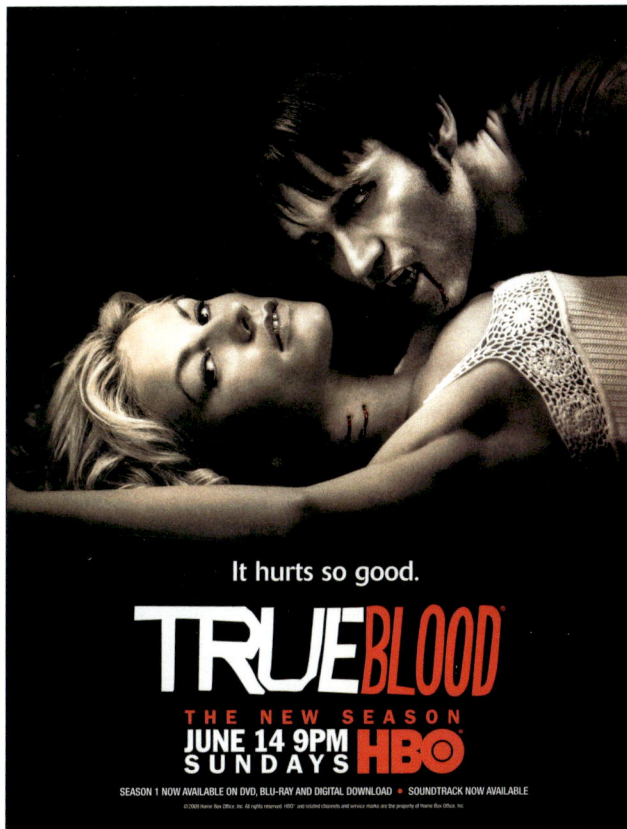

True Blood, 2009

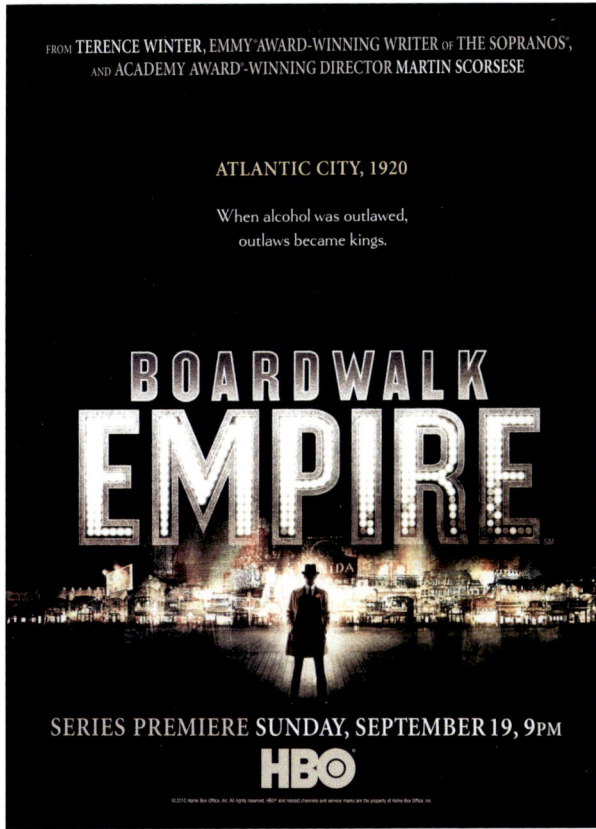

Boardwalk Empire, 2010

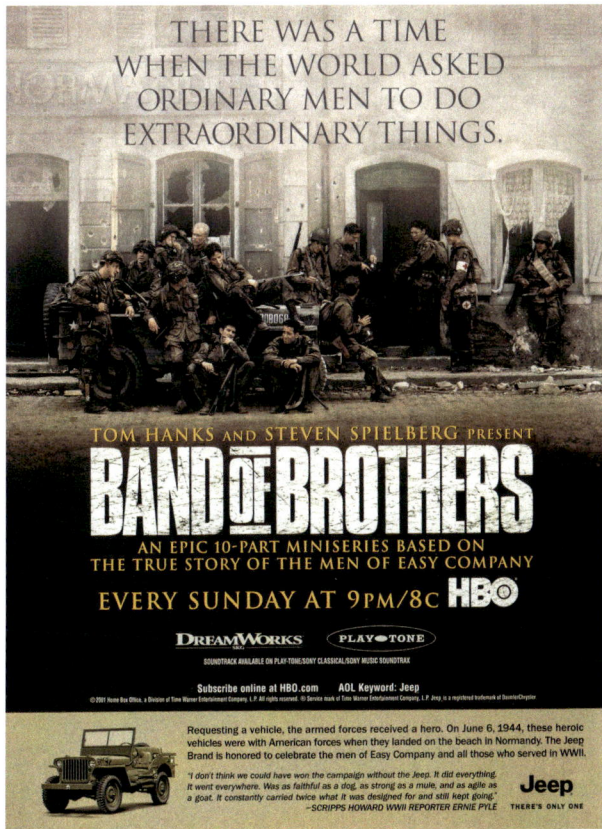

Band of Brothers, 2001

Six Feet Under, 2005

Fuse, 2008

Louie, 2010

Glee, 2010

**music is rebellion.**

**fuse**

www.fuse.tv

*Fuse, 2008*

Can you believe they're all related? Neither can they.

modern family

abc
COMEDY
wednesday
premieres september 23rd 9/8c
Watch an extended preview at abc.com/ModernFamily

Modern Family, *2009*

It's Always Sunny in Philadelphia, 2009

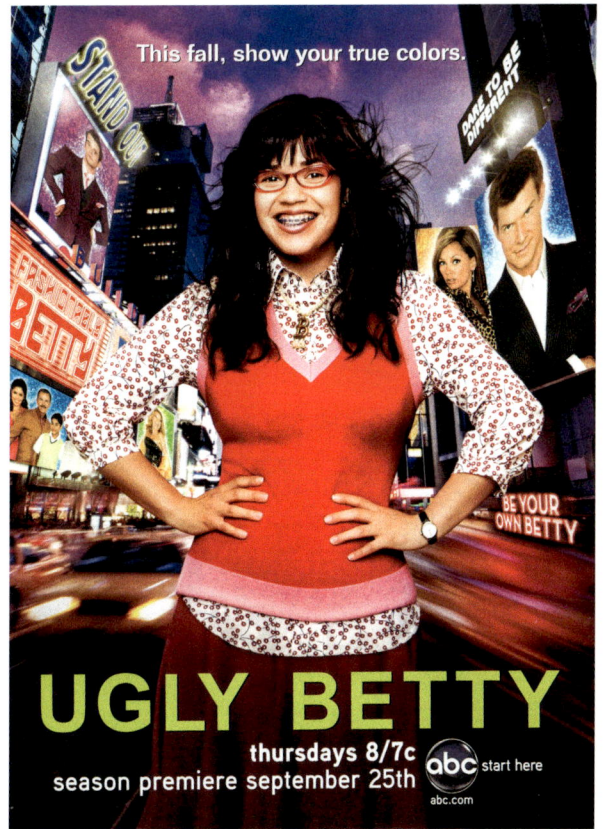

Ugly Betty, 2008

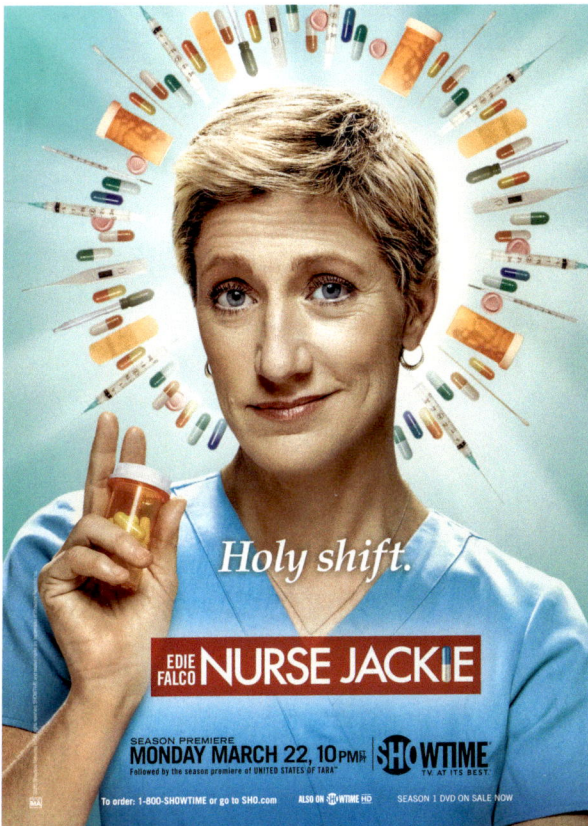

Nurse Jackie, 2010

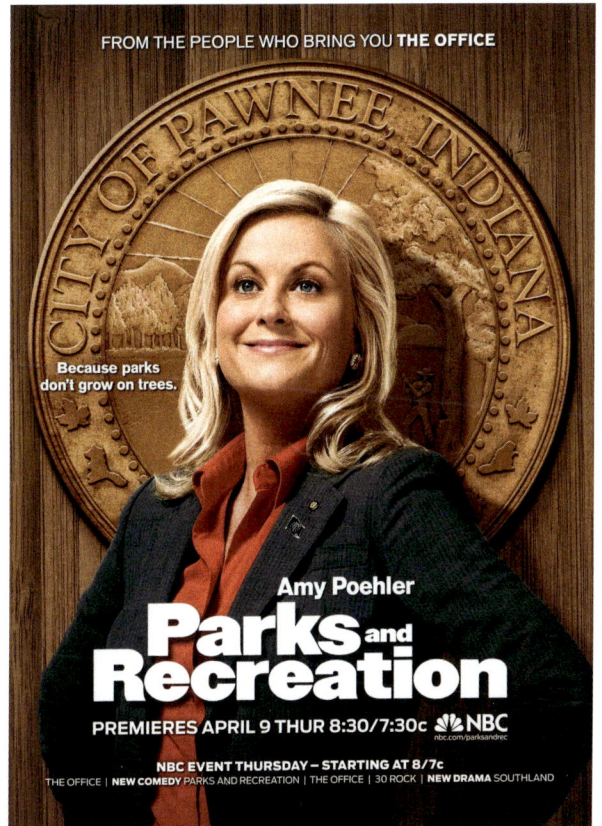

Parks and Recreation, 2009

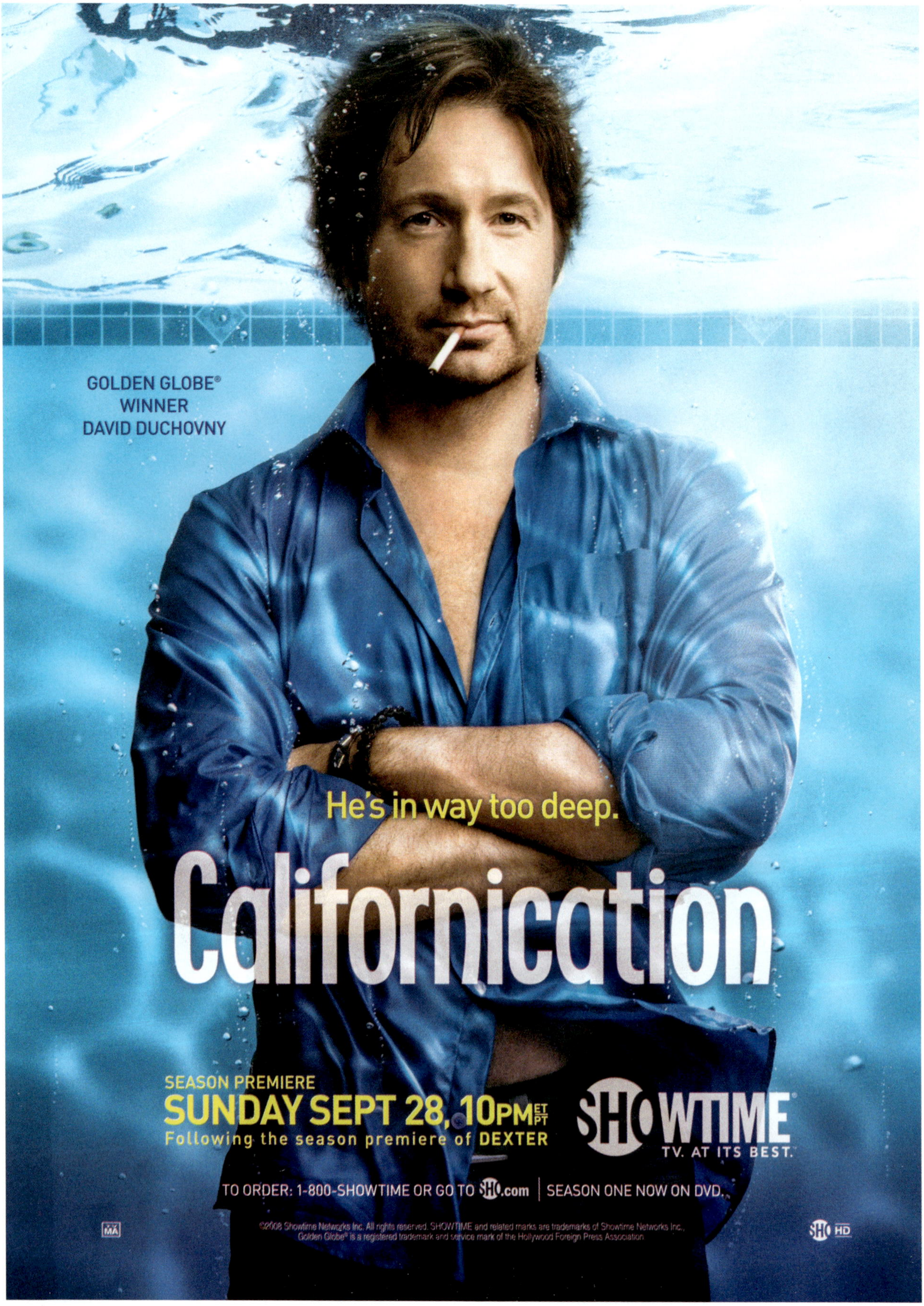


Californication, *2008*

Change [the] Equation

**BReaking**
**Bad**

eries Premiere Jan 20 Sundays 10pm/9c aMC
amctv.com

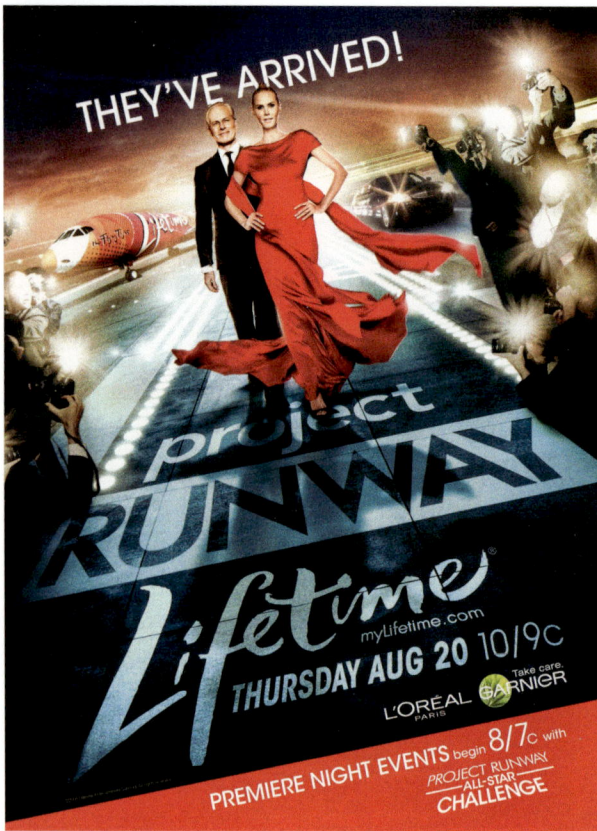

Project Runway, 2009

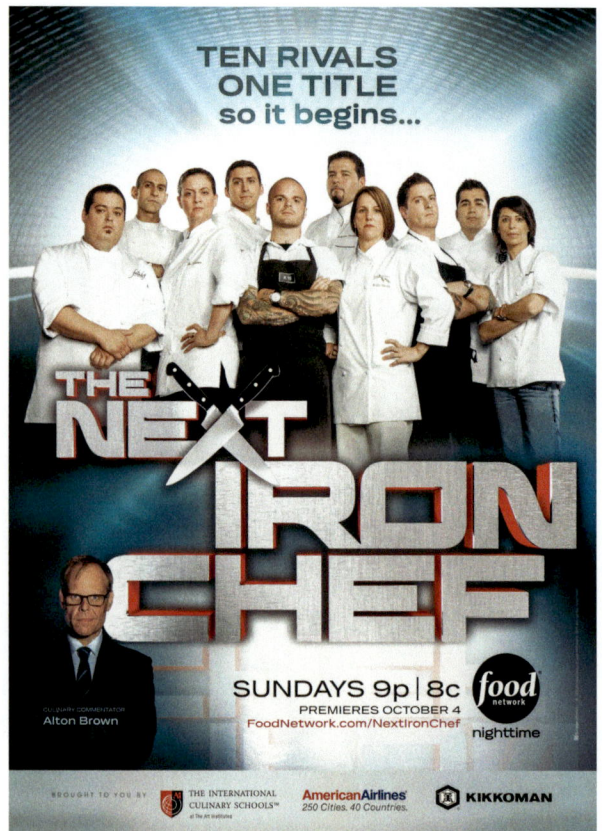

The Next Iron Chef, 2009

American Idol, 2009

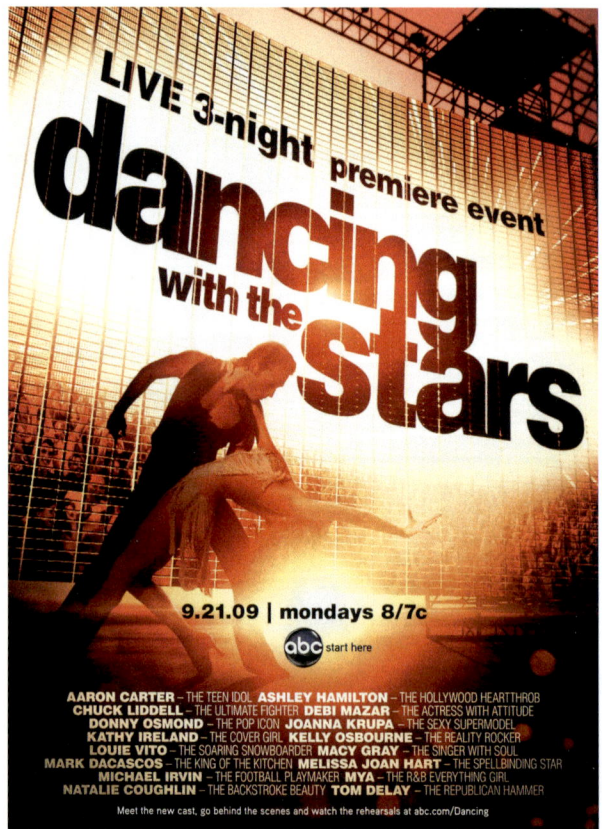

Dancing with the Stars, 2009

The Bachelorette, 2009

Storage Wars, 2010

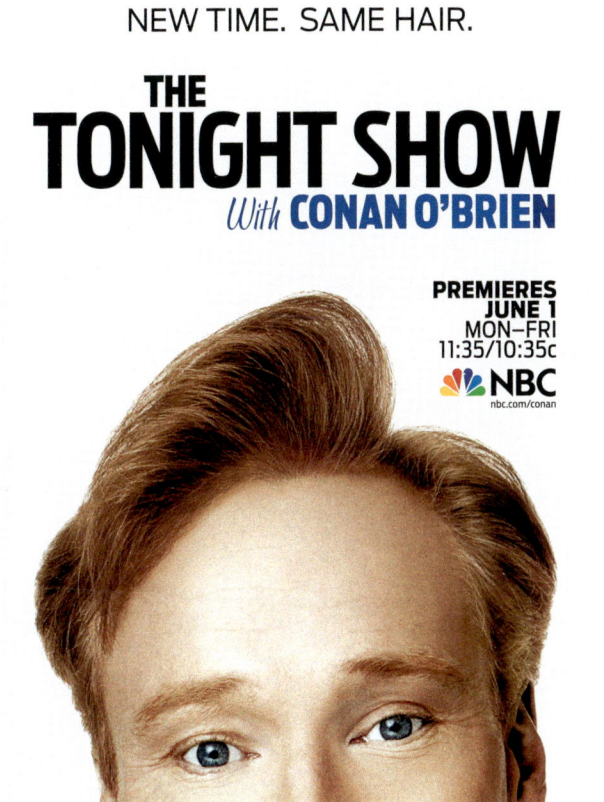
The Tonight Show with Conan O'Brien, 2009

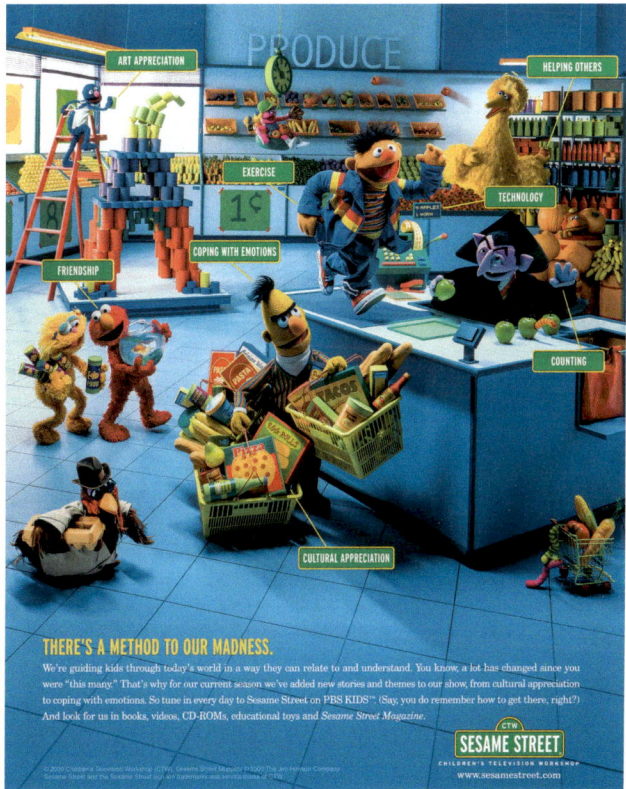
Sesame Street, 2000

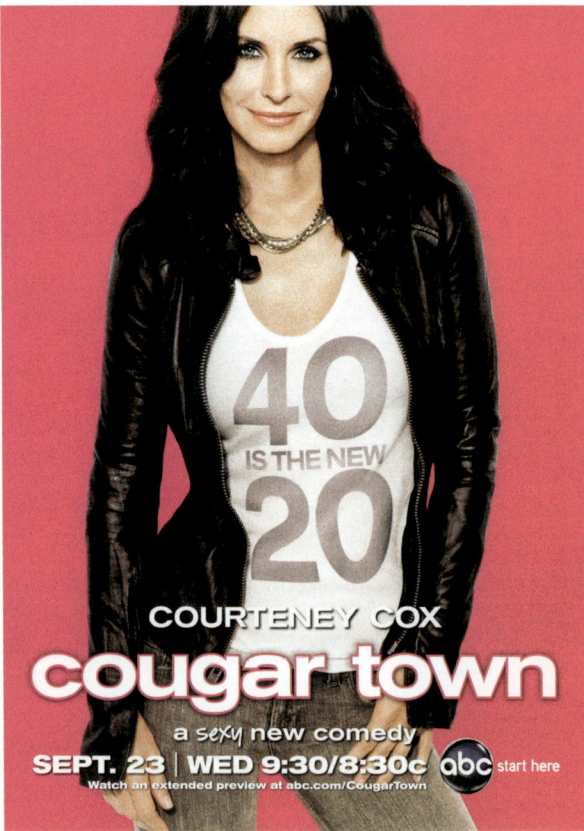

Cougar Town, 2009

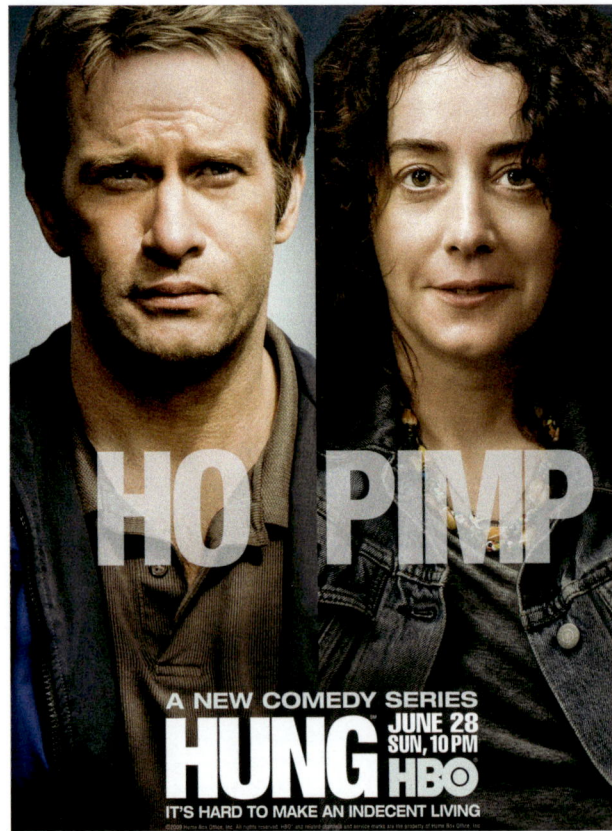

Hung, 2009

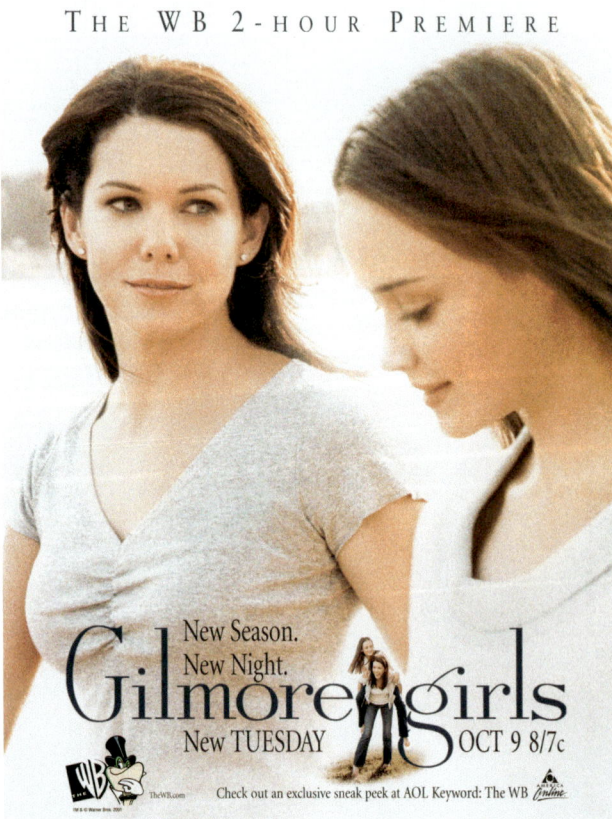

Gilmore Girls, 2009

AbsolutePoker.net, 2009

I Want to Work for Diddy, *2008*

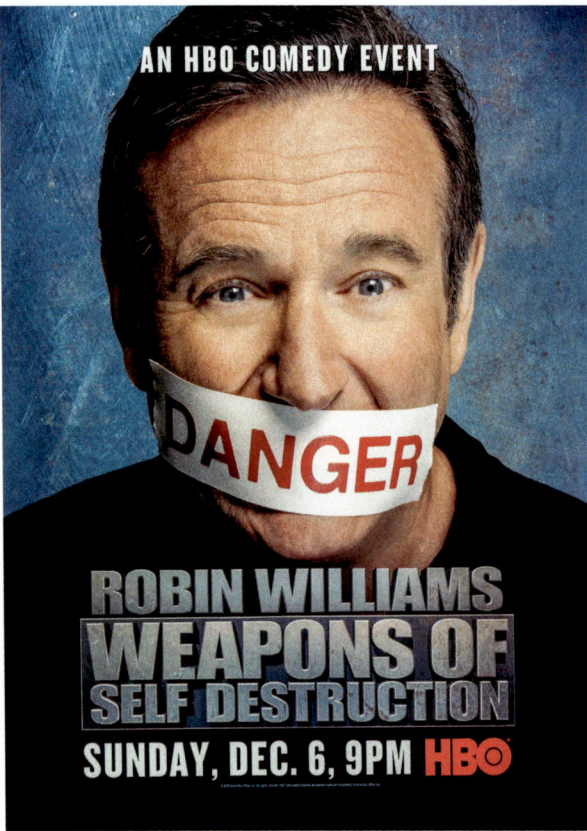

Robin Williams: Weapons of Self Destruction, 2009

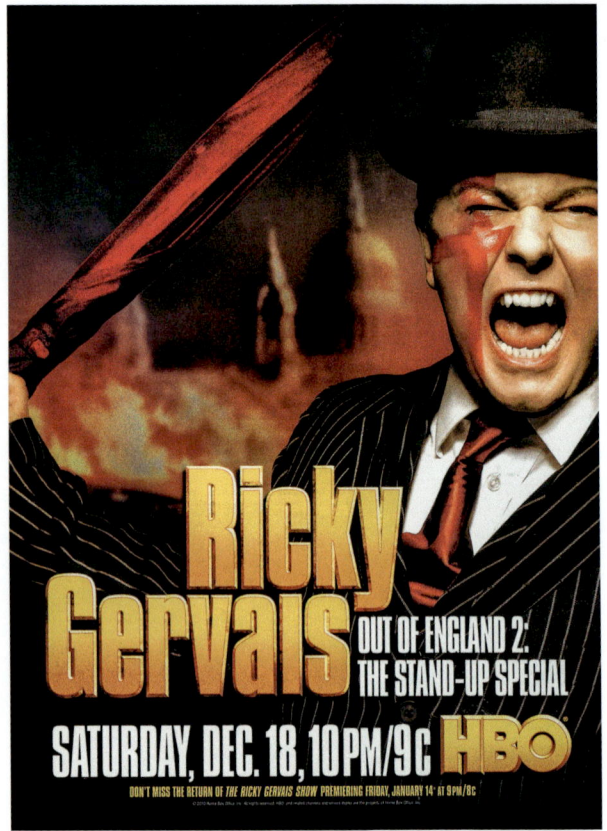

Ricky Gervais: Out of England 2, 2010

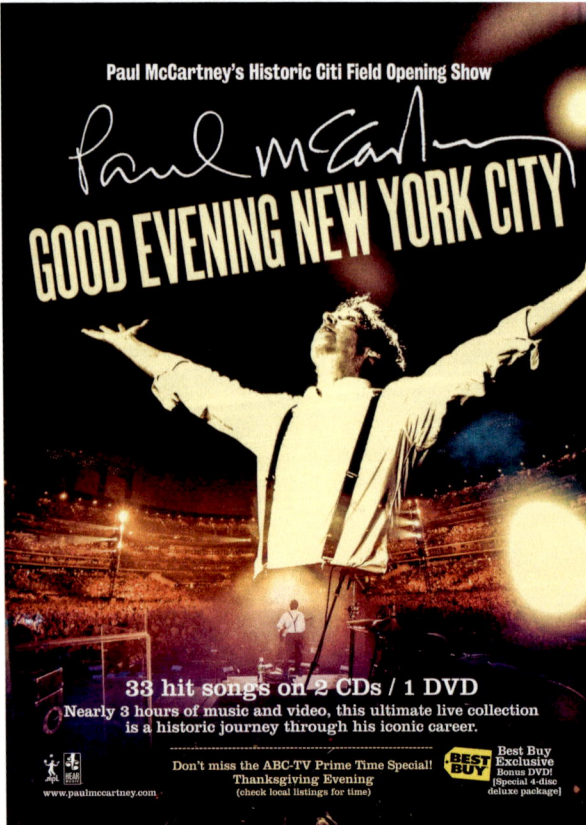

Paul McCartney, 2009

Sunday Night Football, 2008

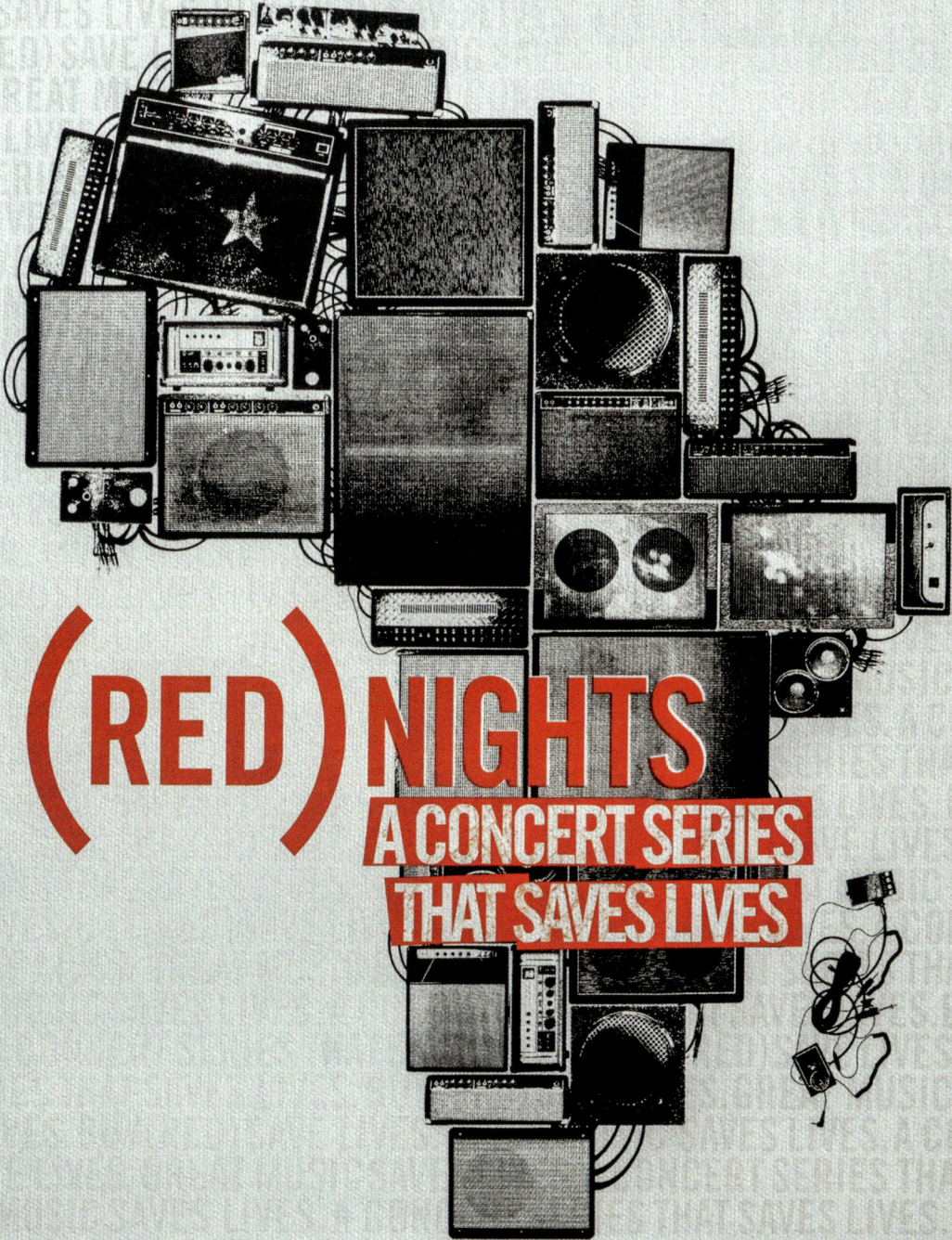

(Red) Nights, 2009

PARAMOUNT VANTAGE PROUDLY CONGRATULATES

CATE BLANCHETT

2006 WOMEN IN HOLLYWOOD AWARD

BABEL

IN SELECT THEATRES OCTOBER 27

www.ParamountVantage.com

PARAMOUNT VANTAGE

Babel, 2006

The Full Monty, 2000

Casino Royale, 2007

The Lord of the Rings: The Fellowship of the Ring, 2002

The Lord of the Rings: The Fellowship of the Ring, 2004

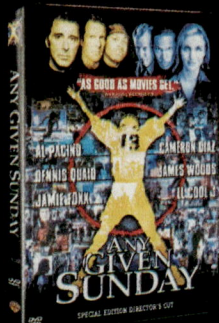
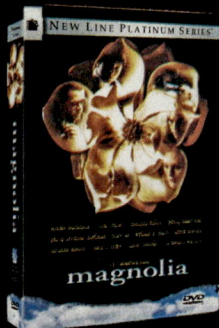
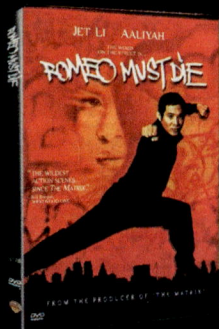
*Netflix, 2000*

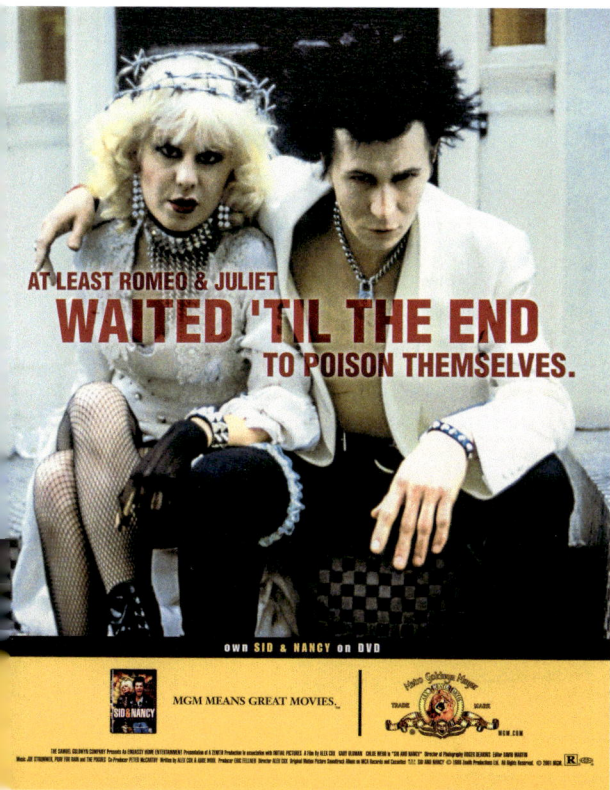

& Nancy, *2001*

Blow, *2001*

e Perfect Storm, *2000*

Madea's Family Reunion, *2006*

EXPLOSIVE ENTERTAINMENT ANY WAY YOU SLICE IT!

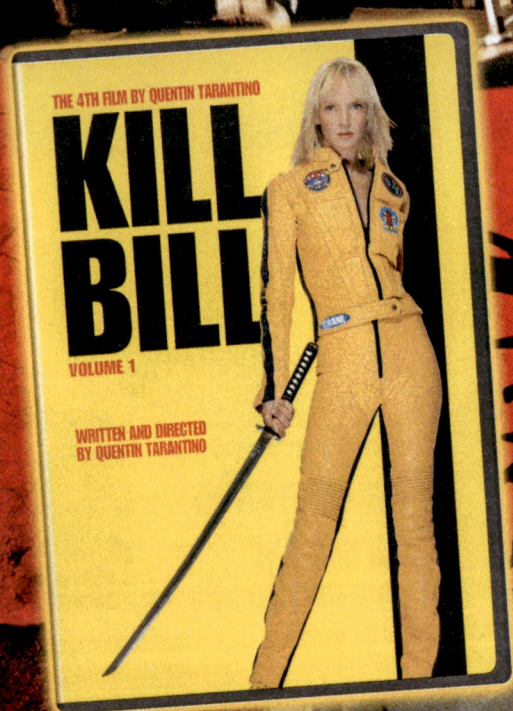

THE 4TH FILM BY QUENTIN TARANTINO

KILL BILL
VOLUME 1

WRITTEN AND DIRECTED BY QUENTIN TARANTINO

OWN THE THRILL
BEFORE THE FINAL KILL

*Volume 1* on DVD April 13th
*Volume 2* in Theaters April 16th

MIRAMAX FILMS PRESENTS A BAND APART A FILM BY QUENTIN TARANTINO UMA THURMAN "KILL BILL" LUCY LIU VIVICA A. FOX MICHAEL MADSEN DARYL HANNAH AND DAVID CARRADINE AS "BILL" GUEST STARRING SONNY CHIBA JULIE DREYFUS CHIAKI KURIYAMA GORDON LIU MICHAEL PARKS MARTIAL ARTS ADVISOR YUEN WOO-PING ORIGINAL MUSIC BY THE RZA EDITED BY SALLY MENKE DIRECTOR OF PHOTOGRAPHY ROBERT RICHARDSON, A.S.C. PRODUCTION DESIGN YOHEI TANEDA DAVID WASCO EXECUTIVE PRODUCERS BOB WEINSTEIN HARVEY WEINSTEIN ERICA STEINBERG E. BENNETT WALSH BASED ON THE CHARACTER OF "THE BRIDE" CREATED BY Q&U PRODUCED BY LAWRENCE BENDER WRITTEN AND DIRECTED BY QUENTIN TARANTINO

R RESTRICTED UNDER 13 REQUIRES ACCOMPANYING PARENT OR ADULT GUARDIAN For Strong Bloody Violence, Language And Some Sexual Content. For rating reasons, go to filmratings.com

A BAND APART

SOUNDTRACK AVAILABLE ON    Kill-Bill.com    Read The Miramax Book

MIRAMAX

Miramax Home Entertainment distributed by Buena Vista Home Entertainment, Inc. Burbank, California 91521. Printed in U.S.A. © Buena Vista Home Entertainment, Inc.

Kill Bill, 2004

▶ Kill Bill: Vol

Monsters vs. Aliens, 2009

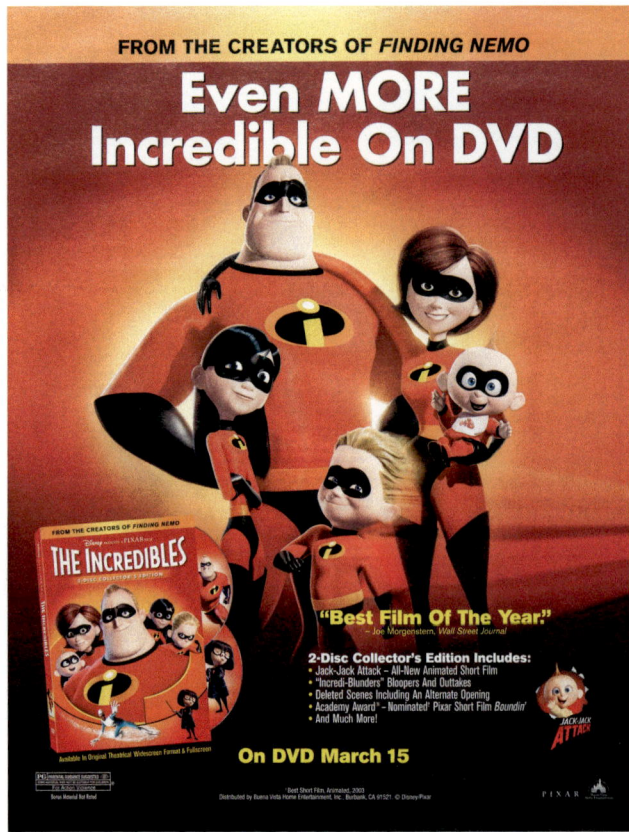

The Incredibles, 2005

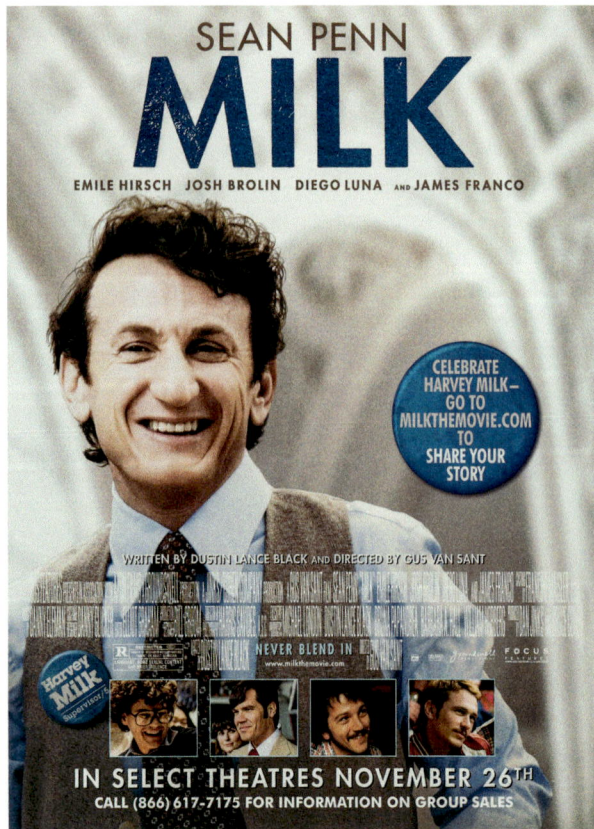

Milk, 2008

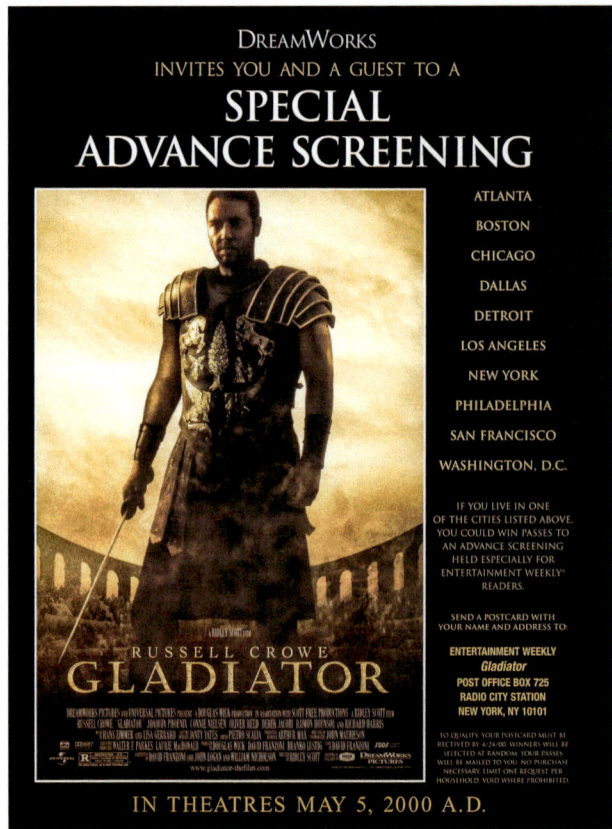

Gladiator, 2000

rnal Sunshine of the Spotless Mind, *2004*

Starsky & Hutch, *2004*

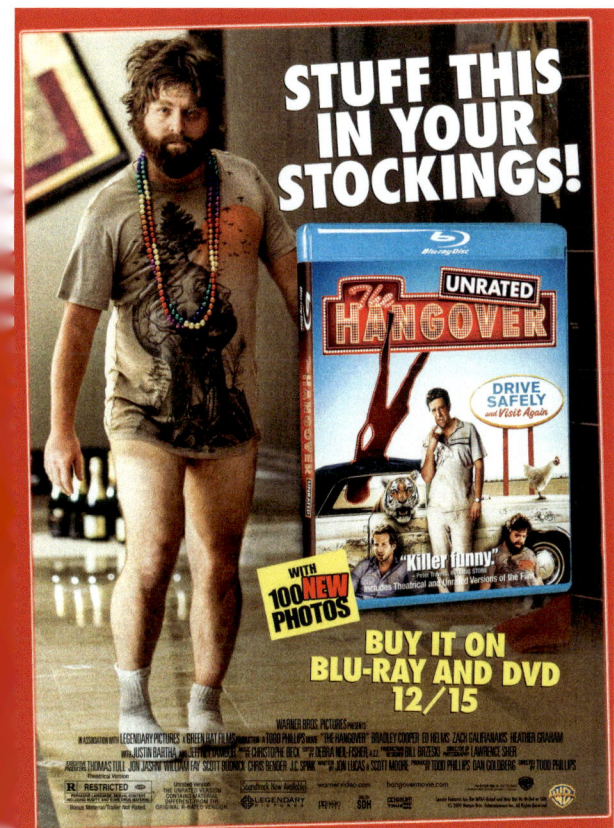

he Hangover, *2009*

Beauty Shop, *2005*

starring in alphabetical order

| GEORGE | MATT | ANDY | BRAD | AND JULIA |
|--------|------|------|------|-----------|
| **CLOONEY** | **DAMON** | **GARCIA** | **PITT** | **ROBERTS** |
| The Idea Man | The Rookie | The Target | The Pro | The Wild Card |

# 12·07·01
## ARE YOU IN OR OUT?

www.oceans11.net   America Online Keyword: Oceans 11

Ocean's 11, 2001

Ocean's 12, 2004

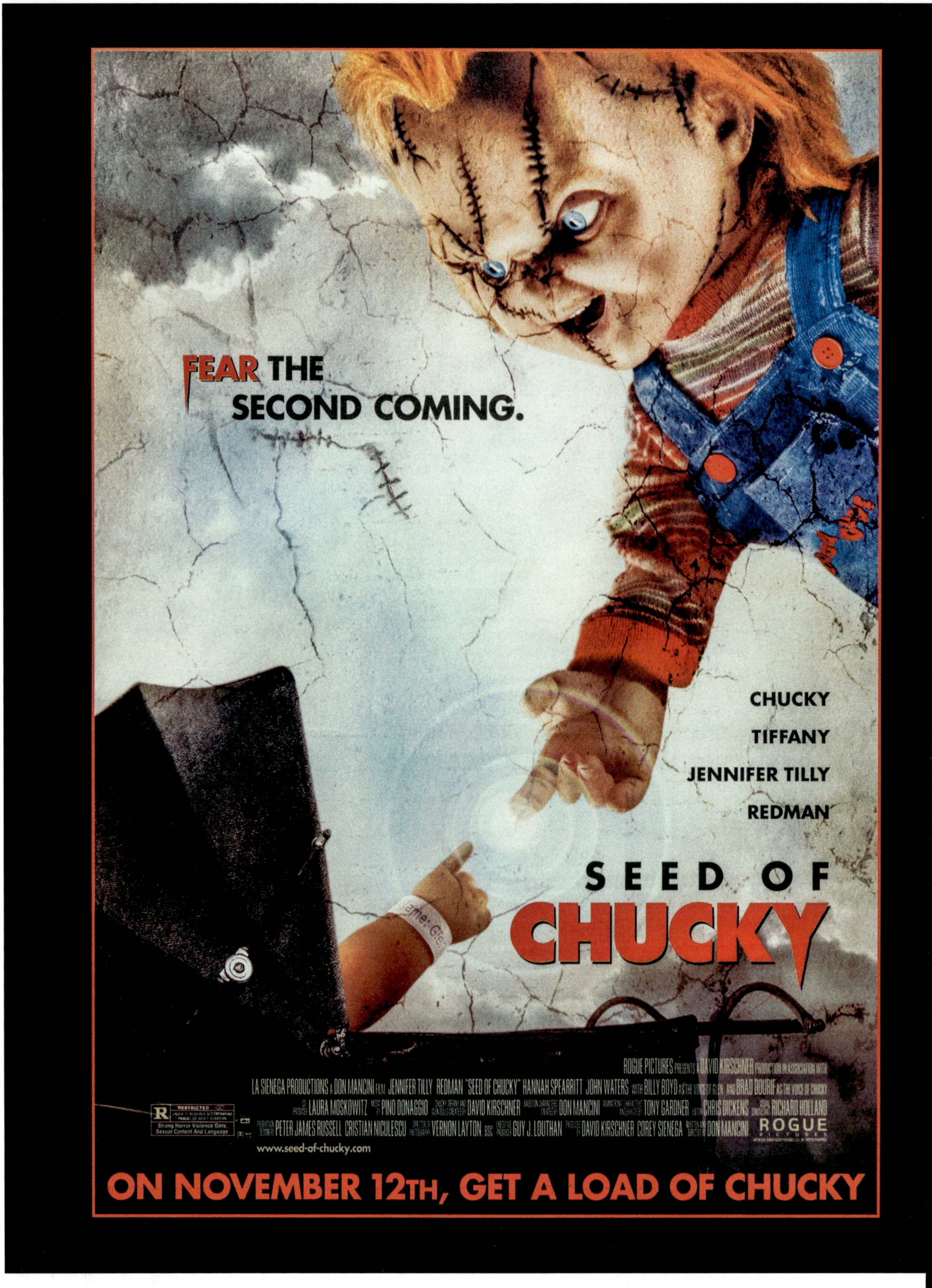


Seed of Chucky, *2004*

Borat, 2007

*NSYNC, 2000*

**BRITNEY SPEARS LIVE FROM LAS VEGAS**

**SUN. NOV.18 8PM ET/PT HBO**®

Look for Britney's new album–*Britney*–
available on Jive Records November 6th

*Britney Spears, 2001*

"DESTINY FULFILLED"

THE HIGHLY ANTICIPATED NEW ALBUM FROM DESTINY'S CHILD

FEATURING THE SCORCHING HITS LOSE MY BREATH AND SOLDIER.

IN STORES NOW.

Album Executive Producers: Mathew Knowles, Beyoncé Knowles, Michelle Williams and Kelly Rowland
destinychild.com  dc-unplugged.com  columbiarecords.com

"Columbia" and ® Reg .U.S. Pat. & Tm. Off. Marca Registrada./© 2004 Sony BMG Music Entertainment. "Sony Urban Music" and ® are trademarks of Sony Corporation.

*Destiny's Child, 2004*

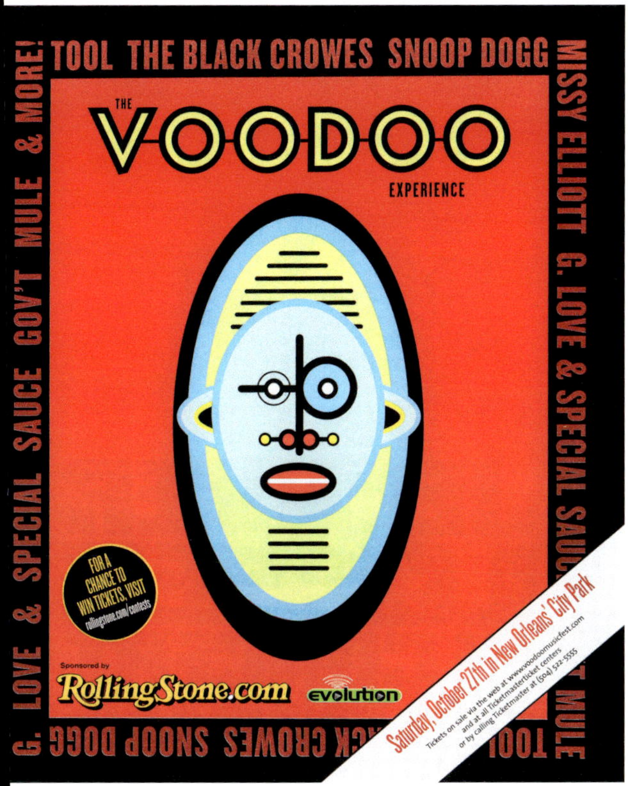

The Voodoo Experience, 2001

Parade, 2004

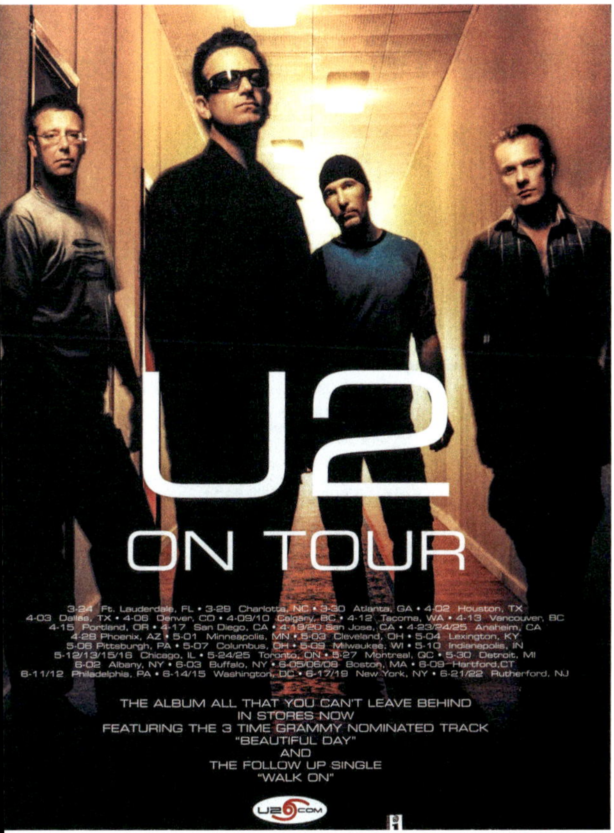

2001

John Mellencamp, 2004

Seal, 2004

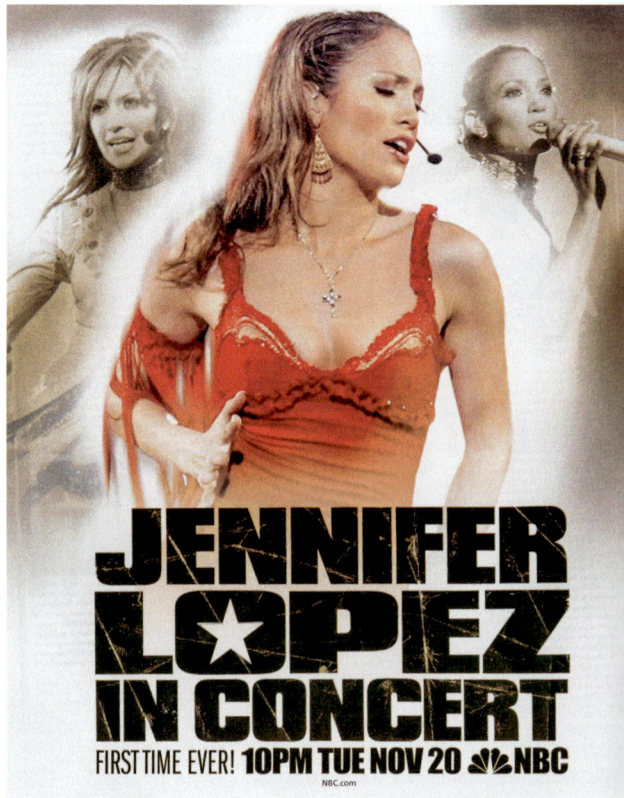
Jennifer Lopez, 2001

Lenny Kravitz, 2004

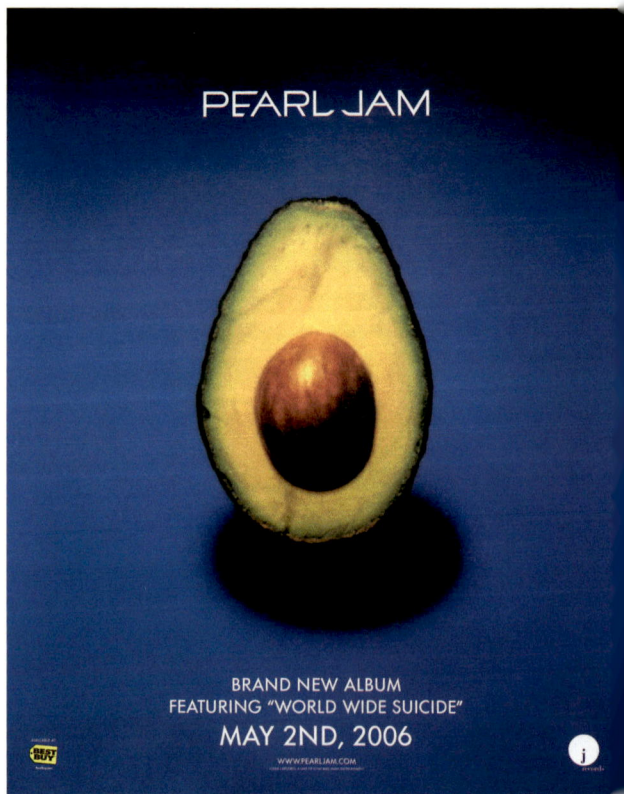
Pearl Jam, 2006

*Tenacious D, 2006*

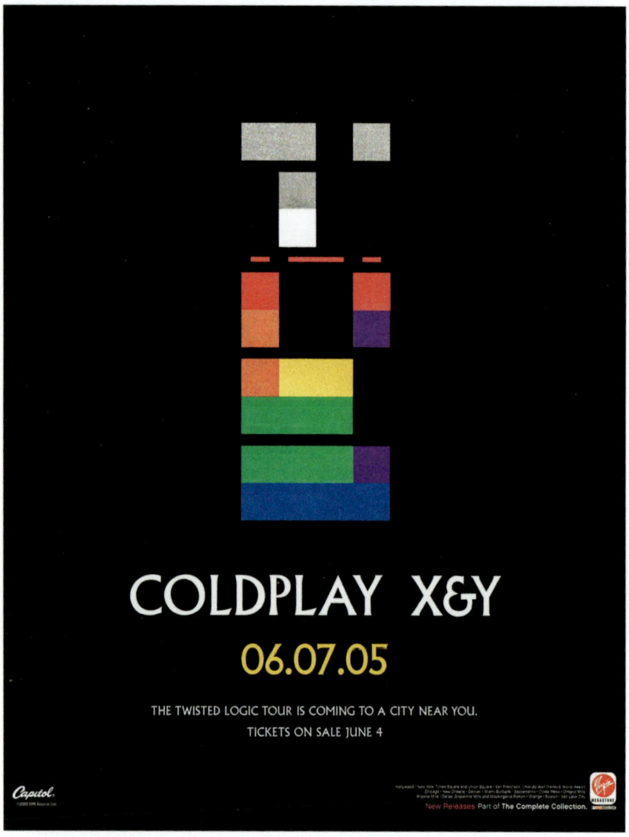

Coldplay, 2005

Jonas Brothers, 2009

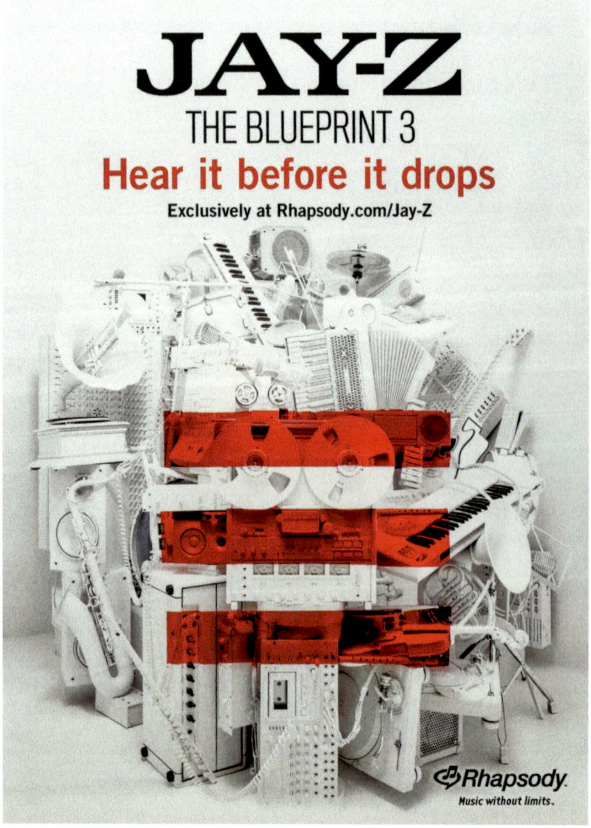

Jay-Z, 2009

Michael Jackson, 2010

**fly**

**Dixie Chicks**

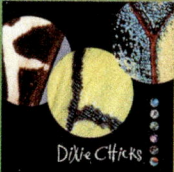

CATCH THE
DIXIE CHICKS
IN THEIR FIRST
TELEVISION
CONCERT SPECIAL
NOVEMBER 20
ON NBC

AVAILABLE AT
TARGET

*Dixie Chicks, 2000*

*E Street Radio, 2009*

Behind the Music, 2009

*MySpace Music, 2008*

AC/DC, 2010

The Black Eyed Peas, 2006

Alicia Keys, 2007

"Weird Al" Yankovich, 2006

Sam Goody, 2000

THERE HAS NEVER BEEN A BAND LIKE THEM.
THERE HAS NEVER BEEN A GAME LIKE THIS.
In stores now. Live on tour 2009.

Guitar Hero, *2008*

Bayonetta, *2010*

Rise to Honor, *2004*

Resident Evil 4, *2005*

Advance Wars: Dual Strike, *2005*

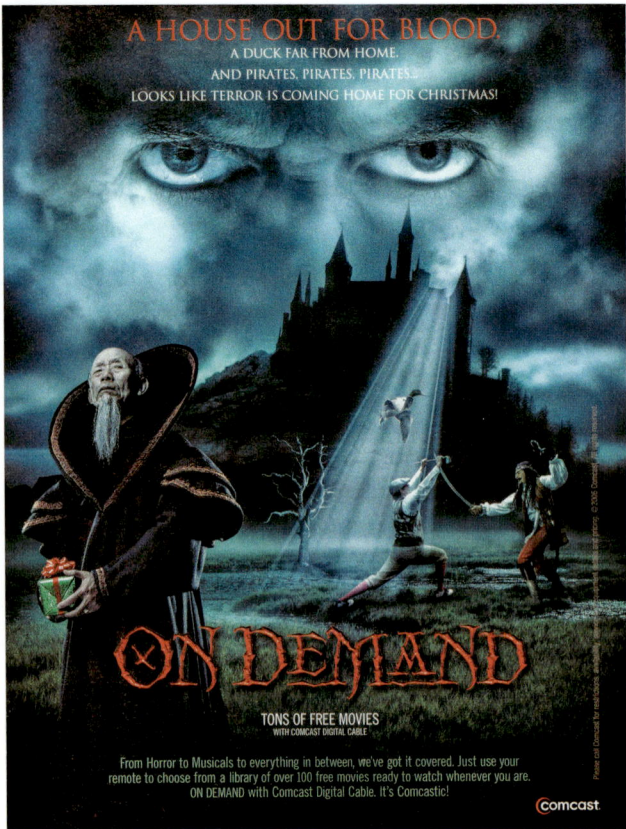

A HOUSE OUT FOR BLOOD.
A DUCK FAR FROM HOME.
AND PIRATES, PIRATES, PIRATES.
LOOKS LIKE TERROR IS COMING HOME FOR CHRISTMAS!

ON DEMAND

TONS OF FREE MOVIES
WITH COMCAST DIGITAL CABLE

From Horror to Musicals to everything in between, we've got it covered. Just use your
remote to choose from a library of over 100 free movies ready to watch whenever you are.
ON DEMAND with Comcast Digital Cable. It's Comcastic!

Comcast

*Comcast, 2006*

BEFORE THE MANSION.
BEFORE THE DISASTER.
EVIL IS BORN.

NINTENDO GAMECUBE.

CAPCOM
capcom.com

*Resident Evil Zero, 2002*

MY PROJECTOR IS MY
BATTLE CRY

Your living room transforms into Armageddon.
This is the quest for ultimate supremacy. With
larger-than-life images, InFocus projectors let you
inflict maximum pain on all who dare challenge
you. Bright, rich colors. Big, bold images. Go ahead.
Let out a primal scream. You've got this battle won.

Learn how InFocus can help you dominate the world. Visit www.infocus.com/playbig or call 866-345-2795.

InFocus
The Big Picture

*InFocus, 2006*

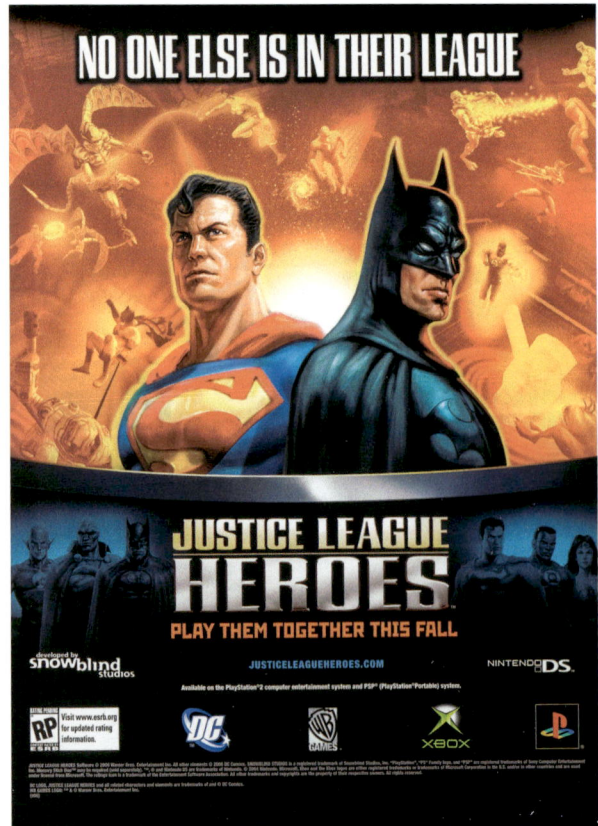

NO ONE ELSE IS IN THEIR LEAGUE

JUSTICE LEAGUE HEROES
PLAY THEM TOGETHER THIS FALL

developed by
snowblind studios

JUSTICELEAGUEHEROES.COM

NINTENDO DS

DC

WB GAMES

XBOX

*Justice League: Heroes, 2006*

FULL-FRONTAL
FEAR.

...ate the 5th anniversary of the most terrifying game series
...er as it mutates onto the PlayStation 2 computer enter-
...ent system. Join Claire Redfield, as she searches for her
...sing brother, Chris, and dig deeper into the evil doings of
...Umbrella Corporation. Flesh eating zombies and bio-tech
...trosities haunt your every move. As an added bonus, this
...cial edition includes never-before-seen cut scenes and
...teractive demo of the highly anticipated, Devil May Cry.

OVER THE EVIL AT
VX.COM

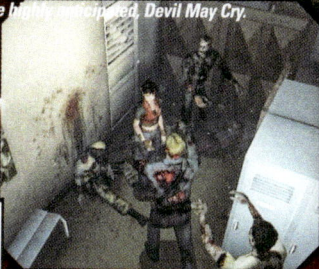

RESIDENT EVIL
CODE: Veronica
X

DEVIL MAY CRY
BONUS
DEMO INCLUDED

CAPCOM    PlayStation 2

Resident Evil – Code: Veronica, *2001*

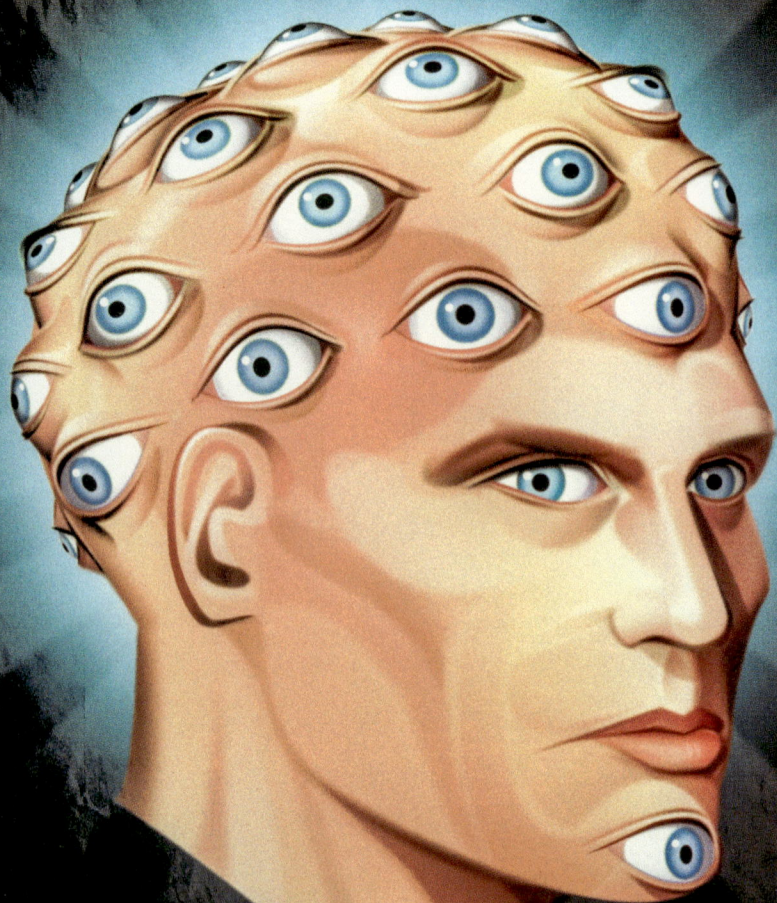

SEE EVERYTHING!

iPIX lets you see across the Internet. Anywhere. Anytime. In any direction.

iPIX

Internet Pictures Corporation
Visual Content Solutions for the Internet

www.iPIX.com

*iPix, 2000*

► Shadow

Sonic Heroes, 2003

Nintendo GameCube, 2001

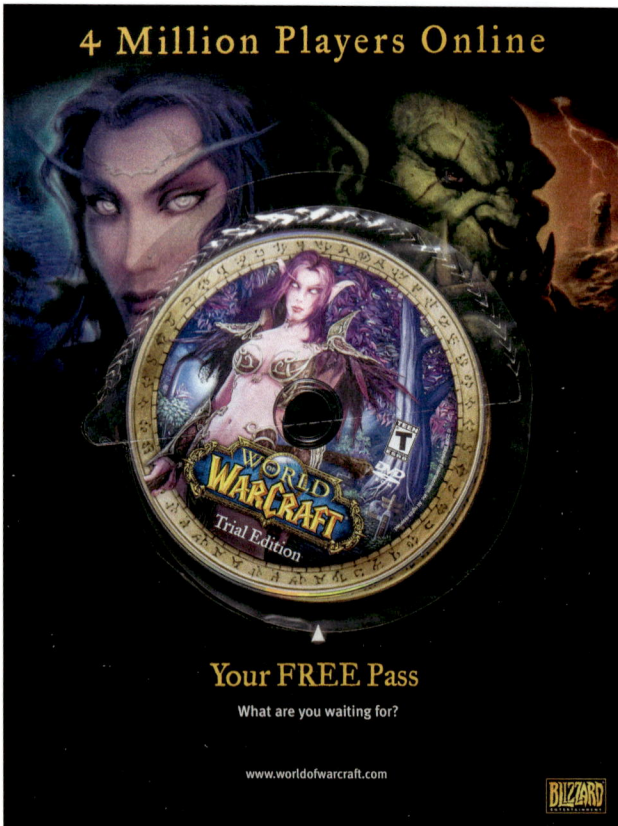

World of Warcraft, 2005

Grand Theft Auto III, 2002

▶ Dungeons & Dragons, 2

APRIL 4 – 16:
**VIOLA DAVIS, GINA GERSHON & ANNIE POTTS**

THE
# VAGINA
## MONOLOGUES
BY
# EVE ENSLER

DIRECTED BY
# JOE MANTELLO

# SPREAD THE WORD

A TRIO OF AMAZING WOMEN LISTED ABOVE WILL SHARE
THE MICROPHONE AT EVERY PERFORMANCE.

April 4 – 16: Viola Davis, Gina Gershon & Annie Potts.
April 18 – 30: Claire Danes, Jenifer Lewis & Mary McDonnell.
*May 2 and beyond* see Theatre Listings and vaginamonologues.com for cast and schedule information.

**WESTSIDE THEATRE • 407 W 43rd St, NYC • Call 212.239.6200**

The Vagina Monologues, *2000*

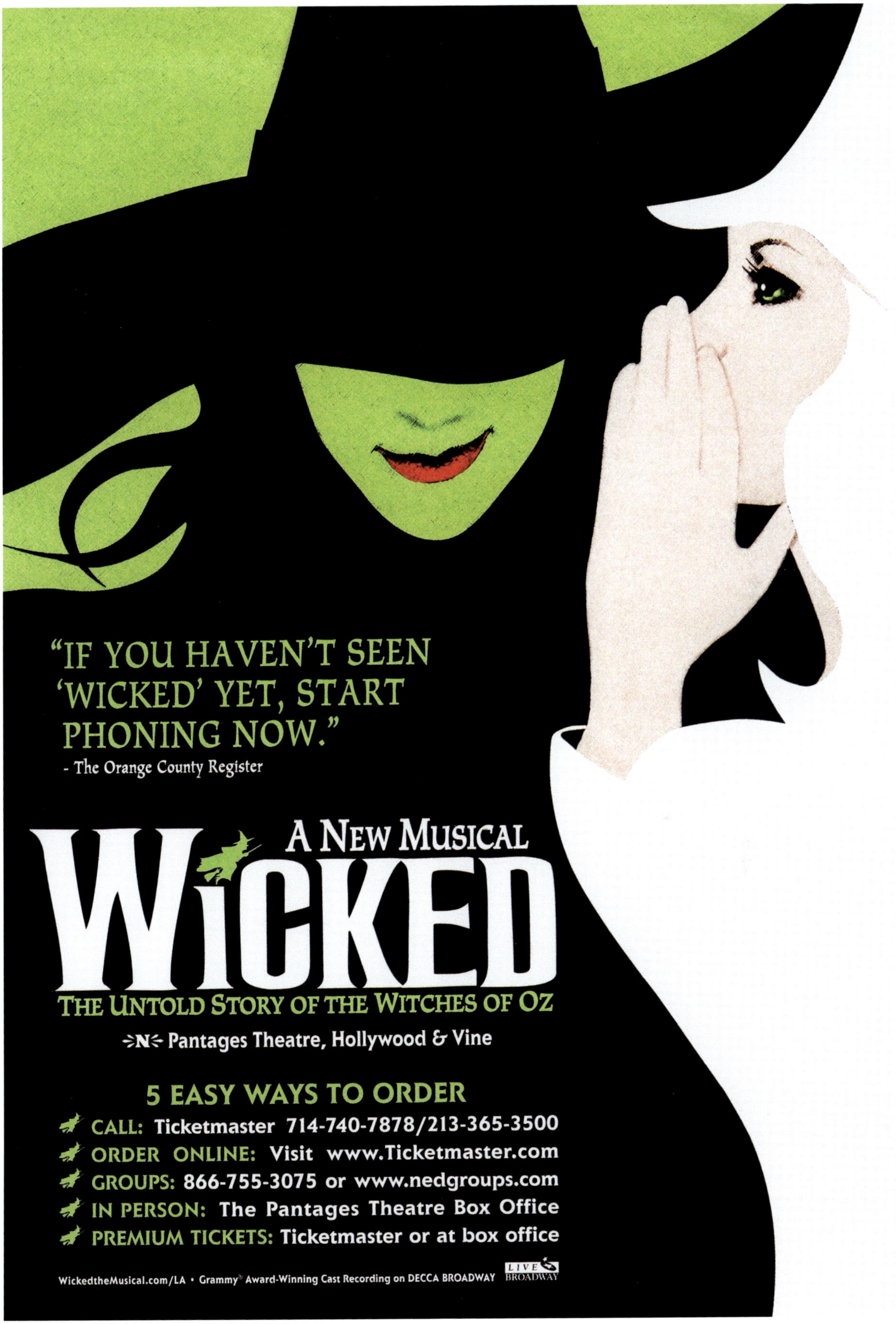
"IF YOU HAVEN'T SEEN 'WICKED' YET, START PHONING NOW."
- The Orange County Register
A New Musical
WICKED
THE UNTOLD STORY OF THE WITCHES OF OZ
Pantages Theatre, Hollywood & Vine
5 EASY WAYS TO ORDER
CALL: Ticketmaster 714-740-7878/213-365-3500
ORDER ONLINE: Visit www.Ticketmaster.com
GROUPS: 866-755-3075 or www.nedgroups.com
IN PERSON: The Pantages Theatre Box Office
PREMIUM TICKETS: Ticketmaster or at box office
WickedtheMusical.com/LA • Grammy® Award-Winning Cast Recording on DECCA BROADWAY
LIVE BROADWAY

Wicked, 2007

# And the winner is...

## Killer Kitchen

Even in the hands of Lady Liberty, a raised knife seems like a sinister approach worthy of promoting a slasher film, rather than saluting a cooking show. Did anybody suggest a whisk or a spoon? Guess there isn't enough violence in the kitchen.

## Küchenkiller

Selbst in der Hand der Freiheitsstatue wirkt ein erhobenes Küchenmesser reichlich düster und eher wie Werbung für einen Slasherfilm als für eine Kochsendung. Ob ihnen jemand zu einem Quirl oder einem Kochlöffel geraten hat? Wahrscheinlich ist es noch zu friedlich in den amerikanischen Küchen.

## Cuisine de tueurs

Même entre les mains de la statue de la Liberté, un couteau brandi reste menaçant et semble plus adapté à la promotion d'un film d'horreur qu'à celle d'une émission gastronomique. Est-ce que quelqu'un a proposé un fouet ou une cuillère, à la place? Sans doute n'y a-t-il pas assez de violence en cuisine.

▶ Top

mia farrow
waffle V-neck henley

your silence.

the gap t-shirt shop

Silk Dress
$69.90

DESIGNED BY MADONNA
IN STORES MARCH 22

H&M

*H&M, 2007*

379

# I AM

a 49-million-woman
majority.
How's that for a
nice round sum?
I am fashion's
new authority.
My size has come.

**Easy-to-wear Stretch Jeans, Sizes 16–26
Plush Fleece Top and Tee,
Sizes 14 / 16W – 26 / 28W**

Great-looki

great-fitting jea

hosiery, linge

and casualwear dedica

exclusivel

plus-size wom

Stretch Jea

Claiborne, 2004

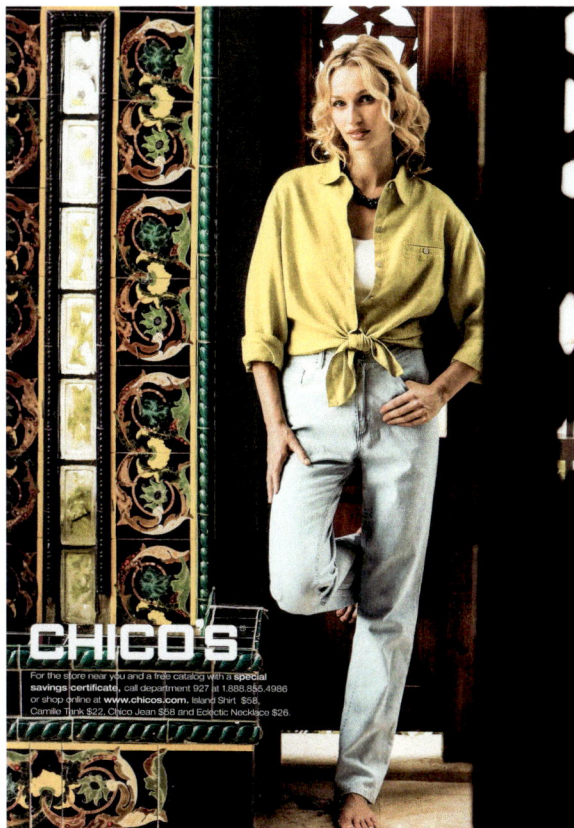

Chico's, 2003

My Size, 2002 ◄ Walmart, 2006

Eileen Fisher, 2004

381

Hazel Clark, 800m runner, wears the Seamless All Sport Hoody.

*Nike, 2001*

*Guess, 2004*

*Guess, 2004*

*get, 2004*

Chiffon dress
$99.90

Turtleneck
$49.90

Karl Lagerfeld
for

# H&M

Launches November 12th in select H&M stores
www.hm.com

*1, 2004*

*Ed Hardy, 2008*

*American Apparel, 2004*

*Fruit of the Loom, 2009*

# Après ski.

**Come see what we're doing at our Community Stores.**

**Lower East Side—NYC**
183 E. Houston St.
New York, NY 10002
Phone: (212) 598-4600

**Noho—NYC**
712 Broadway
New York, NY 10003
Phone: (646) 383-2257

**Soho—NYC**
121 Spring St.
New York, NY 10012
Phone: (212) 226-4880

**West Village—NYC**
373 Sixth Ave.
New York, NY 10014
Phone: (646) 336-6515

**Williamsburg—NYC**
104 N. Sixth St.
Brooklyn, NY 11211
Phone: (718) 218-0002

**Echo Park—LA**
2111 Sunset Blvd.
Los Angeles, CA 90026
Phone: (213) 484-6464

**Little Tokyo—LA**
374 E. Second St.
Los Angeles, CA 90026
Phone: (213) 687-0467

**Los Feliz—LA**
4665 Hollywood Blvd.
Los Angeles, CA 90027
Phone: (323) 661-1407

**West Hollywood—LA**
104 S. Robertson Blvd.
Los Angeles, CA 90048
Phone: (310) 274-6292

**Portland—PTL**
1234 SW Stark St.
Portland, OR 97205
Phone: (503) 721-0700

**Cours Mont-Royal—MTL**
1455 Peel St.
Montreal, QC H3A 1T5
Phone: (514) 843-4020

**Sherbrooke—MTL**
4945 Sherbrooke St. W.
Westmount, QC H3Z 1H2
Phone: (514) 369-2295

**Ste-Catherine—MTL**
1455 Ste-Catherine St. W.
Montreal, QC H3H-1L9
Phone: (514) 932-9922

**St-Denis—MTL**
4001 St-Denis St.
Montreal, QC H2W 2M4
Phone: (514) 843-8887

**St-Laurent—MTL**
3523 St-Laurent Blvd.
Montreal, QC H2X 2T6
Phone: (514) 286-0091

**Queen W. —TO**
499 Queen St. W.
Toronto, ON M5V 2B4
Phone: (416) 703-5146

**Berlin—DE**
Münzstr. 19
10 178 Berlin/Mitte
Phone: 030.280.69.720

**Frankfurt—DE**
Kaiserstr. 23
60 311 Franfurt am Main
Phone: 069.2440.4995

**Carnaby—LON**
3-4 Carnaby St.
London, UK W1F 9DW
Phone: 020.7734.4477

**Coming soon:**
Miami, San Diego, Vancouver,
Paris and many more

## American Apparel™

Made in Downtown LA
Sweatshop Free—Brand-Free Clothes
www.americanapparel.net

American Apparel is a vertically integrated manufacturer and retailer of knit garments for men, women, infants, toddlers and dogs. Producing everything under one roof in Downtown Los Angeles, we are committed to making clothing of the highest quality while pioneering industry standards of social responsibility in the workplace.

All of our 3000 employees, sewing and administrative alike, are paid fairly and have access to basic benefits like healthcare. In our estimation exploitative labor tactics are not only inhumane, but are far less effective than using technology and innovation to advance business.

For more information about our exclusive combed-cotton product line and groundbreaking political mission, please visit our web site.

*American Apparel, 2004*

385

BALI LIVE IT UP

*Bali, 2003*

THERE'S A LOT ON YOUR SHOULDERS. WE RELIEVE THE PRESSURE.

©2002 Playtex Apparel, Inc.

GEL COMFORT STRAP™

Gel-filled straps for the ultimate cushion.

*Playtex* 18 Hour®

www.playtexbras.com

*Playtex, 2002*

BEAUTIFULL-FIGURED

*Luxurious Seamless Stretch panties and coordinating Extreme Comfort bra. Feel as glamorous as you look. Visit fruitforher.com.*

PROVIDING VALUE SINCE 1851

FRUIT OF THE LOOM
Fit for Me

**airwonder**™

**Wonderbra**®

D&G
DOLCE & GABBANA
www.dolcegabbana.it

Valentino, 2000

Chanel, 2008

Valentino, 2000

VERSACE

*Versace, 2000*

Dior

Dior, 2005

YEAR 2000
FIRST STEPS INTO THE NEW CENTURY

Duffle coat
in coated canvas.

NEW YORK  ATLANTA
BAL HARBOUR  BEVERLY HILLS
BOSTON  CHICAGO  DALLAS
HONOLULU  HOUSTON
LAS VEGAS  PALM BEACH
PHILADELPHIA  SAN FRANCISCO
SOUTH COAST PLAZA
WASHINGTON, D.C.
FOR INFORMATION:
1-800-441-4488

HERMÈS
PARIS

Publicis EtNous

*Hermes, 2000*

395

Guess, 2007

Guess, 2008

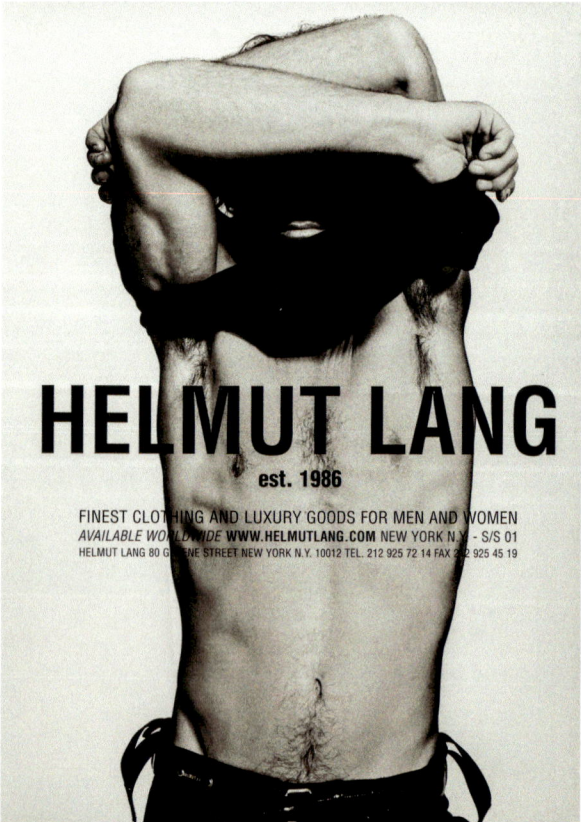

Helmut Lang, 2001

Burberry, 2001

HERMÈS EN ESCAPADE

HERMÈS
PARIS

*Hermes, 2009*

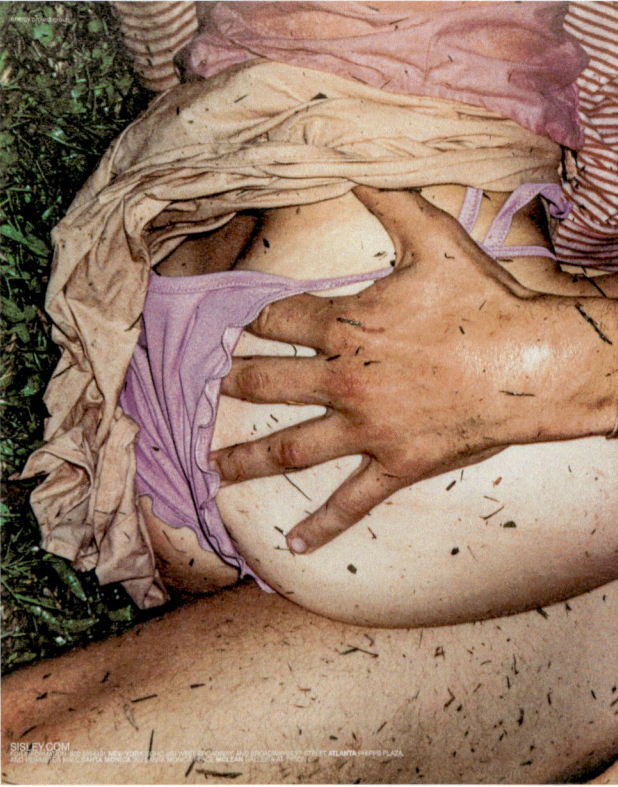

*Sisley, 2001*

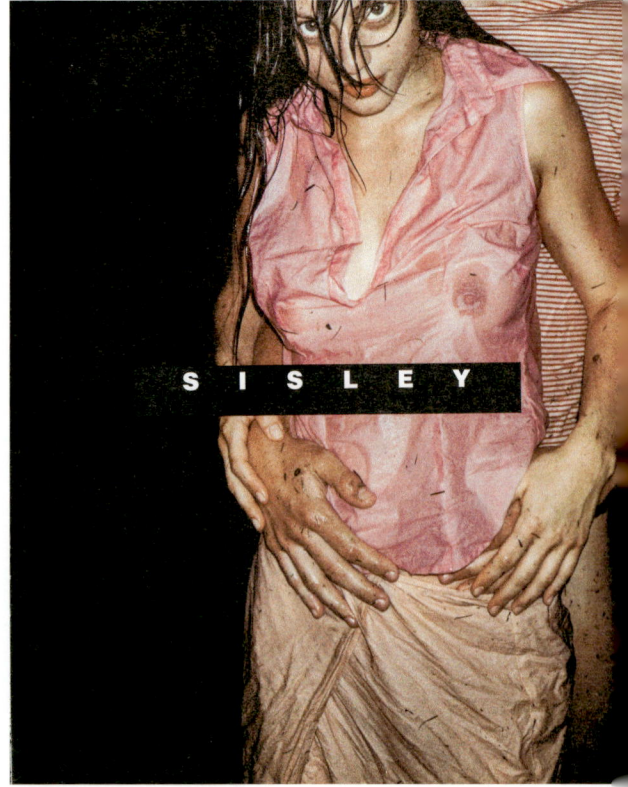

*Sisley, 2001*

*Sisley, 2001*

STELLА McCАRTNEY   STELLА McCАRTNEY   STELLА McCАRTNEY   STELLА

Stella McCartney, 2002

PRADA

Prada, 2000

CESARE PACIOTTI

Cesare Paciotti, 2002

*Tommy Hilfiger, 2003*

Tommy Hilfiger, 2003

Dolce & Gabbana, 2001

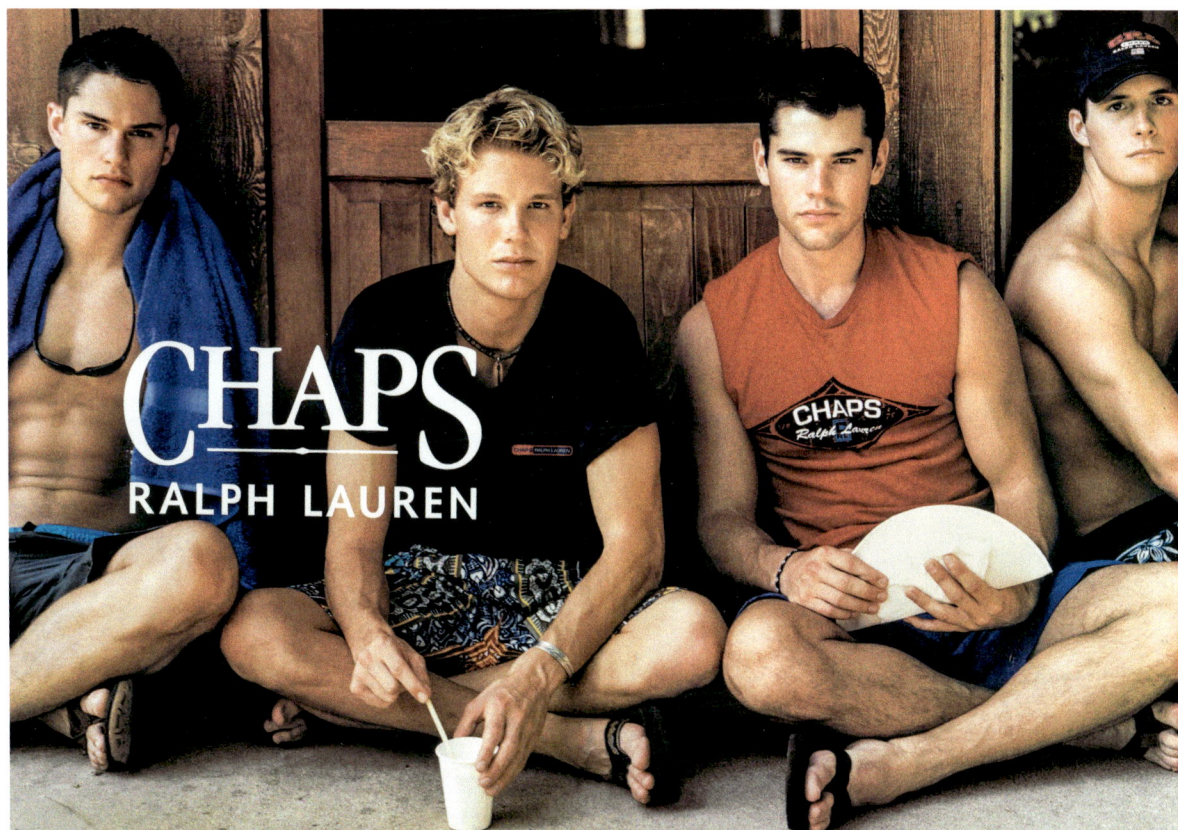

Ralph Lauren, 2001

*Versace, 2002*

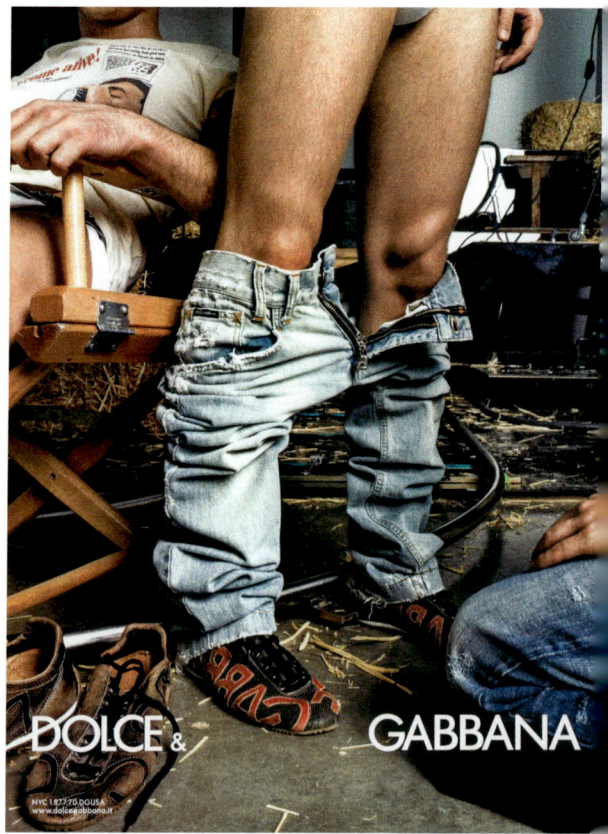

*Dolce & Gabbana, 2006*

*Jean Paul Gaultier, 2001*

*Marc Jacobs, 2010*

Alexander McQueen, 2002

Sisley, 2006

*Prada, 2005*

Versace, 2002

Versace, 2002

Versace, 2002

Versace, 2002

*Just Cavalli, 2006*

*Just Cavalli, 2004*

*Prada, 2001*

Tom Ford, 2008

Tom Ford, 2008

MARC JACOBS

WILLIAM EGGLESTON AND CHARLOTTE RAMPLING PHOTOGRAPHED BY JUERGEN TELLER

Marc Jacobs, 2007

Tommy Hilfiger, 2003

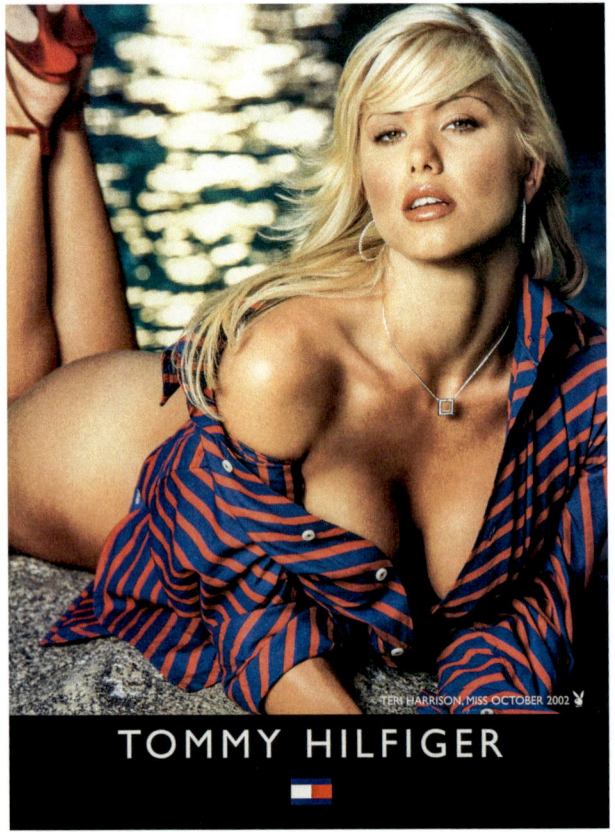

Tommy Hilfiger, 2003

Dolce & Gabbana, 2007

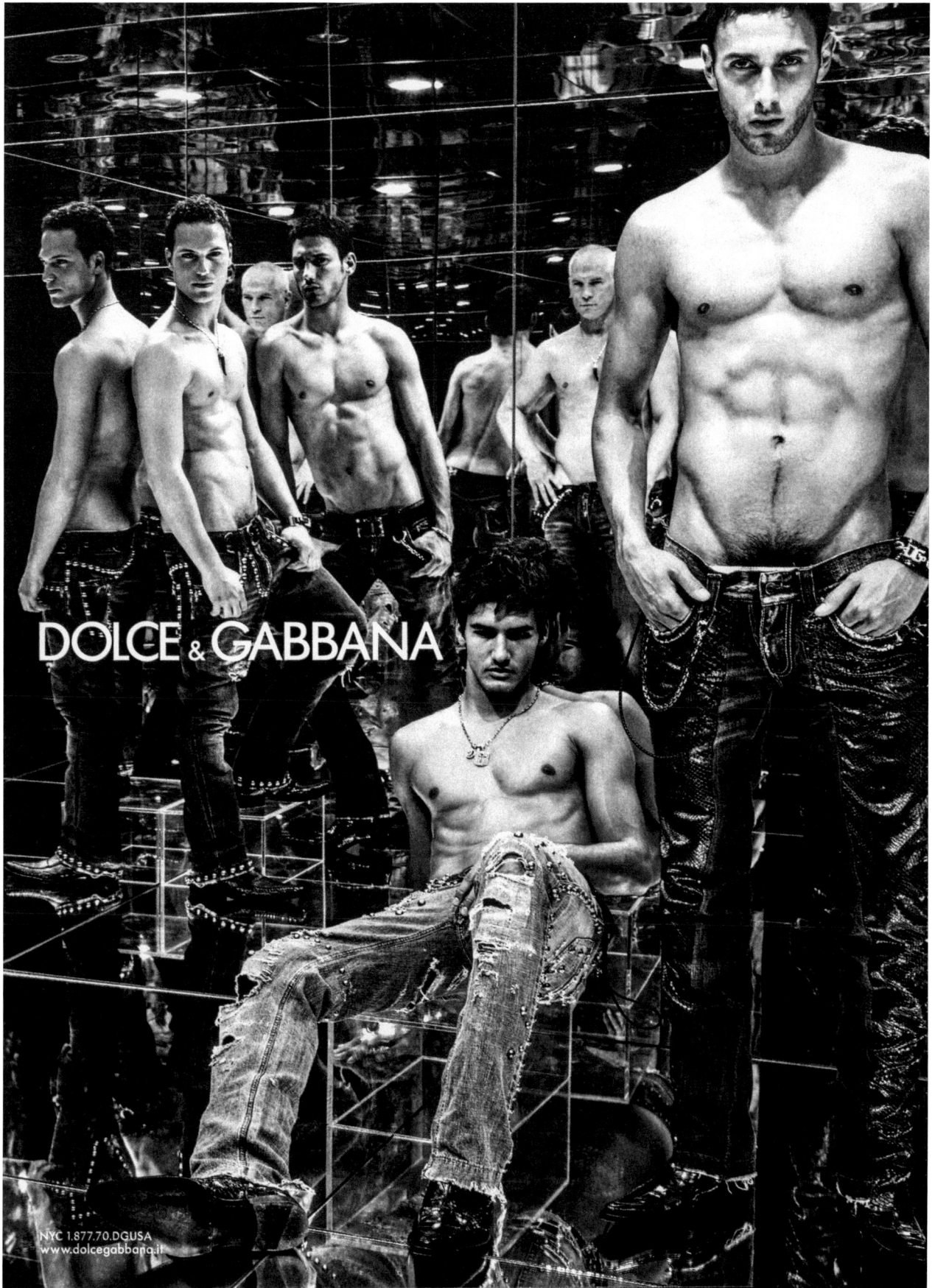

DOLCE & GABBANA

NYC 1.877.70.DGUSA
www.dolcegabbana.it

*Dolce & Gabbana, 2005*

DOLCE & GABBANA

*Dolce & Gabbana, 2001*

ADRIEN BRODY

CHINTZED LINEN JACKET
GRAINED CALF LIGHT SHOES

NEW YORK. BEVERLY HILLS
CHICAGO BOSTON BAL HARBOUR
SOUTH COAST PLAZA
888.880.3462 ZEGNA.COM

THE NEW
COLLECTION FROM
ERMENEGILDO ZEGNA

Zegna

*Zegna, 2004*

MADONNA FOR
VERSACE

*Versace, 2005*

▶ Tommy Hilfiger, 2

H
HILFIGER

Dolce & Gabbana, 2007

Dolce & Gabbana, 2006

*Armani Exchange, 2008*

*Dolce & Gabbana, 2008*

WHEREVER YOU GO >

OCTOGRIP SOLE

MERRELL
™

CHAMELEON VENTILATOR LOW
MEAN OR MELLOW, FAST OR SLOW.
A NEW SPECIES OF FOOTWEAR THAT
ADAPTS TO YOUR ENVIRONMENT.

PERFORMANCE FOOTWEAR
WWW.MERRELLBOOT.COM

888_637_7001

*Merrell, 2001*

*Dr. Martens, 2009*

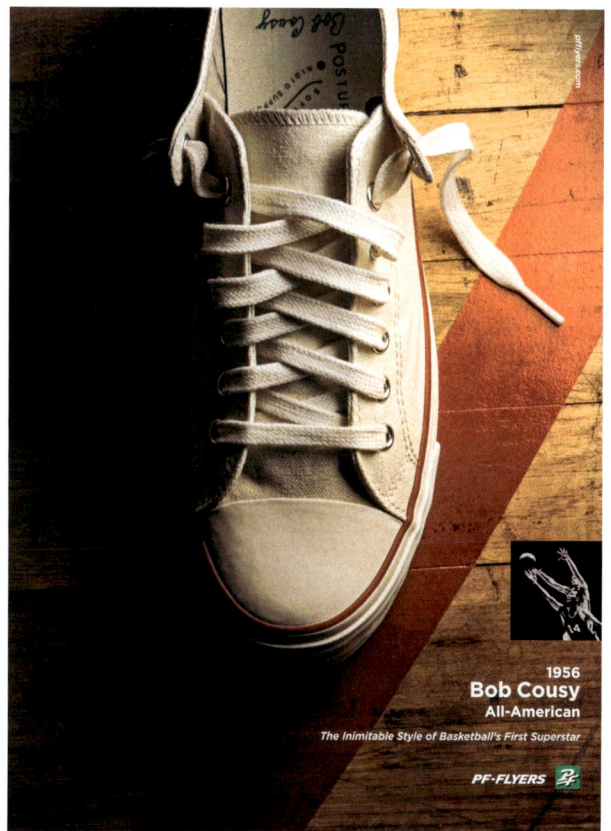

1956
**Bob Cousy**
All-American

*The Inimitable Style of Basketball's First Superstar*

**PF·FLYERS**

*PF-Flyers, 2008*

NIKE SHOX

Boing.

nike.com/nikeshox

2000

Reebok, 2001

Reebok, 2000

Pirelli, 2005

Pirelli, 2005

PopClassic.

*Reebok, 2001*

417

*Tretorn, 2008*

*Havaianas, 2008*

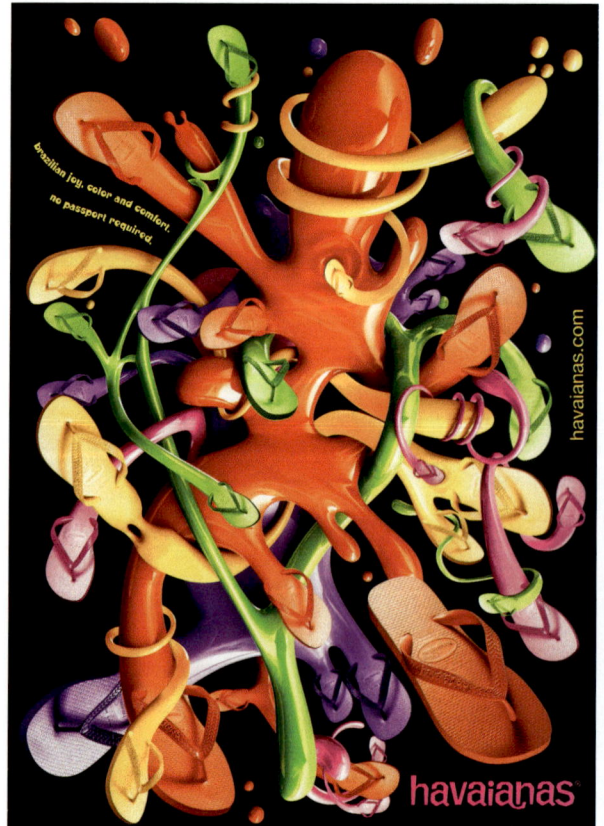

*Havaianas, 2009*

GET
CHUCKED

CLOTHES AND SHOES FOR GUYS AND GIRLS | CONVERSE.COM

CONVERSE®
JOHN VARVATOS

Converse, 2008

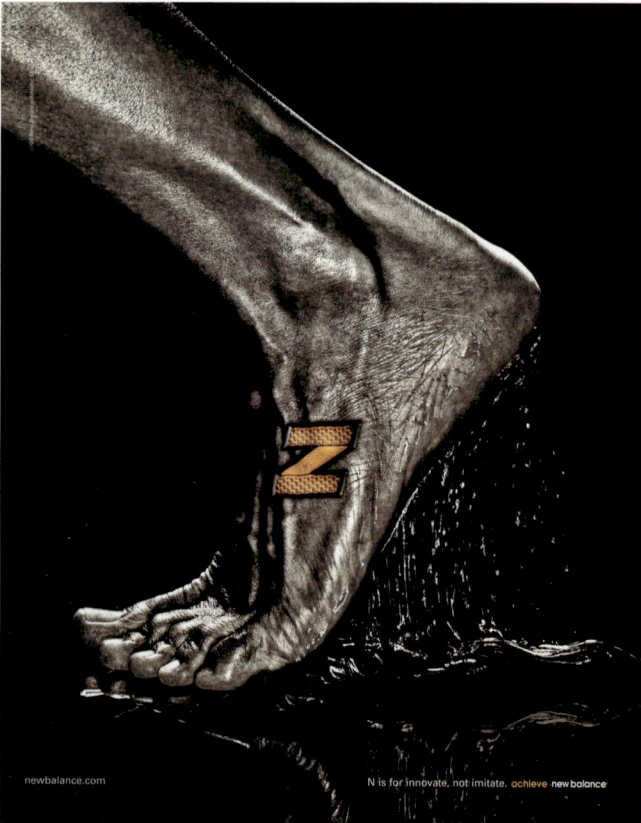

newbalance.com

N is for innovate, not imitate. achieve new balance

New Balance, 2004

reebok
DEFY CONVENTION

Reebok, 2001

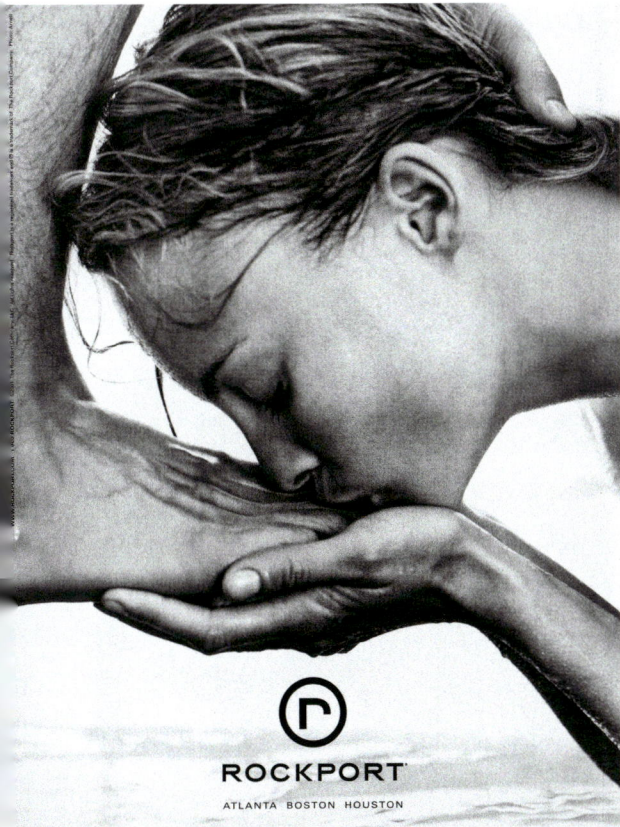

ROCKPORT
ATLANTA BOSTON HOUSTON

ckport, 2001

Diesel, 2002

e, 2006

421

*Nike*, 2001

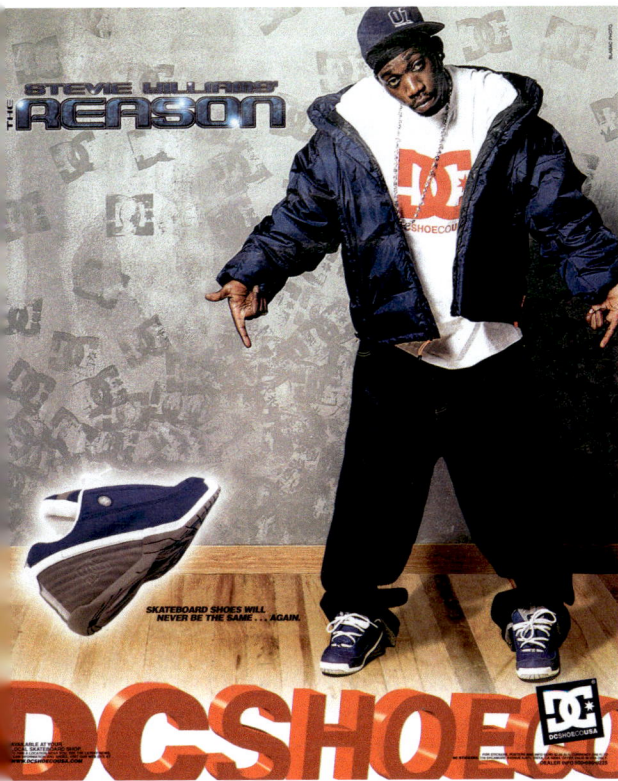

DC Shoes, 2001

DC Shoes, 2004

Adidas, 2006

Nike, 2001

CAMPER

the
walking
society

www.camper.com
t +1 212 7809488

WALK
DON'T RUN

Camper, 2002

ADVERTISEMENT

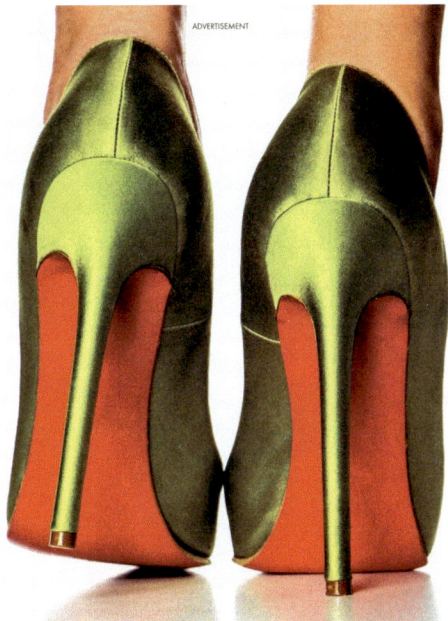

WHERE FASHION CLICKS

# shopvogue.com

**LIVE AUGUST 23.**

SEE ALL OF FALL ON OUR NEW ONLINE LOOK BOOK AT SHOPVOGUE.COM.
ENTER FOR A CHANCE TO WIN DAILY GIVEAWAYS.

NO PURCHASE NECESSARY. Must be at least 18 years of age and a legal resident of one of the 50 United States or the District of Columbia as of the date of entry. Subject to full rules posted on shopvogue.com

opVogue.com, 2005

# PUT A LITTLE ZAPPOS IN YOUR DAY!

Zappos.com

→ MILLIONS OF SHOES, CLOTHES AND BAGS.
→ FREE SHIPPING BOTH WAYS.
→ 24/7 CUSTOMER SERVICE.

Zappos.com
POWERED by SERVICE™

Zappos.com, 2008

310
FASHION & FOOTWEAR COLLECTION

310, 2006

# GET YOUR BOOTS ON

THE CHUCK TAYLOR ALL STAR
OUTSIDER BOOT,
AVAILABLE AT MACY'S.

CONVERSE

Converse, 2010

ugly can be beautiful

crocs

crocs.com

**play hard.
live comfortably.**

ocs, 2007

**nowhere close to normal.**

**crocs**™
crocs.com

Crocs, 2006

ARRIVE IN A CONVERTIBLE.

HAVAIANAS ORIGINAIS DO BRASIL DESDE 1962.

WWW.HAVAIANAS.COM **havaianas**®

Havaianas, 2010

*Dolce & Gabbana, 2002*

S+ARCK | PUMA.
puma.com

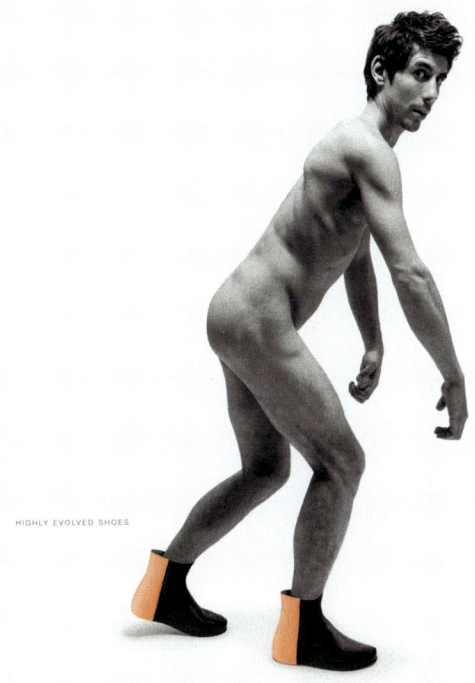

HIGHLY EVOLVED SHOES

HIGHLY EVOLVED SHOES

S+ARCK | PUMA.
puma.com

Puma, 2005

CONVERSE

own it.

THE CONVERSE CHUCK TAYLOR
ALL STAR SNEAKER NOW AT

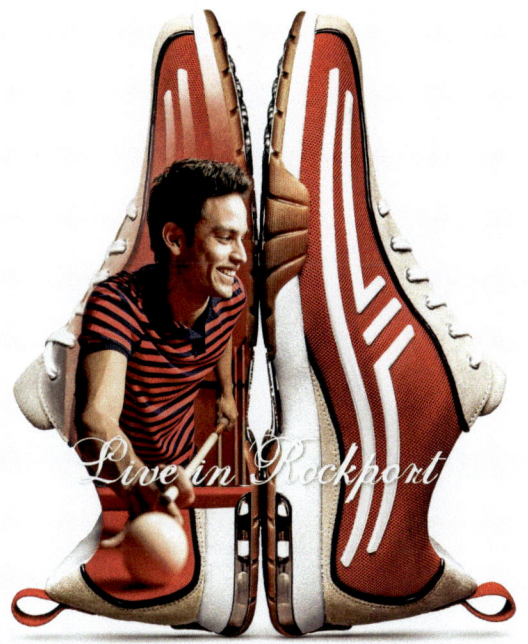

Foot Locker

Foot Locker, 2010

Torsion® System Technology by adidas

Live in Rockport

ROCKPORT® ⓡ The Differences Inside:

ROCKPORT SHOES ARE MEANT FOR A SPECIAL OCCASION. IT'S CALLED LIFE. ROCKPORT.COM

Rockport, 2008

Skechers, 2002

Sean John, 2001

Ugg, 2007

*Diesel, 2005*

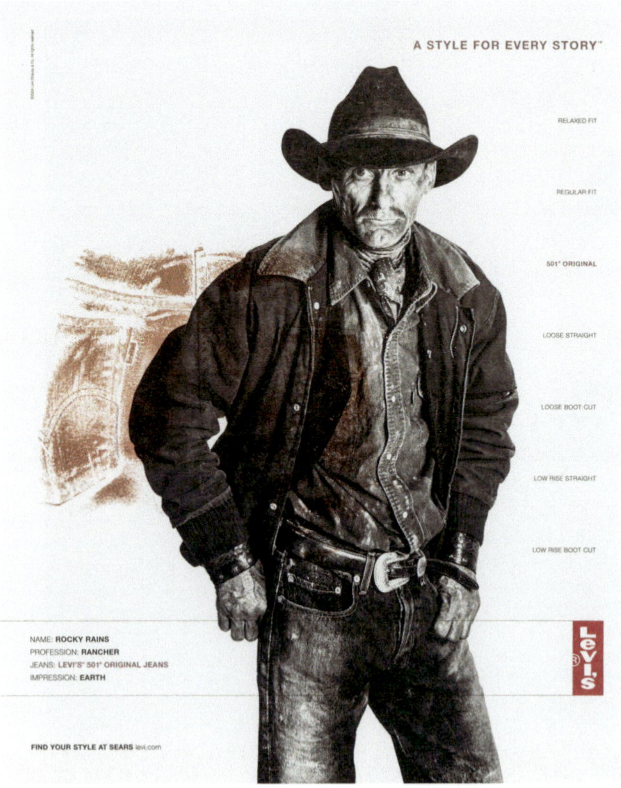


*Levi's, 2004*

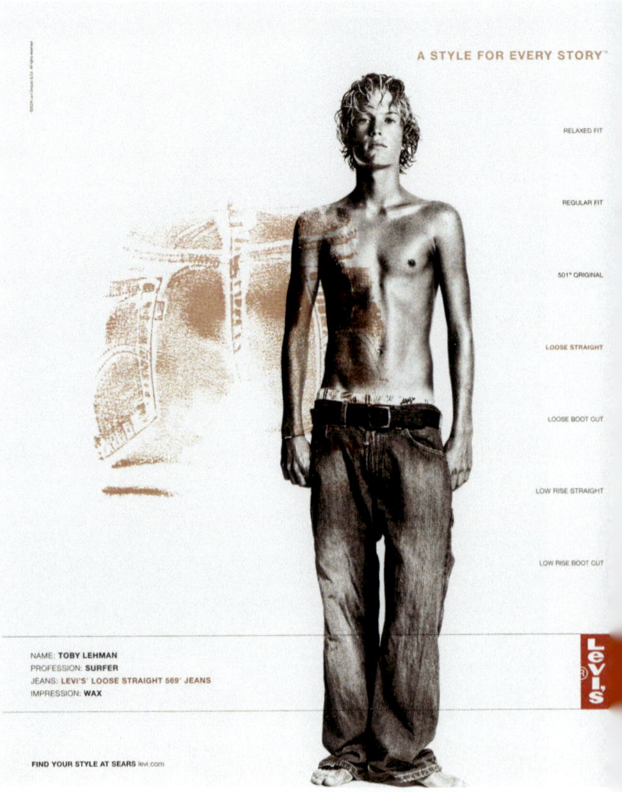


*Levi's, 2004*

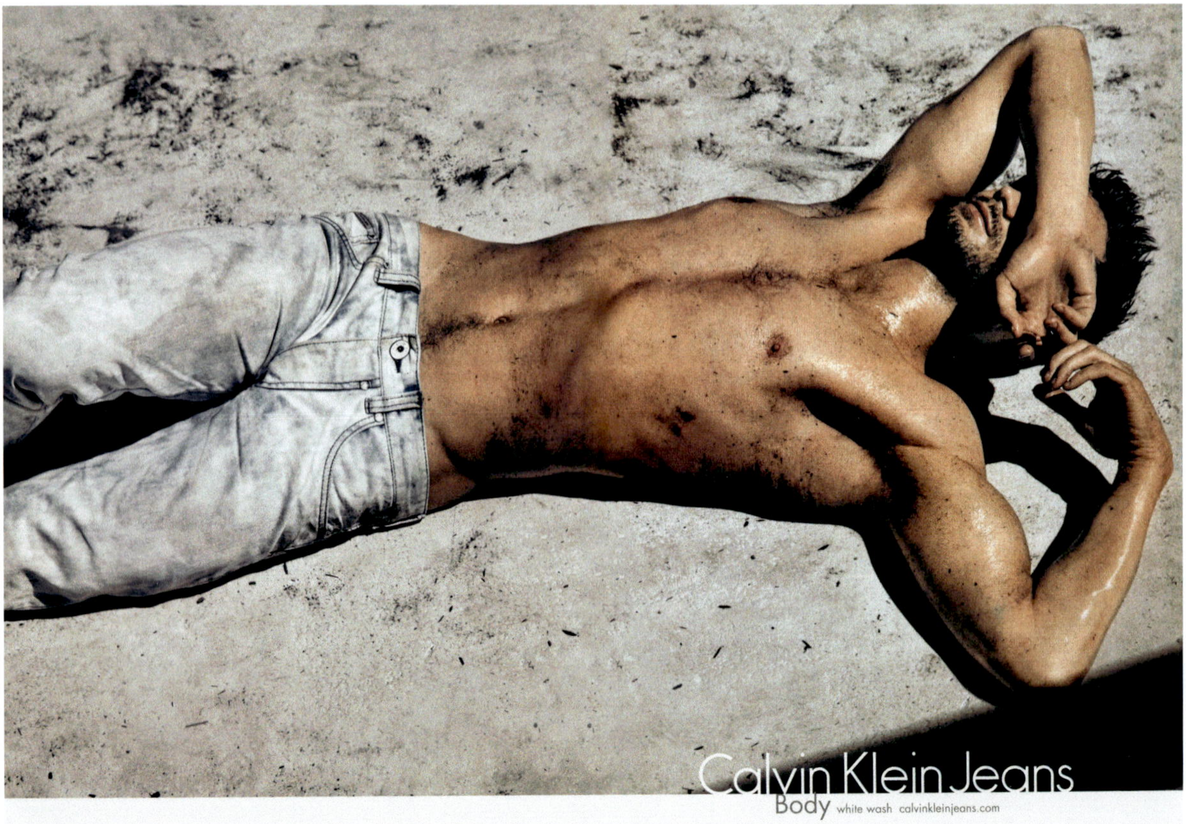


*Calvin Klein, 2010*

*Wrangler, 2004*

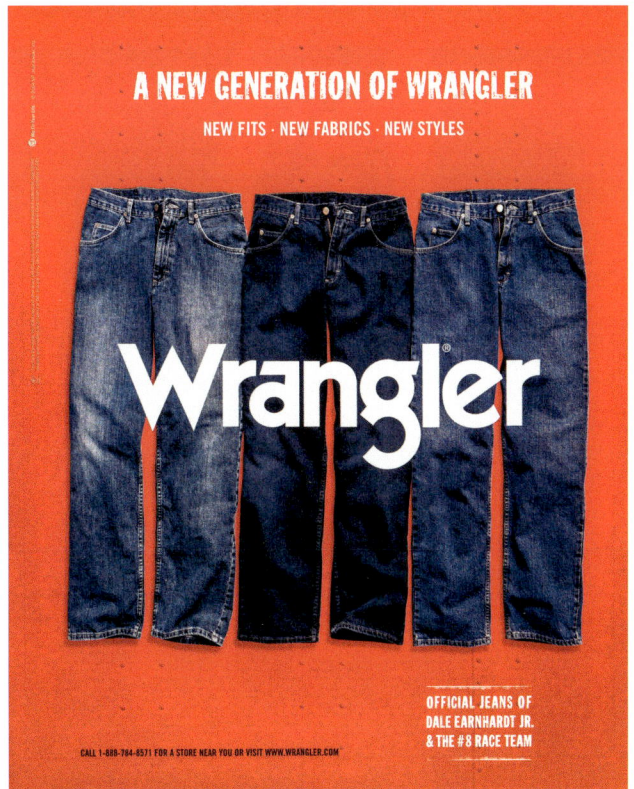

*Wrangler, 2004*

*Levi's, 2004*

*Calvin Klein, ca. 2002*

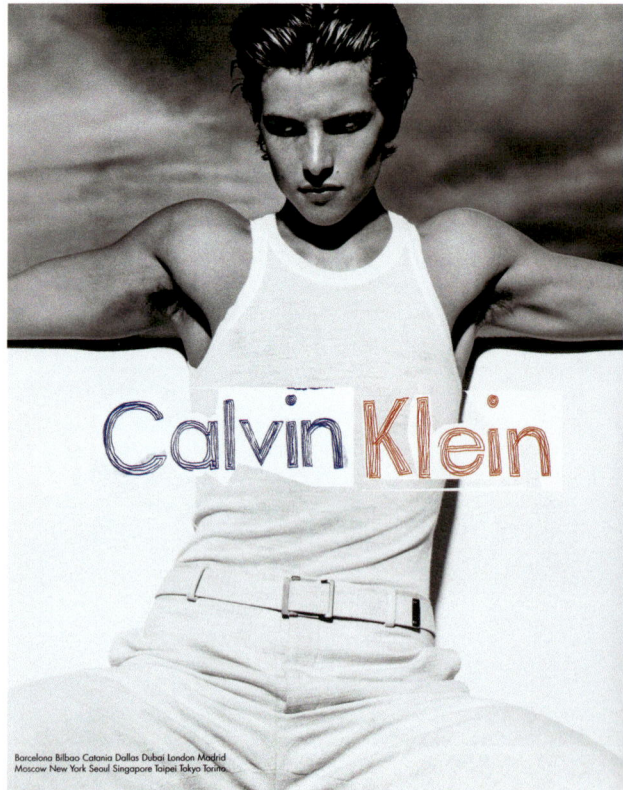

Barcelona Bilbao Catania Dallas Dubai London Madrid
Moscow New York Seoul Singapore Taipei Tokyo Torino.

*Calvin Klein, 2002*

Calvin Klein Jeans
Double Black

*Calvin Klein, 2004*

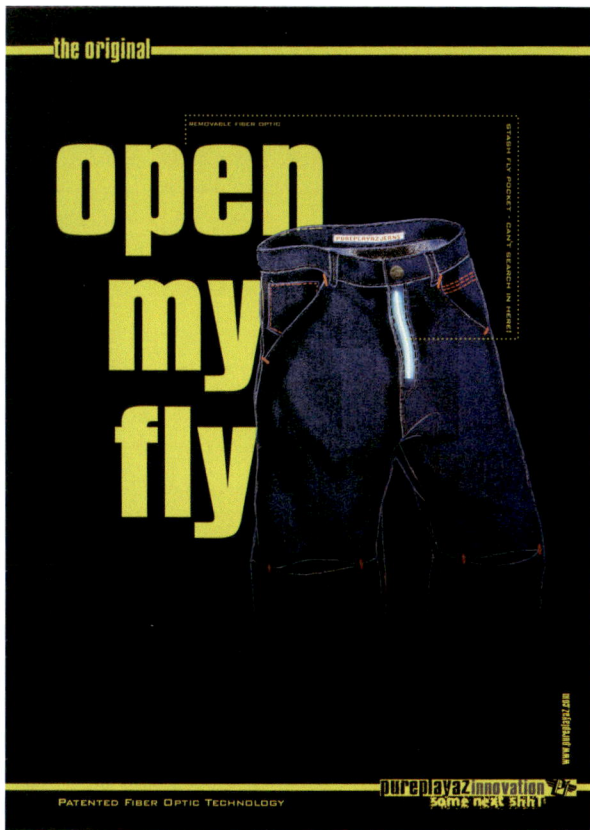

*Pure Playaz, 2000*

*Earl Jean, 2004*

*Calvin Klein, 2004*

*Diesel, 2007*

*Lucky Brand, 2002*

Introducing LUCKY LEGEND
EVERY PAIR MADE BY HAND

LUCKYBRAND.COM

*Lucky Brand, 2009*

Lee, 2009

Levi's, 2010

Nautica, 2005

Levi's, 2007

Giorgio Armani, 2000

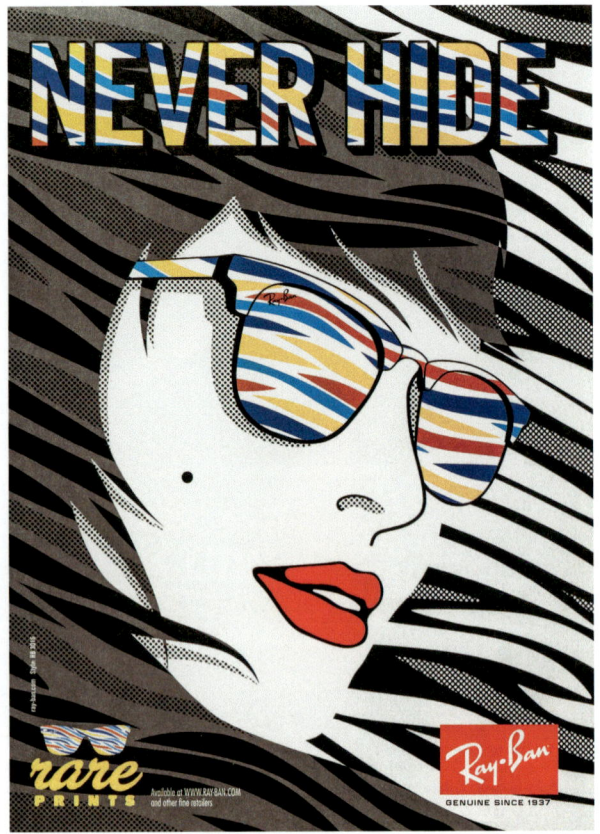

Ray-Ban, 2010

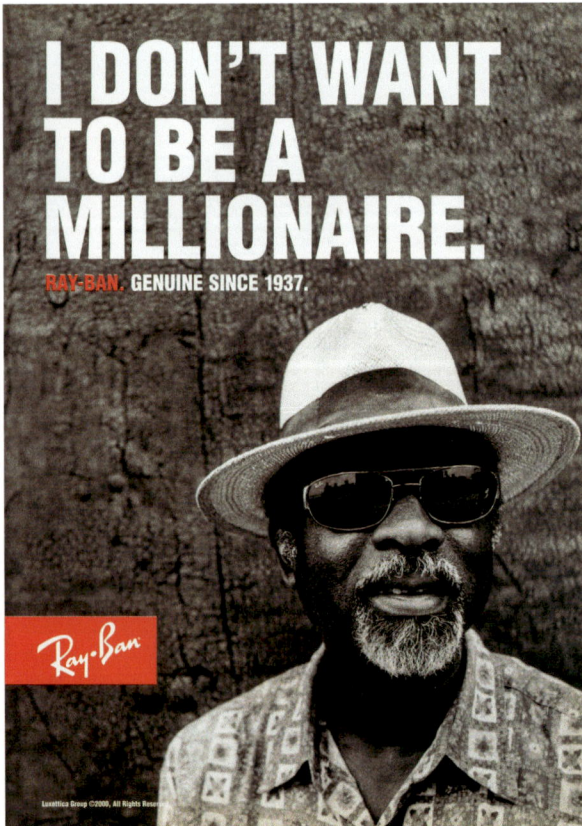

Ray-Ban, 2000

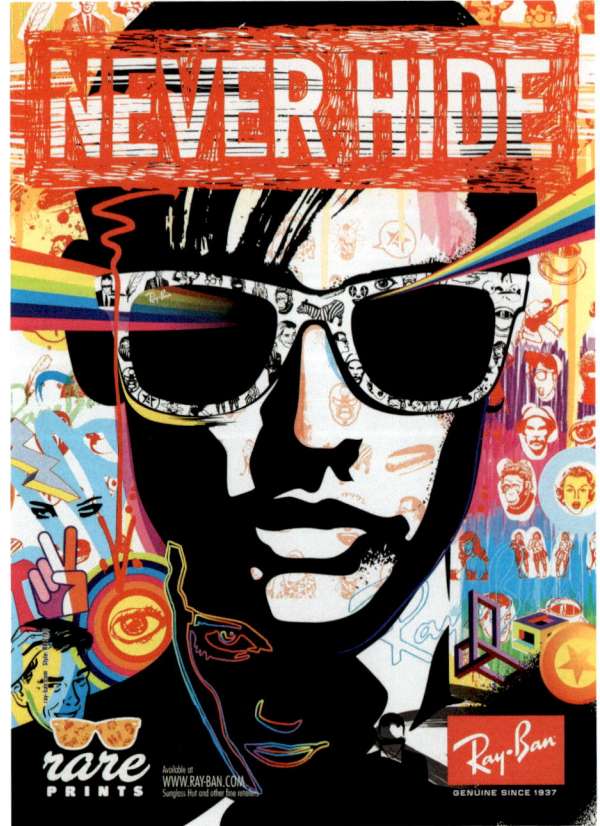

Ray-Ban, 2010

TOM FORD EYEWEAR

*Tom Ford, 2008*

**TechnoMarine** *SPORT*

WATER RESISTANT 200 m / 660 ft

LOG BOOK — LB

THERMOMETER — TP

CHRONOGRAPH — CH

DIVE MODE

COMPASS

DUAL TIME

ALARM

*TechnoMarine, 2004*

Ridiculously easy to use. **TIMEX** **i·Control** setting systems

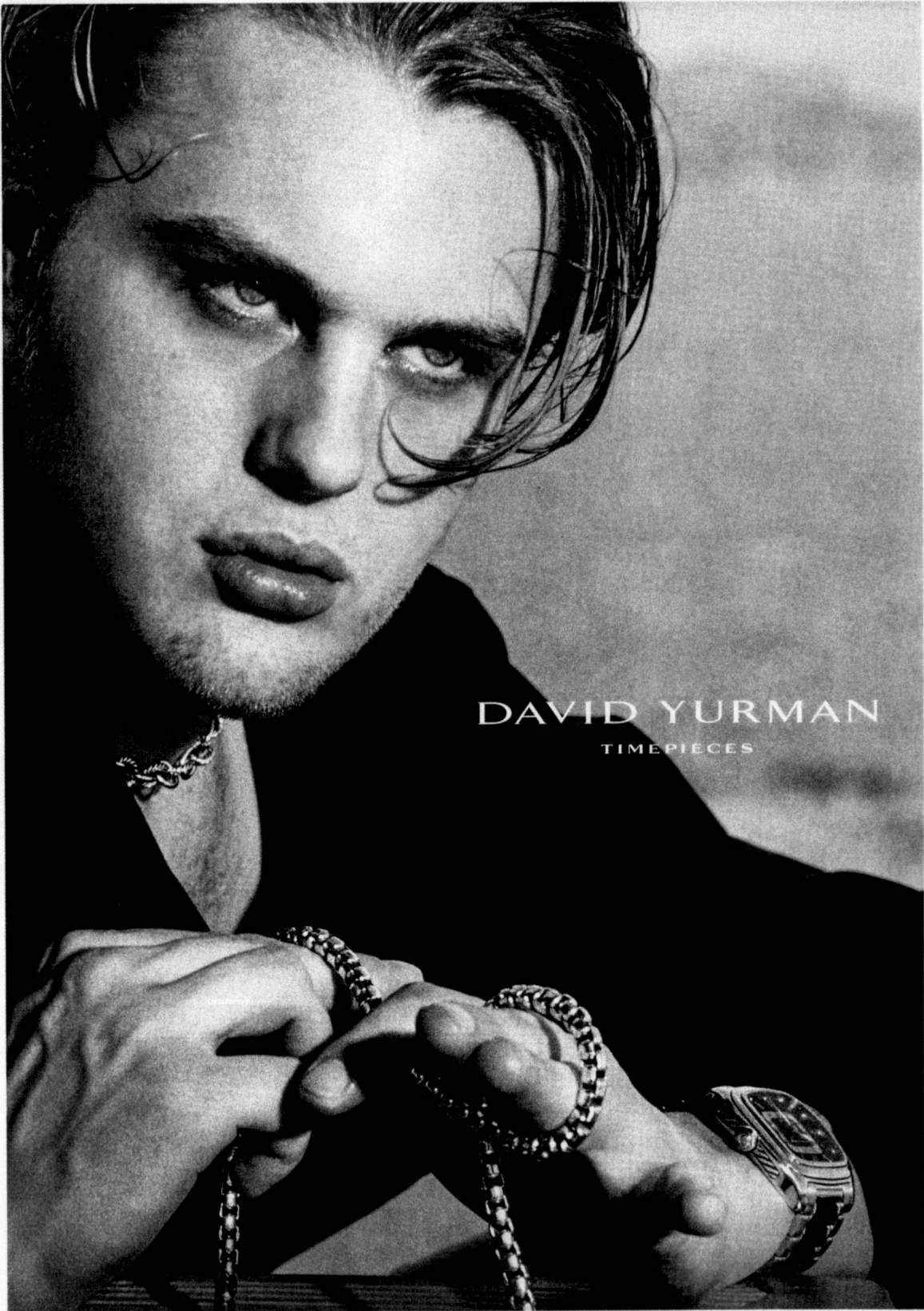

DAVID YURMAN
TIMEPIECES

MADISON AT 64TH   SOUTH COAST PLAZA

*David Yurman, 2004*

52% OF AMERICANS THINK SAME-SEX MARRIAGES
DON'T DESERVE A GOOD RECEPTION.

ARE YOU PUTTING US ON?  -KENNETH COLE

KENNETH COLE new york
KENNETH COLE NEW YORK RETAIL STORES  1 800 KEN COLE  KENNETHCOLE.COM

*Kenneth Cole, 2000*

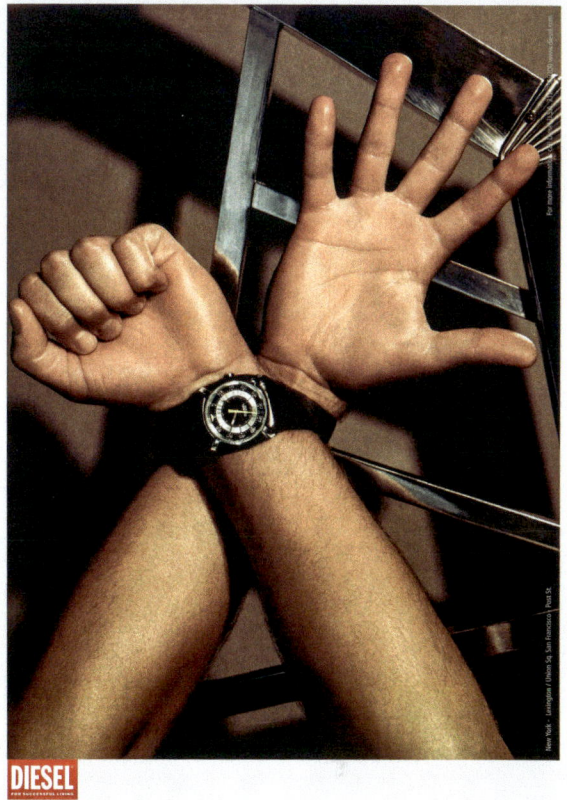

DIESEL

*Diesel, 2005*

THE THINNEST CHRONO IN THE WORLD.

swatch
SKIN
chrono

Swatch Stores:
New York - Los Angeles - Chicago - Miami - San Francisco
Las Vegas - Washington DC - Honolulu - 1.800.8SWATCH

*Swatch, 2001*

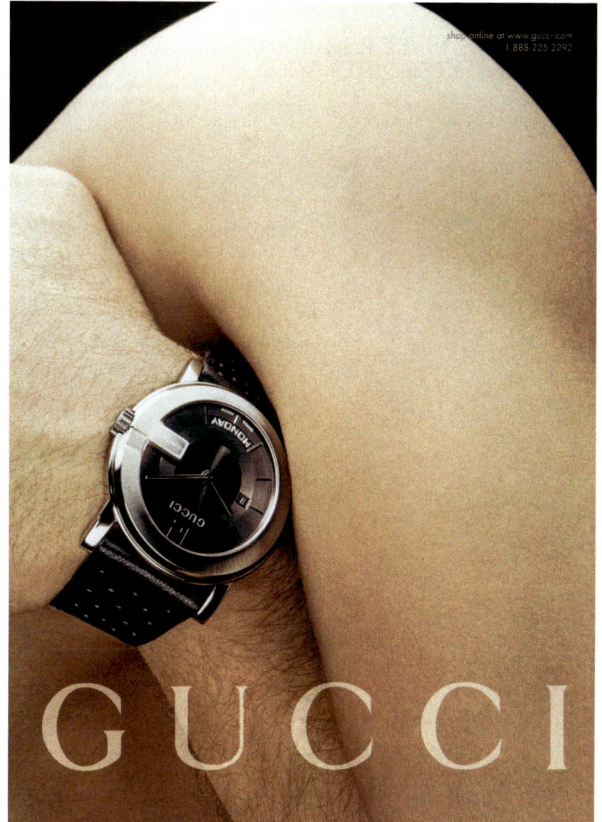

GUCCI

*Gucci, 2004*

*Omega, 2006*

*Omega, 2002*

*Omega, 2004*

007™ VILLAIN COLLECTION BY swatch+

THUNDERBALL
EMILIO LARGO

VISIT HTTP://STORE.SWATCH.COM TO SEE THE 007 VILLAIN COLLECTION

Available at Swatch stores nationwide and select Nordstrom & Bloomingdale's locations.
866.382.4713

*Swatch, 2008*

447

SEIKO®

© 2001 Seiko Corporation of America SKA096

Seiko Science.

Now available

as a fashion

accessory.

Kinetic | www.SeikoUSA.com

*Seiko, 2001*

# PROFESSION: PILOT    CAREER: ACTOR

People are acquainted with the star, the multi-faceted actor. But John Travolta is also a seasoned pilot with more than 5,000 flight hours under his belt, and is certified on eight different aircraft, including the Boeing 747-400 Jumbo Jet. He nurtures a passion for everything that embodies the authentic spirit of aviation. Like Breitling wrist instruments. Founded in 1884, Breitling has shared all the finest hours in aeronautical history. Its chronographs meet the highest standards of precision, sturdiness and functionality, and are all equipped with movements that are chronometer-certified by the COSC (Swiss Official Chronometer Testing Institute). One simply does not become an aviation supplier by chance.    W W W . B R E I T L I N G . C O M

For an authorized Breitling dealer, please call 800 641 7343

**Breitling Navitimer**
*A cult object for aviation enthusiasts.*

BREITLING
1884

INSTRUMENTS FOR PROFESSIONALS™

*Ralph Lauren, 2002*

Abercrombie & Fitch, 2004

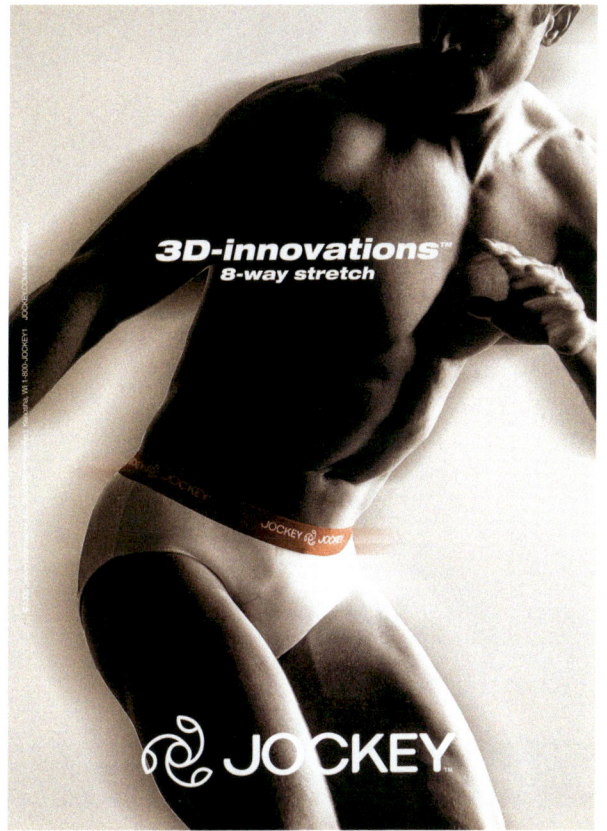

3D-innovations™
8-way stretch

JOCKEY™

Jockey, 2006

DIESEL
FOR SUCCESSFUL LIVING

live fast

High Speed Shopping.diesel.com

el, 2008

*Perry Ellis, 2002*

Available at Macy's and macys.com

David Beckham

EMPORIO ARMANI
UNDERWEAR
shop at emporioarmani.com

*Emporio Armani, 2008*

*Ralph Lauren, 2002*

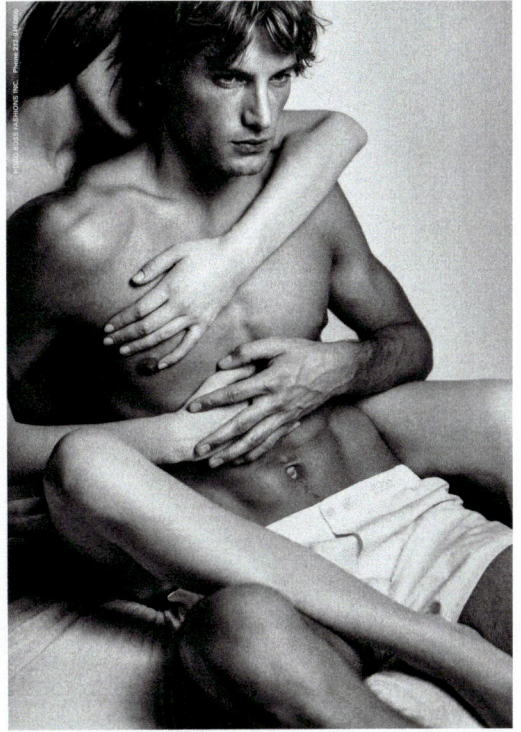

*Hugo Boss, 2002*

*Abercrombie & Fitch, 2005*

**INTRODUCING THE POLO MATCH SHIRT**

NEW YORK  BEVERLY HILLS  CHICAGO  BUENOS AIRES  DUBAI  TOKYO  HONG KONG  LONDON  PARIS  MILAN  MOSCOW

RALPHLAUREN.COM

*Ralph Lauren, 2007*

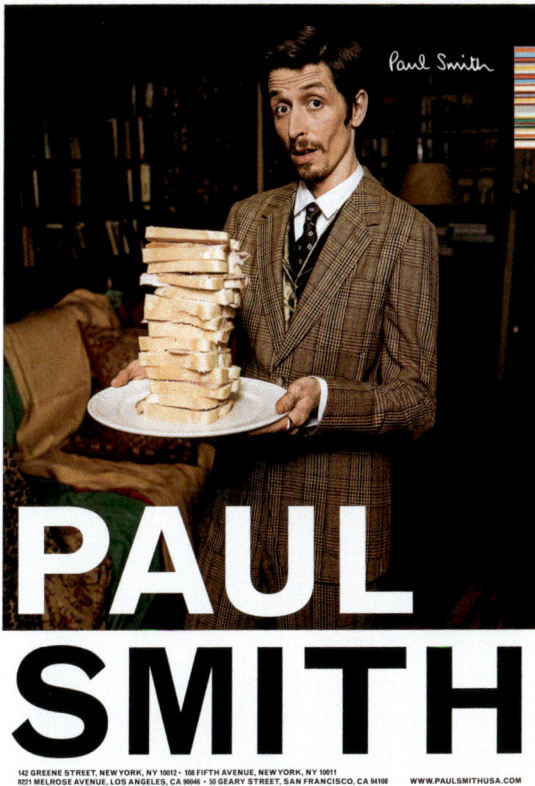

*Paul Smith, 2009*

*Banana Republic, 2008*

*Gap, 2002*

*G-Star Raw, 2008*

STACY ADAMS®
collection

*Stacy Adams, 2005*

▶ *Avirex*

COLOR

IZOD

*Izod, 2005*

Kidrobot, 2009

Gap, 2009

Op, 2009

G-Unit, 2007

Zoo York, 2004

Gap, 2004

Le Tigre, 2004

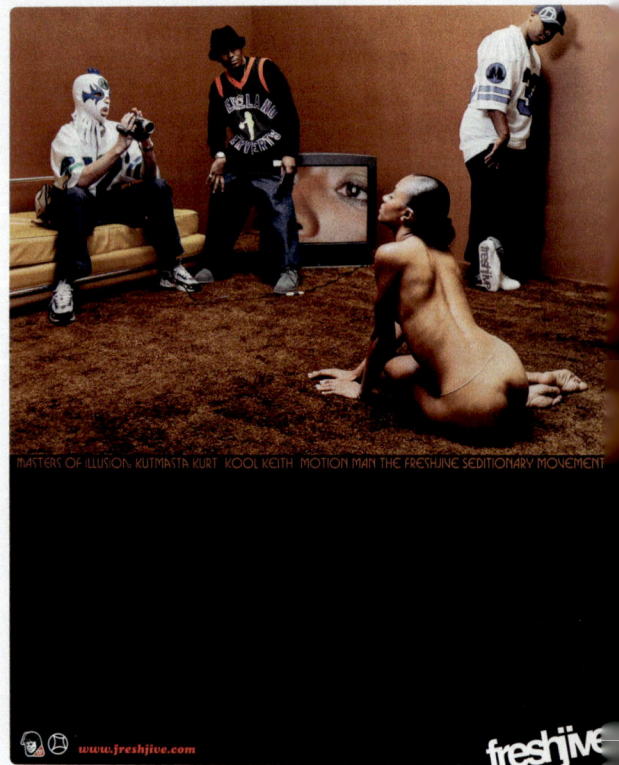

Freshjive, 2001

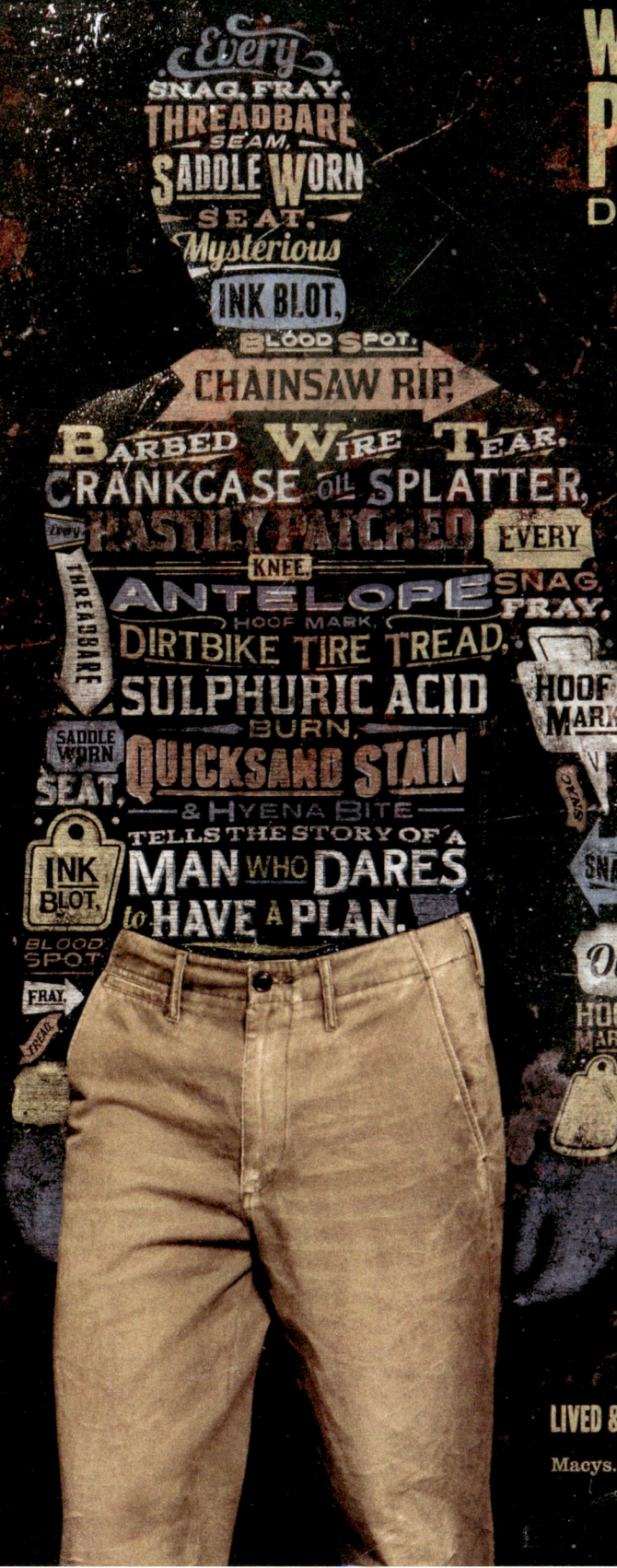

Dockers, 2009

*Sean John, 2004*

JORDAN TWO3

*Jordan Two3, 2002*

*Russell Athletic, 2001*

*Fred Perry, 2005*

steven tyler
concert T

your voice.

philip burke

*Gap, 2006*

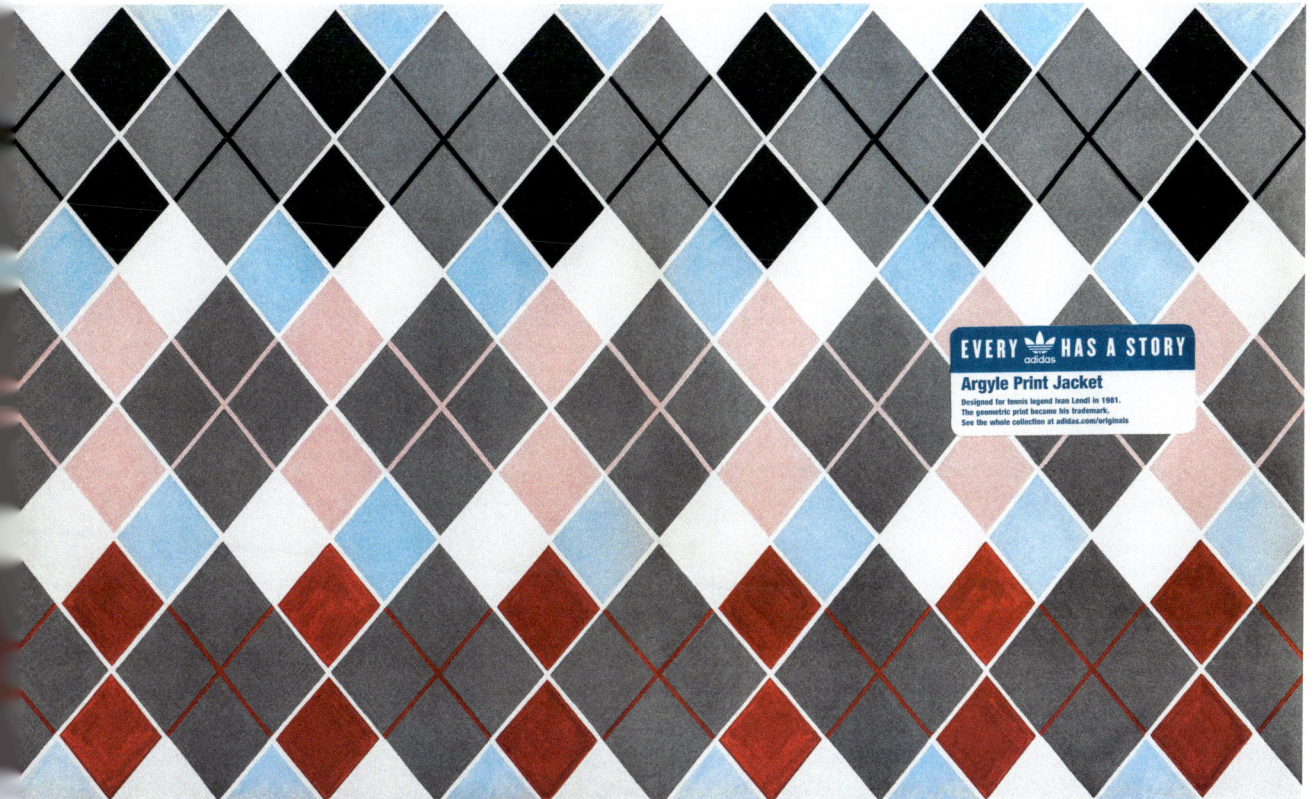

EVERY [adidas] HAS A STORY

**Argyle Print Jacket**

Designed for tennis legend Ivan Lendl in 1981.
The geometric print became his trademark.
See the whole collection at adidas.com/originals

*didas, 2002*

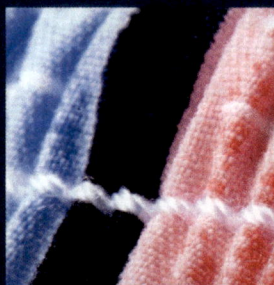

*Vilebrequin, 2008*

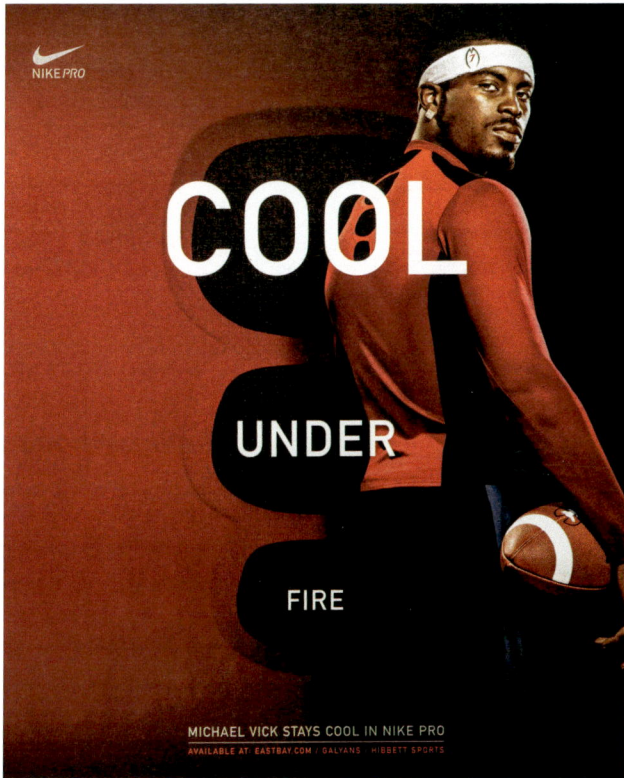

*Nike, 2004*

*Patagonia, 2008*

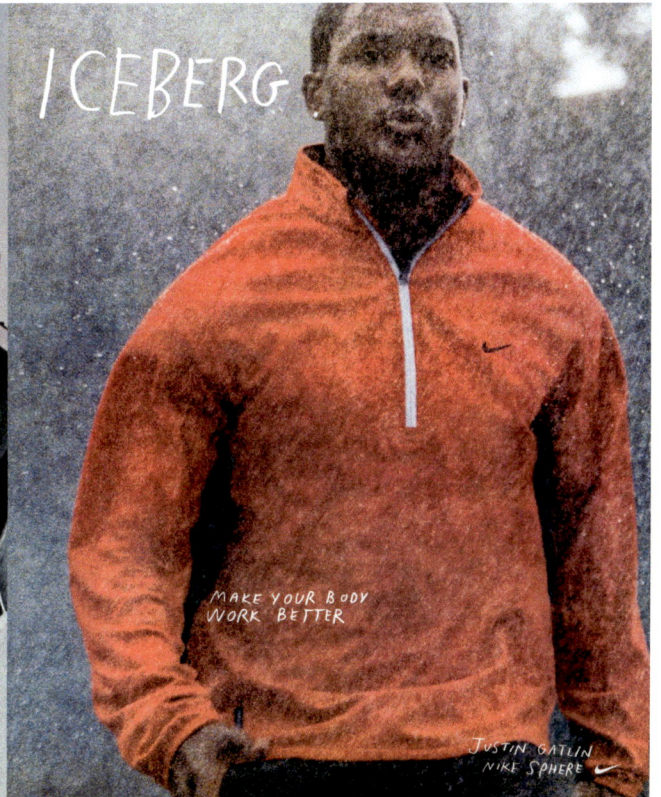

*ike, 2004*

▶ *Nike, 2010*

LEBRON JAMES, SF
OPPOSING TEAMS DON'T
REALIZE I WAS A FOOTBALL
PLAYER FIRST I CAN TAKE
THOSE HITS AND GIVE
A FEW BACK TOO.

NIKE (swoosh logo)

PREPARE
FOR COMBAT

NIKEBASKETBALL.COM

KOBE BRYANT, SG
I'LL DO WHATEVER IT
TAKES TO WIN GAMES.

"why Andy Warhol? why not Andy Warhol.
you can't do better than Andy Warhol!"

Paul Frank

*Paul Frank, 2005*

**PRADA**
Vitello Daino calfskin tote $1760, Tory Burch
Crinkle Reva Metallic Ballet Flats, exclusively
at Saks, $250

This classic texturized
metallic leather tote
features the signature
jacquard lining

*Prada, 2009*

*Tommy Hilfiger, 2000*

Ben Hudson and Alex Pascale. Secret Service. Year 2033.

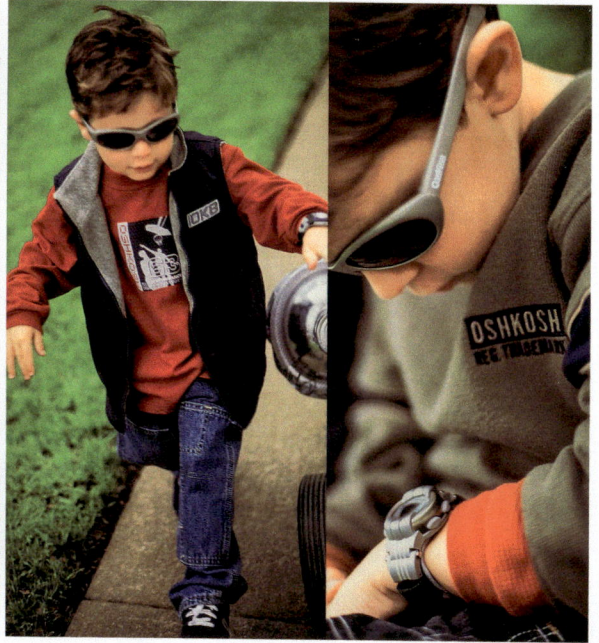

OSHKOSH
www.oshkoshbgosh.com

WHAT THE FUTURE WEARS

*Oshkosh, 2000*

How do you dress a doll who's more than 12" tall?

*Barbie*
Style

*Barbie Style, 2000*

*Barbie*
Style

Girls dress Barbie. Barbie dresses girls.

*Barbie Style, 2000*

back to school

paulfrank.com – facebook.com/paulfrank – paulfrank.com/blog

**PAUL FRANK**
industries

*Paul Frank, 2010*

Ralph Lauren, 2004

Pretty Perfect, 2010

g, 2003

Small Paul, 2006

# And the winner is...

## Luxurious Pleasure

Gucci, Gucci, Gucci. Where did the class go? Stooping to sophomoric suggestions of an enhanced male appendage and self-gratification is hardly the territory of a respected luxury brand. Thankfully, the fashion house came to its senses as the decade pressed on and the focus boomeranged back to fashion sans priapic symbols.

## Luxusbefriedigung

Gucci, Gucci, Gucci. Ich dachte, bei euch geht es um Klasse? Sich auf das Halbwüchsigenniveau eines angedeuteten männlichen Geschlechtsteils und Selbstbefriedigung hinunterzubewegen, ist ja nun wirklich nicht das angestammte Territorium einer respektablen Luxusmarke. Glücklicherweise kam das Modehaus im Verlauf des Jahrzehnts wieder zu Verstand und wandte sich abermals dem Fokus auf Mode ohne priapeische Symbole zu.

## Luxe et volupté

Gucci, Gucci, Gucci... Mais où est donc passé le chic ? S'abaisser à suggérer un appendice mâle au garde-à-vous façonné en solitaire, avec une subtilité de carabin, ce n'est pas digne d'une marque de luxe respectable. Heureusement, la maison a repris ses esprits en fin de décennie pour revenir à une mode exempte de symboles priapiques.

ALL-AMERICAN

▶ Gu

The sweet taste of honey and graham comes to Life.® life Honey Graham is full of surprises.

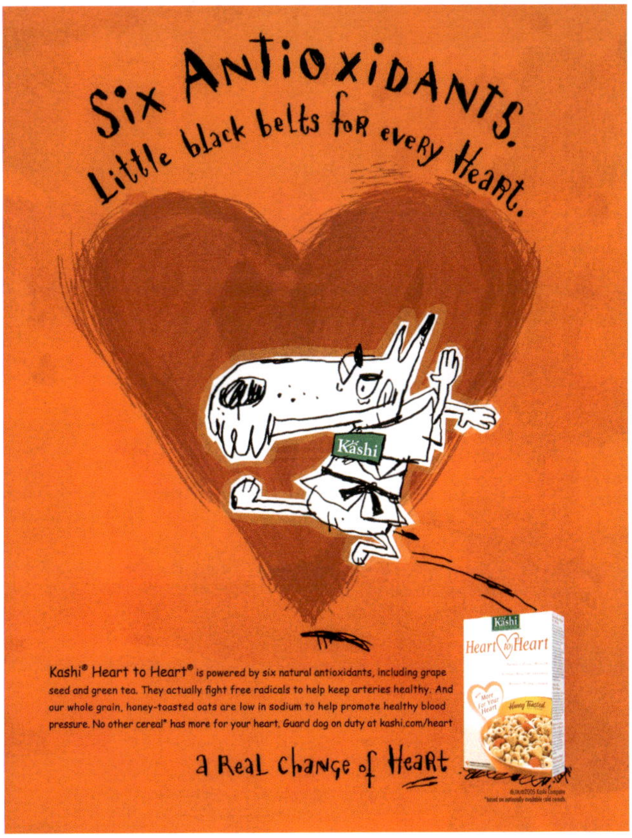


Kashi, 2005

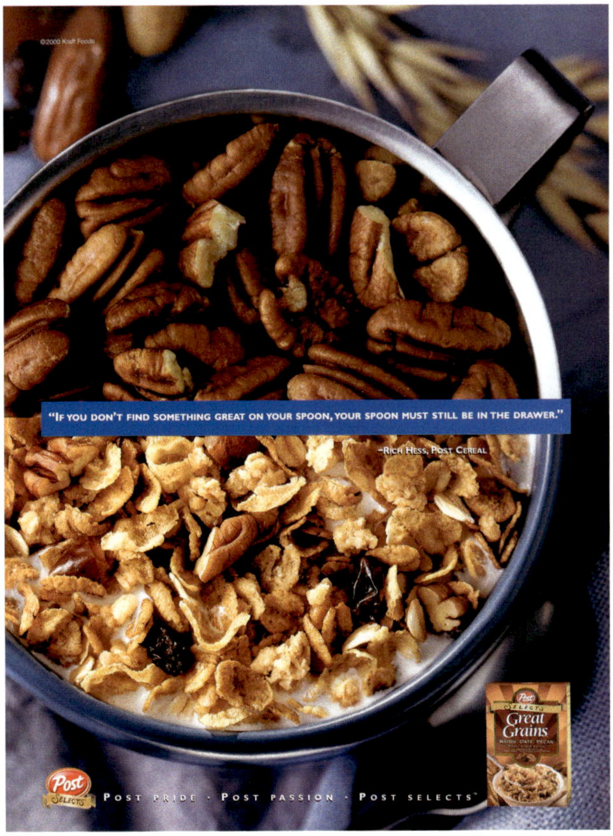


Post, 2000

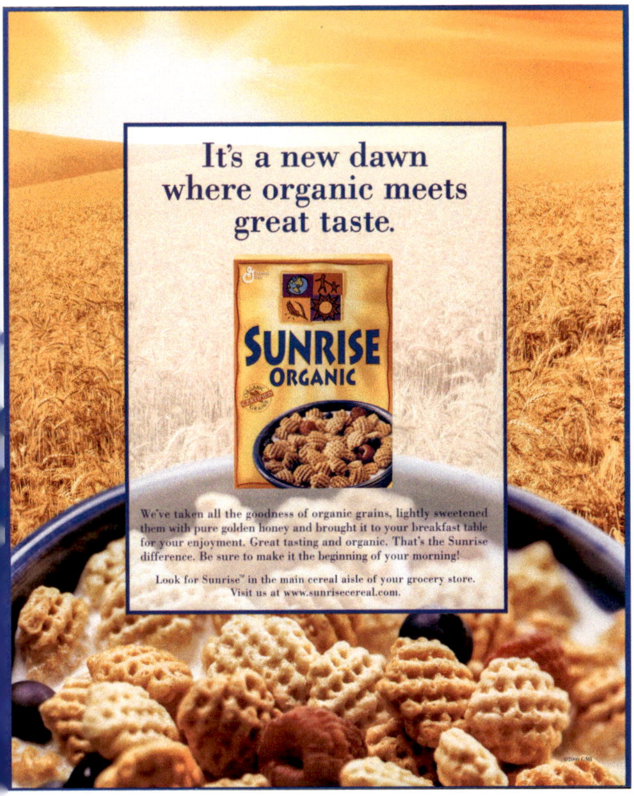


General Mills, 2000

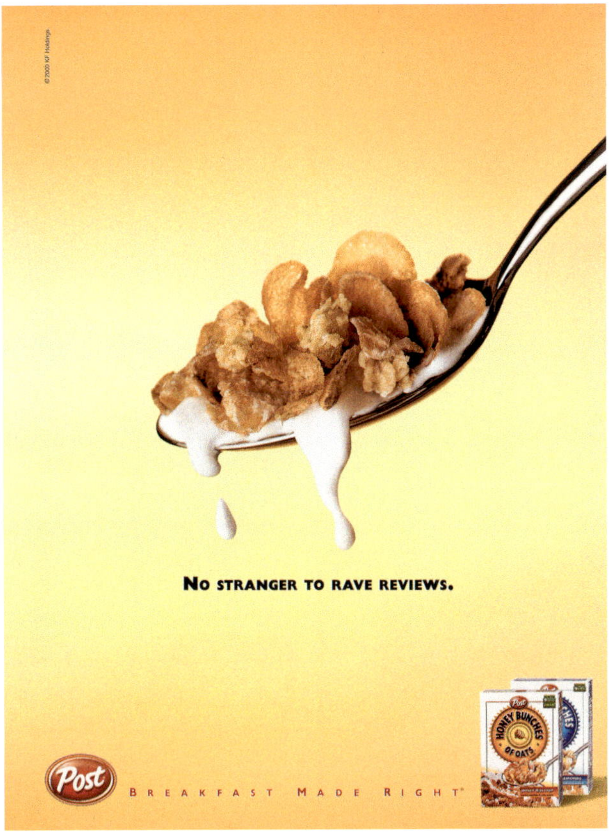


Post, 2000

What satisfies a hungry woman?

NEW!
Post
Shredded Wheat with Real Strawberries

*Post, 2008*

# OH, THE SHAME.

## CURIOUSLY STRONG

**ONE BAD MOTHERPUCKER**

THE CURIOUSLY STRONG SOURS

*Altoids, 2004*

*Altoids, 2001*

*Orbit, 2007*

*Wrigley's, 2002*

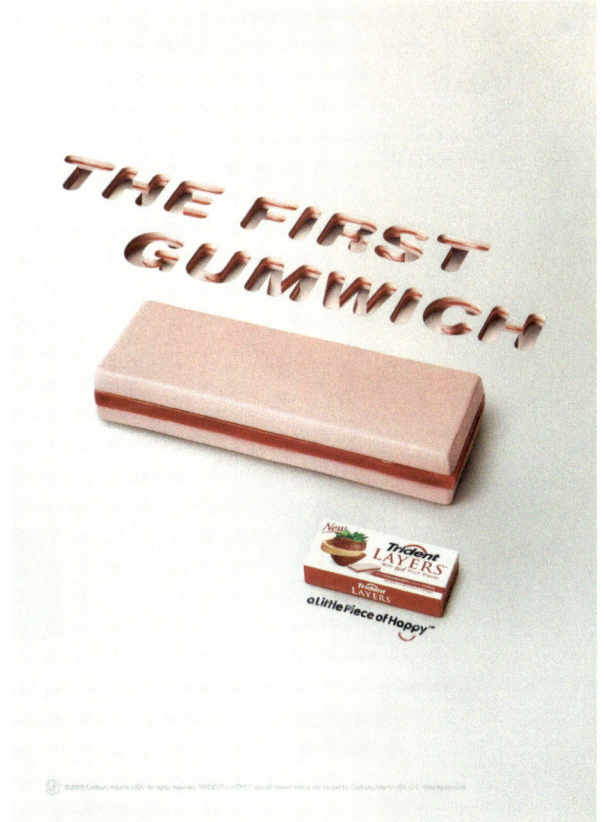

*Trident, 2010*

© 2006 McDonald's

Starving Artist?
I don't think so.

Dollar M Menu

Whether it's a Double Cheeseburger, fries,
or Hot Fudge Sundae, I can create anything
from a meal to a snack out of McDonald's®
Dollar Menu. Enjoying good food every day
doesn't make me less talented. Take a look
at my work. I call this my happy period.

For more information on the artist, Hebru, check out 365black.com

i'm lovin' it®

*McDonald's, 2006*

Taco Bell, 2004

McDonald's, 2004

st, 2001

National Pork Board, 2008

Warm milk has met its match.

Wendy's Late Night Pick-up Window
is open 'til midnight or later.
So, you can get a
hot 'n juicy Classic Single,
Classic Double with cheese
or Classic Triple with cheese,
and eat great, even late.

*Wendy's, 2004*

OVEN MITTS
SOLD SEPARATELY.

COME IN AND TRY THE NEW FRESH TOASTED
CHICKEN BACON RANCH TODAY.

fresh TOASTED

SUBWAY
eat fresh.

*Subway, 2005*

-Mr. Wendy

"I HAD A NIGHTMARE:
I DREAMT WENDY'S
WASN'T OPEN LATE."

Classic Double with cheese

It was horrible. Luckily it was only a dream.
Wendy's Pick-Up Window is open 'til midnight
or later so you can order anything on
the menu like a hot 'n juicy Classic Double
with cheese, made fresh and eat great, even late!
Sweet dreams.

-Mr. Wendy, "Unofficial" Spokesman

At participating locations.

*Wendy's, 2004*

You don't have to go to Salt Lake City to taste the glory.

*McDonald's, 2000*

McDonald's, 2010

McDonald's, 2008

Jack in the Box, 2001

McDonald's, 2001

DISCOVER
THE POWER OF
PROTEIN
IN THE LAND OF
LEAN BEEF

BEEF
IT'S WHAT'S FOR DINNER

BeefItsWhatsForDinner.com | Funded by The Beef Checkoff

*The Beef Checkoff, 2008*

# GO BUCK WILD

with the
**WHOPPER JR.**
now only a **BUCK** on the
NEW BK™ VALUE MENU.
Price and participation may vary.

BURGER KING®

HAVE IT YOUR WAY®

*Burger King, 2006*

Kraft Heinz, 2005

Capri-Sun, 2006

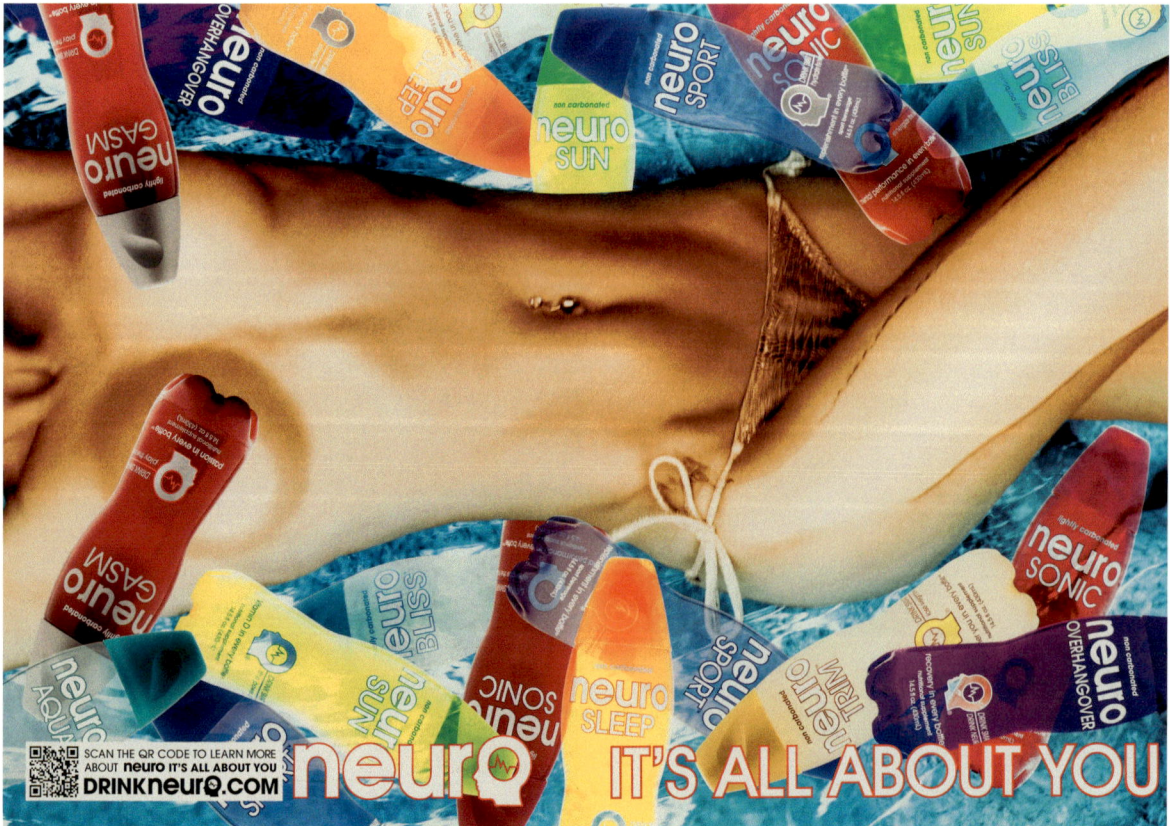

Neuro, 2001

AN OVERLY CAFFEINATED WORLD
DESERVES A SENSIBLY CAFFEINATED WATER.

new

20 calories

a touch of caffeine
20 mg*

3 B vitamins

propel
invigorating water
beverage
strawberry

It's how Propel does Energy Water.

*Propel, 2008*

497

*Glaceau, 2010*

*Izze, 2008*

*Gatorade, 2010*

*Snapple, 2009*

▶ *Fiji, 2008*

# Every drop is green.

FIJI Water is not merely the best-tasting water, it is also an environmentally responsible choice. Together with Conservation International, we are helping to save Fiji's largest owland rainforest, the Sovi Basin, in perpetuity. We're also reducing $CO_2$ emissions across our product's entire life cycle. This includes our raw materials, the eventual recycling of our bottles and every process in between. We then offset the remaining carbon footprint by 120%, making FIJI Water not just carbon-negative, but positively green.

**fijigreen.com**

*L'original*

*Smart Water, 2009*

*Evian, 2000* ◄ *Sanpellegrino, 2001*

*Brita, 2006*

Diet Rite, 2003

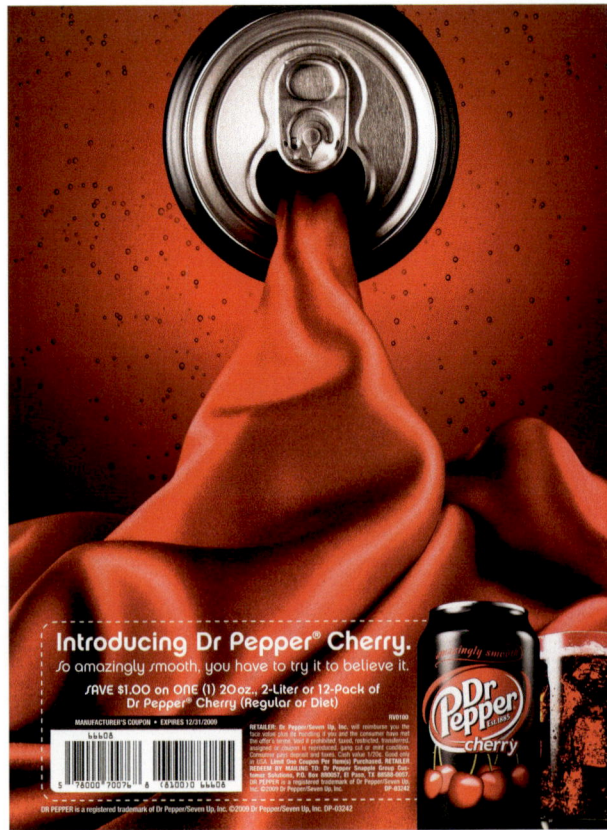

Dr. Pepper, 2009

electrolyte enhanced hydration.
vapor distilled purity.
the answer for tom brady.

Smart Water, 2008

► Mountain Dew, 2004

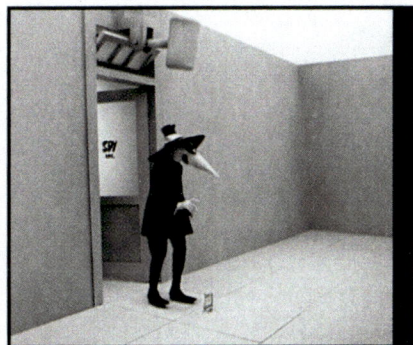

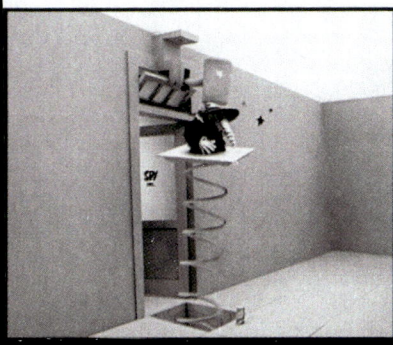

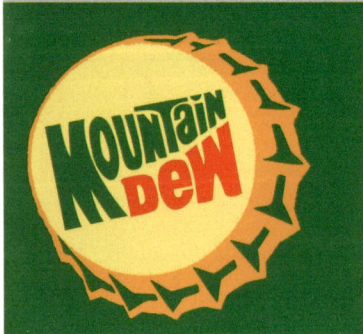

*Mountain Dew, 2004*

ONEIFY.COM

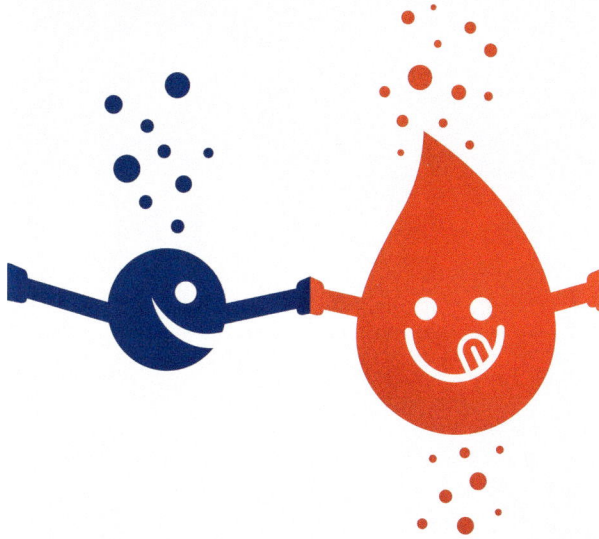

**ONE CALORIE AND FULL FLAVOR. ONEIFY.**

One calorie and full flavor have come together in Pepsi ONE. Now sweetened with SPLENDA Brand Sweetener, made from sugar so it tastes like sugar. Finally, a diet cola that's at one with your taste buds.

*Sweetened with Splenda*

PEPSI ONE, ONEIFY and the Pepsi Globe design are trademarks of PepsiCo, Inc.

*Pepsi, 2005*

**POP STAR!**

Vol. 1, Issue 2

THE LIGHT, REFRESHING WEEKLY

Diet Pepsi and entourage keep cool before a HOT night!

DIET PEPSI: TELL-ALL CONFESSION!!!

**"MILLIONS CAN'T GET ENOUGH OF ME!"**

diet PEPSI

LIGHT · CRISP · REFRESHING

THE 411

WORLD EXCLUSIVE!

THE **ULTIMATE** CELEB LOWDOWN: How to Keep Light, Crisp and Refreshing Through Any Drama!

ON KEEPING IT REAL.
DIET PEPSI—THE ONE CELEB EVERYONE WANTS TO KNOW!

DIET PEPSI, DIET PEPSI LIME, DIET PEPSI WILD CHERRY and the Pepsi Globe design are registered trademarks of PepsiCo, Inc.

*Pepsi, 2006*

make it loud. make it break decibel records. make it a sonic boom. make it a big deal. make it real. make it a song. make it a move-ment. make it so huge that it swallows up the whole scene. make it blow the doors off. make it make your idols scratch their heads. make it a reason to get up in the morning. make it rattle off the walls and make it an echo you'll remember for your whole life.

*Coca-Cola, 2005*

Great taste has its benefits.

Diet Coke PLUS

Great taste + vitamins and minerals

*Coca-Cola, 2008*

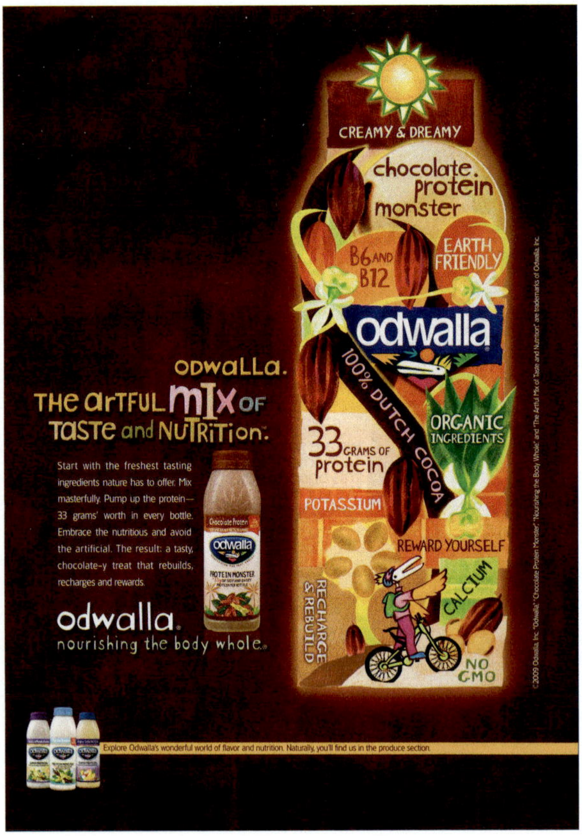


*Odwalla, 2009*

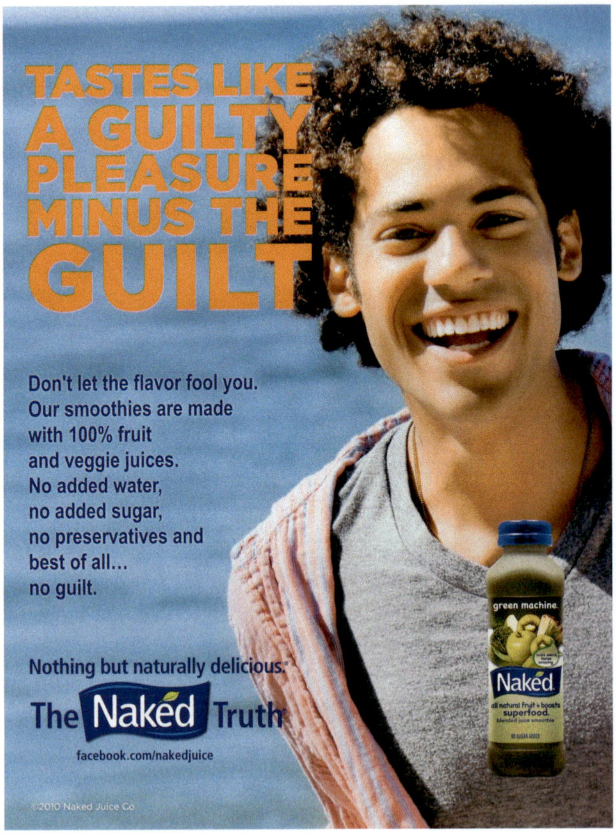


*Naked Juice, 2010*

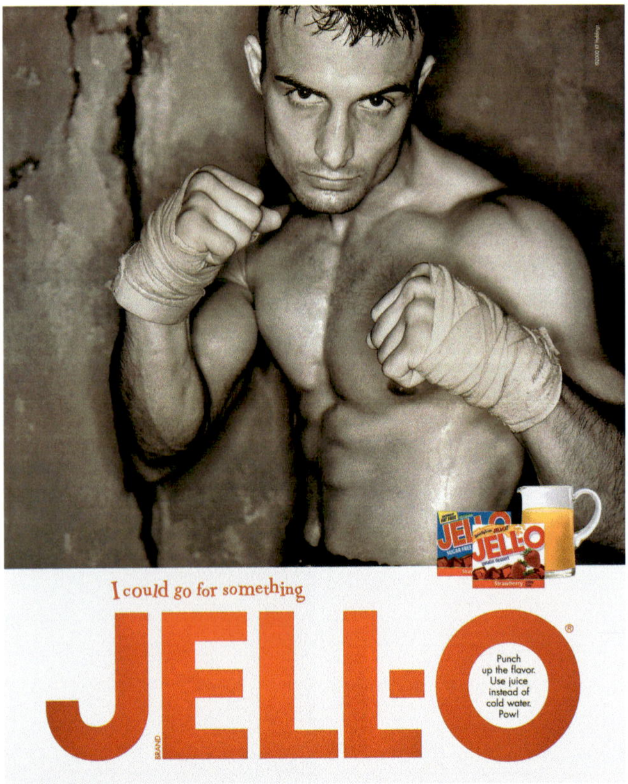


*Jell-O, 2000*

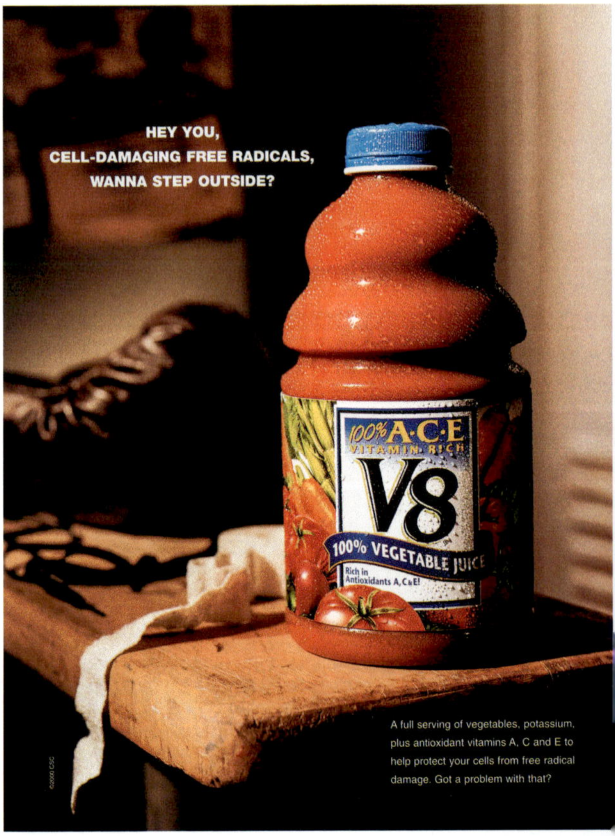


*V8, 2001*

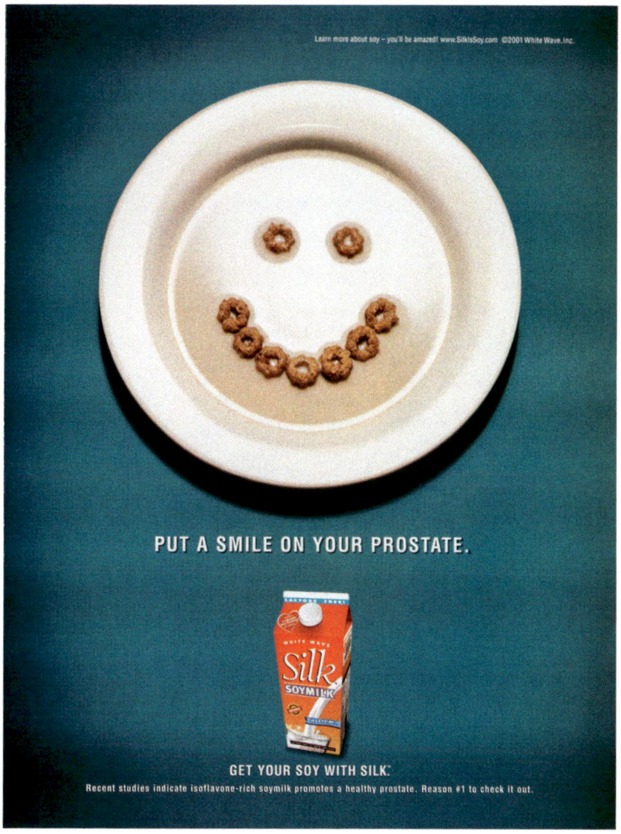


*Silk, 2001*

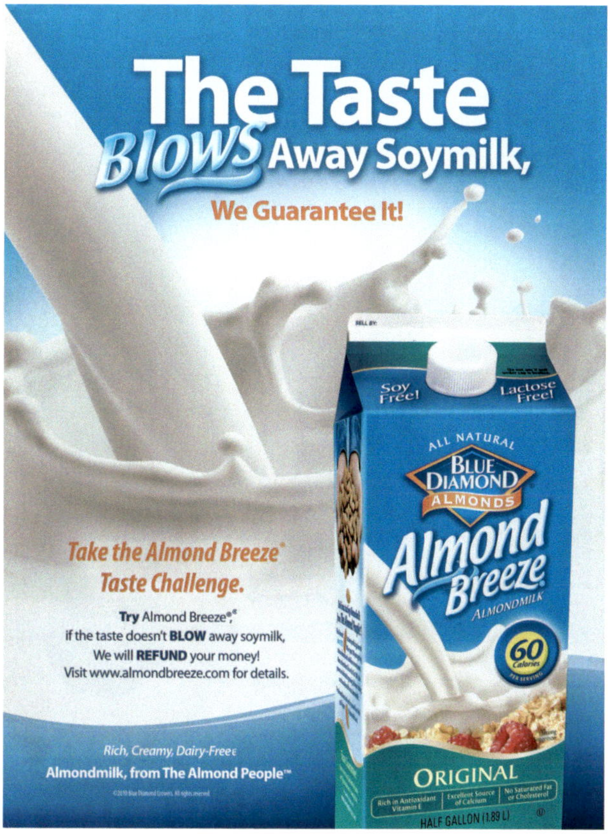


*Blue Diamond Almonds, 2010*

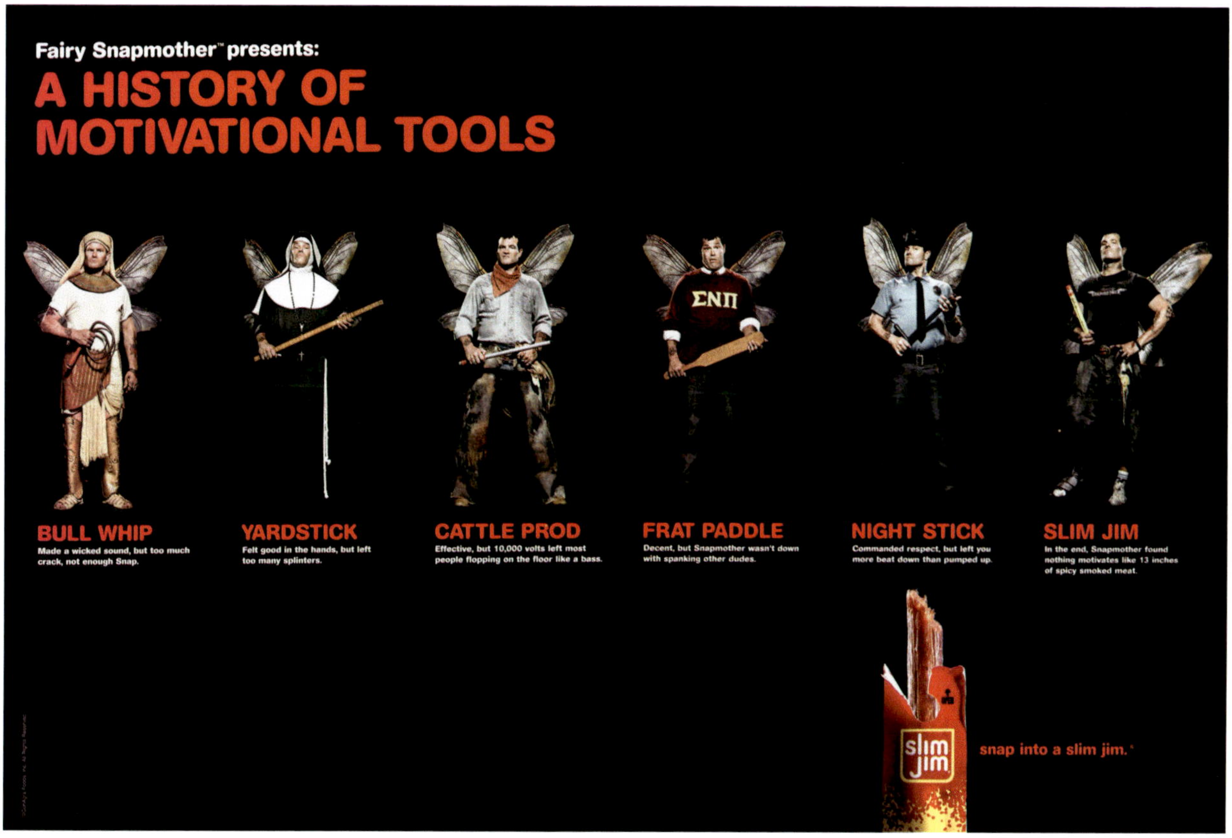


*Slim Jim, 2005*

Help get them going.
With Quaker Chewy® bars made from whole grain Quaker oats.

Go humans go

miss milk?

TONY

Now you can enjoy the great taste of milk and cereal again with
LACTAID® Milk. 100% real milk. Calcium-rich, lactose-free and delicious.

Available in Whole, 2%, 1%, Fat Free, and Calcium Fortified. **Lactaid**. Real milk.

*Lactaid, 2004*

miss milk?

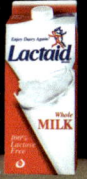

Get milk back in your life.
Lactaid® is real milk. 100%
wholesome and delicious.
But it's lactose free, so
it's easy on your stomach.

**Lactaid**. It's milk.

Available in Whole, 2%, 1%, Fat Free, and Calcium Fortified.

*Lactaid, 2002*

## A fresh new look.
## The same delicious milk.

The LACTAID® Milk
you know and trust
looks different on
the outside, but inside
it's the same **delicious**
and **wholesome**
**real milk** that's
**100% lactose-free**
so it's **easy to digest**.

100% LACTOSE FREE

REDUCED FAT MILK

**Lactaid**

Enjoy Milk
Again!         Taste
Goodness

NEW LOOK!

REDUCED FAT
**MILK**

100% LACTOSE FREE

EASY TO DIGEST

NEW LOOK IN STORES
SOON!

lactaid.com

*Quaker, 2009* ◄ *Lactaid, 2010*

## Drink to
## prostate health.

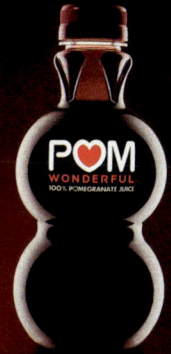

P♥M
WONDERFUL
100% POMEGRANATE JUICE

Sometimes, good medicine can taste great. Case in point: POM Wonderful.®
A recently published preliminary medical study followed 46 men previously
treated for prostate cancer, either with surgery or radiation. After drinking 8 ounces
of POM Wonderful 100% Pomegranate Juice daily for at least two years, these
men experienced significantly longer PSA doubling times. Want to learn more
about the results of this study? Visit pomwonderful.com/prostate. **Trust in POM.**

pomwonderful.com

*POM, 2008*

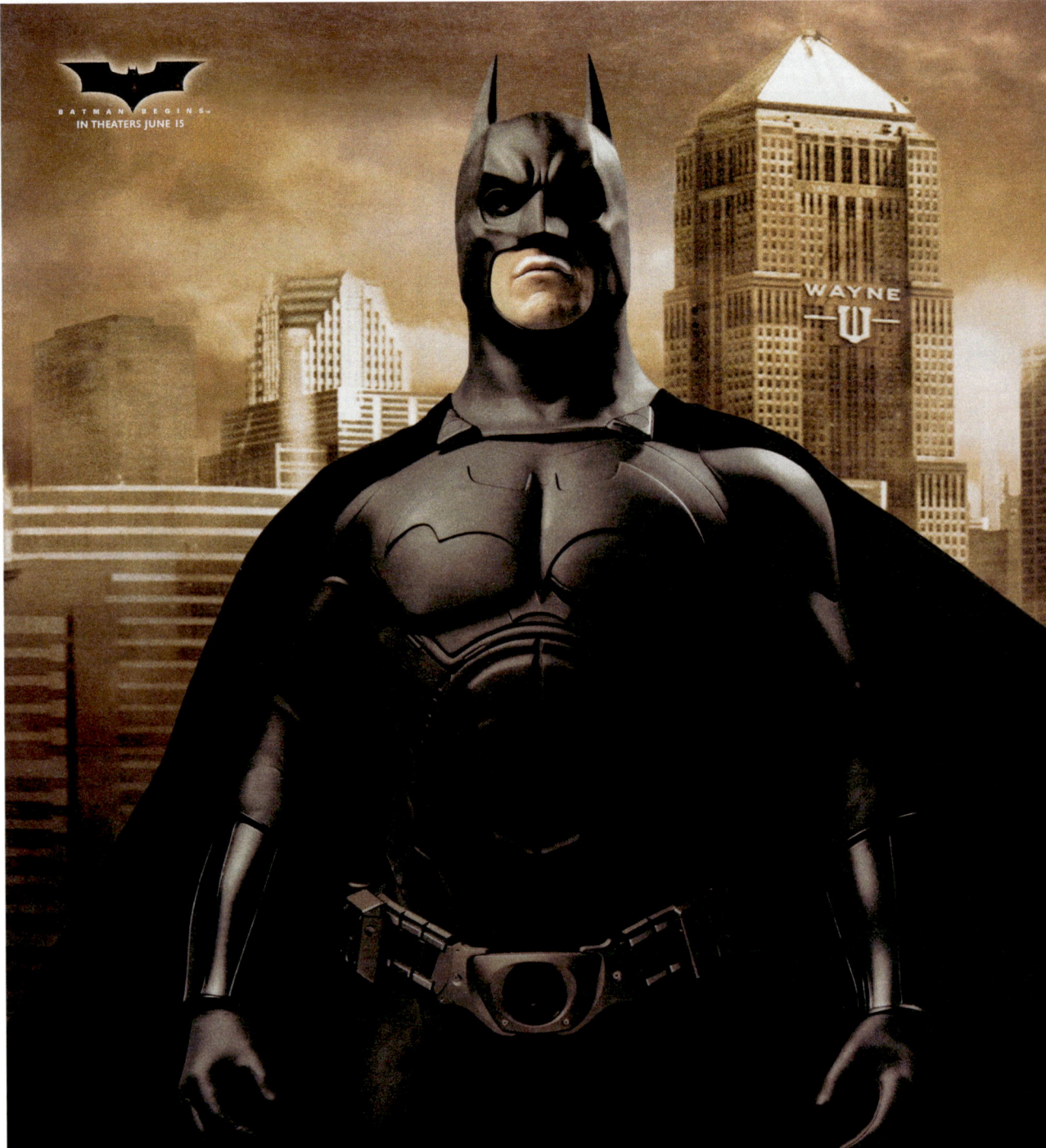

America's Milk Processors, 2005

Super.
That's how milk makes you feel. The calcium helps bones grow strong, so even if you're not from Krypton™ you can have bones of steel.

# got milk?®

SUPERMAN
RETURNS.
JUNE 30

*America's Milk Processors, 2006*

Want strong kids?

Milk has nine essential
nutrients your kids'
active bodies need.
Which means you'd better
remember to save
some for yourself.

got milk?

*America's Milk Processors, 2000*

I'm still standing.

Want strong bones?
Drinking enough
lowfat milk
now can help prevent
osteoporosis later.

got milk?

*America's Milk Processors, 2001*

got milk?

Lean machine.

When it comes
to winning titles,
perfect form helps.
So I serve up milk.
Studies suggest
people pursuing a
healthy weight could
lose more weight
and burn more fat by
including 24 ounces
a day of lowfat or
fat free milk in their
reduced-calorie
diet, instead of
8 ounces or less.
That's what I call
a nice return.

milk
your diet. Lose
weight!

*America's Milk Processors, 2006*

got milk?

Want strong
bones?

Your bones
grow until
about age 35
and the calcium
in milk helps.
After that,
it helps keep
them strong.

*America's Milk Processors, 2000*

The Peanut Butter Deluxe Licuado.

gotmilk.com has all kinds of licuado recipes. This indulgent Mexican drink has a banana, REESE'S® Peanut Butter Cups, ice and 1 cup of milk.

*America's Milk Processors, 2002*

Milk mustaches don't last long when you're a sponge.

Which means I may have to drink another glass of yummy chocolate milk.

Or two.

Or three.

Or four.

CHOCOLATE got milk?

SpongeBob SquarePants YOU WISH

*America's Milk Processors, 2001*

Haute cowture.

Trick or treat? There's no trick to it. The 9 essential nutrients in lowfat or fat free milk make it the perfect after-treat treat for your whole family. So this Halloween, dress up your costume with a look that's always in style. Wunderbar!

got milk?

*America's Milk Processors, 2008*

whymilk.com

Dairy Torres.
I'm a natural in water. But after a workout, my natural choice is milk. It's a strong starting block for wellness. The protein helps build muscle, plus its unique mix of nutrients helps me refuel. Three glasses of lowfat or fat free milk a day. Lap it up.

Drink well. Live well.
got milk?

*America's Milk Processors, 2009*

thedavidbeckhamacademy.com

Goal by Beckham.
Body by milk.

Heads up. The protein in milk helps build muscle and some
studies suggest teens who choose it tend to be leaner. Staying active,
eating right, and drinking 3 glasses a day of lowfat or fat free milk
helps you look great. So grab a glass and get in the game.

got milk?

www.bodybymilk.com

DAVID BECKHAM ©2006 AMERICA'S MILK PROCESSORS

*America's Milk Processors, 2006*

▶ *America's Milk Process*

Father knows best.
Want to win? Milk has 9 essential nutrients active bodies need.
In other words, it's the greatest.™

got milk?®

Avocados from Mexico

the amazing avocado™

# vitamins, minerals & great ideas.

With nearly 20 essential vitamins and minerals and even more ways to serve them, Avocados from Mexico add a rich, creamy texture to meals you make every day. Slice them on a salad, spread them on a sandwich, or dice them into soup. Visit our website for more ways to get the benefits of avocados and the smiles of your family.

discover all the health benefits @ theamazingavocado.com

*Mexican Hass Avocado Importers, 2010*

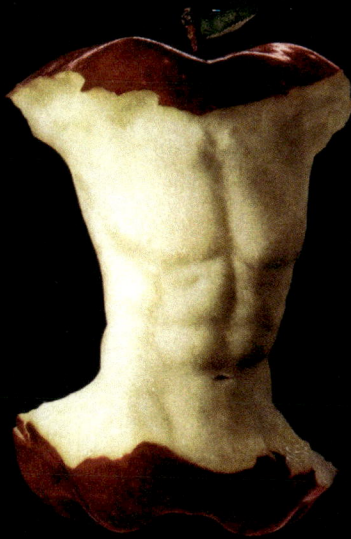

IF YOU BLOW
**THIS DIET**
YOU'RE ONLY OUT 89 CENTS.

THE 3-APPLE
A DAY PLAN

A WASHINGTON
APPLE
BEFORE EACH MEAL

Washington Apples, the official diet pill of Gold's Gym.®
www.3appleplan.com

*Washington Apples, 2003*

517

bluebunny.com

So good, it speaks for itself.

BLUE BUNNY
PREMIUM
Bunny Tracks

LOADED WITH INDULGENCE. COWABUNGA.

Chocolate so good
it'll give you the chills.

DoveBar®

Fall madly in
Dove

the amazing avocado™

**delicious ideas are in bloom.**

Everywhere you look, there are great new recipes for Avocados from Mexico. Slice them into any salad or spread them on any sandwich. They're a simple, natural way to add creamy texture and rich flavor, not to mention nearly 20 vitamins, minerals and phytonutrients in a 1-ounce serving. Pick up some avocados in the produce department today, and taste for yourself.

discover all the health benefits @ theamazingavocado.com

PEANUTS:
ENERGY for the good Life.
nationalpeanutboard.org

*Mexican Hass Avocado Importers, 2010*

*National Peanut Board, 2010*

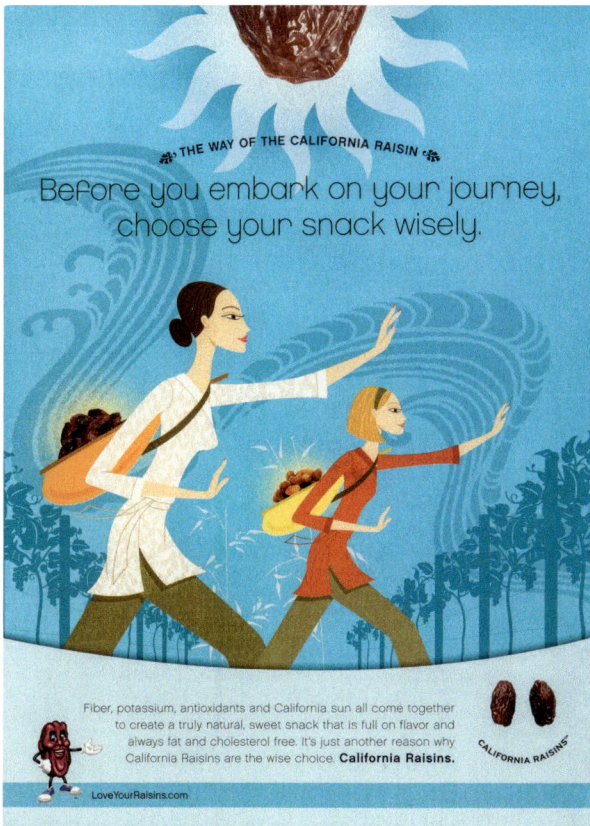

*Häagen-Dazs, 2008 ◄ California Raisins, 2009*

*California Raisins, 2010*

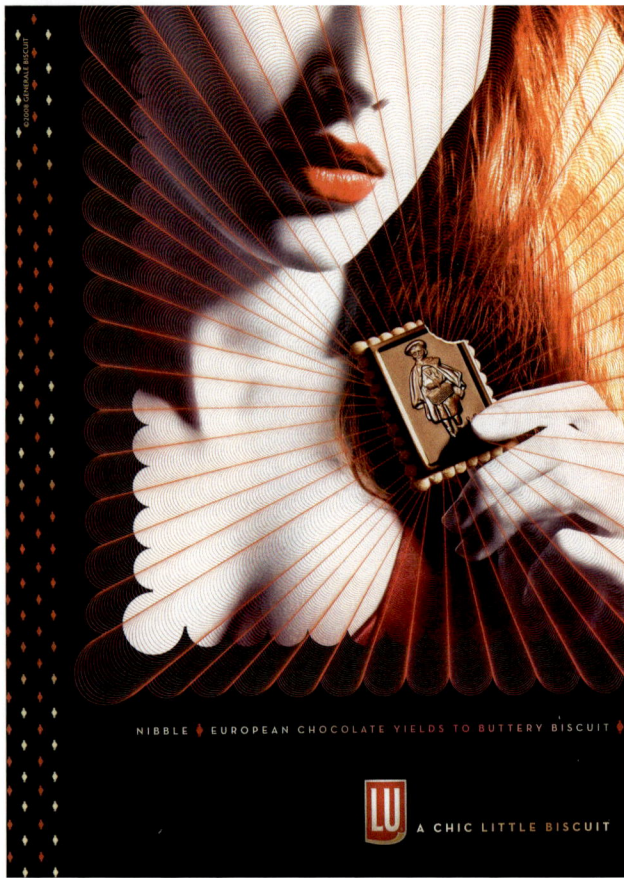

LU, 2008

Ben & Jerry's, 2009

Starbucks, 2004

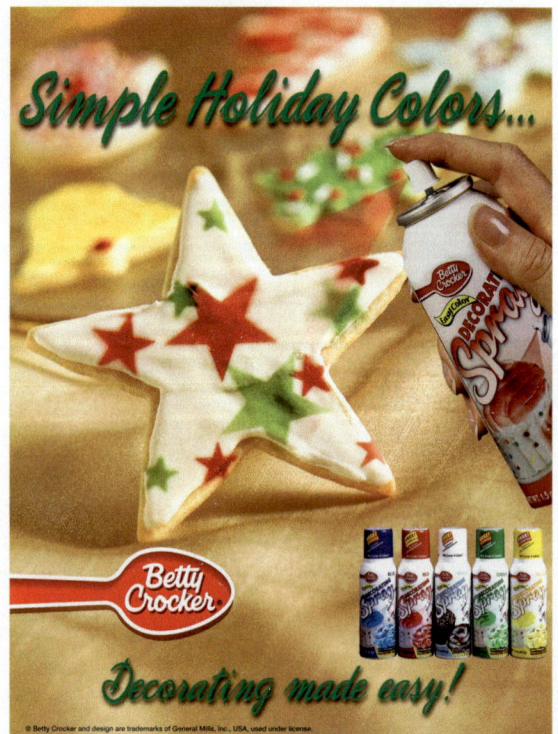

Betty Crocker, 2002

▶ Bear Naked, 200

*Oreo, 2010*

*Kellogg's, 2003*

*Ritz, 2000*

*Pepperidge Farm, 2002*

Hope for a Blizzard

Add tempting Torani flavoring
syrups to coffee. Hot cider. Cocoa.
Sparkling water. Even champagne.
Then spread cheer to anyone who
drops by, from in-laws to Santa Claus.
Call us at 1-800-775-1925 for a free
recipe booklet, or visit www.torani.com

**Torani Sparkler**
1 T. Torani syrup (try Vanilla,
    Raspberry or Caramel)
6 oz. champagne or sparkling cider
Stir together gently.
Drink to having a snow day.

Torani®

LIFE IN COLOR

525

America's Dairy Farmers, 2000

Kraft Heinz, 2000

Five Brothers, 2000

Hidden Valley, 2009

**EYE CANDY**

WHAT DOES THIS LUSCIOUS CHOCOLATE "M&M'S"® WEAR TO STAND OUT FROM THE GUYS IN THE BAG? ATTITUDE. PHOTOGRAPHY BY ELFIE SEMOTAN. FASHION BY WYLIE MORAN.

Green is wearing white vinyl boots with signature silver buckles, $625, by Cass. Ivory cotton gloves with pearl buttons, $285, by Rafael Lampon. Candy coat, about 50¢, available in bags of "M&M's"® Chocolate Candies.

www.m-ms.com
© Mars, Incorporated 2000

*Mars, 2000*

527

the NEW
however-you-want-it
frappuccino®
blended beverage

BOOOM!

Caffeinated
CARAMEL
ATTACKS

ADD
extra
COFFEE

COSMIC
Collision
OF
COFFEE
&
CARAMEL

**Extra Coffee**
Caramel Frappuccino®

Blended Beverage

Visit Frappuccino.com to create your own.
Come to Starbucks to try it today!

Express your Looooooooove!

*Starbucks, 2010*

*Lavazza, 2006*

*Jif, 2010*

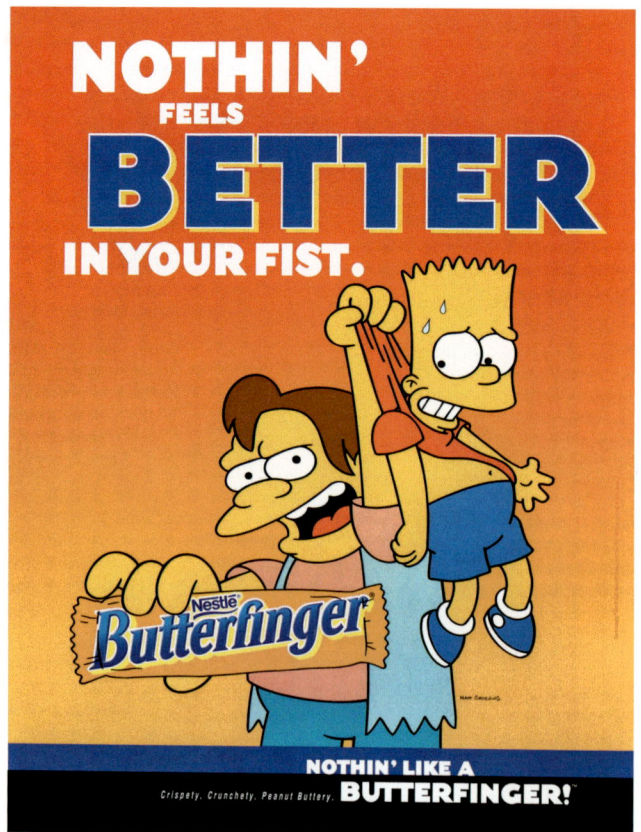

*Nestlé, 2001*

*PAM, 2009*

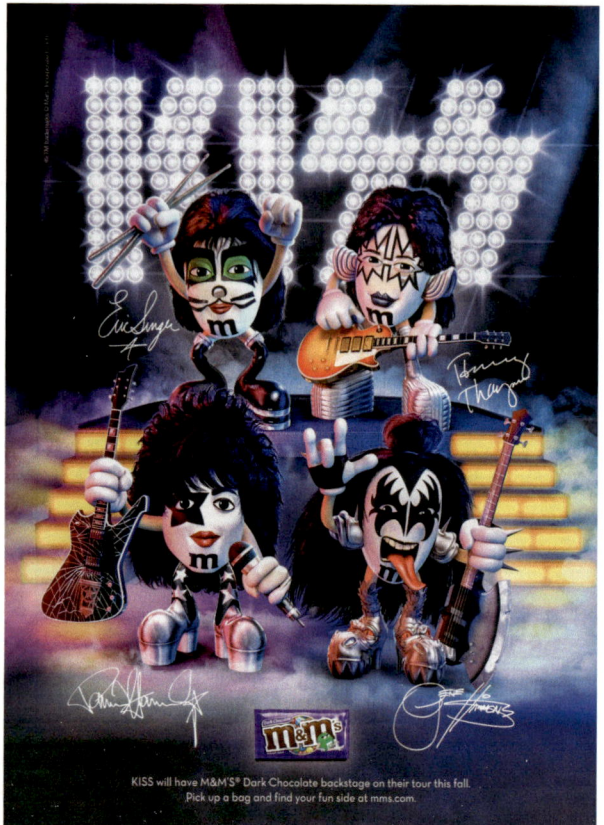

*Mars, 2009*

if one is good, a handful must be better.

Starburst
isn't life juicy?

*Mars, 2001*

SALT LAKE 2002 GAMES SUPPLIER

-Lenny Krayzelburg, 25
*Swimmer*
3X Olympic Gold Medalist
PowerBar user since 1996

©PowerBar

"There are a lot of guys willing
to put in the time and kill
themselves training. Which would
be okay, if **PowerBar** that was
all it took."   **Be great.**

PowerBar HIGH PERFORMANCE ENERGY BAR
VANILLA CRISP FLAVOR

*PowerBar, 2001*

# WHAT ARE YOU HUNGRY FOR?

To keep the edge, I train with 110% intensity.
It's what drives me to outdo my
last workout and helps me get results.

*- Carlos Garcia, Firefighter*

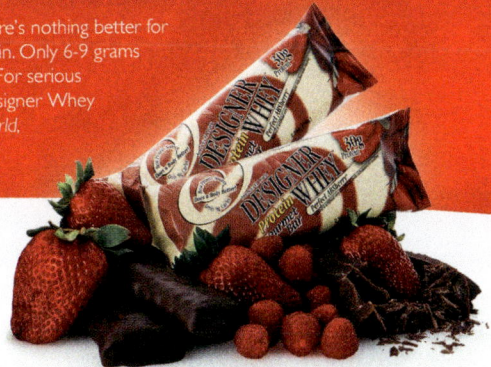

*Next Proteins, 2001*

533

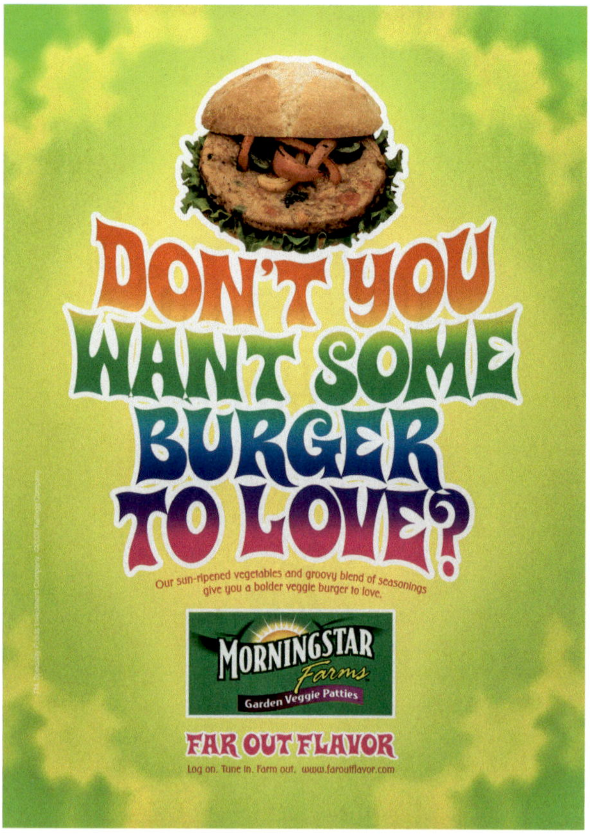


*Morningstar, 2000*

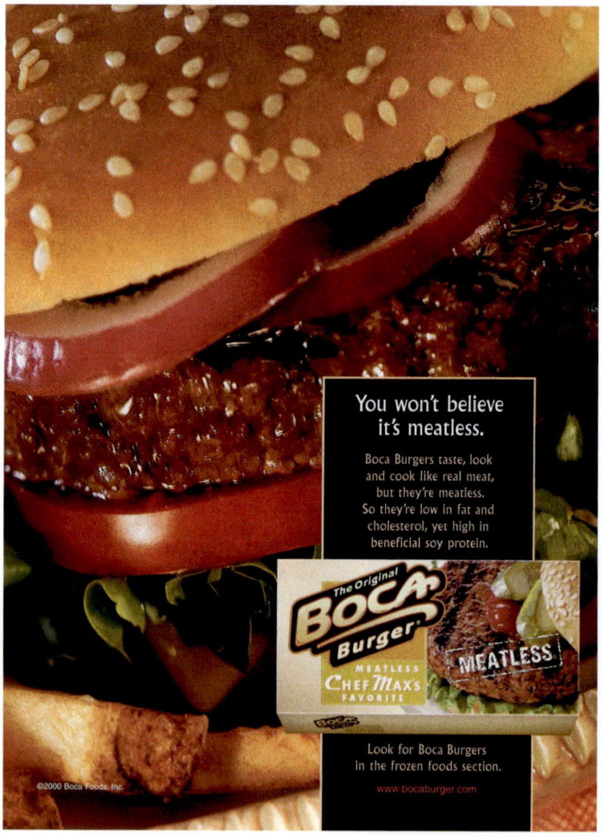


*Kraft Heinz, 2000*

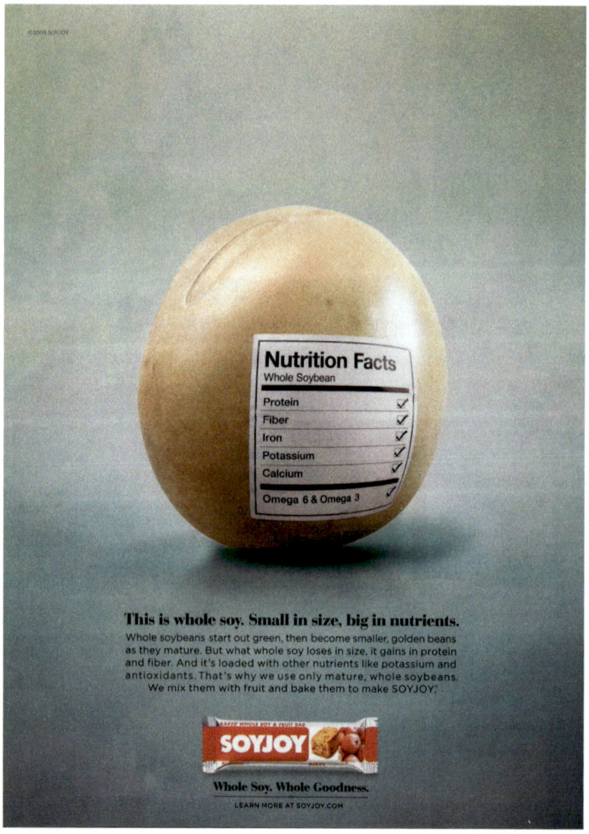


*SOYJOY, 2010*

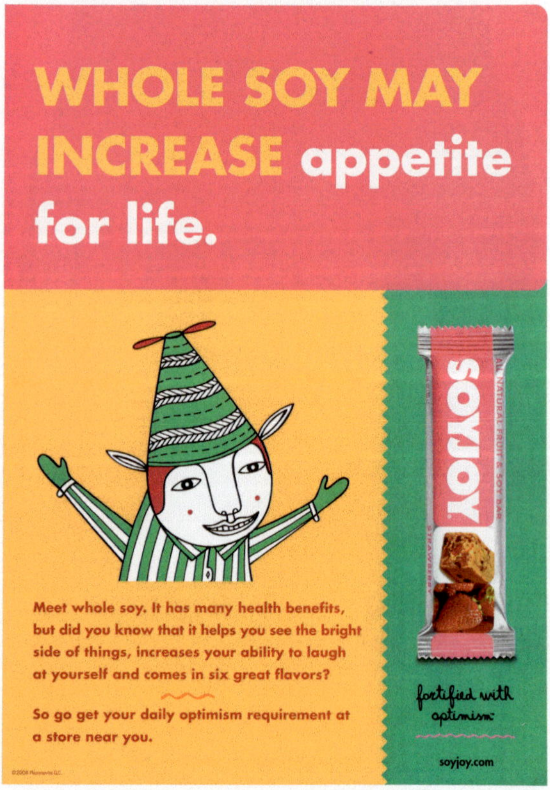


*SOYJOY, 2008*

# DURING THE DUST BOWL, SOYBEANS DID MORE THAN JUST REVIVE THE EARTH. THEY HELPED REVIVE AMERICA.

The 1930s. The Great Depression turned the land of opportunity into a land of despair. Struggling farmers, in an attempt to reap greater profits, cultivated large tracts throughout the Great Plains. This removed precious nutrients and moisture from the soil, putting a great strain on the land. Couple that with cattle overgrazing and a drought courtesy of Mother Nature, and the Dust Bowl was born.

Enter the soybean. Packed with soil-replenishing nitrogen, it gave back to the land what crops like corn and wheat stripped away. Planted in large quantities, and utilized in crop-rotation practices first developed in ancient China, soybeans helped suppress erosion and hold the ground together.

With the stabilization of the land helping to stabilize the economy, America was slowly pulled out of the Great Depression. Thanks in part to the amazing soybean – for over 5,000 years an integral part of cultures and diets.

Today, it's this same historic soybean that we take, mix with fruit, and bake to make every SOYJOY.®

*Packed with Soy. Baked in History.*™

SOYJOY.COM

© 2009 SOYJOY

MYHUNGER.COM

Ball Park

©2007 Sara Lee Corporation.

# HUNGER GETS
## WHAT HUNGER WANTS

*Ball Park, 2007*

*Ball Park, 2010*

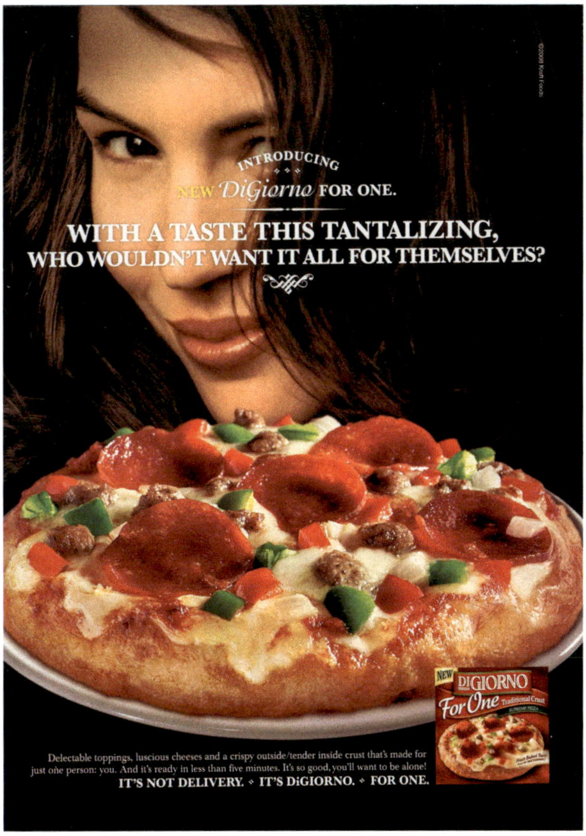

*DiGiorno, 2008*

*Kraft Heinz, 2003*

*Oscar Mayer, 2006*

Mars, 2004

Italian Trade Commission, 2004

Ragu, 2008

Kraft Heinz, 2010

▶ Italian Trade Commission, 20...

The Italian food collection.

cayenne

Italian Trade Commission - New York
Government Agency

AGNESI
DIVELLA
Garofalo
RUMMO
Unione Industriali Pastai Italiani

FALL-WINTER. SPRING-SUMMER.
Every season is the perfect occasion to discover the great creations of Italian gastronomy: Chianti Classico Black Rooster wine, Parmigiano-Reggiano® cheese, Prosciutto di Parma and the pasta produced by some of the members of UNIPI, the Italian pasta association. This elegant collection of inimitable flavors is available to you at fine restaurants and specialty stores.

PARMIGIANO REGGIANO

PARMA
Prosciutto di Parma

APPLY LIBERALLY TO HUNGER PAINS.

FEED YOUR NFL SIZE HUNGER. NEW CAMPBELL'S® CHUNKY®BBQ BURGER SOUP. *IT FILLS YOU UP RIGHT.*®

*Campbell's, 2007*

▶ *Green Giant, 2000*

CAN I PICK 'EM
OR WHAT

## smiles are something you never need to budget.

Our bologna has just 4 grams of sugar. PB&J has 16. And it's made with premium beef, no fillers. So in these times of tough choices, *Oscar Mayer* Beef Bologna is one choice that's sure to make everyone happy.

For the love of b-o-l-o-g-n-a.

*Oscar Mayer, 2009*

## WITH 100% REAL CHEESE, IT'S MAC & CHEESE TO THE MAX.

Look for it in the frozen food section! It's microwavable!

MAXARONI IS PACKED WITH AS MUCH CALCIUM AS A GLASS OF MILK AND HAS THE NEW CHEESY TASTE KIDS LOVE.

*Nothing Comes Closer to Home.*

*Stouffer's, 2002*

## Moms who know say "No" Less

As a mom you have to say "no" a lot. With Kid Cuisine you can say "yes"!

A full serving of veggies

The fun stuff kids love

The protein kids need

Calcium for growing bodies

The goodness of whole grains

Real ingredients like white meat chicken

Kid Cuisine® meals come with good stuff you want and fun stuff kids love. Learn more at sayyestoyourkids.com

### Kid Cuisine

The more you know, the less you "no".™

*Kid Cuisine, 2010*

## Good Corn Dog!

**State Fair** Corn Dogs...You will love the convenience, the kids will love the great taste.

• Easy to make. Just pop them in the microwave.

• Honey-dipped in corn bread batter to deliver a delicious sweet taste.

The only corn dogs with juicy **Ball Park** franks inside.

In your grocer's freezer.
www.ballparkfranks.com
© 2002 Sara Lee Corporation.

*Ball Park, 2002*

**Matt Horton**
Former Muffin Maker

*Kellogg's, 2000*

TURN ON TASTE BUDS YOU
NEVER KNEW YOU HAD.

T.G.I. FRIDAY'S® COMPLETE SKILLET MEALS.
EAT BOLD, NOT BLAND.

*TGI Fridays, 2009*

You Wonder: Does she practice that look or does it come naturally?

You'll never
have to Wonder
about the goodness of new
Wonder Smartwhite. It has the
Fiber of 100% whole wheat,
the Calcium of 8 oz of milk
and Vitamin D. Plus that
great Wonder taste
your family loves.

*Wonder, 2010*

ONLY CAMPBELL'S
IS MADE WITH
FRESH EGG NOODLES.
32 FEET
IN EVERY CAN!

So many, many reasons it's so...
M'm! M'm! Good!

*Campbell's, 2010*

To make the very best bacon,
we take the slow road.

Oscar Mayer bacon is carefully selected, hand-trimmed and naturally
hardwood smoked for hours. Because there are no shortcuts to that
one-of-a-kind Oscar Mayer flavor America says is the best.

For the love of bacon.

*Oscar Mayer, 2009*

▶ *Uncle Ben's, 2010*

DOGGIE DENTURES
Because brushing is just too hard.

Or, there's DENTASTIX.
The treat that's clinically proven to reduce up to 80% of tartar buildup.
Dogsrule.com

®/TM Trademarks ©Mars, Incorporated 2010.

Pedigree, 2010

Cats everywhere are having a hard time smelling their litter boxes.    freshstep.com

*Fresh Step, 2010*

# And the winner is...

## BlāK to the Drawing Board

Well, actually, the loser was BlāK, Coca-Cola's major miscalculation that blending the flavors of Coke and coffee would be a winning combo. Bowing to the rise of coffee as the preferred "trendy" beverage of millions of Americans, Coca-Cola introduced the product with a resounding thud. The soda was a definitive failure and joined New Coke, OK, Vault, and Green Tea Coke on the company's shelf of shame.

## BlāK zurück ans Reißbrett

BlāK war kein Winner, sondern ein waschechter Loser. Coca-Colas totale Fehlkalkulation, dass ein unwiderstehliches Getränk dabei herauskommen würde, wenn man Cola und Kaffee zusammenkippte. Coca-Cola beugte sich dem neuen Trend von Kaffee als dem hippen Getränk von Millionen Amerikanern und knallte uns diese Flasche auf den Tisch. Aber das Gebräu reihte sich mit New Coke, OK, Vault und Green Tea Coke in die erfolglosen Schandflecken der Firmengeschichte ein.

## BlāK, au piquet

En fait, le vrai perdant a été BlāK, la grosse erreur de calcul de Coca-Cola, qui a cru que mélanger les arômes du Coca et du café lui rapporterait le gros lot. Le café est alors la boisson «branchée» préférée de millions d'Américains et Coca-Cola s'emballe. Le soda fait un flop monumental et rejoint les New Coke, OK, Vault et autres Coca au thé vert dans la vitrine de la honte.

▶ Coca-Col

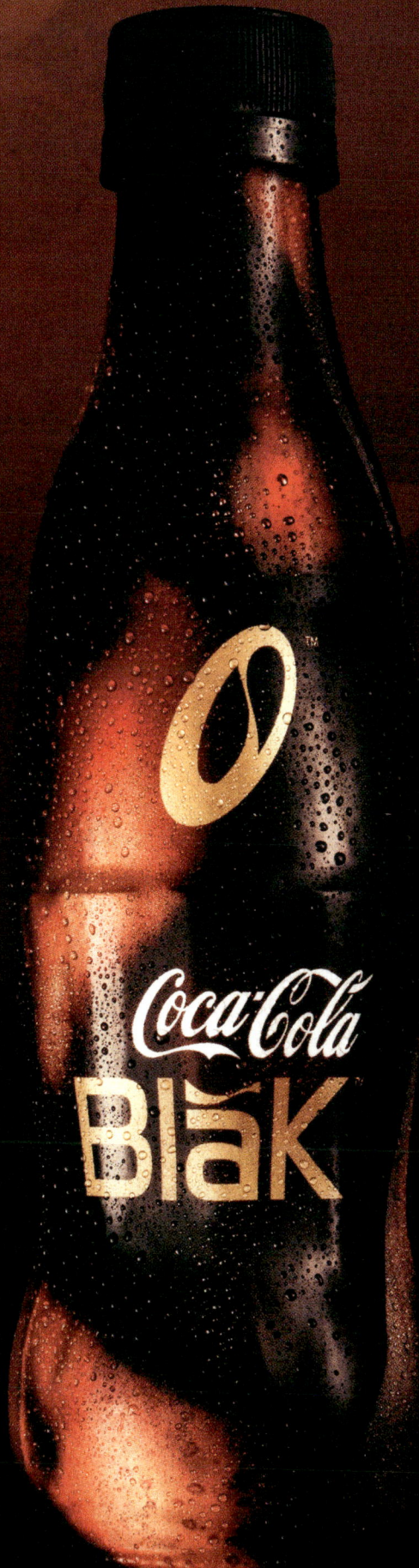

*Trojan, 2007* ◄ *Chanel, 2001*

*Introducing*

A NEW TEAM OF FRAGRANCES

# RALPH LAUREN

THE BIG PONY COLLECTION

*Ralph Lauren, 2010*

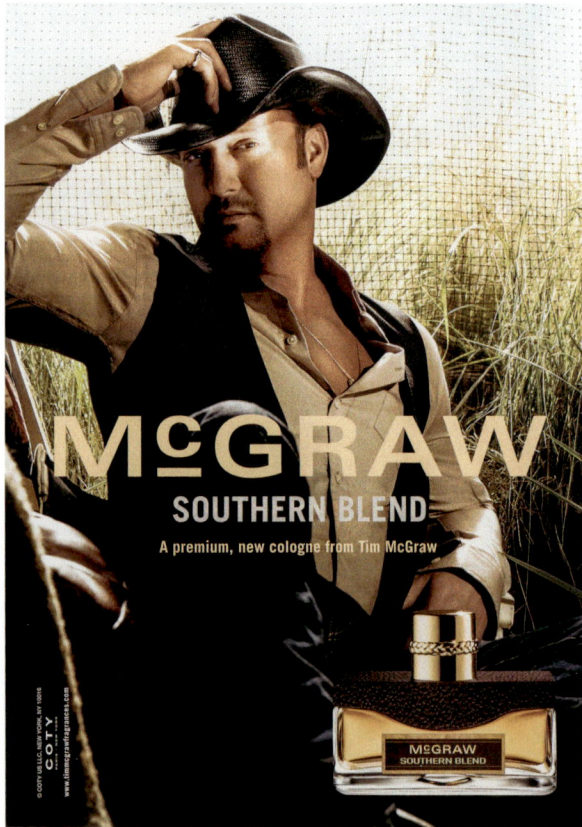

*McGraw, 2009*

*Stetson, 2006*

*Donald Trump, 2004*

*Paris Hilton, 2005*

*Celine Dion, 2004*

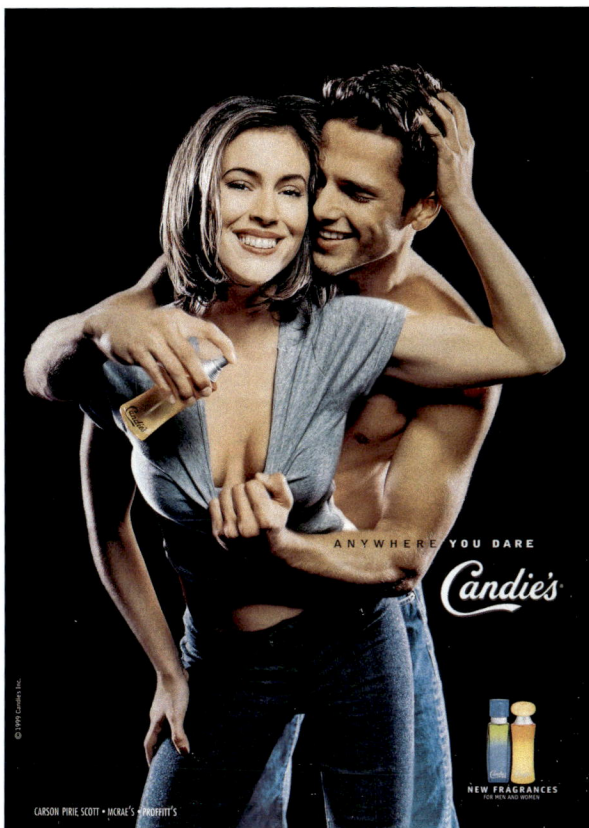

*Candies, 2000*

*Paris Hilton, 2005*

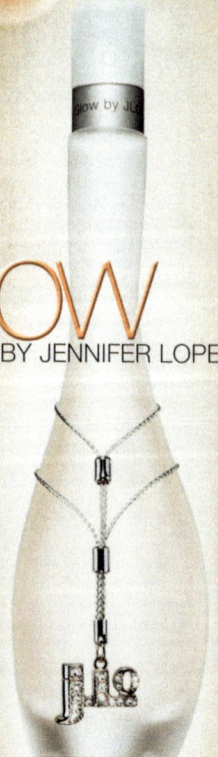

FRESH-SEXY-CLEAN. it's the **Glow**
THE NEW FRAGRANCE BY JENNIFER LOPEZ

Glow by JLO

Available at
Fine Department Stores

*Jennifer Lopez, 2002*

www.jenniferlopez.com/fragrances

*Elizabeth Taylor, 2003*

*Avon, 2009*

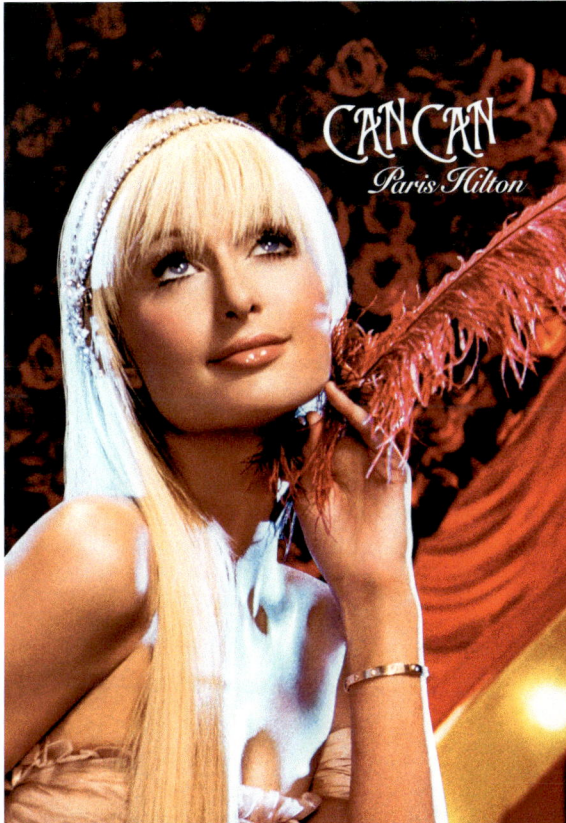

*Paris Hilton, 2007*

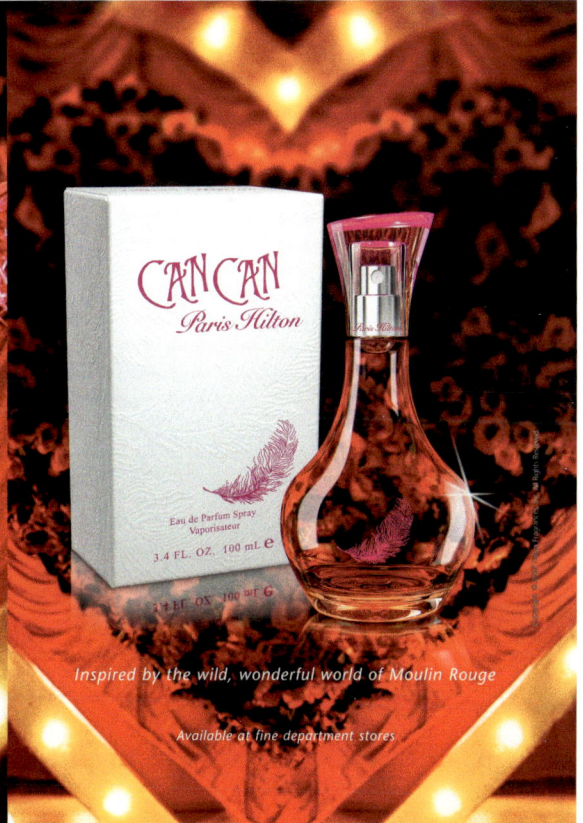

Usher, 2008

Chanel, 2003

Tommy Hilfiger, 2004

Aramis, 2004

*Michael Jordan, 2004*

*David Beckham, 2007*

*Elizabeth Arden, 2003*

*Liz Claiborne, 2004*

*Dunhill, 2002*

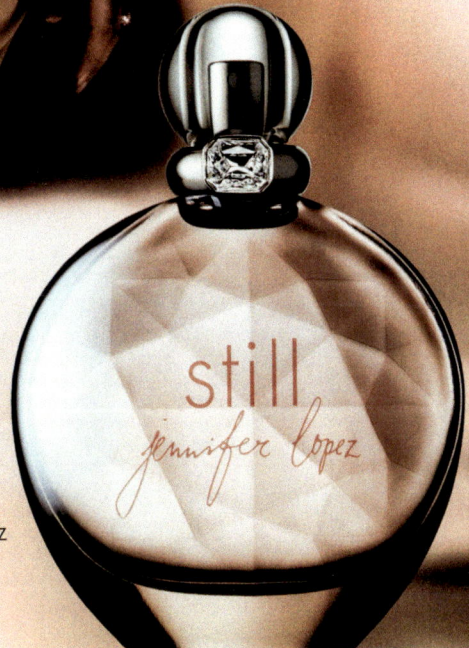

in the eye
of the storm
i am

## still
*jennifer lopez*

still
*jennifer lopez*

a new fragrance premiere by jennifer lopez

ROBINSONS-MAY    HECHT'S    FILENE'S    FOLEY'S

*Jennifer Lopez, 2003*

IRINA PHOTOGRAPHED BY JUERGEN TELLER

# DAISY
## MARC JACOBS

THE NEW FRAGRANCE FOR WOMEN
**SAKS FIFTH AVENUE / NORDSTROM / NEIMAN MARCUS**

*Marc Jacobs, 2007*

▶ *Yves Saint Laurent, 2000*

OPIUM
the fragrance from
Yves Saint Laurent

CHANEL

*Chanel, 2003*

*Giorgio Armani, 2000*

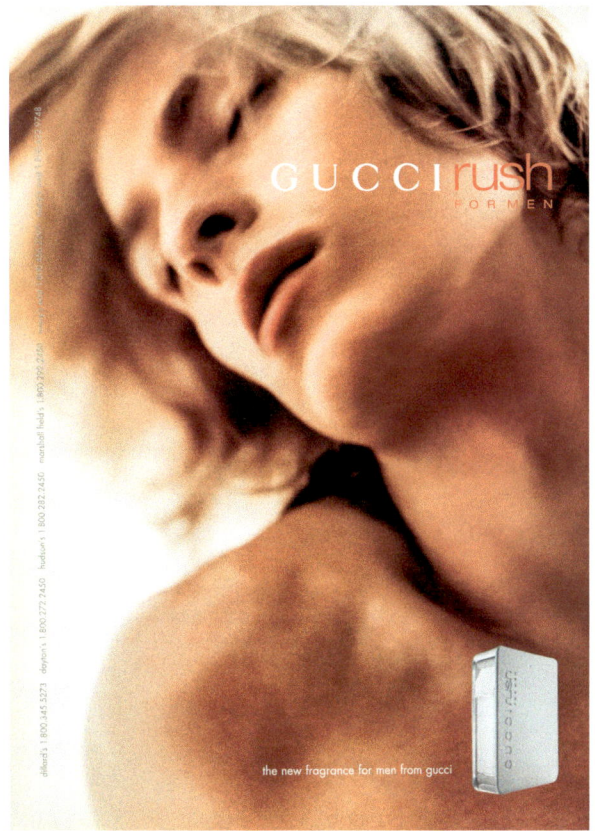

*Gucci, 2000*

*Calvin Klein, 2003*

*Burberry, 2004*

Lacoste, 2008

Roberto Cavalli, 2004

Dolce & Gabbana, 2006

DiRTy ENGLiSH

LIFT TO SMELL

THE

www.juicycouture.com

Juicy Couture

Fragrance for men

*Juicy Couture, 2008*

Davidoff

Cool Water

EAU DE
TOILETTE

Available at Fine Department Stores

*Davidoff, 2000*

Ralph Lauren, 2004

Tom Ford, 2007

Calvin Klein, 2003

Calvin Klein, 2009

*Ralph Lauren, 2004*

*Givenchy, 2002*

*Dolce & Gabbana, 2001*

*Vera Wang, 2004*

DOLCE & GABBANA
*Parfums*

*Dolce & Gabbana, 2001*

Stetson, 2003

Pierre Cardin, 2007

Calvin Klein, 2007

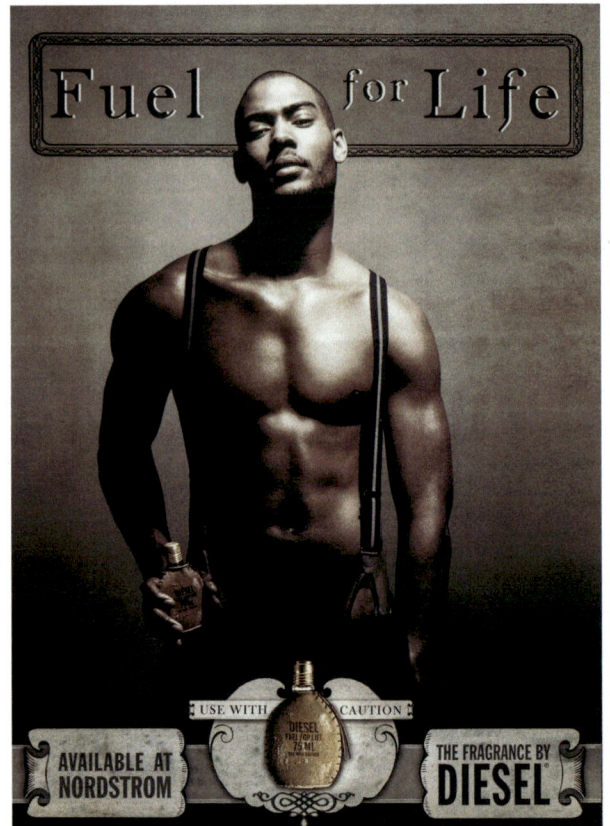
Diesel, 2007

▶ Lucky Brand, 2001

Get Lucky!
XXXOOO

 *Lucky You* **LUCKY BRAND**

NEW FRAGRANCES FOR MEN AND FOR WOMEN

DILLARD'S • CARSON PIRIE SCOTT

Jean Paul GAULTIER

"CLASSIQUE"

Jean Paul Gaultier, 2009

Jean Paul Gaultier, 2000

THE NEW FRAGRANCE FOR MEN

# MARC JACOBS
# BANG

MARCJACOBSBANG.COM    MARC JACOBS PHOTOGRAPHED BY JUERGEN TELLER

AVAILABLE AT FINE DEPARTMENT STORES AND MARC JACOBS BOUTIQUES

*Marc Jacobs, 2010*

*Tom Ford, 2007*

TOM FORD

THE FIRST FRAGRANCE FOR MEN FROM TOM FORD.

*Tom Ford, 2007*

◁ THERE'S A NEW COWBOY IN TOWN.

*Stetson, 2003*

**Chatting got you hoarse?**

Treat your throat®

Soothe your dry, scratchy throat with the delicious cooling relief of Halls Fruit Breezers.® In no time flat you'll start to feel like yourself again. Now go call someone and let 'em know.

Use as directed. **hallsfruitbreezers.com**

*Halls, 2005*

FOR A **BETTER-LOOKING TOMORROW.**

Vicks NyQuil. The nighttime, sniffling, sneezing, coughing, aching, fever, best sleep you ever got with a cold... medicine.

VICKS *breathe life in*™

*Vicks, 2009*

Don't let nasal congestion get in between you and your sleep.

*Breathe Right.* ADVANCED

Opens your nose to relieve nighttime congestion the instant you put it on. For as long as you have it on.

It's your right to Breathe Right. GET 2 FREE STRIPS AT BREATHERIGHT.COM

*Breathe Right, 2010*

**Mucinex·D says the less sinus pressure the merrier.**

When mucus packs into your sinuses, you need Mucinex D. It breaks up mucus that causes congestion and sinus pressure. And thanks to a unique dual-release formula, one dose lasts for a full 12 hours. So when mucus moves into your sinuses, kick it out with Mucinex D.

**Mucinex** Mucinex in. Mucus out.®

Use as directed.

www.mucinex.com   AVAILABLE AT THE PHARMACY COUNTER

*Mucinex, 2009*

**Moms are 73% friendlier to alien invaders when they don't have a sinus headache.**

Now the strength of Motrin IB is combined with a powerful decongestant so you can get to your sinus pain and pressure before it gets to you. And it's nondrowsy. Good thing This is no time to space out.

**Motrin** Sinus Headache Caplets

Life is too good to feel bad.®

*Motrin, 2000*

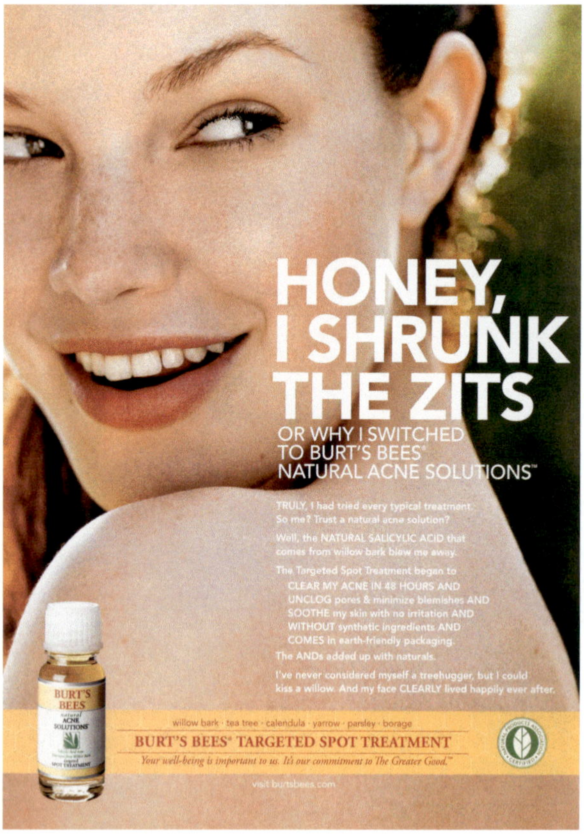


Burt's Bees, 2009

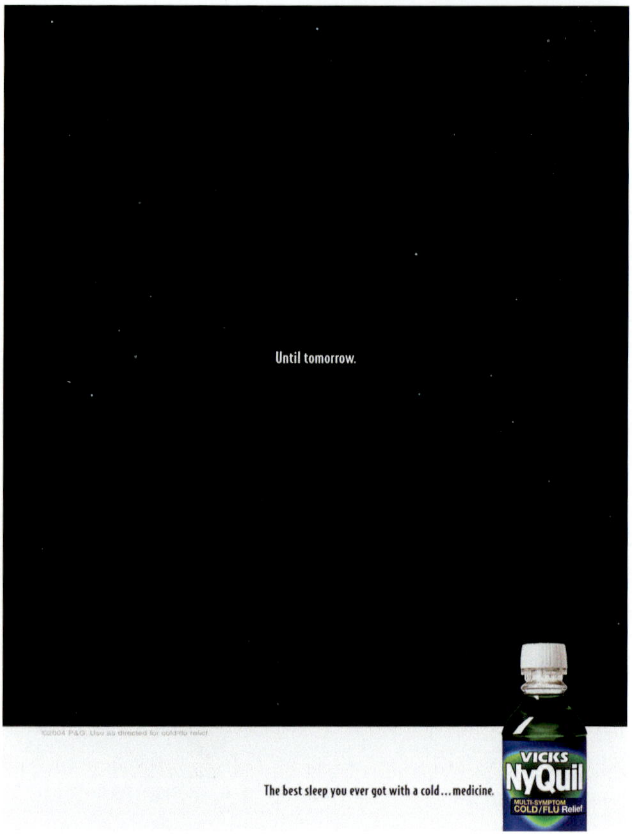


NyQuil, 2005

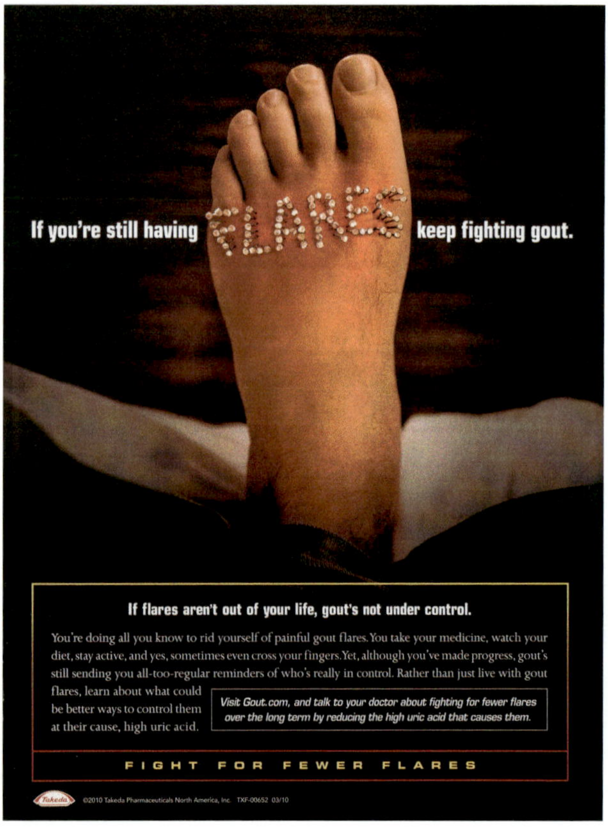


Takeda, 2010

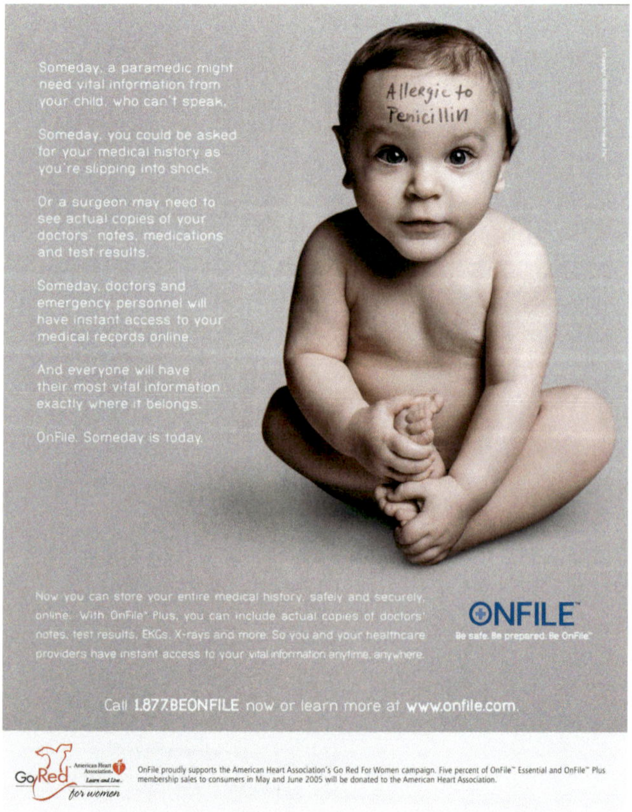


OnFile, 2005

IF HEP C WAS ATTACKING YOUR FACE INSTEAD OF YOUR LIVER, YOU'D DO SOMETHING ABOUT IT.

READY TO FIGHT BACK?

YOU'LL NEVER BE STRONGER THAN YOU ARE TODAY TO STOP THE DAMAGE HEP C IS DOING TO YOUR LIVER. Talk to your doctor now about prescription treatment. Patients in clinical studies overall had a better than 50% chance of reducing the Hep C virus to undetectable levels. Response to treatment may vary based on individual factors. So log on or call, then talk to your doctor to find out if treatment is right for you. And help put Hep C behind you.

HepCSource.com          866-HepCSource          866-437-2768

The Twisty TIE

The TAXidermy Cat

The fetal gRASShoppeR

The unhappy Meatball

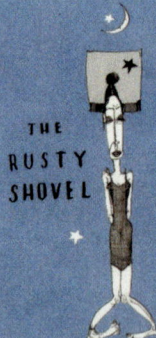

THE RUSTY SHOVEL

THE Angry Tree

The uncooked MACARONI

The PLANK

THE UNI-LEG

The MOST coverage of any ULtra thin pad* Sleep comfortably and

MOVE FReeLY.™

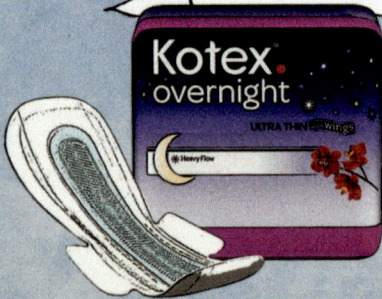

Kotex overnight
ULTRA THIN wings
Heavy Flow

Get your free sample at movefreely.com†

The Sleephoweveryouwant

*Kotex, 2009*

Always, 2000

Tampax, 2009

Kotex, 2004

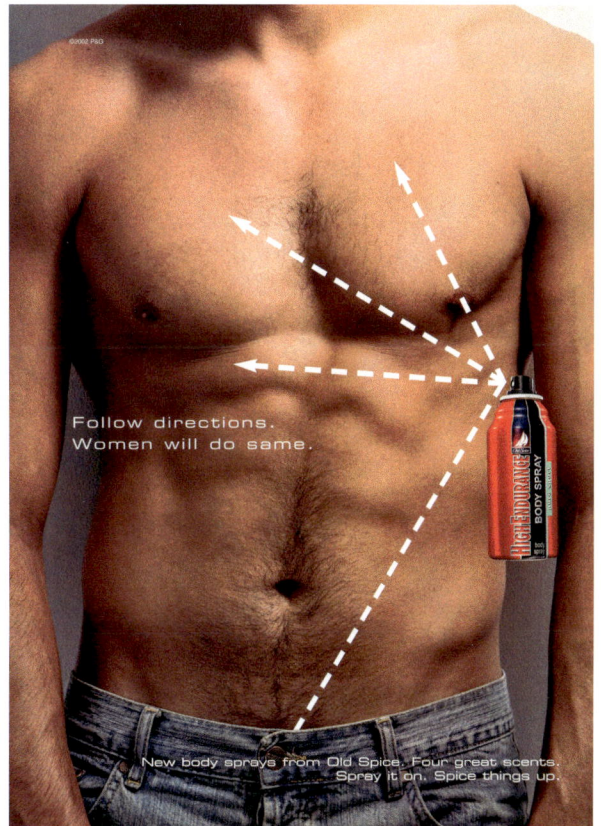

Old Spice, 2002

**SADLY, ABOUT 7,400 KIDS END UP IN THE HOSPITAL EACH YEAR BECAUSE OF PROBLEMS DUE TO CHICKENPOX.**

And tragically, about forty children lose their lives. Help protect your child against chickenpox. Learn more by visiting **www.chickenpoxinfo.com**. And be sure to talk to your doctor.

*3.3 million cases of chickenpox per year in children under 15 years of age in the United States from most recent data (1980–1990)

**MERCK**
Vaccine Division

References: 1.) CDC: Prevention of Varicella: Recommendations of the Advisory Committee on Immunization Practices (ACIP). MMWR *45 (RR-11)*: 1-36. July 12. 1996. 2.) Conrad. D.A.: New and Improved Vaccines, Postgraduate Medicine (Vaccines): 114. October, 1996.
Copyright © 1999 by Merck & Co.. Inc. All rights reserved.

D02629/2x(908)-VRV

*Merck, 2000*

**Frustrated by frequent urges in your internal plumbing? Annoyed you can't always do things spur of the moment?**

**There's a treatment you can discuss with your doctor.**

Frequent bladder urges can sometimes get in the way of doing things spontaneously. So talk to your doctor today to see if prescription VESIcare can help.

Taken once a day, VESIcare can reduce frequent urges and may help effectively manage bladder leakage, day and night. It doesn't have to be a pipe dream.

**Call (800) 403-6565**
**vesicare.com**

Here's what you'll receive:
- Information about overactive bladder
- $25 savings check*
- Talk to your doctor guide

**Important Safety Information**

VESIcare is for urgency, frequency, and leakage (overactive bladder). VESIcare is not for everyone. If you have certain types of stomach, urinary, or glaucoma problems do not take VESIcare. While taking VESIcare, if you experience a serious allergic reaction, severe abdominal pain, or become constipated for three or more days, tell your doctor right away. In studies, common side effects were dry mouth, constipation, blurred vision, and indigestion.

**Please see important product information on the following page.**

*Subject to eligibility. Restrictions may apply.

**VESIcare®**
**(solifenacin succinate)**
tablets

Partnership for Prescription Assistance

If you don't have prescription coverage, visit pparx.org, or call 1-888-4PPA-NOW (1-888-477-2669)

*VESIcare, 2006*

evolve. be a man. use a condom every time. nobody likes a pig.

TROJAN
trojanevolve.com

*Trojan, 2007*

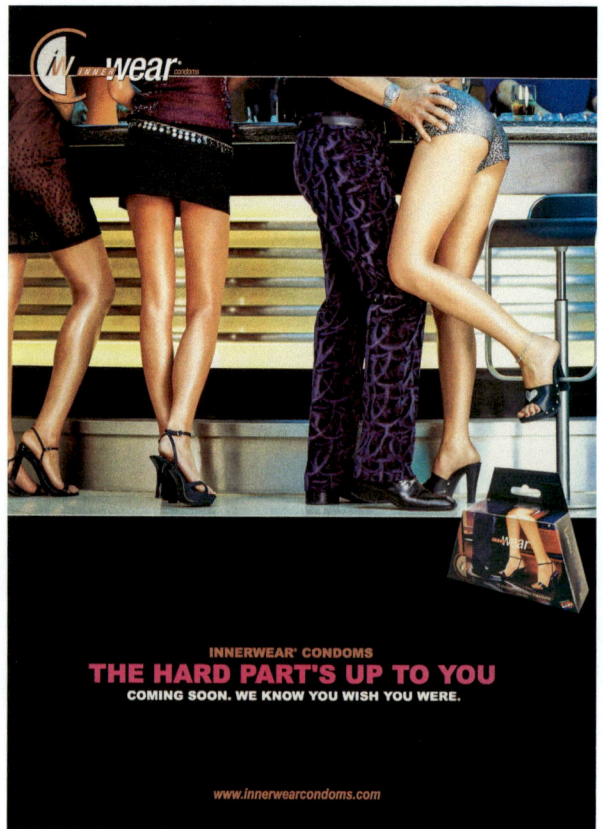

INNERWEAR' CONDOMS
THE HARD PART'S UP TO YOU
COMING SOON. WE KNOW YOU WISH YOU WERE.

www.innerwearcondoms.com

*Innerwear Condoms, 2002*

Getting
that
'let's-go-again'
look
that's my pleasure

durex
avanti
BARE
NEXT-TO-NOTHING FEEL

Durex® Avanti BARE™. A new material for a next-to-nothing feel.
Discover new pleasures at thatsmypleasure.com

*Durex, 2009*

TAKE 'EM OFF. PUT IT ON. GET IN HERE.

FEEL MORE
WANT MORE
GET MORE

The LifeStyles' X2' is the only condom infused
inside and out with Excite' Gel. That means
you'll feel more stimulation than ever. As far
as what it does for her, well, do as she says.
You'll thank us later.

LifeStylesX2.com

LifeStyles
X2
Electrifying Safe Sex

*LifeStyles, 2009*

Never
making it
to the
bedroom

that's my pleasure

durex®

avanti
BARE
NEXT-TO-NOTHING FEEL

Durex® Avanti BARE™. A new material for a next-to-nothing feel.
Discover new pleasures at thatsmypleasure.com

*Durex, 2009*

TURN A SPARK INTO A BLAZE.
K-Y® BRAND INTRIGUE™ HEAT.™
INTENSE WARMING PERSONAL LUBRICANT.

For a sample of K-Y® Brand INTRIGUE™ go to www.keeplifesexy.com

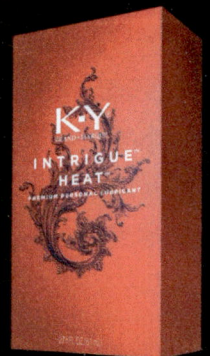

K•Y®
KEEP LIFE SEXY™

K-Y, 2008

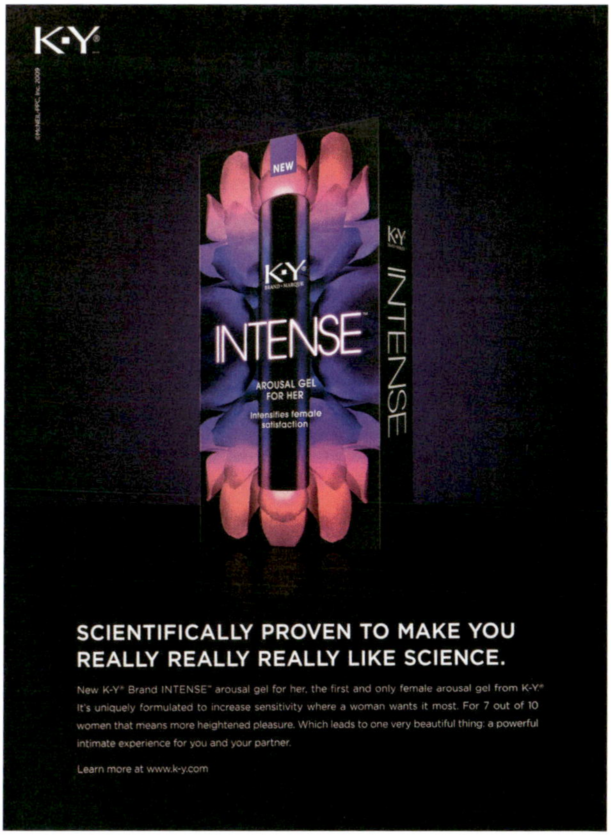


*K-Y, 2009*

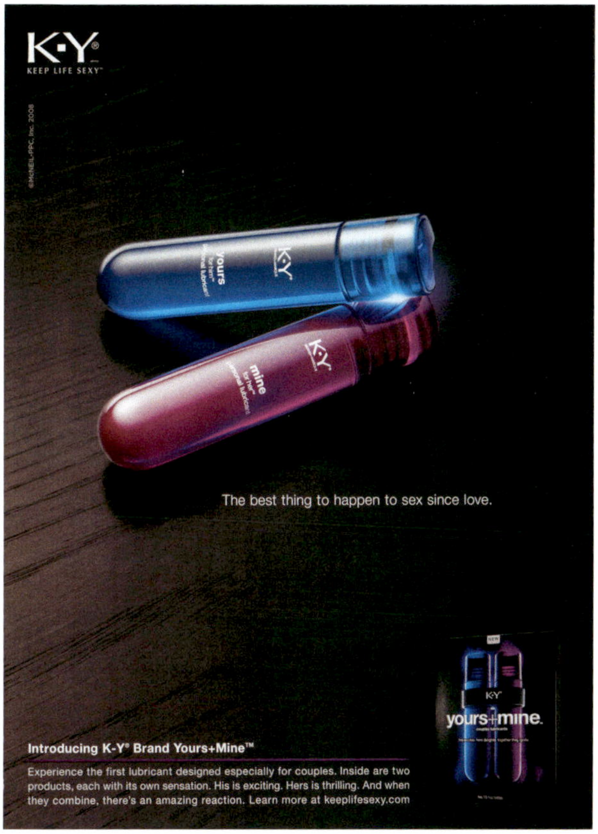


*K-Y, 2008*

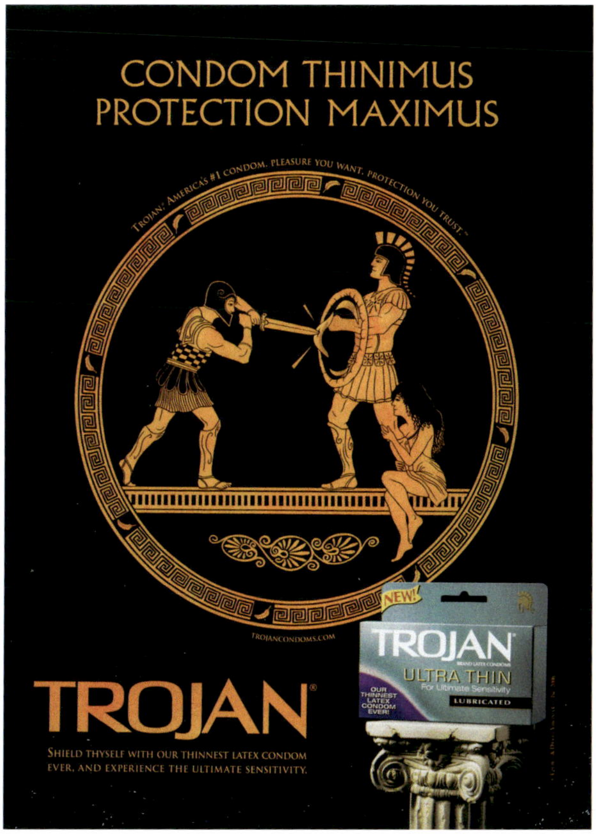


*Trojan, 2007*

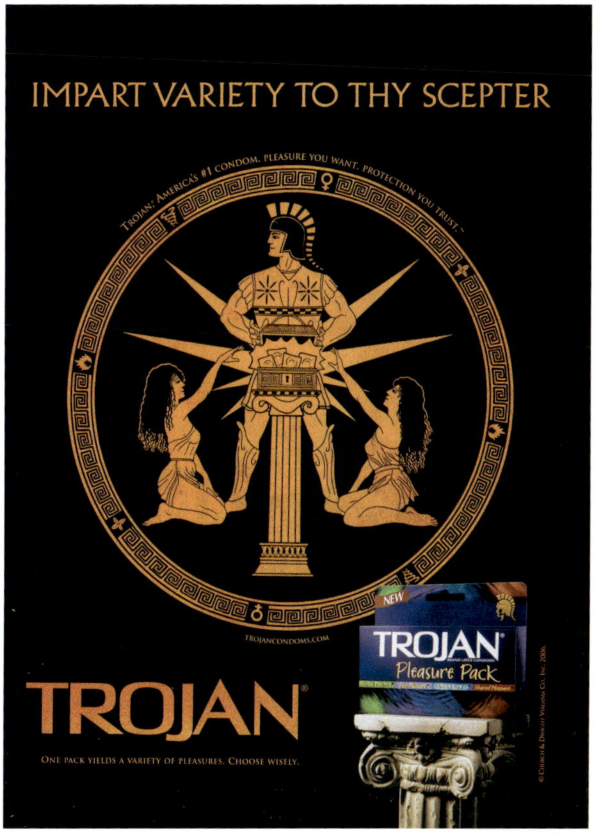


*Trojan, 2007*

WHEN WILL YOU NEED IT?

Nothing is stronger than Red Zone from Old Spice. It's the strongest form of wetness protection ever made for guys. If you don't think so, call 1-800-PROVE-IT.

*Old Spice, 2001*

WANT TWO THINGS IN ONE THING?

INTRODUCING LIVE WIRE.
BODY WASH. MOISTURIZER. STRIPED TOGETHER.
IT'S TWO PRODUCTS IN ONE AWESOME PRODUCT.

BODY WASH
MOISTURIZER

Old Spice

AND TRY OUR NEW SCENT IN GAME DAY HIGH ENDURANCE
BODY WASH FOR AN EXHILARATING CLEAN THAT GOES INTO OVERTIME.

BODY WASH

*Old Spice, 2009*

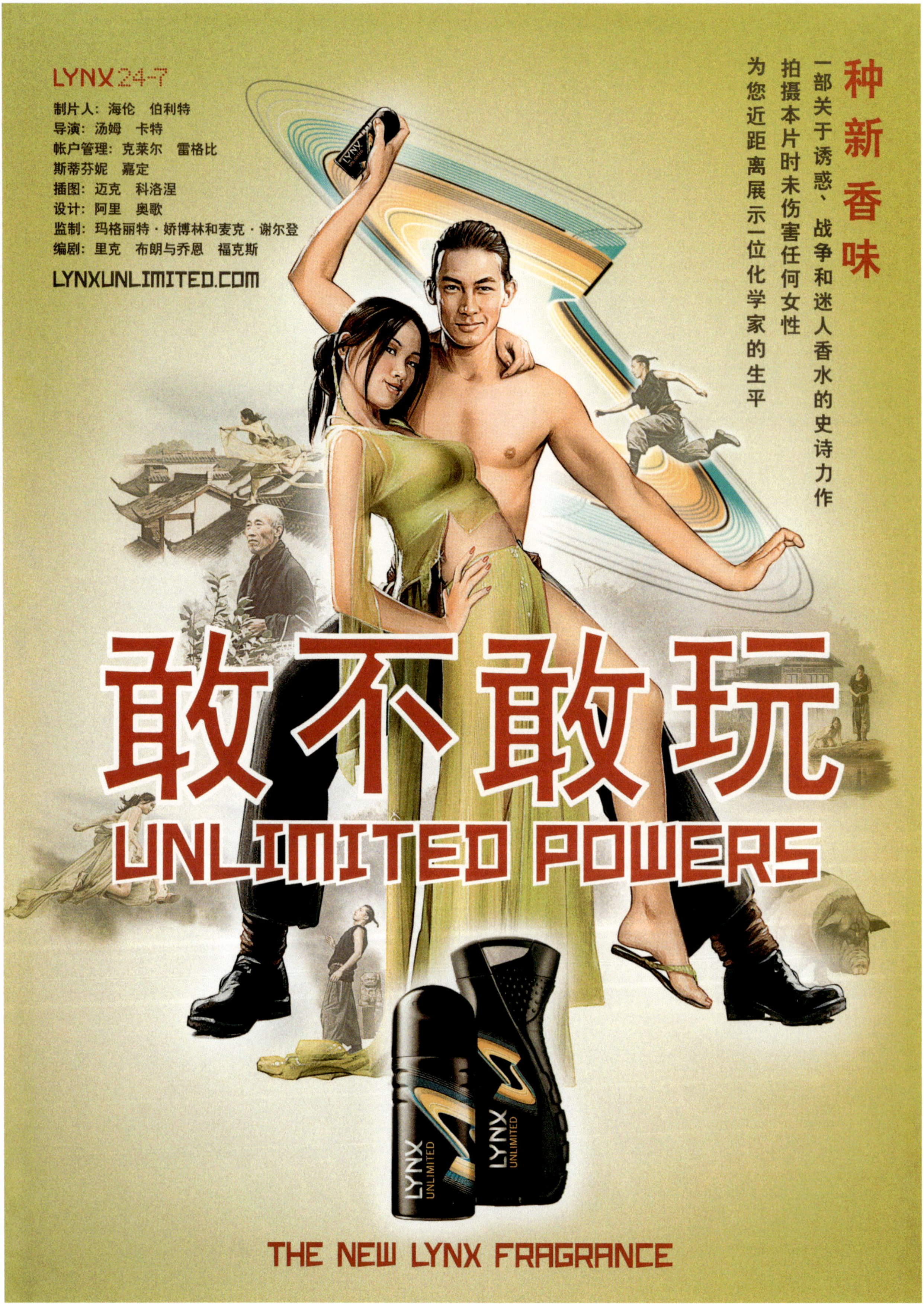

种新香味
一部关于诱惑、战争和迷人香水的史诗力作
拍摄本片时未伤害任何女性
为您近距离展示一位化学家的生平
LYNX 24-7
制片人：海伦　伯利特
导演：汤姆　卡特
帐户管理：克莱尔　雷格比
斯蒂芬妮　嘉定
插图：迈克　科洛涅
设计：阿里　奥歌
监制：玛格丽特・娇博林和麦克・谢尔登
编剧：里克　布朗与乔恩　福克斯
LYNXUNLIMITED.COM
敢不敢玩
UNLIMITED POWERS
LYNX UNLIMITED
LYNX UNLIMITED
THE NEW LYNX FRAGRANCE


*Lynx, 2005*

Polamolecule ①a

Formulated to give you fuller, thicker-looking
hair in one week. Guaranteed.**

 **head & shoulders.**

**Official Shampoo of the NFL**

NFL

Imagine. Millions of tiny yet powerful Troy Polamolecules, cleaning your
head every time you shampoo to leave you with fuller, thicker-looking hair.
Yeah, they don't really look like that, but still, you'll feel like there's a little
Troy in every bottle of Head & Shoulders Hair Endurance.

*Vs. Unwashed Hair

Go to **TroysHair.com** for a chance to win a trip and primo tickets to Super Bowl XLV.

*Head & Shoulders, 2010*

total control. total performance. Introducing adidas anti-perspirants and deodorants.

*Adidas, 2001*

TURN HEAT INTO soft silky hair

*Thermasilk, 2003*

Who does your hair?

CLINIQUE simple hair care system

Introducing Clinique's simple system of hair care specialists. Designed to cleanse, condition, style. And custom-fit to your hair type. For the healthiest results. The best effects. The look you want. At the Clinique counter. No appointment necessary. Get precision-fit hair care at www.clinique.com

*Clinique, 2000*

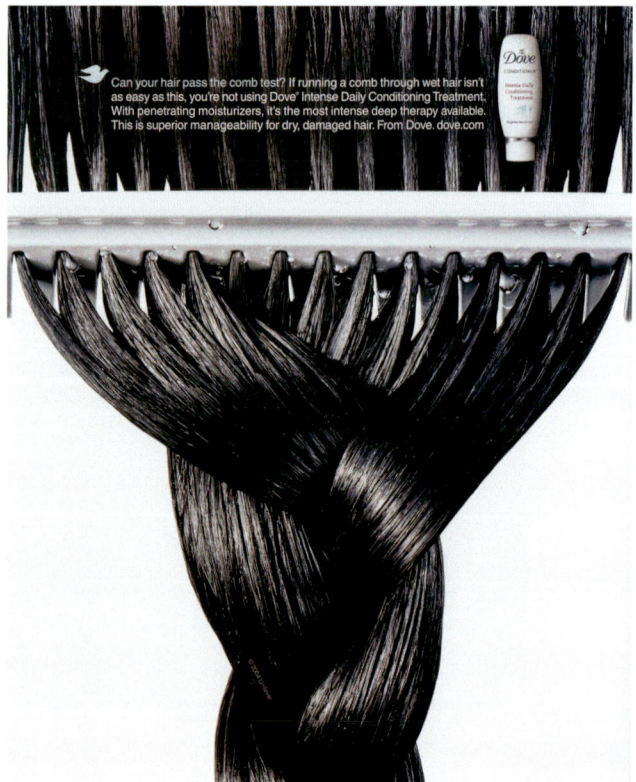

Can your hair pass the comb test? If running a comb through wet hair isn't as easy as this, you're not using Dove® Intense Daily Conditioning Treatment. With penetrating moisturizers, it's the most intense deep therapy available. This is superior manageability for dry, damaged hair. From Dove. dove.com

*Dove, 2004*

Old Spice, 2007

You can't go too far to make a child smile.

Crest is going all the way to Zimbabwe. And Brazil. And India. And Vietnam. Since 1994, Crest has provided educational materials to Health Volunteers Overseas. It's helped bring oral health to countries where dental care is hard to find. So for the children of Chegutu village, the world is no wider than a smile.

©1999 Procter & Gamble  OJAN99374  For more information about this program go to www.hvousa.org

Creating smiles every day.

Crest

Crest, 2000

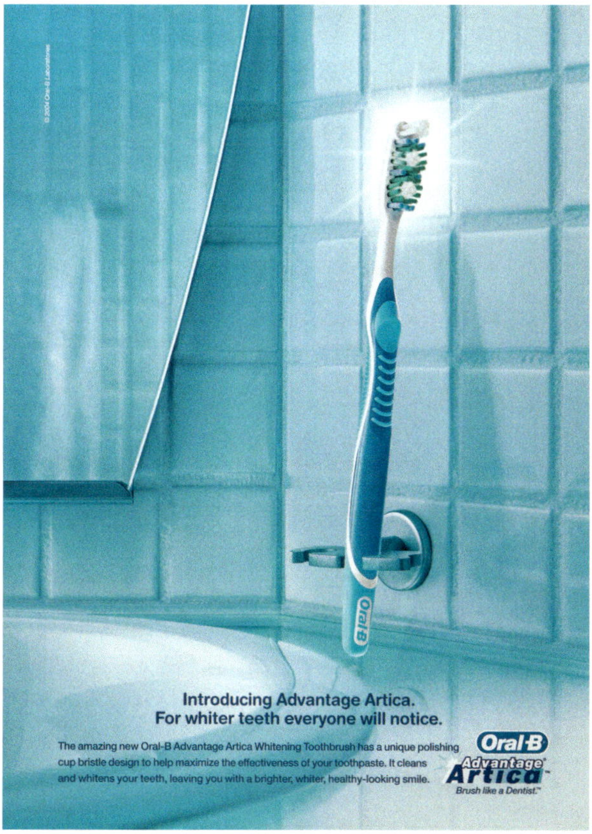


Oral-B, 2004

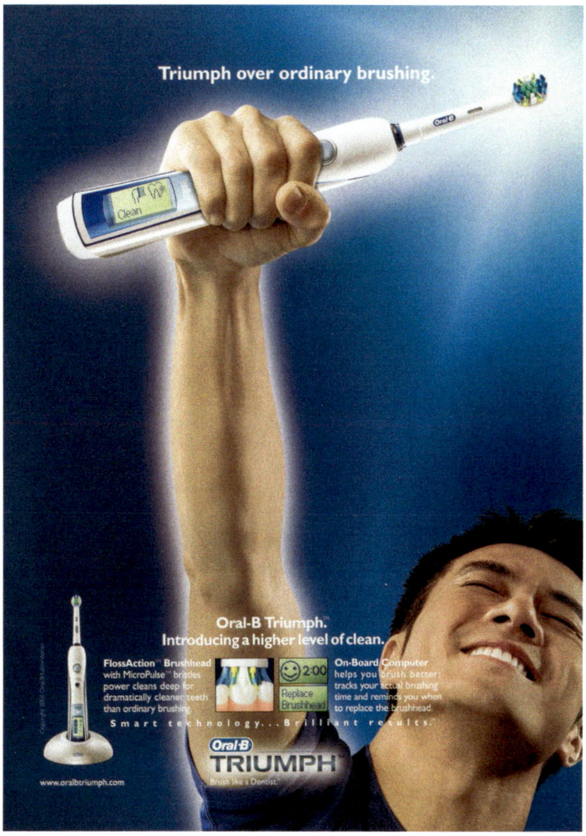


Oral-B, 2006

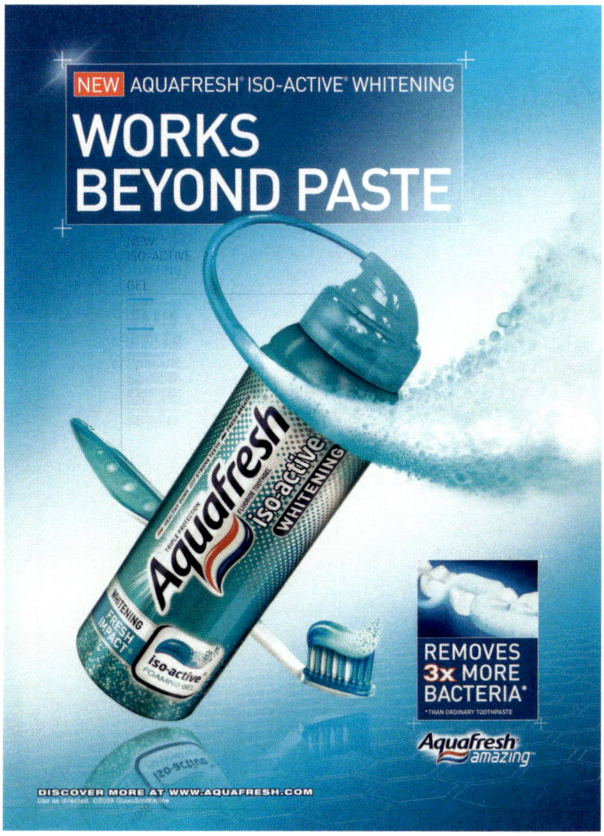


Aquafresh, 2009

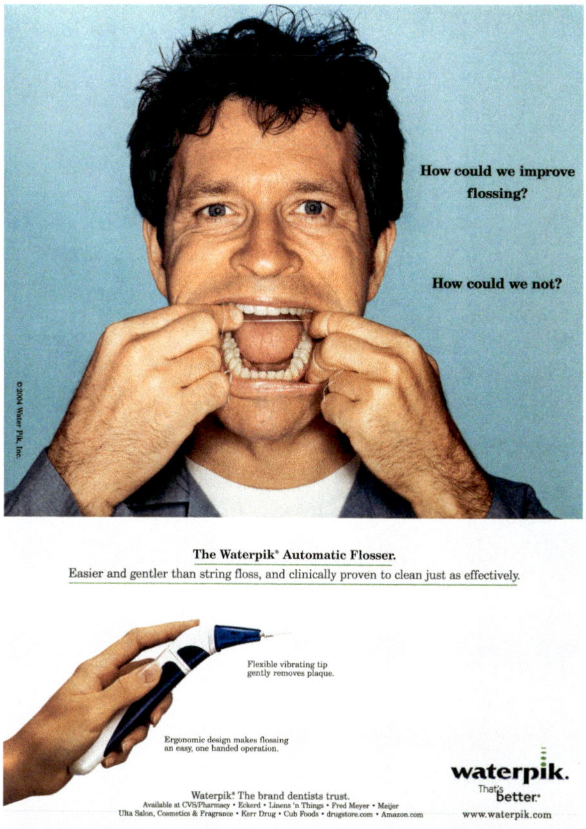


Waterpik, 2004

# And the winner is ...

## All Around Loser

It doesn't get much weirder than this! AXE DRY Anti-Perspirant & Deodorant took the extraordinary step of combining a charming model, a glass of wine, and a Venetian gondolier with a stubby, mutated foot, which has a vaguely vaginal hairy armpit for a face, and threw in a meaningless tagline to sell its product. The ad begs the question: "Who would buy this?"

## Der Totalversager

Noch abartiger geht es wohl kaum! Das AXE DRY Deo entschied sich für den außergewöhnlichen Schritt, ein charmantes Model, ein Glas Rotwein und eine venezianische Gondel mit einem mutierten Beinstummel zu verbinden, dessen Gesicht aus einer vage an weibliches Schamhaar erinnernden Achselbehaarung besteht, und hoffte dann, das Produkt mit einem aussagelosen Slogan zu verkaufen. Dabei wirft diese Anzeige nur eine große Frage auf: „Wer würde so was kaufen?"

## La crème du pire

Peut-on imaginer plus improbable? La pub pour le déodorant anti-transpirant AXE DRY réussit l'exploit d'associer un charmant mannequin, un verre de vin, un gondolier vénitien et un pied mutant replet à une aisselle poilue vaguement vulvaire en guise de visage. La question se pose : « Qui achèterait ça? »

ALL-AMERICAN

► Axe

Dry Pits Win

New AXE DRY Anti-Perspirant & Deodorant
*available in sticks & gels · www.theaxeeffect.com*

FR. HI-SPD INT. SND. MSGS. FASTR. GR8!

You get a comfy bed; shouldn't your computer get a free high-speed connection?* Fair is fair at Holiday Inn. For reservations, call 1-800-HOLIDAY, visit holiday-inn.com, or call your travel agent.

*Holiday Inn, 2005*

*W Hotels, 2004*

PORTRAITS *of* PENINSULA

THE PENINSULA
H O T E L S

*Air France, 2000* ◄  *The Peninsula Hotels, 2007*

*W Hotels, 2003*

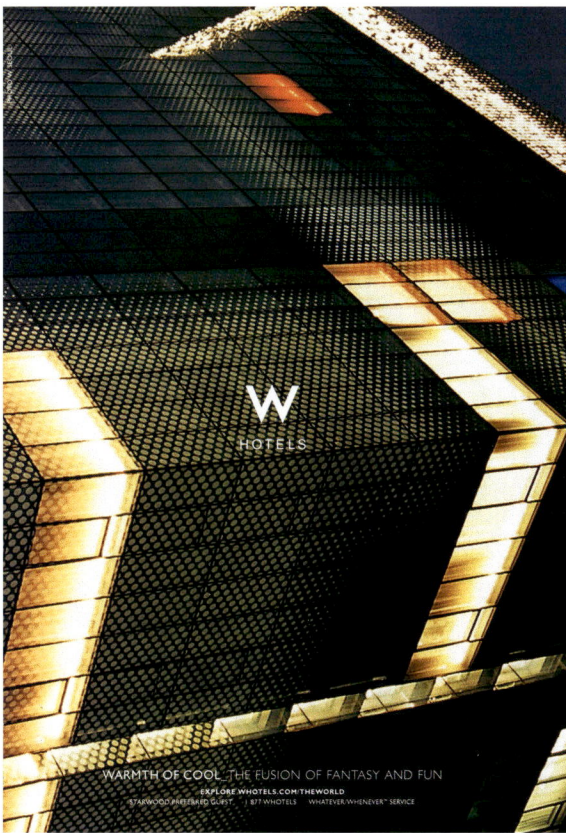

W Hotels, 2005

The Standard, 2008

Renaissance Hotels, 2008

ALWAYS GO TO BED EARLY.
AT LEAST BEFORE NOON.

CAESARS PALACE
LAS VEGAS

LIVE FAMOUSLY.®

800.634.6661 • caesarspalace.com

Must be 21 or older to gamble. . ... ...o Stop Before You Start.® Gambling Problem? Call 1-800-522-4700. ©2006, Harrah's License Company, LLC. 40802

*Caesars Palace, 2006*

Our newly-remodeled rooms provide the perfect respite from the raucous fun of Coyote Ugly™, our bar & dance saloon, the non-stop action of ESPN Zone™, the good times and tall ales of Nine Fine Irishmen™, our authentic Irish pub, and the eroticism of ZUMANITY™ - Another Side of Cirque du Soleil™ - a show so stimulating, you might just find yourself heading straight back to that room of yours, for anything but rest and relaxation.

You went upstairs for some rest and relaxation.
Yeah, good luck with that.

*Ya Gotta love this town.* NEW YORK · NEW YORK
THE GREATEST CITY IN LAS VEGAS

3790 Las Vegas Boulevard South · Las Vegas, Nevada 89109 · nynyhotelcasino.com · 1-800-NY-FOR-ME
DFW/A

New York-New York, 2004

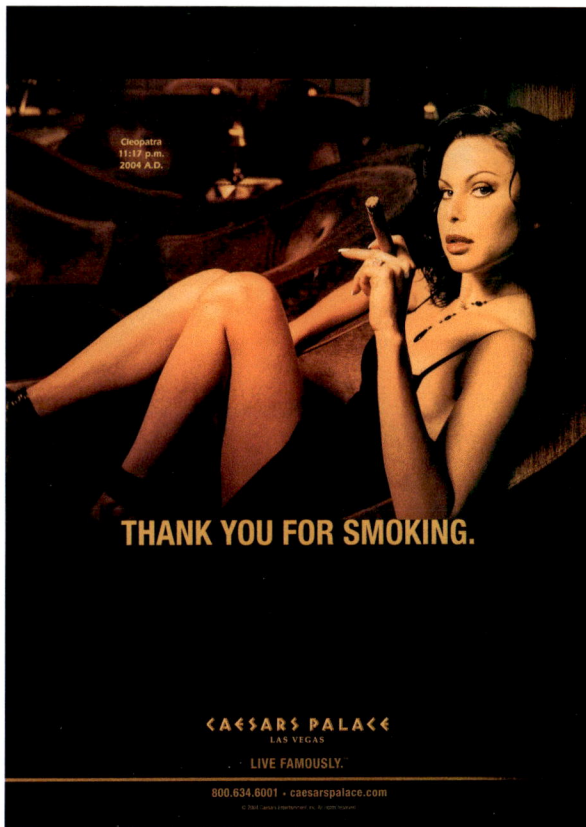

Cleopatra
11:17 p.m.
2004 A.D.

THANK YOU FOR SMOKING.

CAESARS PALACE
LAS VEGAS
· LIVE FAMOUSLY. ·

800.634.6001 · caesarspalace.com

Caesars Palace, 2004

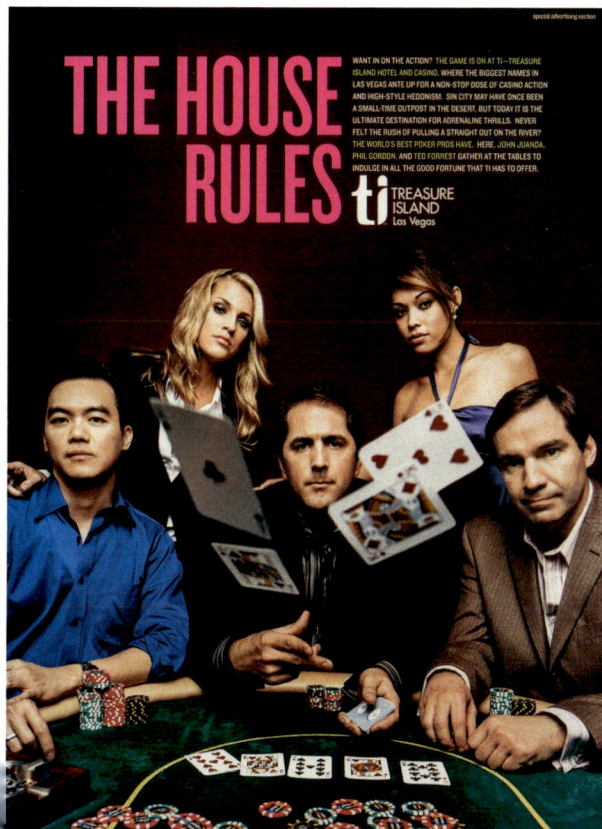

THE HOUSE RULES

WANT IN ON THE ACTION? THE GAME IS ON AT ti—TREASURE ISLAND HOTEL AND CASINO, WHERE THE BIGGEST NAMES IN LAS VEGAS ANTE UP FOR A NON-STOP DOSE OF CASINO ACTION AND HIGH-STYLE HEDONISM. SIN CITY MAY HAVE ONCE BEEN A SMALL-TIME OUTPOST IN THE DESERT. BUT TODAY IT IS THE ULTIMATE DESTINATION FOR ADRENALINE THRILLS. NEVER FELT THE RUSH OF PULLING A STRAIGHT OUT ON THE RIVER? THE WORLD'S BEST POKER PROS HAVE. HERE, JOHN JUANDA, PHIL GORDON, AND TED FORREST GATHER AT THE TABLES TO INDULGE IN ALL THE GOOD FORTUNE THAT ti HAS TO OFFER.

ti TREASURE ISLAND Las Vegas

Treasure Island, 2005

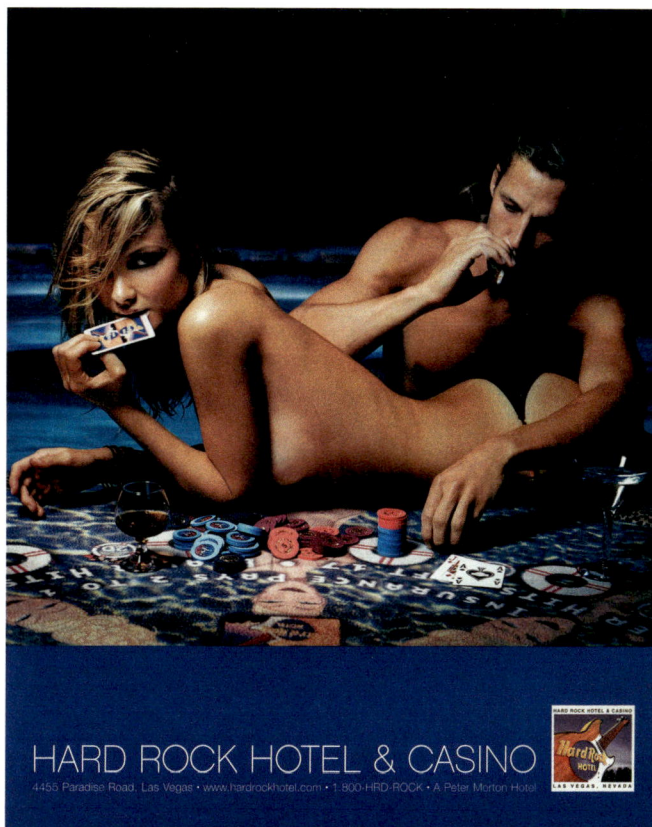

HARD ROCK HOTEL & CASINO
4455 Paradise Road, Las Vegas · www.hardrockhotel.com · 1-800-HRD-ROCK · A Peter Morton Hotel

HARD ROCK HOTEL
LAS VEGAS, NEVADA

Hard Rock, 2004

Rio, 2008

Caesars Palace, 2004

Crystal Cruises, 2001

Paris Las Vegas, 2009

Hard Rock, 2001

MONTECARLO.COM

FOE
PAW

Monte Carlo
LAS VEGAS RESORT & CASINO

4 STYLISH POOLS AND A SWIMSUIT SHOP.    UNPRETENTIOUSLY LUXURIOUS

*Monte Carlo, 2009*

*Paris Las Vegas, 2008*

Caesars Palace, 2006

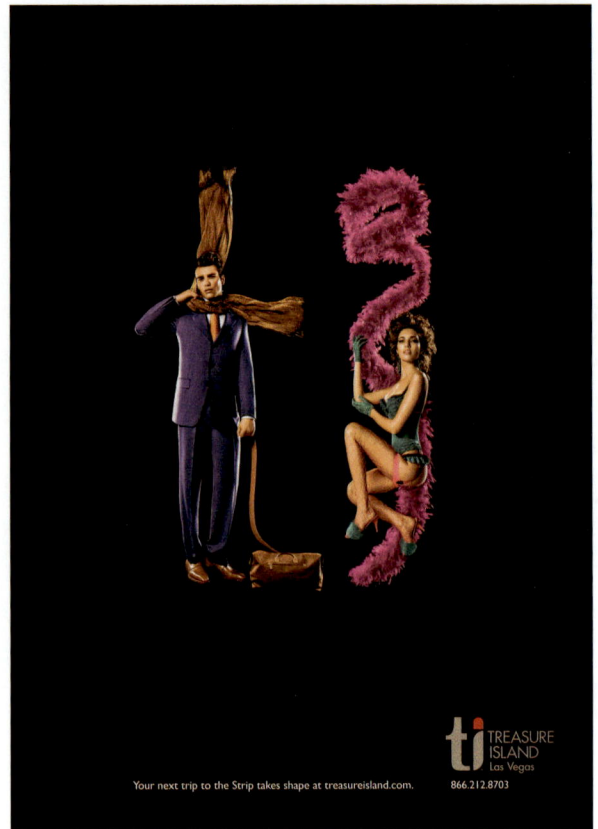

Treasure Island, 2005

Visit Las Vegas, 2005

Paris Las Vegas, 2008

▶ Cirque du Soleil, 2008

The rough trail taught you what's most important in life –
sometimes the day's end calls for more than a campfire.

Grab life. Immerse yourself in a day full of adventure and a night full of fun.
More to discover and definitely more than you expect, all waiting here for you. For
your free travel packet, call 1-866-366-9286 toll-free or visit arizona**guide**.com.

ARIZONA
GRAND CANYON STATE

*Arizona, 2008*

Outrun a monster *at* gohawaii.com/films

HAWAI'I
THE ISLANDS OF ALOHA

Hear Dan Moore's story about surfing the colossal waves of Peahi (*Jaws*) on Maui or take a
surfing lesson on the tranquil waves of historic Waikīkī Beach. Watch these breathtaking short
videos and other stories of Hawai'i. Then start planning your own adventure at gohawaii.com.

*Hawaii, 2008*

EMAAR

The Address.

Armani Hotel | Retail | Residences | Spas | Corporate Suites

BURJ DUBAI

No.1, Burj Dubai Boulevard, Dubai, UAE
www.burjdubai.com

*Burj Dubai, 2005*

▶ *Bellagio, 2006*

SUPERIORITY COMPLEX.

BELLAGIO®
LAS VEGAS

Embrace extravagance at Las Vegas' first and only AAA Five Diamond resort casino

877-987-7775 • bellagio.com

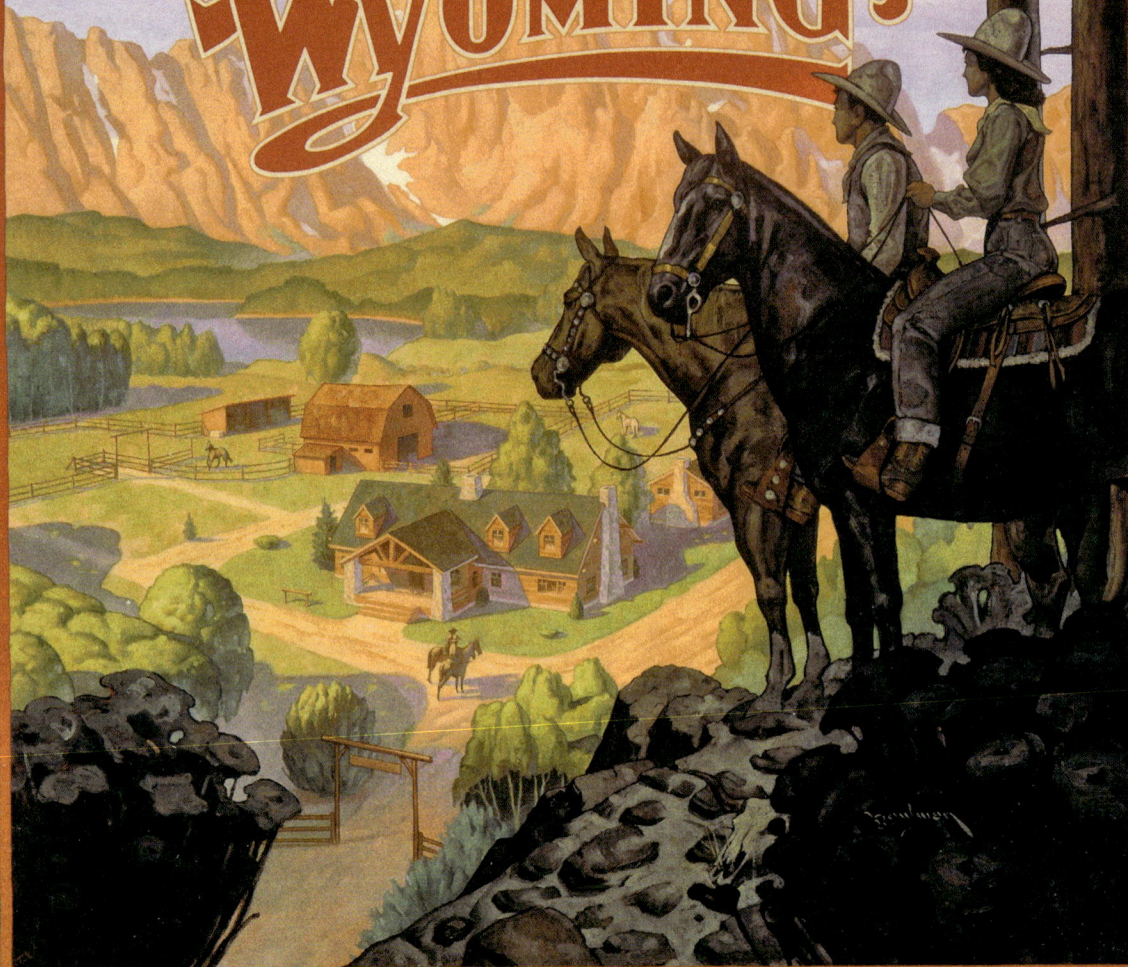

*Wyoming, 2009*

Elephants have greeting ceremonies for friends
returning from voyages. Secretly, I hoped that
when I come back, they'll remember me as
much as I'll remember them.

Go to www.southafrica.net/adventurerswanted

SOUTH AFRICA
It's possible

South Africa, 2009

Be one with the captivating. Be one with this Caribbean gateway to the Maya world. Be one with this
Hemisphere's largest barrier reef. As one of the last unspoiled places, you'll feel an intimate connection
to authentic experiences in Belize. All just a two-hour flight from the U.S., in the only English-speaking
country of Central America. Call 800-624-0686 or visit TravelBelize.org/his. And just be, in Belize.

BELIZE
MOTHER NATURE'S
BEST KEPT SECRET

Be one with Belize

Belize, 2009

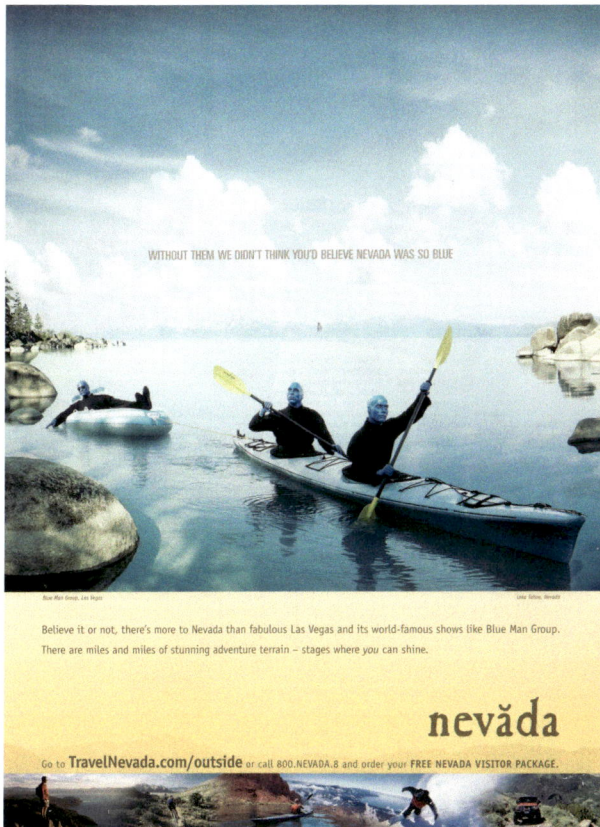

WITHOUT THEM WE DIDN'T THINK YOU'D BELIEVE NEVADA WAS SO BLUE

Believe it or not, there's more to Nevada than fabulous Las Vegas and its world-famous shows like Blue Man Group.
There are miles and miles of stunning adventure terrain – stages where you can shine.

nevăda

Go to TravelNevada.com/outside or call 800.NEVADA.8 and order your FREE NEVADA VISITOR PACKAGE.

Nevada, 2008

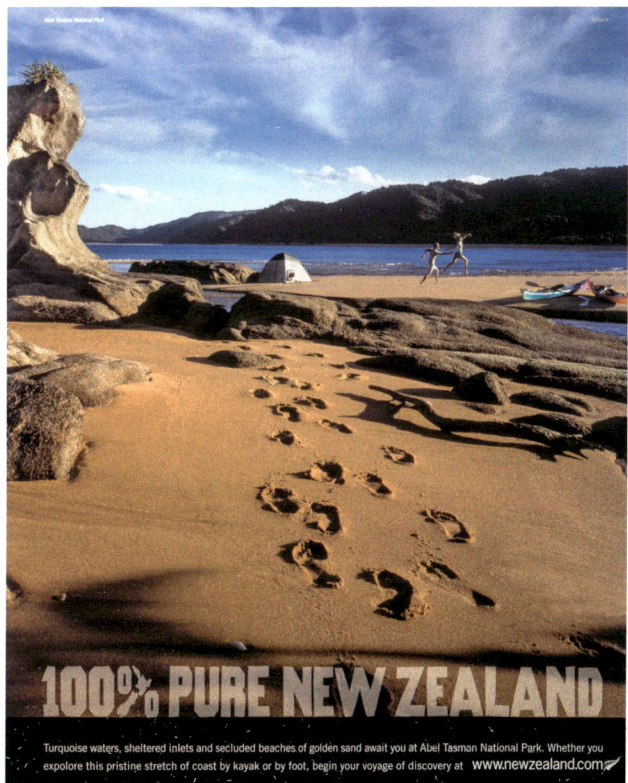

100% PURE NEW ZEALAND

Turquoise waters, sheltered inlets and secluded beaches of golden sand await you at Abel Tasman National Park. Whether you
explore this pristine stretch of coast by kayak or by foot, begin your voyage of discovery at www.newzealand.com

New Zealand, 2006

YES, THIS IS ACTUALLY NEVADA. THANK YOU VERY MUCH.

Lamoille Canyon

Believe it or not, there's more to Nevada than fabulous Las Vegas. There are miles

and miles of stunning adventure terrain – stages where *you* can shine. The possibilities are wide open.

nevăda
WIDE OPEN

Go to **travelnevada.com/outside** or call 800.NEVADA.8 and order your **FREE NEVADA VISITOR PACKAGE.**

*Nevada, 2007*

*Where every Cinderella story comes true.*

Scarlett Johansson as Cinderella

DisneyParks.com
*407-W-DISNEY*

Disney Parks, 2007

**You think you've got problems?** Try being one of the hundreds of vineyards in New York State. To succeed here, the wine has to be just as good as what the city offers. It's taken hard work and sleepless nights. Did I grow the best grapes? Did I check every vat? Did I leave the stove on?

Neurotic Vineyards.
Another reason, I ♥ NY

For scenic vineyards, farm-fresh cuisine and a million other reasons to ♥ New York, visit iloveny.com
©2008 NYS Department of Economic Development. All rights reserved.

New York, 2008

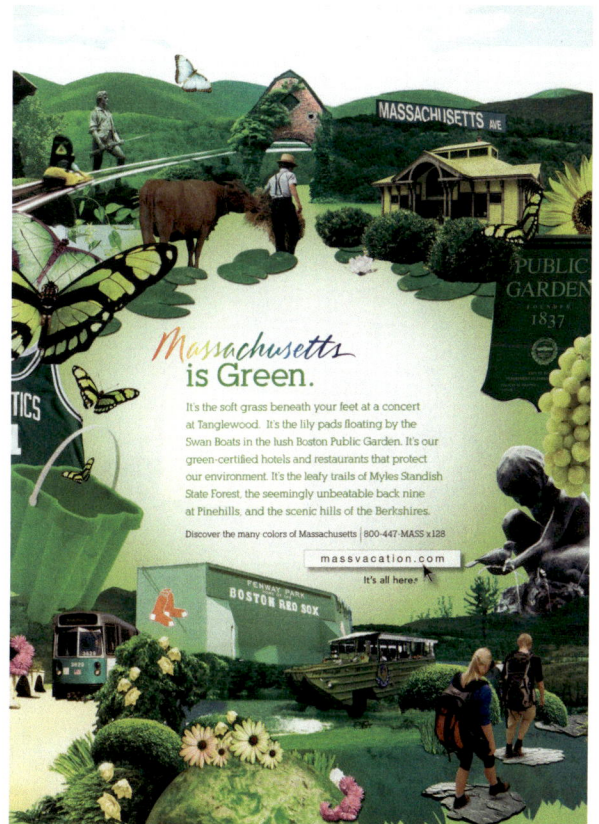

*Massachusetts*
**is Green.**

It's the soft grass beneath your feet at a concert at Tanglewood. It's the lily pads floating by the Swan Boats in the lush Boston Public Garden. It's our green-certified hotels and restaurants that protect our environment. It's the leafy trails of Myles Standish State Forest, the seemingly unbeatable back nine at Pinehills, and the scenic hills of the Berkshires.

Discover the many colors of Massachusetts | 800-447-MASS x128

massvacation.com

It's all here.

Massachusetts, 2009

*This is not* A JOURNEY THROUGH THE LOOKING GLASS.

IT IS THE WORK OF A MODERN-DAY NATIVE AMERICAN ARTIST. A TESTAMENT TO ANCESTRAL TRUTHS THAT STRETCH BACK TO THE BEGINNING OF TIME. COLLECTORS WILL FIND ART LIKE THIS IN ARIZONA. WHERE THE EARTH ITSELF HAS THE ANSWERS YOU SEEK.

FOR YOUR FREE TRAVEL PACKET, CONTACT THE ARIZONA OFFICE OF TOURISM AT 1-800-239-0692 OR VISIT ARIZONAGUIDE.COM

**ARIZONA**
GRAND CANYON STATE

Wayne Beyale

*Arizona,* 2001

THE SEVEN MOST
FAMOUS BOWLS
IN SKIING.
BE SURE TO PACK
AN APPETITE.

vail.com

VAIL. Like nothing on earth.

*Vail, 2008*

We the People

Recharge
your faith
in democracy.

★ Visit the JFK Presidential Library and Museum · Columbia Point, Boston · jfklibrary.org ★

*JFK Presidential Library and Museum, 2008*

SOUL
SUSTENANCE

MIAMI
movements

◆ provocative art · gustatory delights · cultural consciousness · MiamiMovements.com ◆

*Miami, 2007*

*Royal Caribbean, 2002*

# Club Med

Whether it's windsurfing or horseback riding, you choose your fun. At Club Med, you can challenge yourself with a vast array of sports, like waterskiing, tennis and golf. Then dance the night away in our disco. Freedom of choice is the rule here, from our extensive menu of activities to our enticing buffets of international cuisine including unlimited wine and beer with lunch and dinner. And virtually everything is included. So, choose a vacation where the fun never ends: Come to Club Med.

## Fun is hard work.
## Go ahead, exhaust yourself.

1-800-CLUB MED
OR CALL YOUR TRAVEL AGENT
clubmed.com

Re-new

MR COOK, I LET YOUR WIFE KNOW YOU'LL BE 30 MINS LATE.
ORBITZ

At Orbitz, every ticket includes 24/7 Customer Care. Now you and your family can receive flight delay and gate info via cell phone. Another travel mission accomplished at WWW.ORBITZ.COM.

*Club Med, 2001*

*Orbitz, 2003*

► *San Francisco Museum of Modern Art, 2008*

# TAKE YOUR TIME
## OLAFUR ELIASSON
### THROUGH FEB 24

**San Francisco Museum of Modern Art**
151 Third Street    415.357.4000    www.sfmoma.org

**SFMOMA**

*Take your time: Olafur Eliasson* is organized by the San Francisco Museum of Modern Art. Lead support is provided by Helen and Charles Schwab and the Mimi and Peter Haas Fund. Generous support is provided by the Bernard Osher Foundation, the Barbro Osher Pro Suecia Foundation, and Collectors Forum. Additional support is provided by Patricia and William Wilson III, the Andy Warhol Foundation for the Visual Arts, the National Endowment for the Arts, and the American-Scandinavian Foundation. Support for education programs has been provided by Helen Hilton Raiser in honor of Madeleine Grynsztejn. Media support is provided by *Dwell* magazine.

Olafur Eliasson, *One-way colour tunnel* (installation view), 2007; Courtesy the artist; Tanya Bonakdar Gallery, New York; and neugerreimschneider, Berlin; © 2007 Olafur Eliasson

## More legroom. Our equivalent to the pat on the back.

At United, we want to reward you for a job well done. That's why we are the only airline with Economy Plus® throughout our fleet—a special section up front where our most frequent flyers can enjoy up to five inches of extra legroom. Voted "Best Premium Economy Class in the World" by the readers of *Business Traveler*, it's just one of the many ways we reward you for all your hard work.

united.com    A STAR ALLIANCE MEMBER

**UNITED**
It's time to fly.®

*United Airlines, 2005*

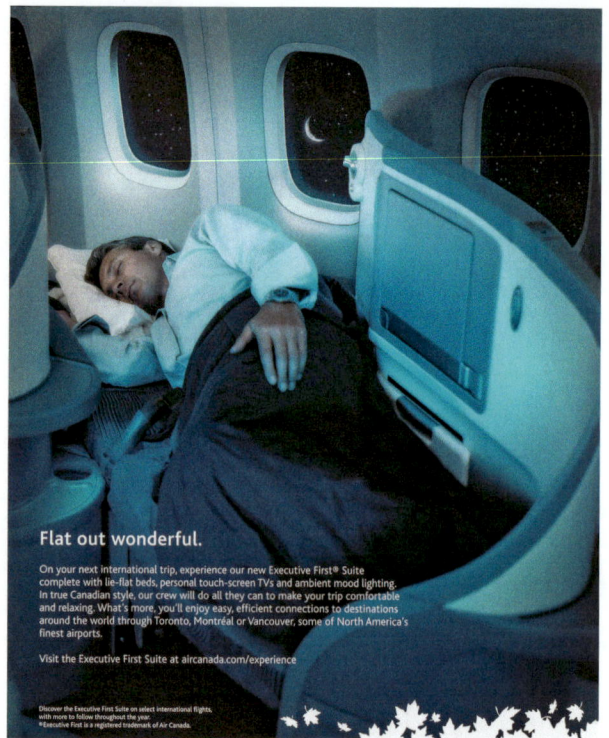

## Flat out wonderful.

On your next international trip, experience our new Executive First® Suite complete with lie-flat beds, personal touch-screen TVs and ambient mood lighting. In true Canadian style, our crew will do all they can to make your trip comfortable and relaxing. What's more, you'll enjoy easy, efficient connections to destinations around the world through Toronto, Montréal or Vancouver, some of North America's finest airports.

Visit the Executive First Suite at aircanada.com/experience

Discover the Executive First Suite on select international flights, with more to follow throughout the year.
®Executive First is a registered trademark of Air Canada.

STAR ALLIANCE

**AIR CANADA**
The freedom to fly your own way

*Air Canada, 2008*

## YOU JUST CAN'T DOWNLOAD THIS.

They say
life is an adventure.
Prove them right.
250 cities. 40 countries. One airline.

*We know why you fly* **AmericanAirlines**
AA.com

*American Airlines, 2009*

www.koreanair.com

From departure to arrival, the world is a step closer with Korean Air

**Excellence in global network** Korean Air now connects 6 continents including South America with its new direct flights between Los Angeles and Sao Paulo, Brazil. With flights to 116 cities in over 38 different countries. Korean Air's fast and convenient global network serves you anywhere around the world in style.

Excellence in Flight
**KOREAN AIR**

*Korean Air, 2008*

There are people who shoulda, coulda, woulda.
And there are people who are glad they did.

**UNITED**
It's time to fly.℠

united.com   A STAR ALLIANCE MEMBER ✺®

*United Airlines, 2004*

627

**L'Espace 127.**
**It gives a whole new meaning to the phrase**
**"fresh off the plane."**

With seats designed for extra comfort, a personal video entertainment system, two in-flight bars and gourmet cuisine, no wonder our Business Class passengers are always fresh on arrival. For reservations, contact your travel professional, call Air France at 1-800-237-2747, or visit us at www.airfrance.com. Our frequent flyer program partners are Continental Airlines and Delta Air Lines.

**AIR FRANCE**
Making the sky the best place on earth

*Air France, 2000*

Less time flying,
More time
exploring Asia

**The fastest service from New York to Bangkok, non-stop.**

Arrive more time for the cultural richness of an Asian adventure in Thailand and beyond. Our new Southeast Asia Silk Express is the fastest service from New York to Bangkok, the gateway to Southeast Asia. Discover new pleasures when you step aboard our brand new Airbus A340-500 and experience unparalleled pampering, with more comfort, more space, more personal entertainment, and more legendary Royal Orchid service.

For more information, please call your local travel agent or Thai Airways at 1-877-THAI AIR. www.thaiairways.com

**THAI, Smooth as silk.**

**Thai**
A STAR ALLIANCE MEMBER

*Thai Airways, 2005*

**The perfect trip starts at southwest.com/gaytravel**

Southwest Airlines® is proud to offer a section of our web site dedicated to the gay and lesbian community. At southwest.com/gaytravel, you'll find helpful information on gay-friendly destinations, special deals, and events around the country along with travel tips to fabulous places. Whether it's business or pleasure, Southwest is taking freedom to new heights.

**SOUTHWEST**
southwest.com/gaytravel

*Southwest Airlines, 2008*

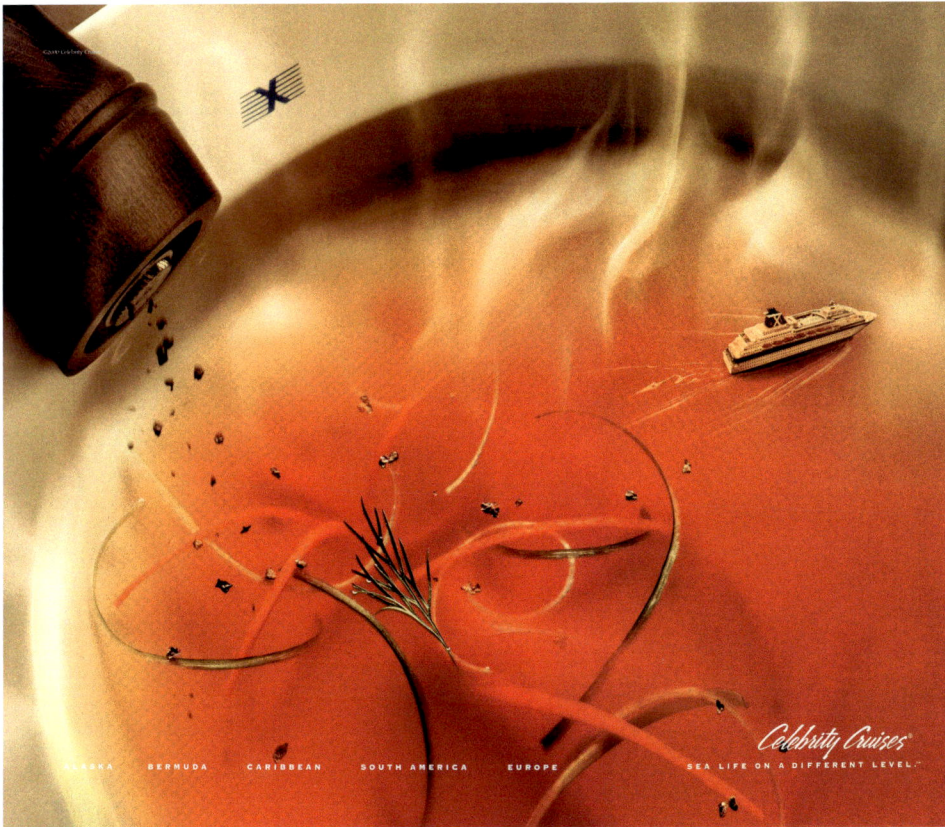

*Celebrity Cruises, 2000*

*JetBlue, 2010*

Everyone dreams.
Some people are
just more active
participants.

UNITED
It's time to fly.™

*United Airlines, 2004*

Pregame. Postgame. None of it matters if you don't
BRING YOUR "A" GAME.

*Fig. 1 Hot Dog*

*Fig. 2 Drumstick*

*Fig. 3 Cheeseburger*

*Fig. 4 Corn on the Cob*

*Fig. 5 Shish Kebab*

*Fig. 5 Rib Eye*

Fill up the fridge. Find your friends. Fire up the grill. Do just about anything, and go just about anywhere
with an RV. Go to GoRVing.com for a free video and visit an RV dealer. WHAT WILL YOU DISCOVER? Go RVing.

*Go RVing, 2008*

FRIENDS DON'T LET FRIENDS
MISS FISHING TRIPS.
On the water memories aren't made, they're caught. To
discover all the ways boating and fishing can enrich your life,
visit takemefishing.org.
TAKE ME FISHING™
takemefishing.org

*Take Me Fishing, 2008*

*California, 2009*

631

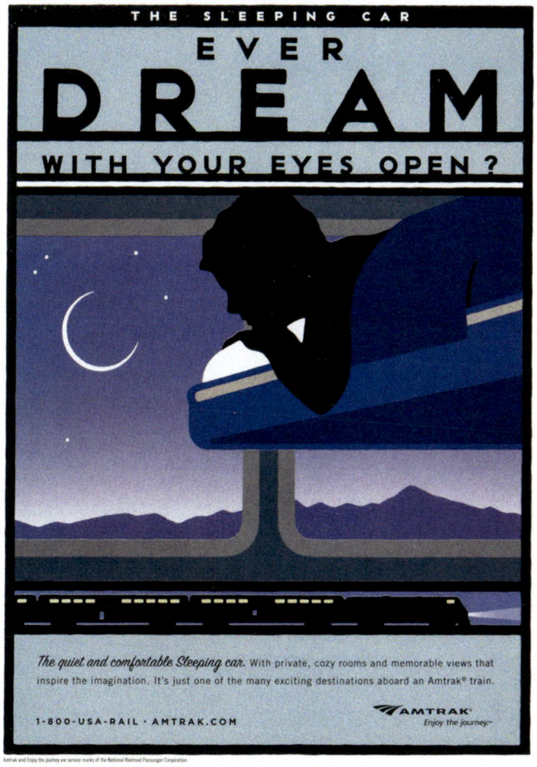


Amtrak, 2005

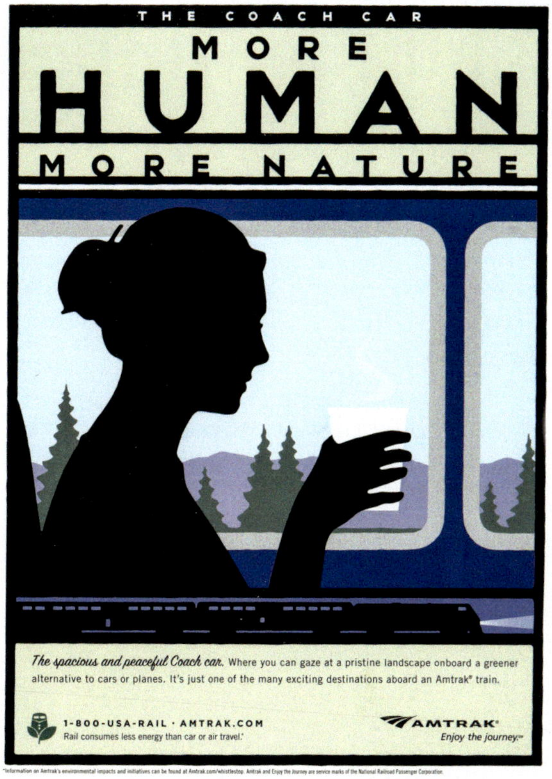


Amtrak, 2005

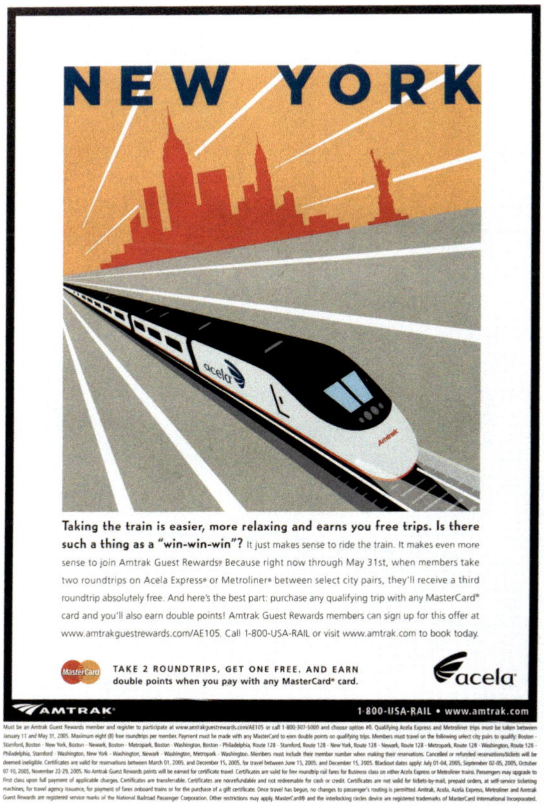


Amtrak, 2005

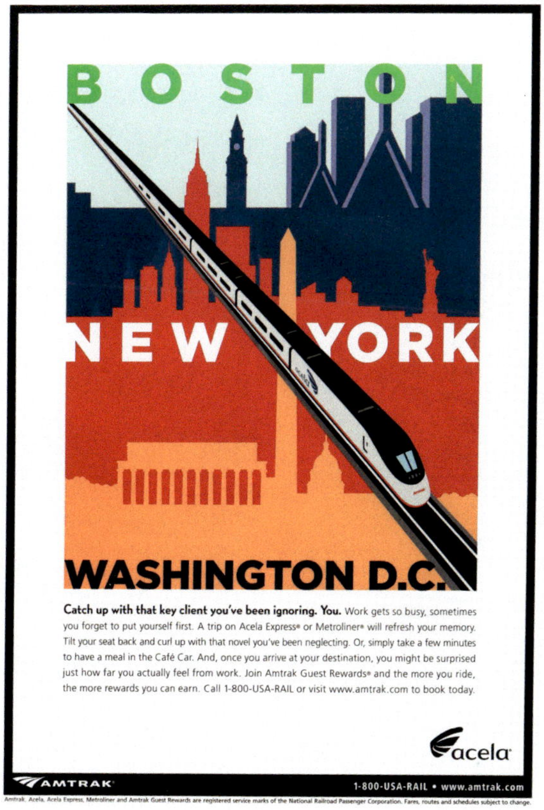


Amtrak, 2005

# And the winner is...

## Butt Out

Royal Caribbean Cruises enlists its customers to "Get out there" and enjoy the sites. But while spinning in the A.M. is suggested, followed by onshore sightseeing, the choice of gazing at the supple back end of a statue gives pause to the couple's activities once back aboard the ship. What kind of antics is the cruise line suggesting?

## Arsch hoch

Royal Caribbean Cruises fordert seine Kunden zum Sightseeing auf: „Get out there." Aber während morgens der Spinning-Kurs und danach Kultur beim Landgang angesagt sind, muss man sich bei der Wahl dieses knackigen Statuenpos, den das Paar betrachtet, doch fragen, was bei den beiden als Nächstes auf dem Programm steht, sobald sie wieder an Bord sind. Was die Kreuzfahrtlinie da wohl im Sinn hatte?

## Balade suggestive

Le croisiériste Royal Caribbean encourage ses passagers à « sortir prendre l'air » et profiter de la vue. Mais quand il suggère d'interrompre son séjour à bord pour une excursion culturelle à terre, ce couple choisit d'admirer les fesses potelées d'une statue. Quel autre type de distractions la compagnie aurait-elle pu suggérer?

▶ Royal Caribbean,

# 20th Century America at Your Fingertips

The best of American consumer output is showcased in these comprehensive volumes presenting the buying habits, economic preferences, and cultural trends as viewed in advertisements from various decades of the 20th century.

**All-American Ads of the 40s, 50s, 60s, 70s, 80s & 90s**
Jim Heimann
Multilingual edition in:
English / Deutsch / Français

**"Anyone who approaches with questions about how people lived, ate, felt and consumed in earlier decades will find the TASCHEN ad books an excellent investment."**
*— The Toronto Star*

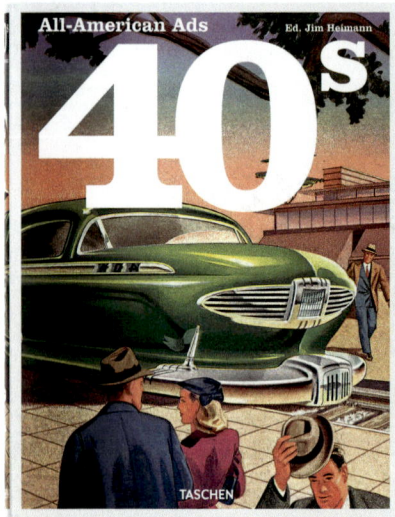

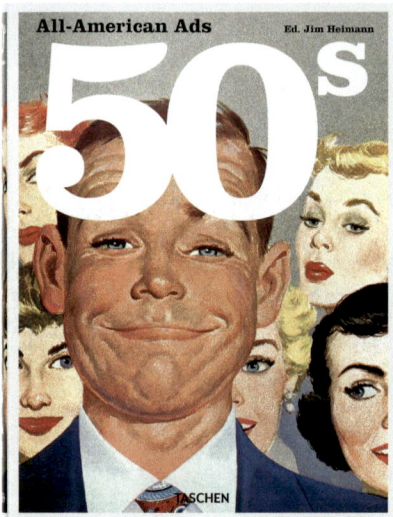

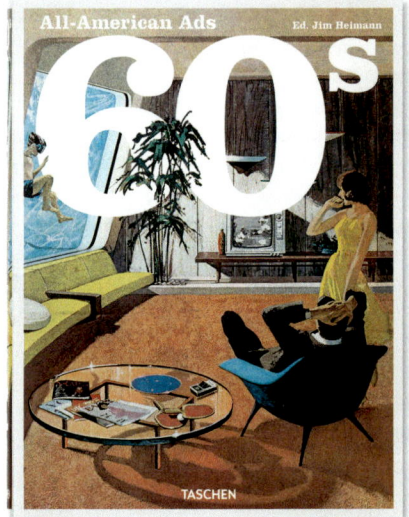

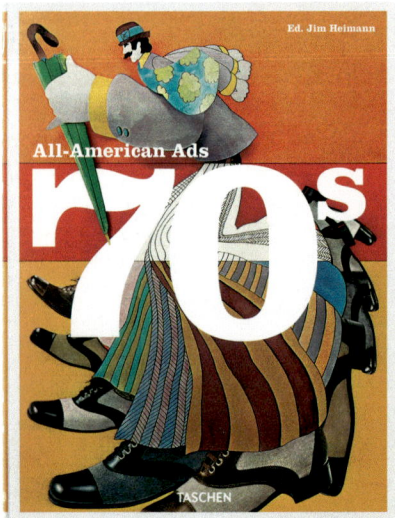

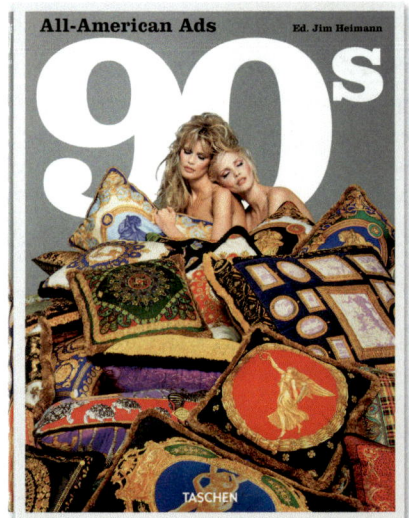